P9-ASK-602

Washington Matthews

Washington Matthews
(Photograph, Courtesy National Archives)

Washington Matthews

Studies of Navajo Culture, 1880–1894

Edited by
KATHERINE SPENCER HALPERN
and SUSAN BROWN McGREEVY

Published in cooperation with the Wheelright Museum of the American Indian

University of New Mexico Press
Albuquerque

First Edition

Library of Congress Cataloging-in-Publication Data
Washington Matthews: studies of Navajo culture, 1880-1894 /
edited by Katherine Spencer Halpern and Susan Brown McGreevy.
—1st ed.
p. cm.
"Published in cooperation with the Wheelwright
Museum of the American Indian."
Includes bibliographical references and index.
ISBN 0-8263-1631-x (hardcover)
1. Navajo Indians. 2. Matthews, Washington, 1843–1905.
3. Anthropologists—Southwest, New—Biography.
I. Halpern, Katherine Spencer, 1913– .
II. McGreevy, Susan Brown, 1934– .
III. Wheelwright Museum of the American Indian.
E99.N3M448 1997
305.8972—dc21 97-13901
CIP

To the generations of hataałii*—past, present and future—*

whose wisdom and ceremonial knowledge have

enriched generations of scholars.

Contents

PART TWO Selections from the Papers of Washington Matthews

Unpublished Papers

Papers Published in Hard-to-Find Journals

PART THREE Washington Matthews' Bibliography

Foreword

Washington Matthews belonged to what is undoubtedly the most unappreciated and ignored generation of American anthropologists—the first generation. Unlike most scholarly disciplines, American anthropology originated not in the universities but rather in the museums. The first anthropologists were not drawn from the academic world but from the public world of government service, law, medicine, and business. Initially, the common elements that united these individuals were the desire to understand other peoples and to preserve a record of the rapidly changing lives of the American Indians. Their classrooms were reservations and their professors were the Indians themselves. No other generation of anthropologists has ever had such intense and personal knowledge of the peoples whose lives they were studying. Frequently dismissed by later generations of academically trained anthropologists as merely descriptive ethnographers, these men and women were the first to breach the ethnocentrism which blinded the American academic world to the value of non-western cultural traditions and in doing so laid the foundation for a new discipline. Confronting the prevailing racist ideas and stereotypes, they demonstrated through their writings that American Indians were rational peoples with cultural traditions far richer and more complex than ever imagined. While their theoretical concepts were more implicit than explicit, and the ideas which they did formally voice were more modest by contemporary standards, many of these ideas were truly revolutionary for the late nineteenth century.

A medical doctor by training, Washington Matthews was an Army surgeon. His interest in American Indians and anthropology began in 1865 when he was assigned to Fort Berthold in the Dakota Territory. One of the few diversions at this isolated post was to be found in the nearby village of Arikaras, Hidatsas, and Mandans, and Matthews filled his leisure hours by studying the Hidatsa language. By 1880 he had already established himself as a published researcher, and his reassignment that year to Fort Wingate, New Mexico, was arranged by the Bureau of American Ethnology of the Smithsonian in order to allow him the opportunity to study the Navajos. With only a few exceptions, Matthews spent the rest of his life and career studying and writing about the Navajos.

Navajo life in the 1880s was in many ways very different from Navajo life even in the early years of the twentieth century. The Navajo war of 1863–64 and the subsequent Navajo imprisonment at the Bosque Redondo until 1868 had left the Navajos impoverished. However, less than a dozen years later, the Navajos through their own industry had rebuilt their herds to levels far beyond those of earlier periods. With farms, good hunting, and a million or more sheep, goats, and other livestock, there was no poverty or want among the Navajos. With the exception of the Osages, the Navajos were the richest group of Native Americans in the United States. Prosperity and geographical isolation had temporarily protected them from the deleterious effects of government programs and Anglo-American contact. Few government officials ventured far beyond Fort Defiance, and few Navajos bothered to visit the agency. Except for intervening in the Navajo conflicts with local Anglos and Hispanics, government agents followed a laissez-faire policy toward the Navajos. Attempts to educate them failed. Out of a population of between 13,000 and 15,000 Navajos, not more than a few dozen spoke English. Missionaries had come and gone to no avail. Trading posts were few since Navajo needs for Anglo-American goods were still limited. Yet the 1880s were also a time of change—but change on Navajo terms and change born out of prosperity not privation. Wealth and cultural cohesion marked the 1880s as a "golden age" for the Navajos. Thus it was that the Navajo world which Matthews saw and recorded was markedly different from that observed by later generations of anthropologists. Matthews' Navajo world was comprised of an economically self-sufficient and culturally autonomous people who had to be dealt with on their own terms.

This extraordinary prosperity would end in the 1890s as Anglo and Hispanic ranchers crowded the margins of the Navajo range. Drought and resultant overgrazing would destroy most of their livestock. Government officials would establish Courts of Indian Offenses to change "objectionable" sociocultural practices, and increasing numbers of children would be forced to attend government schools. Missionary activities on the reservation would intensify, and the number of trading posts would multiply as economic necessity forced the Navajos to become more integrated into the national and regional economies.

Matthews and other American anthropologists in the 1880s were not confronted by a lack of "theory." In fact, if anything, they were troubled by an overabundance of "theories" concerning the nature and character of non-western peoples. There were the evolutionary theories drawn from the natural sciences. There were the various concepts of "primitive man" espoused by social philosophers. Finally, there were the all-pervasive stereotypes of American Indians so firmly embedded in American popular culture that they were accepted by even most members of the academic community as unquestioned "truth." All of these theories shared one thing: they were based on ignorance. What anthropology lacked at the time was any significant substantive knowledge of American Indians, or non-western peoples, which could either confirm or refute these ideas. The issues which most immediately concerned these early anthropologists were research methods and strategies. How might one study and record the culture of another people? From the broad array of cultural traits and institutions present within any culture, which aspects should one focus on? While today we see these issues as merely "methodological" questions, we must remember that implicit in the choice of research methods and strategies are certain "theoretical" assumptions.

Matthews' early research had been primarily concerned with Hidatsa language and customs. Now, in his new role as official "scientific collaborator" with the Bureau of American Ethnology, his research interests broadened. Although he had made substantial contributions to early physical anthropology and had even written on the epidemiology of Indian tuberculosis, Matthews' most lasting contribution would be his ethnographic studies of the Navajos. Without any formal direction, he developed his own methodology and techniques for the study and recording of cultural data. Initially, he concentrated on the study of the Navajo language, but soon focused his research on particular aspects of Navajo culture. While most of his Navajo research was concerned with rituals and mythology, he also dealt with culture change (silversmithing and weaving), ethnobotany, and even social organization. In his general fieldwork, he utilized a technique that later anthropologists would formally define as "participant observation." In his systematic observations and his meticulous field notes, he set standards for field research that others would later emulate. His greatest legacy, however, was a published series of detailed descriptions of Navajo culture upon which future generations of anthropological researchers would build.

Anthropology owes a debt of gratitude to Katherine Spencer Halpern and Susan Brown McGreevy for organizing and editing this volume and to James Faris, Charlotte Frisbie, David McAllester, Nancy Parezo, and Paul Zolbrod for their contributions. Their chapters, together with a selection of Matthews' published and unpublished works, present a clear picture of the broad range of interest and expertise of one of America's most gifted ethnographers and insightful anthropologists. This volume provides Navajo researchers with a long-needed introduction to Matthews' studies. However, its significance goes well beyond the boundaries of Navajo studies. As a contribution to the history of anthropology, it calls for reappraisal of the role of Matthews and his contemporaries in the development of the discipline.

Garrick Bailey
October 1994

Preface

The roots of the discipline of Navajo studies can be traced to Washington Matthews' pioneering work of the late nineteenth century.[1] Between his periods of fieldwork in New Mexico, Matthews also was an active participant in the burgeoning anthropological community centered in Washington, D.C. However, in spite of the importance of his role in early American anthropology, recognition of his accomplishments has been largely neglected by the profession. The archive of the papers of Washington Matthews at the Wheelwright Museum has provided the editors and contributing authors with the raw material for placing Matthews' work in appropriate perspective.

Approximately three decades after Matthews' last assignment at Fort Wingate (1890–94), Mary Cabot Wheelwright, Bostonian aristocrat and student of comparative religions, became interested in Navajo ceremonialism. For fifteen years, beginning in the early 1920s, she worked with eminent Navajo ceremonial practitioner, Hastiin Klah, documenting Navajo ceremonies and their associated narrative texts.[2] In 1937, with Klah's assistance, she founded the House of Navajo Religion, later called the Museum of Navajo Ceremonial Art, and since 1976, the Wheelwright Museum of the American Indian. Among her most significant acquisitions for her museum was the archival collection of the papers of Washington Matthews. Wheelwright's respect for Matthews' work is apparent from commentary in her autobiographical journal, "Journey Towards Understanding" (1955:14):

> I read Washington Matthews' book on Navaho religion as my Bible on the subject. No one ever did a better job on it than this U.S. Army surgeon. . . . Later I found that all his deposit of records . . . diaries of ceremonies . . . and his papers had been

left at Berkeley University. No one had looked at them for fifteen or twenty years, so I asked to have these records given to the Museum of Navaho Ceremonial Art, which was finally done.

Correspondence between Wheelwright and the University of California, Berkeley, indicates that the museum's prominence as a center for Navajo studies was the principal catalyst for the move. In his letter of March 23, 1951, T. D. McCown, Chairman of the Anthropology Department explained:

> Today we are sending you and the Museum of Navaho Ceremonial Art the manuscripts and other materials belonging to Washington Matthews. . . . We believe that effective use can best be made of the materials by having them in your custody. This is . . . an outright transfer of materials. (Wheelwright Museum archives)

The transfer was formally approved by the Museum's Board of Trustees at their meeting of October 11, 1951. Thus the Museum became the repository for this important archive of Navajo studies. The Washington Matthews Papers consist of his ethnographic and linguistic field notes, notebooks, manuscripts, vocabulary cards, photographs, and sketches, together with a portion of his correspondence with contemporaneous scholars. The collection also contains some newspaper and journal articles on American Indian subjects of interest to Matthews as well as notes on his reading. By far the largest part of the collection derives from his Navajo research covering the years from 1880 to his death in 1905. A few items, dating from his earlier army assignments, pertain primarily to his work with the Hidatsas and Modocs.

By the late 1970s the condition of the collection had deteriorated severely due to age and frequent use. In 1980 McGreevy, then director of the Museum, applied for a grant from the National Historical Publications and Records Commission to reproduce the Matthews Papers on microfilm. In the early stages of the project it was decided that the value of the microfilm edition would be significantly enhanced by the inclusion of relevant materials from other repositories, principally the National Archives, the Southwest Museum in Los Angeles, and the University of California at Berkeley. Thus, a considerable body of correspondence, military records, and other memorabilia was added in order to complete the microfilm edition. The *Guide to the Microfilm Edition of the Washington Matthews Papers*, written by Halpern and published by the University of New Mexico Press in 1985 (copyright Wheelwright Museum of the American Indian), not only provided a valuable tool for scholars wishing to study the collection, but also contributed further insights into Matthews' life and work.[3]

In 1986, one year after the completion of the microfilm project, and one hundred years after Matthews' initial work among the Navajos, we organized a symposium for the eighty-fifth annual meeting of the American Anthropological Association. "Washington Matthews and the Beginning of Navajo Studies: A Centennial Retrospective of His Contribution to American Anthropology" was the first major forum exclusively devoted to examining the significance of Matthews' accomplishments. We invited anthropologists working in the field of Navajo studies to contribute papers. In addition, there were two papers that concerned Matthews' work in physical anthropology: Charles Merbs (Arizona State University) discussed Matthews' research pertaining to the paleopathology of the Hohokam skeletal remains uncovered during the second Hemenway expedition (1887), and Steven J. Kunitz (University of Rochester) presented a paper on Matthews' medical writings on Indian tuberculosis.

In the aftermath of the symposium we began to discuss the possibility of a publication, based on the presented papers, that would also include selections from Matthews' field notes and correspondence, as well as some of his early, currently inaccessible published articles. After further consideration, we decided to limit the volume to Matthews' work among the Navajos. Although James C. Faris and Paul Zolbrod were not among the participants in the AAA session, because of their recent and important contributions to Navajo studies, we asked them to join us. This volume is thus comprised of an examination of Matthews' Navajo studies as viewed from diverse late-twentieth-century perspectives, as well as original source material pertaining to Matthews' encounters with late-ninetieth-century Navajo culture.

The process of compiling this book has shown that Matthews' Navajo studies continue to comprise a resource for further work, especially research concerning continuity and change in musical, artistic, and ceremonial traditions. Oswald Werner (Northwestern University), who presented a paper on Matthews' linguistic studies at the symposium, further suggests that investigation of the problems presented by Matthews' Navajo orthography would contribute to the history of Navajo linguistics and simplify further research. Although the recent republication of Matthews' *Navajo Legends* by the University of Utah Press (1994) contains a "Note on Orthography" by Robert W. Young (pp. 301–303), much work remains. A computerized program that fully analyzes all versions of Matthews' orthography as compared with that in use today (based on Young and Morgan) would be an important first step.

As Navajo educator Grace Anna McNeley observes, "The work of Matthews is now being utilized in ways he could scarcely have imagined, not only by *bilagáana* [Anglo] scholars . . . but also by modern Navajos as a secondary source of knowledge to supplement that of their fathers and grandfathers" (1994:xiv). Thus, in addition to providing seminal research on Navajo culture, Matthews also has left us a rich potential for future study.

The substance of Part One of this volume is clearly the result of the time and work that each author has contributed. We are greatly appreciative of their support and cooperation in bringing this project to fruition. We also wish to acknowledge the work of Robert Poor, whose biography of Matthews has been an important source of information for us.

In addition, we want to thank the following persons and institutions for their assistance: The Carlisle Barracks, Carlisle, Pennsylvania; Jeff Grathwohl, University of Utah Press; Michael Harrison, the Michael and Margaret B. Harrison Western Research

Center, University of California (Davis); The National Archives, Washington, D.C.; National Anthropology Archives, Smithsonian Institution, Washington D.C; Paul S. Sledzik, National Museum of Health and Medicine, Institute of Pathology, Washington D.C.; The Southwest Museum, Los Angeles, California.

Our research for this project has been greatly facilitated by the libraries of the Museum of New Mexico in Santa Fe. We especially want to thank Laura Holt, librarian, Laboratory of Anthropology; Judith Sellers, librarian, Museum of International Folk Art; Orlando Romero, librarian, History Library; and Arthur Olivas and Richard Rudisill of the Department of Photo Archives, History Library. We also appreciate the advice and information provided by anthropologists David M. Brugge and Jennie R. Joe.

Finally, our appreciation to Lynette Miller, curator of collections, and Jonathan Batkin, director of the Wheelwright Museum, for their continued help and encouragement throughout the lengthy period of the book's parturition.

Susan Brown McGreevy
and Katherine Spencer Halpern
Santa Fe, New Mexico, 1994

Notes

1. While the alternative spelling "Navaho" is used in some references, the "j" spelling is preferred by the Navajo Nation and is therefore used throughout this volume, with the exception of direct quotes in which the "h" spelling appears. Navajos refer to themselves as *Diné*, meaning "the People." Navajo orthography in the contributed papers conforms to standards established by Robert W. Young and William Morgan, Sr. in the revised edition of *The Navajo Language, A Grammar and Colloquial Dictionary* (1987). Matthews' idiosyncratic orthography is retained in all quotes and references from his work.

2. *Hastiin* in Navajo means man, or mature man. Klah is the Anglicized *tł'aii*, meaning left-handed in Navajo.

3. Throughout this volume references to the Matthews Papers will be cited as "Guide", followed by page number where the item is described and in some cases also by item number (denoted by #) or by microfilm frame number (denoted by f.).

List of Contributors

GARRICK BAILEY is well known for his research on Navajo history. His publications include *Historic Navajo Occupation of the Northern Chaco Plateau* (with Roberta Glenn Bailey, University of Tulsa Faculty of Anthropology) and *A History of the Navajos; The Reservation Years* (with Roberta Glenn Bailey, 1986). He is currently Professor of Anthropology at Tulsa University.

GLORIA EMERSON, Diné (Navajo), is an artist and educator from Shiprock, New Mexico. She has most recently been affiliated with the Institute of American Indian Arts in Santa Fe, New Mexico, where she worked in cultural research, in curriculum development and as an administrator. Emerson also has worked in community development, education and social services on the Navajo reservation and is currently an advocate for Native languages.

JAMES C. FARIS is Professor of Anthropology at the University of Connecticut. His study of the Navajo Nightway ceremony that involved not only extensive archival and library research, but also intensive work with current Navajo Nightway *hataałii*, culminated in his publication of *The Nightway, A History and a History of Documentation of a Navajo Ceremonial* (1990). Of particular relevance to this volume is the information about Washington Matthews that emerged from his research for that publication.

CHARLOTTE J. FRISBIE has been involved with Navajo studies since 1962. Trained in ethnomusicology and anthropology, she is currently a Professor of Anthropology and Department Chairperson at Southern Illinois University at Edwardsville. Among her publications on Navajo topics are *Kinaaldá: A Study of the Navaho Girl's Puberty*

Ceremony (1967; 1993); *Navajo Blessingway Singer: The Autobiography of Frank Mitchell, 1881–1967* (ed. with David P. McAllester, 1978); and *Navajo Medicine Bundles or "Jish"* (1987).

KATHERINE SPENCER HALPERN has published on Navajo mythology and has worked in Navajo medical anthropology. Her publications include *Reflections of Social Life in the Navaho Origin Myth* (1947) and *Mythology and Values: An Analysis of Navaho Chantway Myths* (1957). She is Professor Emerita, American University, and is currently a Research Associate at the Wheelwright Museum, where she served as research anthropologist for the microfilm edition of the Washington Matthews Papers.

DAVID P. MCALLESTER attended his first Navajo ceremonial, a summer performance of the Enemyway, in 1936. Since then, Navajo music of all kinds has been the principal focus of his studies. He is one of the founders of the Society for Ethnomusicology and is a past-president and former editor of its journal. He is Professor Emeritus of Anthropology and Music, Wesleyan University. His books include *Enemy Way Music* (1954); *The Myth and Prayers of the Great Star Chant and The Myth of the Coyote Chant* (1956); and *Navajo Blessingway Singer* (ed. with Frisbie: see above).

SUSAN BROWN MCGREEVY began her work in Navajo studies in 1970 and has continued her research in art and culture change among the Navajos. She was Director of the Wheelwright Museum from 1978 to 1982. During her tenure, she was project director for the microfilm edition of the Washington Matthews Papers. Selected Navajo publications include "What Makes Sally Weave? Survival and Innovation in Navajo Basketry Trays (1989); *Anii Ánáádaalyaa'ígíí: Recent Trends in Navajo Art* (with Bruce Bernstein, 1988); "The Other Weavers: Navajo Basket Makers" (1985) and *Woven Holy People: Navajo Sandpainting Textiles* (1982). McGreevy is currently a Research Associate at the Wheelwright Museum.

NANCY J. PAREZO is Curator of Ethnology, Arizona State Museum, and Professor of American Indian Studies and Research Professor of Anthropology at the University of Arizona. She served as Anthropology Program Officer for the National Science Foundation from 1987 to 1988 and received the Distinguished Service Award from the Institute for Museum Services in 1989. Her recent publications include *Navajo Sandpainting: From Religious Act to Commercial Art* (1983); *Daughters of the Desert* (with Barbara A. Babcock, 1988); and *Hidden Scholars: Women Anthropologists and the Native American Southwest* (1993).

PAUL G. ZOLBROD comes to Native American studies by way of medieval and early Renaissance literature. Originally trained to examine Old English manuscripts and Early English printed texts, he subsequently began to explore the process by which

Native American oral traditions found their way into print and how that conversion influenced Anglo-European readers and affected people like the Navajos. He is author of *Diné Bahane': The Navajo Creation Story* (1984), along with numerous essays and articles on ethnopoetics and medieval and Renaissance poetry. Zolbrod was formerly Frederick F. Seeley Professor of English at Allegheny College, Meadville, Pennsylvania.

PART ONE

Essays

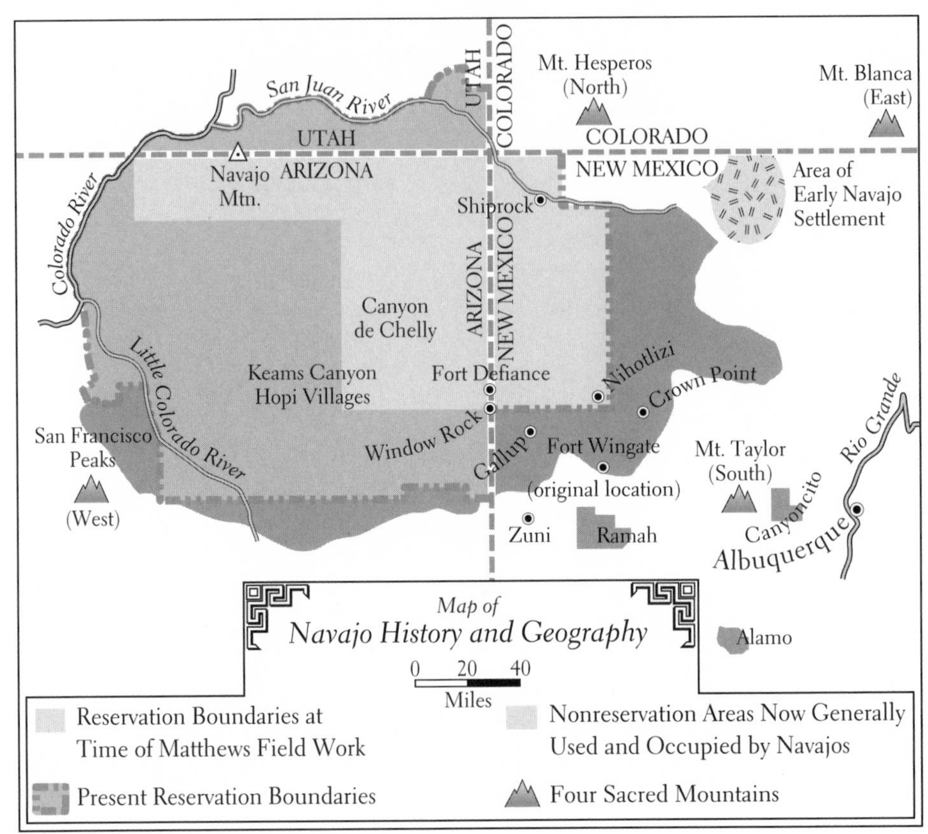

Adapted from Williams (1970), Maps 2 and 3

Washington Matthews: Army Surgeon and Field Anthropologist in the American West, 1843–1905

KATHERINE SPENCER HALPERN

Washington Matthews, who came to Navajo country in 1880, was the first serious student of Navajo ethnography. An army surgeon of a natural scholarly bent, he made his most important contribution to the new field of anthropology as a self-taught field worker; the standard of disciplined and scientific field investigation that he set was unusual in nineteenth century American anthropology. His Indian studies were begun independently during early army assignments in Dakota Territory in the 1860s and '70s. By 1880 his work had become recognized and encouraged by John W. Powell through his newly established Bureau of Ethnology at the Smithsonian Institution, and Matthews' assignment to Fort Wingate, New Mexico, was arranged so that he could open up the new field of Navajo research. Navajo scholars have long recognized Matthews as the founder of Navajo studies, and his publications on Navajo religion and mythology are among the earliest and best anthropological works to present American Indian beliefs and ritual with appreciation, understanding, and scholarly care.

Among his colleagues and friends in the Southwest were Frank H. Cushing at Zuni, Alexander M. Stephen in Hopi country, John G. Bourke with the Apaches and western Pueblos, and southwestern historian Adolph F. A. Bandelier. They were all pioneers in the study of southwestern Indian cultures, and their correspondence reflects the excitement, human interest, and dedication that they brought to this new field of anthropological inquiry.

In the late 1880s, between two field assignments in New Mexico, Matthews was detailed to the Army Medical Museum in Washington, D.C., where he also made early contributions to anthropometry and physical anthropology. In Washington he was part of the lively scientific and intellectual community that centered around the Smithsonian Institution, the Army Medical Museum, the National Geographic Society, and the Anthropological Society of Washington. His Navajo reports were published in the early Annual Reports of the Bureau of [American] Ethnology, and when the new anthropological journals were launched in the late 1880s, the *American Anthropologist* and *Journal of American Folklore* became his regular publishing media. This preliminary essay will provide an overview of Matthews' life and work and set the stage for the specialized accounts of his work in the essays that follow.[1]

Washington Matthews was born in 1843 in Ireland, the elder son of Nicholas Blayney Matthews, a physician. After his mother's early death his father brought his two young sons to the United States, and by 1851 they had settled in Dubuque, Iowa. Matthews studied medicine with his father and at the University of Iowa in Keokuk. Little is known about his early life, but military records, beginning with his first army contract in 1864, give the outlines of his army career. He spent most of the years 1865–72 at posts on the Upper Missouri (Forts Union, Berthold, Rice, Stevenson, and Buford). His initial opportunity for close contact with Indians came in the summer of 1865 during his assignment, at age twenty-two, to Fort Berthold. Close by was an Indian village inhabited by Arikaras, Hidatsas, and Mandans, and one of the entertainments of this small isolated garrison consisted of visiting the medicine lodge at night to watch the Indians perform their public songs, dances, and ceremonials (Matthews 1897b: 261). In 1867 Matthews wrote to Spencer F. Baird, Secretary of the Smithsonian, asking for vocabulary blanks and grammars to help in his study of Fort Berthold languages (Guide: 78), but he must have relied primarily on devising his own methods of investigation. Unfortunately, all of his notes from this time were destroyed in a fire in his quarters in January 1871. Nevertheless, Matthews was able to reproduce enough from memory to publish a volume on the *Ethnography and Philology of the Hidatsa Indians* (1877).[2] The introduction to a reprint of this work edited by Robert F. Spencer (1971: xxiii–xxv; see Poor, App. 2: 108–9) comments that although Matthews worked within a now-outdated framework of universal linguistic categories, he succeeded in evaluating Hidatsa on its own terms, giving a sense of the semantic categories of the language and of the patterns of Hidatsa thought, which, in Spencer's words, was "no mean feat considering the status of linguistic science of the day."

There is evidence that during these Dakota years Matthews had a son named Berthold by the daughter of an Indian chief; the boy's mother died of tuberculosis soon after his birth, but Matthews apparently maintained interest in his welfare (Schevill Link 1960: 318; Guide: 59).[3] His personal friendships with Indians are indicated in early army records that mention going on hunting parties with them. His younger half-brother Alphons joined him for one of these expeditions, and two long letters written more than thirty years later appear to be from Alphons describing his trips back to Fort Berthold country in 1903 and 1904 and recalling mutual memories as well as giving information on the present state of their old Indian friends (Guide: 43–44).

After brief assignments in New York and Maine from 1872 to 1875, Matthews spent five years at various posts in California (1875–80), where he participated in the Nez Perce and Bannock campaigns. While stationed at Alcatraz Island, he obtained from a Modoc prisoner a vocabulary that has remained in manuscript at Berkeley (Guide: 69).

In 1877 he married Caroline Wotherspoon, daughter of an army doctor. In this period his correspondence shows that he was in touch with V. F. Hayden, Elliott Coues, Garrick Mallery, and Powell regarding his own work in Dakota Territory and California (Guide: 78), and it was apparently this contact with Powell that opened up the opportunity for his transfer to New Mexico and his Navajo work. At this time he became an official "scientific collaborator" of the Bureau of Ethnology, an unpaid position that conferred scientific status and affiliation on the holder (see Parezo's paper in this volume, note 2).

Navajo Fieldwork

Matthews carried out his major Navajo fieldwork during two assignments at Fort Wingate, New Mexico, from 1880 to 1884 and again from 1890 to 1894. These first investigations centered on subjects that were readily accessible—the Navajo material arts of silver-smithing and weaving (1883a; 1884a). Recognizing from the beginning the need for a firm basis in linguistics, Matthews instituted systematic vocabulary collection, which he continued throughout his Navajo work.[4] Although Matthews never brought this linguistic work to full formulation, he published an early paper on Navajo botanical terms and their native classification system (1886e). In this article, and more fully in a popular lecture titled "Natural Naturalists" prepared for delivery to the Philosophical Society of Washington in October of 1884, Matthews expressed his respect for the extent and accuracy of Navajo botanical knowledge, pointing to instances where their terms reflect a closer and more discriminating observation of nature than our own.[5]

Matthews soon began to gain access to the more esoteric aspects of Navajo culture that became his special interest—their healing ceremonies and mythology. During his first years of fieldwork, the Mountain Chant, with the spectacular public events of the Fire Dance on its final night, appears most frequently in his field notes. He first recorded a Fire Dance in November 1882 on a trip to Keams Canyon, where under the guidance of Alexander M. Stephen he observed an all-night performance (Guide: 54, Notebook #467); his popular account of this performance was published under a pseudonym (1884b). It was not until the fall of 1884 that he had his first sight of the series of sandpaintings, or drypaintings that accompany this chant. His excitement at this discovery of Navajo drypaintings is vividly conveyed in his 1884 report to Powell (Guide: 46, see item #190 reproduced in Part Two of this volume; see also Parezo's paper, this volume) and in a later letter to Cushing, who had become a friend and confidant during their fieldwork association at Zuni and Wingate (Guide: 81). Matthews' observations on both of these occasions were incorporated in a major publication, *The Mountain Chant* (1887a), that became the first description in full detail of the ritual and origin myth of a Navajo ceremonial.[6]

In March 1884 Matthews was recalled to the Army Medical Museum in Washington, D.C., where he remained until 1890. Here, in addition to his museum research in physical anthropology, he found time to work on his Navajo field data. In the fall of

1885 he brought the Navajo medicine man, Tall Chanter, to Washington to help check his field notes on ceremonies.[7] In addition, he took two field trips to Navajo country, one in the fall of 1884 when he discovered drypaintings, and the other in the fall of 1887 on his return from visiting the Hemenway Expedition site in Arizona. During these Washington years he began the steady stream of Navajo publications (over thirty items) that continued into the early 1900s.

By March 1890 Matthews was again settled at Fort Wingate for a four-year period of intensified work on Navajo ritual and myth, now with primary focus on the major nine-night ceremony, the Night Chant. His field notebooks reveal the richness of the data he was collecting. Nine notebooks are devoted primarily or partly to the Night Chant (Guide: 53–54); two of them give hour-by-hour accounts of the ceremony (#589, 11/1891; #632, 12/1891–1/1892, in which Matthews helped to prepare the ceremonial properties). By this time, the medicine men had come to see him as a fellow medical practitioner and were urging their knowledge upon him, and both Tall Chanter and Laughing Singer had become principal informants (Guide: 53–54, Notebook #674). Matthews reported enthusiastically in letters to Cushing on the "great strides" in his knowledge of Navajo rites, and he spoke repeatedly of his efforts, ultimately successful, to obtain the newly available phonograph to record ceremonial songs (Guide: 82).

Early in this second field assignment Matthews began to suffer physical difficulties (deafness, vertigo, and muscular incoordination), which some writers have attributed to a stroke. The Navajos themselves interpreted them as a consequence of the dangers of his contact with the powerful ceremonies.[8] Nevertheless, Matthews pursued his field studies with vigor and persistence until illness finally forced him to return to Washington in May 1894.

Friends and Colleagues in Fieldwork

Fortunately for Matthews, Fort Wingate in the early 1880s was situated at the gateway to Southwest Indian country. It was a point of departure and supply for military men, government officials, scientists, even artists and writers. Among these were a few self-taught field anthropologists who, like Matthews, were beginning to lay the foundations for our knowledge of southwestern cultures. Chief among Matthews' friends were Cushing at Zuni, Stephen at Keams Canyon with the Navajo and Hopi, and Bourke, whose interests stemmed from his Plains and Apache experiences. Adolph Bandelier, whose historical and archaeological investigations in the Southwest had already become well known, and Hermann F. C. ten Kate, newly arrived from Holland with European training in physical anthropology, were also cordially received by Matthews at Wingate, but they later developed closer ties with Cushing as members of his Hemenway Expedition. All shared a deeply felt appreciation and respect for the Indian friends and ways of life that they were encountering.

Matthews and Cushing appear to have established a close friendship during their early years of fieldwork.[9] Cushing had come to Zuni in the summer of 1879 with the Smithsonian's first southwestern ethnological expedition and had stayed on to live in

Zuni and pursue there his own unorthodox but creative ideas about "participation" in the culture he was observing. Before Matthews arrived at Fort Wingate, Powell had alerted him to Cushing's work, and after Cushing had spent a week with him, Matthews reported positively to Powell:

> I was very much pleased with him. He seems to be a young man of keen observation and sound judgment. I would feel inclined to place great reliance on any report he might make. He has certainly got the confidence and regard of the people among whom he is living. I predict a useful future for him if he perseveres as he has begun. (Guide: 78, National Anthropological Archives, Smithsonian Institution, #171)

Cushing's first mention of Matthews, in a letter to Powell and Baird dated 13 January 1881, describes him as "a thorough ethnologist"; soon thereafter he refers to him as "an esteemed friend and collaborator" (1/16/1881); and still later (6/10/1881) as "My ever kind and true friend" (Green 1990: 147–48). In letters to Cushing, Matthews came to express himself freely, revealing his enthusiasm and delight at the unfolding discoveries of fieldwork and, in concert with Cushing, voicing appreciation for some of their colleagues and criticism of others. Matthews was some fourteen years older than Cushing and his letters reflect a protective attitude of encouragement for Cushing's work and concern for his persistent ill health.[10]

During these early years Matthews' army diary (Guide: 72–73) records meetings at Wingate and Zuni with others of these friends. In early 1883 Bandelier spent two weeks in Zuni; on the return to Fort Wingate he was injured in a wagon accident and spent some time in the post hospital and with Matthews (Green 1990: 276–77; Bandelier 1970: 57–58). Bandelier's journal entry dated 17 March 1883 refers to Matthews as "an excellent man—a man of science," and in a letter to Lewis H. Morgan's widow dated 18 March 1883, he reassures her regarding the state of anthropological work in the Southwest, that in Cushing's and Matthews' hands ". . . the work to be done is better cared for than it would be in mine" (Green 1990: 276–77). In the autumn of 1883 ten Kate stopped at Fort Wingate on his way to visit Cushing. While Matthews' relations with Bandelier and ten Kate were cordial, these men both seemed especially captivated by Cushing's dramatic and imaginative approach in his Zuni investigations, and Cushing later chose them to participate in the Hemenway Expedition that attempted to trace Zuni history to its roots in southern Arizona. Matthews and Cushing make clear in their correspondence that they respected and appreciated these colleagues, but this was not true for some others, notably for Matilda and James Stevenson at Zuni and later Jesse W. Fewkes and his work on the second Hemenway Expedition. These scientists were frequently the object of Cushing's and Matthews' criticism and scorn for what the two men believed was insensitivity and exploitation in dealing with both Indians and their anthropological colleagues. In the spring of 1884 Matthews and Cushing were both recalled from the field to Washington and their activities diverged for a time, until they met again under different circumstances in connection with Cushing's Hemenway Expedition.

John G. Bourke, an officer in the Apache campaigns who had come to know and appreciate his Apache scouts and had developed broad Indian interests, also found Fort Wingate to be a gathering place for congenial colleagues. He first met Matthews there in the spring of 1881, and he returned in the summer and again in November for a two-week stay with Cushing at Zuni (Green: 185–93).[11] This was the beginning of lifelong friendships with both Matthews and Cushing. In the summer of 1887, when Bourke and Matthews were both based in Washington, it was Bourke who arranged to have Matthews sent to the aid of Cushing when he became ill during his work on the Hemenway Expedition (Porter 1986: 276–77). Bourke's journal describes Cushing's later despondency over what he saw as his failure in this expedition, and his comments to Bourke about Matthews in May of 1889 reveal Cushing's feeling of estrangement from Matthews over events in the expedition: "Matthews is the only man to compare with you (as an ethnologist), but his training had [*sic*] made him narrow. He cares more for skeletons and crania than anything else."[12] During this period Matthews seems to have maintained his own protective feelings and efforts in Cushing's behalf, and he joined Bourke in defense of Cushing's reputation. All three stood together in their criticism of Fewkes, Cushing's successor as leader of the Hemenway Expedition, for his reliance on the work of others that they felt amounted to plagiarism, especially the exploitation of Stephen's notes and information about the Hopi (Matthews' letters to Cushing, 7 January 1891 and 18 November 1891, see Guide: 81–82; Porter 1986: 277–78). By the late-1880s Matthews and Bourke were both in Washington and had become active in the Anthropological Society of Washington (ASW) and the American Folklore Society (AFLS). Together they arranged a program of the ASW in 1890 on the "gentile systems" of the Navajo and Apache. Matthews was elected president of the AFLS for 1895 (JAFL 1895: v. 8, 339) and Bourke for 1896 (JAFL 1896: v. 9, 69). But in the spring of 1896 Bourke's health began to fail rapidly and he died in June (see Matthews' obituary of him 1896c).

Early in his Navajo fieldwork Matthews also became acquainted with Alexander M. Stephen, a Scotsman with a mineralogy degree from the University of Edinburgh, who had come West originally as a prospector. He had settled near Keams Canyon, where he developed an interest in the Navajos and Hopis, and the trader Thomas Keam was his firm supporter (Green 1990: 389; Parsons 1936: xx–xxiv; Stephen was a relative of Keam, information from Nancy Parezo). One of Matthews' earliest opportunities to observe a Mountain Chant had been under Stephen's tutelage on a trip to Keam's Canyon in November 1882 (see Matthews 1884b and 1887a). Matthews continued to maintain contact with Stephen on Navajo matters, and their letters reflect their mutual interests and esteem.[13] Stephen's premature death of tuberculosis in 1894 cut short his important contribution to southwestern anthropology and left him a shadowy but highly respected figure to later scholars.

The Years in Washington

Scholars who know Matthews through his Navajo studies may not be aware of his substantial work in physical and medical anthropology. From 1884 to 1890 at the Army

Medical Museum he was part of their small staff of army surgeons (with J. S. Billings, Curator; Jacob Wortman, anatomist; Daniel Lamb; and Robert Fletcher) working on anthropometric techniques, and he authored some seven papers on cranial and skeletal measurements and equipment (1885b, 1885e, 1886a, 1886b, 1886c, 1886d, 1889a).[14] However, Matthews' major work in physical anthropology resulted from his contacts with the Hemenway Expedition. When he was sent to the aid of Cushing at the archaeological site in southern Arizona and found that no provision had been made for collecting the human remains lying uncovered, he arranged with Cushing and Wortman to have them preserved and sent to the Army Medical Museum for analysis. He became the principal author of the resulting report (1893a), which was recognized in a contemporary review (Baker 1895) and later by Hrdlicka (1914: 543–45) as an important early contribution to the physical anthropology of the American Indians.[15]

During this first period in Washington, Matthews was active in a number of local scientific societies, giving lectures at the Philosophical Society of Washington, the National Academy of Science, the U.S. National Museum, and at meetings of the newly organized Anthropological Society of Washington. He served on the first editorial committee of the *American Anthropologist* (published by the ASW) and frequently contributed articles and reviews to it.[16] In a series of articles on the problem of tuberculosis among Indians (1886g, 1887c, 1887d, 1888c), he compiled what epidemiological information he could find on the high rate of tuberculosis in American Indian populations. His discussion focused on the importance of social factors in the unfavorable conditions of their changing life style under white pressures.[17]

On returning to Washington in 1894 Matthews was able, despite failing health, to continue his Navajo writing. He completed two major publications: *Navaho Legends* (1897a), which contains the lengthy story of tribal origins together with origin stories of two principal curing ceremonies; and his magnum opus *The Night Chant* (1902a), with full description of its ritual actions, its songs and prayers, and its mythological background. For the remainder of the decade Matthews maintained an active schedule of writing, publication, and participation in scientific meetings. He became increasingly active in folklore circles. At the annual meeting of the American Folklore Society in 1894 he gave a demonstration of Navajo songs by means of his phonograph recordings, explaining the use of this recently available device. It was at this meeting that he was nominated to serve as president of the AFLS for 1895. In the following years he continued to give papers at scientific meetings and published several theoretical articles on the characteristics of ceremony and myth (1894c, 1897b, 1898b, 1899b, 1902b).

By the turn of the century Matthews' circle of friends and colleagues was changing and his own activities had become more limited. The early friends with whom he had shared the discoveries of fieldwork had died—Stephen in 1894, Bourke in 1896, and Cushing in 1900 (Matthews contributed to his obituary, 1900c). But new relationships took their place. With James Mooney, a younger Washington colleague, he had established a friendship of mutual respect and trust based on the bond of their Irish heritage, a similar ethnographic outlook, and common interests in issues of Indian welfare. In 1885 at the beginning of his career, Mooney seems to have welcomed Matthews' counsel on conducting fieldwork, and Matthews' later reviews of Mooney's publications (1897c on the Ghost Dance Religion, and 1901d on the Kiowa Calendar History) were positive, although brief. While both had been associated with Powell and the Bureau of American Ethnology, neither fully accepted Powell's rigid evolutionary doctrine, and both carried their research in other directions—Matthews to his intensive examination of Navajo religion and curing, and Mooney to develop his ethnohistorical interests.[18]

In 1896 Matthews joined with the musicologist John Comfort Fillmore in publishing two companion articles on Navajo songs in the popular western journal *Land of Sunshine* (Matthews 1896b; Fillmore 1896).[19] Charles Fletcher Lummis, editor of this journal, a writer himself and founder of the Southwest Museum in Los Angeles, began a cordial correspondence with Matthews in 1899 that lasted for the rest of Matthews' life. Lummis' letters are enthusiastic in their appreciation of Matthews and his work, and this new friendship became an important professional and personal support at this time in Matthews' life, when he was contending with increasing physical difficulties and strained financial circumstances. In this correspondence Lummis frequently urged Matthews to visit him in Los Angeles, but by this time Matthews insisted that his physical condition would not allow him to make the trip. However, Lummis was finally able to meet him on two of his own trips to Washington. Their close friendship may seem unusual in light of Lummis' scorn for what he saw as the academic posture of most anthropologists (see Whitaker 1992). Lummis seems to have felt that Matthews' unpretentious but solid fieldwork was not being fully recognized by his peers; his own designation for Matthews was "the dean of American ethnologists" (Lummis 1905).[20]

After 1900 Matthews began a series of general articles for F. W. Hodge's *Handbook of American Indians* (1907 and 1910), six of which were published.[21] In 1903 he made an agreement with A. L. Kroeber and F. W. Putnam leaving his papers to their newly established anthropology department at the University of California in return for a small subsidy and with the understanding that the young philologist Pliny Earle Goddard would carry on his Navajo work.[22] During these last years Matthews' health had been declining seriously, and on 20 April 1905, he died in Washington at age sixty-one.

In several respects Matthews' work was unusual for his time. First, he set an early standard for thorough and exact ethnographic observation and description. With no guides available for anthropological field research, he devised his own methods. His notes reveal his meticulous recording in field observations and his exhaustive search for details. He recorded ceremonies in hour-by-hour accounts with drawings of drypaintings and ritual paraphernalia. Recognized in his own day by both European and American scholars as models of ethnographic description (see, e.g., Buckland 1893; Durkheim and Mauss 1963; Hodge 1903; Newell 1903), these accounts have remained an unchallenged foundation for the work of later anthropologists on Navajo ceremonialism and myth.

The second aspect of his work, unusual for the time, was his ability to understand the native viewpoint and his intellectual respect for it. In one reviewer's words (Newell, review of *The Night Chant*, 1903):

> For the first time it was possible to attain a true comprehension of native character and thought; the alien races with which Anglo-Americans had lived for three centuries, without penetrating further than the surface of their mentality, were revealed in the clear light of their own intellectual conceptions.

This appreciation for the native view was evident in his early Hidatsa publication, where he was able to view their language in its own terms, and again in his early Navajo work on plant names, where he marshaled evidence to show the extraordinary extent of their "close and discriminating study of nature" and their ability to "generalize and classify." On a personal level Matthews' notebooks and correspondence show a feeling of deep human appreciation for the Indians with whom he was working.

Matthews was also different from some other anthropologists of his time in his lack of interest in the strong evolutionary commitment of Powell and his followers in the Bureau of American Ethnology. Not that Matthews explicitly rejected the basic ideas of social evolution (in fact, he used such common terms of the time as "savage," "heathen," "pagan"); rather he chose to work on a different level—the intensive focus of his Navajo ethnography.

In sum, Matthews appears as a self-made and independent scholar. He found his own way into linguistic and anthropological research with a minimum of academic training. He undertook the study of Navajo religion at a time when there was no model for such investigation, and his work became a model for the long line of Navajo scholars who have followed.

Notes

1. The only existing biography of Matthews is by Robert M. Poor, written as an anthropology Master's thesis at the University of Nevada, Reno, in 1975 (University Microfilms No. M-8323). Poor brings together what is known of Matthews' life and work. This biography and Poor's cooperation were of invaluable help in the early stages of our work on Matthews. A few other obituaries and brief biographical references are noted in the *Guide to the Microfilm Edition of the Washington Matthews Papers* (Guide: 9–12), including obituaries by Mooney (1905) and Newell (1905) and two brief notes by Schevill Link (1948–49 and 1960).

2. Matthews published a Grammar and Dictionary of Hidatsa (with an "Introductory Sketch of the Tribe") in 1873, and an Hidatsa English Dictionary in 1874, both in Shea's Library of American Linguistics, ser. 11, nos. 1 and 2 (New York: Cramoisy Press). These two were revised and consolidated and published in 1877 as the *Ethnography and Philology of the Hidatsa Indians*, U.S. Geological and Geographic Survey, Miscellaneous Publication no. 7 (Washington: GPO), reprinted in 1971 by Johnson Reprint Editions with an introduction by Robert Spencer. The ethnographic portion was reprinted in 1969 in the *Plains Anthropologist* 14(45) with an introduction by Waldo Wedel. Both Wedel and Spencer praise this pioneer work. It was this publication that brought Matthews the LL.D. degree from the University of Iowa in 1888 (Wedel's introduction: 176).

3. A letter written April 14, 1951, from Mrs. Dorothea M. Waller, a niece of Washington Matthews, to Margaret Schevill (Link) was received by the Wheelwright Museum in November 1993 to be included in the Washington Matthews Collection. The letter, a gift from James Schevill, son of Margaret Schevill, and his wife, Margot Blum Schevill, was in a response to Margaret Schevill's request for information about Matthews' son Berthold, and it throws further light on

Berthold Matthews' life and his father's continuing responsibility for him. Mrs. Waller had been told that Berthold's mother was the daughter of a Gros Ventre chief, that Matthews had taken the little boy to a mission to be cared for and educated, that Matthews had accepted full responsibility for his son, had kept up contact and correspondence with him, and had given him some land near Baker, Oregon, where Berthold resided for a time. Berthold was still alive when Matthews died in 1905. Mrs. Waller said that Berthold was reported to have had difficulties with drinking, that he had entered the University of Iowa law school but she thought that he probably had not graduated. He was reported to have written to his father that he was proud of his father but also proud of his mother's people. She had been told that in Eastman's "Indians of Today" there was a reference to a child of Dr. Matthews but otherwise no published reference to him. She wrote that "Dr. Matthews felt no need for secrecy," but she left to Mrs. Schevill the decision whether it was wise to let this history be known.

4. Evidence of this vocabulary collection appears throughout his papers, especially in the field notes and notebooks (Guide: 50–56). Powell's Introduction to the 4th Annual Report of the Bureau of [American] Ethnology for 1882–83 carries notice of Matthews' linguistic work (xliii–xliv), and Pilling (1892) quotes a letter from Matthews dated 22 September 1891, reporting:

> My work on the Navajo language is growing but is in such a chaotic state as yet that I cannot give you a very satisfactory account of it. I have, I think, grammatic material to fill 200 or 250 printed quarto pages, and I have about 10,000 words in my dictionary. My collection of texts and translations—songs, prayers, myths, rituals, etc.—would fill a good size volume of themselves. It will take time and leisure to put them in shape however.

The Matthews Papers contain five metal file boxes of vocabulary cards transcribed from field notes, containing Navajo words and phrases (see Guide: 50, 56, item 767, microfilm rolls 6, 7, and 8).

5. In October 1884 Matthews was on a field trip to the Southwest, so J. S. Billings of the Army Medical Museum read the paper for him. For the published abstracts of this lecture, see Matthews 1885a. The manuscript of this lecture is reproduced in the Appendix to Poor (1975: 131–39) and is included in the selections from Matthews' papers in the present volume.

6. Four field notebooks contain hour-by-hour accounts of the Mountain Chant: #467, 1882; #214, 1884, which records his first sight of drypaintings; #468, 1887; and #474 (see Guide: 54). The Mountain Chant publication was reviewed in England by A. W. Buckland (1893). In the Mountain Chant (1887a: 441, par. #145) Matthews indicated that he had left out a portion of the dramatic action that might be offensive to readers. In 1889 H. Ayme, a surgeon and self-professed scientist, complained to the Smithsonian at this "prudery" and suppression in a scientific publication and asked for access to the full record. Matthews prepared a full description of the sexual joking behavior in the performance that he had witnessed on 5 November 1882, together with a translation of the accompanying dramatic dialogue that his friend A. M. Stephen had obtained the following day from one of the actors. This "Suppressed Part of the Mountain Chant" was privately printed in a four-page pamphlet at Fort Wingate (1892c) and has since been accessible in the National Anthropological Archives of the Smithsonian and in the Matthews microfilm (Guide: 22, #68). It is also reproduced in Part Two of this volume.

7. Matthews' own statement (1902a: #42) that Tall Chanter's visit was in 1884 is apparently in error. His correspondence with Powell (Guide: 78–79) places it a year later. Poor discusses this apparent error (1975: 36, #79).

8. Schevill Link attributes his physical difficulties to a stroke some time in 1892 (1948–49: 4). An army retirement board attributed them to "a severe attack of grippe sustained in the spring of 1891" (see letter of the Secretary of War dated 23 September 1895, contained in the medical reports of Matthews' disability retirement, Guide: #72).

9. Matthews' correspondence with Cushing is in the Hodge-Cushing Collection of the

Southwest Museum in Los Angeles. Twelve of Matthews' letters, from 1881 to 1884, show the early development of their personal friendship, the enthusiasm with which they undertook fieldwork, and their comments on various scientific and political visitors. (These letters are reproduced in the microfilm of the Matthews Papers, see Guide: 81–82). Cushing's journal and correspondence covering the years 1879–1884, published with detailed annotation in Green 1990, reveal his side of the relationship with Matthews. After Matthews and Cushing left New Mexico in 1884, their correspondence is less regular; there are six letters from Matthews and one from Cushing in the years 1884–1890, and six from Matthews during his second assignment at Fort Wingate from 1890 to 1894.

10. When Cushing was away on short exploring trips, Matthews' letters show this concern for his health and encouragement for his work (Green 1990: 175–76, 237). During Cushing's long trip East in 1882 with Zuni companions, Matthews reported to him what was happening at Zuni and Wingate. Cushing was married during this trip, and the cordial reception the newlyweds received on their return to Wingate apparently reassured him of Matthews' approval of his bride; his journal entry for 18 September 1882 notes: "Dr. and Emma good friends, thank God . . ." (Green 1990: 240). In celebration of this homecoming Matthews had composed a ballad titled "The Pagan Martyrs" that took as its theme the Zuni steadfastness in their own religion in the face of the injustices of their Spanish conquerors (see Zolbrod's paper in this volume). Sylvester Baxter, a writer and newspaper correspondent from the East who had visited Wingate and Zuni, published several popular articles on Cushing's Indian activities, and he included Matthews' ballad in his account of Cushing's trip East with his Zuni companions (Baxter 1882; Green 1990: 240–41, note 11, p. 401).

11. Bourke's diary (ed. Lansing B. Bloom, 1936, nos. 1–3) gives an account of his first Zuni visits in the spring and summer of 1881, and Porter (1986: 113–40) also describes them, as well as his two-week stay with Cushing in November 1881.

12. Accounts of Matthews' contacts with the Hemenway Expedition appear in several sources. Early accounts are: Matthews 1893a and 1900a; Bourke 1936: 204; Lamb n.d.: 92; Hrdlicka 1914: 543–45. Later descriptions include Poor 1975: 41–45; Hinsley 1983: 60–61; Porter 1986: 276–77; Green 1990: 308. When Matthews returned to Washington after his trip to help Cushing in 1887, he arranged to have his colleague, Dr. Jacob Wortman, of the Army Medical Museum, return with equipment to preserve the bones that were being uncovered and bring them back to the Museum for analysis (Lamb n.d.: 92). Cushing had appointed as the expedition's physical anthropologist ten Kate, who collaborated with Wortman in an archaeological report on the hyoid bone for the Berlin 1888 International Congress of Americanists (Wortman and ten Kate 1890), but ten Kate's field observations for the expedition were primarily of the Pima, Papago [Tohono O'odham], and other living tribes of the area, with comparative data on skulls from the excavations (he acknowledges that Matthews provided him with information on these skull measurements) (ten Kate 1892). However, the major analysis of the excavated skeletal material was performed by Matthews, as presented in his publication of 1893a. Among Matthews' military records of 1888–89 is a thirty-two-page exchange of correspondence between J. C. Billings, Matthews, Cushing, and Fewkes regarding a dispute in which Billings, acting for the Army Medical Museum, refused to send a selection of skeletons from the expedition to the Berlin exhibit of 1888 since there was no assurance that they would be returned (Guide: 74–75). In the papers presented by the Hemenway Expedition at the Berlin Congress (Cushing 1890; Wortman and ten Kate 1890; Bandelier 1890) there is no mention of Matthews' analysis of the skeletal material. As Poor (1975: 45) and Bourke (1936: 204) have indicated, there seems to have been a temporary cooling of Cushing's friendship with Matthews, apparently related to some of these events of the Hemenway Expedition.

13. Stephen published several early articles on the Navajos (see Stephen 1893), and his 1885 recording of their origin myth was edited by Olive Bushnell (1930). The Matthews Papers con-

tain four letters from Stephen to Matthews (Guide: 45, items 184–185, 71, 295); a copy of a fifth is in Notebook 674 (Guide: 56). They discuss mutual Navajo interests (including detailed lists of clans), and they are friendly but formal in a graceful and polished writing style. Green says that the Hodge–Cushing Collection contains a few letters from Stephen to Cushing, envelope 87 (Green 1990: 268–72) that presumably date from 1882–84. One dated 15 December 1883 to Cushing published in Green (1990: 312) is lighter and livelier in style than Stephen's letters to Matthews—and full of literary allusions.

14. Paul Sledzik, in a symposium paper (1989), summarizes the historical development of the research program of the Army Medical Museum (now the National Museum of Health and Medicine, Armed Forces Institute) and the participation of early army surgeons in it. He cites Matthews' work in developing anthropometric methods and equipment and in analyzing the Hemenway skeletal remains.

15. Baker comments on the "thoroughness and care with which this investigation was conducted" and praises it as "one of the most exhaustive examinations of a small group of skeletons that has ever appeared" (1895: 87–89). Hrdlicka's review article of early developments in American physical anthropology discusses Matthews work at the Army Medical Museum, listing ten of his publications in physical anthropology, and judges the Hemenway volume as a "contribution of lasting value" (1914: 544–45). In the light of more recent interest in paleopathology of the Hohokam, Merbs (a participant in the 1986 AAA Symposium on Matthews) finds Matthews' work "a worthy pioneer effort . . . commendable for its accuracy and in pointing the way for future researchers." He goes on to say: "Matthews appears to have possessed the skill to become a first-rate palaeopathologist, but the discipline barely existed in his time and his strongest interests seemed to lie elsewhere" (Merbs 1986).

16. Matthews contributed twelve articles, twenty-one reviews, and nine brief notes to the *American Anthropologist* from its first issue in 1888 to 1904. A volume of *Selected Papers from the American Anthropologist, 1888–1920*, edited by Frederica de Laguna was published in 1960. It contains facsimile pages of the Table of Contents for the first two volumes, 1888 and 1889, and Matthews is the only author who occurs in both volumes (with a total of three articles, eight reviews, and five brief comments). However, there is surprisingly little recognition of Matthews' ethnographic work in de Laguna's volume. His linguistic work is discussed by Goddard (pp. 398–99), and his physical anthropology is described in some detail by Hrdlicka (pp. 343–45). The introduction to the section on Ceremonialism refers to his 1892 article on "Butts and Tips," and in the section on Ethnography he is cited briefly by Swanton and by Lowie.

17. As part of the AAA symposium on Matthews' work in 1986, the medical sociologist Stephen Kunitz gave a paper on Matthews' writings on Indian tuberculosis. Kunitz viewed this work in the context of early epidemiological thinking when public health measures were concerned primarily with social reform to improve living conditions of the poor and when the causal role of the tubercular bacillus was just becoming known. Matthews had calculated from his own materials and from correspondence with medical colleagues the proportionate contribution of tuberculosis to total mortality among a wide variety of tribes. He recognized that the means of leading a healthy life under indigenous tribal conditions had been taken away by white contact, and he tended to see the most humane solution for problems of Indian welfare in a policy of education and assimilation. Hrdlicka (1909: 2) says: "Original research in this subject may be said to have been begun in the 'eighties' by Dr. Washington Matthews."

18. This brief sketch of Matthews' relationship with Mooney is based on Moses' biography of Mooney (1985: esp. 21, 86, 104, 232–33) and Hinsley's picture of the intellectual position of anthropologists and their relationships in the early Washington scene (Hinsley 1981: 210–22). Matthews joined with Mooney in protesting federal neglect of the Cherokees (Judd 1967: 67). The three brief letters from Mooney in the Matthews Papers (Guide: 44) contain no significant per-

sonal data on their relationship; however, some of their common interests are reflected in their writings and in Mooney's obituary of Matthews (1905).

19. In the Matthews Papers there are eight letters from Fillmore from 1895 to 1896 regarding their articles on Navajo music (Guide: 46–47, 83). Fillmore had moved to California, and he may have been the stimulus to Lummis' contact with Matthews.

20. Newell's obituary (1905) noted that Lummis was to prepare a biographical account that presumably was never published. However, Lummis was presumably the unnamed correspondent who wrote to the *Nation* on 7 July 1905 an appreciative tribute to Matthews:

> . . . no other one man has known so intimately much about any one aboriginal tribe as Matthews did. His studies of the Navajo are the most exhaustive thing of their sort in all our anthropology. He was an extremely modest man, without the gift of popularity, either in his writings or in his intercourse. Of an extremely sweet and unselfish disposition, and much beloved by those who knew him, there was not a bit in him of self-seeking or pushing to the front. He accepted, with a whimsical patience, but with his eyes open, his latter-day function as the original source from which a hundred 'popularizers' built up notoriety for themselves, without credit to him. He was a real martyr—using that abused word without abuse—both to his duty as an army surgeon and his duty as a scientist; and the great mass of accurate and intimate research that he has left to us will always remain among the chiefs of the corner in our scientific edifice. I do not feel easy that such a man should be forgotten in his death by the *Nation*.

The Charles Fletcher Lummis Collection in the Southwest Museum contains the Lummis-Matthews correspondence (also reproduced in the Microfilm Edition of Matthews' Papers, see Guide: 83–85). The Lummis papers also contain the *Scrap Book of Dr. Washington Matthews* (indexed as "92 Matthews, Washington—Biography"). This is a large, old-fashioned scrapbook filled to a bulky four to five inches thick with clippings and memorabilia dating from 1887, mostly about Matthews' lectures, activities, and publications, which conveys the contemporary public impression of his work as reflected in newspaper notices and reviews.

21. In the Matthews Papers there are seven items of correspondence between Matthews and Hodge as editor of the *American Anthropologist*, and six regarding Matthews' articles for Hodge's *Handbook of the American Indians* (Guide: 44). The F. W. Hodge Collection in the Southwest Museum contains forty-two letters from Matthews to Hodge beginning in 1887 concerning the Hemenway Expedition, Matthews' contributions to the *American Anthropologist* 1892–1904, and his articles for Hodge's *Handbook* (Guide: 82). Matthews received remuneration for six of his articles that were published in this *Handbook*, which was sponsored by the Bureau of American Ethnology, and there are drafts of several that were not published (on "Medicine," "Family," "Culture Heroes," "Mourning," "Navajo Mortuary Customs") (Guide: 56, 62).

22. The Matthews Papers contain twelve letters to Putnam and Kroeber regarding these arrangements and eight items of correspondence between Matthews and Goddard regarding Goddard's proposed fieldwork to help complete their final publication on myths, prayers, and songs of the Night Chant (Matthews, with Goddard 1907). In this correspondence Matthews offers advice to Goddard from his own experience with Navajo informants (Guide: 45–46). (See selections from this correspondence in Part Two of this volume.)

Matthews' Studies of Navajo Arts

SUSAN BROWN McGREEVY

A century after his research among the Navajos, historical perspective confirms that Washington Matthews' pioneering work has had lasting influence on subsequent studies of Navajo culture and Native American art. The scientific methodology characteristic of his investigations has provided a wealth of detailed information acquired during a particularly critical period in the development of Navajo arts. Furthermore, his respect and appreciation for the creative accomplishments of the Navajos reflect ideological assumptions that were not generally acceptable at the time, but presaged future concerns with problems inherent in ethnocentric bias. Matthews' pivotal analyses of Navajo art forms have continued to inform and enrich ensuing generations of scholars.

Setting

Since their arrival in the Southwest, some 500–1,000 years ago, the Navajos have continuously and selectively adapted ideas and technologies from neighboring Pueblo, Hispano, and Anglo cultures, translating each external influence into a distinctively Navajo idiom. Navajo arts were an integral part of everyday life. Objects were made for a variety of utilitarian and ceremonial functions, yet the care and attention to the creation of beauty transcended necessity. Navajo creativity is embodied within the fundamental, philosophical concept of *hózhǫ́*, loosely translated as "beauty," but embracing "the intellectual notion of order, the emotional state of happiness, the physical state of health, the moral condition of good, and the aesthetic dimension of harmony" (Witherspoon 1987:7).

Over the years, the *Diné* developed a viable socioeconomic system, based on farming and sheepherding.[1] Trading with neighboring Spanish and Pueblo communities was an important part of Navajo life. Mutual raiding also was a frequent occurrence. Beginning in 1848 with the American acquisition of the Southwest, a number of military campaigns were initiated to solve the "Navajo Problem." The principal objective of U.S. policy was to coerce the Navajos into submitting to government control. Finally, in 1863–64, military forces under the command of Kit Carson initiated a militarily successful, but morally reprehensible, "scorched earth" campaign. Carson's troops destroyed crops, livestock, and food caches, ultimately starving the people into submission. It has been estimated that between 8,000 and 9,000 Navajos were forced to make the brutal "Long Walk" of over 400 miles to Fort Sumner (Bosque Redondo) in southeastern New Mexico. However, due to "poor planning, abuses in the supply system and the unsuitability of the location" (Bailey and Bailey 1986:10), the Bosque Redondo experiment was a catastrophic failure. In 1868 the U.S. government established a new reservation in an area adjacent to the *Dinétah* (original Navajo homeland). Only 7,000 Navajos had survived to settle there (Bailey and Bailey 1986:27).

Washington Matthews' first posting on the Navajo Reservation in 1880 thus coincided with a pivotal point in Navajo history, a period in which the Navajos were adapting to life on the newly established reservation. Matthews' assignment at Fort Wingate also occurred during the developmental phase of American anthropology. As early as 1841, the National Institute (later to become the Smithsonian Institution) recognized the value of enlisting the assistance of army officers stationed at various outposts to gather information about neighboring Indian tribes. However, this policy did not become institutionalized until 1879 with the organization of the Bureau of Ethnology (later the Bureau of American Ethnology) under the leadership of Major John Wesley Powell.

Research sponsored by Powell and the Bureau was heavily influenced by social evolutionary theory. Under Powell's aegis, the objective of field work and the collection of raw data was to establish a scientific rationale for "civilizing" the Indians. As Hinsley asserts, ". . . science in 19th-century America was a moral enterprise" (1981:285). Powell's primary goal was to compile a complete classification of American Indian languages, with a secondary emphasis on studying the lifeways of the peoples who spoke them. He was impressed with Washington Matthews' previous accomplishments among the Mandans and Hidatsas and viewed him as a likely candidate to initiate a program of Navajo studies.

Thus Matthews' assignment to Fort Wingate occurred as a direct result of Powell's influence. Although his earlier work had provided some experience in ethnographic investigation, Matthews was perforce working in a methodological vacuum; guidelines for systematic anthropological field work were yet to be developed. In spite of his rigorous analytical and problem-solving skills, his pursuit of scientific objectivity was nonetheless constrained by the prevailing sociopolitical sentiments of the time. Although he did not, indeed could not, escape the pervasive climate of Social Darwinism, Matthews' Navajo studies are nonetheless consistently informed by an exacting and independent mind. Matthews' respect and appreciation for the intellectual integrity of indigenous belief systems and the caliber of native artistic accomplishments were shared by only a handful of scholars. Not surprisingly, Cushing, Bourke, Mooney, and Stephen were the colleagues Matthews respected most (see Halpern this volume). Powell occasionally found the individualism shared by these confreres cause for consternation. In 1891 he protested:

> When brought into close contact with the Indian, and into intimate acquaintance with his language, customs and religious ideas, there is a curious tendency observable in [some] students to over-look aboriginal vices and to exaggerate aboriginal virtues. It seems to be forgotten that after all the Indian is a savage. (quoted in Hinsley 1981:180)

"Industrial Arts"

SILVERWORK As part of his official duty as post surgeon at Fort Wingate, Matthews submitted routine reports to the army.[2] These chronicles indicate that although his responsibilities at Wingate were heavy, his professional obligations did not deter him from pursuing his Navajo research. He began with a systematic study of the language,[3] soon followed by investigations into various aspects of what Matthews called "industrial arts" (i.e., silversmithing and weaving). By 1882 Powell was importuning Matthews to submit a report about Navajo ritual and mythology. However, Matthews knew that his studies of Navajo ceremonialism were far from complete and his compulsion for detail and accuracy prompted his reluctance to comply with Powell's request.[4] In a letter dated 13 May 1882 from Matthews to J. C. Pilling, clerk of the Bureau and Powell's trusted friend and amanuensis (Hinsley 1983:164), Matthews makes a strong case for his material culture research.

> However if the major [Powell] must have myth and nothing else for his next report, I will send him what I have. . . . But I think I can send him something of equal or greater value. Our ethnographic literature is meager in . . . descriptions of Indian industrial arts. Now my notes on the working of metal by these [Navajo] Indians are about as complete as they are likely to ever be; and I could . . . prepare a very readable little essay . . . on this subject. (Guide:77, Roll 10, f. 565–566)

This "very readable little essay," entitled "Navajo Silversmiths," was Matthews' first publication about the Navajos, and also the first substantive monograph to be written on the subject. It was included in the 2nd Annual Report of the Bureau of [American] Ethnology for 1880–1881. The study is unique in several respects: it furnishes a wealth of detailed information about silversmithing technology, provides insights into Matthews' field work methodology, and places the development of the art in chronological perspective.

The Navajo smith, Atsidi Sani (*'atsidii sání*, meaning "old smith"), is most generally credited with being the first Navajo to work with silver. According to his nephew, Grey Moustache, Atsidi Sani learned to work with iron from a Mexican smith, but "it was not until the Navajo came back from Fort Sumner that he learned how to make silver jewelry" (Adair 1944:4). Although Matthews freely confesses that he does not know "when and how the art of working metals was introduced among them [Navajos]," he also observes that "old white residents . . . tell me that the art has improved greatly within their recollection; that the ornaments made fifteen years ago do not compare favorably with those made at the present time" (1883a:167). Thus, this study, made during the early years of the post–Bosque Redondo period, is of particular value in documenting the formative stages of silversmithing among the Navajos.

The research strategy Matthews devised for his study also merits scrutiny. His predilection for carefully observing and recording details with meticulous accuracy departed from the more common practice of relying on descriptions provided by "informants." Matthews arranged for a local silversmith to build a forge "in an out-house on my own premises . . . where I could constantly observe him" (1883a:168), and sometime later "engaged two of the best [silver] workmen in the tribe to come . . . and work under my observation for a week" (1883a:175).

As a result of this experience, Matthews was able to document the silversmithing process with exacting precision, step-by-step in chronological order. He recounts (1) the construction of forge, bellows, anvil, and crucible; (2) the types of tools utilized during and after the forging process; and (3) the repertoire of silver objects made at the time. Matthews' publication also includes a number of illustrations that further illuminate the state-of-the-art of silversmithing during this important early period.[5] Some years later, in his monograph *Navaho Legends*, published in 1897, he provides further insights into the continued development of the art.

> There are a few silversmiths in the tribe, whose work, considering the rudeness of their tools and processes, is very artistic. . . . In a treatise entitled, "Navajo Silversmiths," the author described the art as it existed in 1881, but the work has improved since that time. (1987a:19)

As the first systematic account of Navajo silverwork, Matthews' study has provided subsequent generations of anthropologists with a highly useful research tool. In his book *The Navajo and Pueblo Silversmiths*, John Adair observes, "The report of Dr. Washington Matthews is the only old historical account of silversmithing which we have" (1944:16). Adair additionally comments, "With his usual thoroughness and precision of detail Matthews extensively described the technology of the craft as it existed in the 1880s. . . . he is an <u>invaluable</u> source of information" (1986: personal communication).

TEXTILES Matthews' study of silversmithing was rapidly followed by his monograph on textile arts, "Navajo Weavers" (1884a). His appreciation for the craft is obvious from the opening paragraph, "It may be safely stated that with no native tribe in North America . . . has the art of weaving been carried to greater perfection than among the Navajos" (1884a:371). In a later publication he further observes:

> It is in the art of weaving that the Navahoes [*sic*] excel all other Indians within the borders of the United States. In durability, fineness of finish, beauty of design and variety of pattern, The Navaho blanket has no equal. (1897a:20)

Weaving had long been a significant activity for Navajo women. The Navajo creation story relates how the *Diné* emerged into this world after passing through a series of underworlds. At some point in the mythological past, Spider Woman instructed Navajo women to weave on an upright loom that Spider Man taught Navajo men to make. Weaving with cotton had been practiced since prehistoric times by the Pueblo peoples of New Mexico and Arizona. When the Spaniards came to new Mexico in the late sixteenth century, they brought flocks of churro sheep with them, thus providing the raw material for weaving with wool.[6]

While the dates and circumstances of the origin of Navajo weaving seem likely to remain undocumented, the most convincing evidence favors Pueblo antecedents (Rodee 1987:63; Kent 1985:2; Wheat 1981:3). The earliest Navajo textiles recovered from archeological sites dating from between 1750 and 1800 are of two major types: women's dresses and men's shoulder blankets. Both styles relate directly to Pueblo prototypes. By the early nineteenth century, new materials and influences were at work on the eclectic consciousness of Navajo weavers. Although garments were woven primarily for Navajo use, textiles also constituted an important trade commodity. Indeed, Navajo textiles were so admired that by 1800 "Navajo weaving was the most valuable product of New Mexico" (Wheat 1978:13).

"Navajo Weaving" briefly discusses the influence of the Pueblos on the development of Navajo weaving and includes a passing reference to the introduction of sheep into the Southwest by the Spaniards; however, the principal value of Matthews' study is contained in his rich and graphic documentation of process, beginning with shearing the sheep. Matthews' exegesis conforms to the same unerring, scrupulous standards previously established in his silversmithing publication. His report is made visually explicit through the use of diagrams and illustrations, including examples of textiles that he collected himself.[7] However, there is one interesting oversight. His description of loom construction is flawed by the curious omission of the culturally significant fact that Navajo men are responsible for building the loom.[8]

This 1884 study also provides some enlightening observations concerning traditional native dyes.[9] Most authorities have argued that prior to the introduction of commercial dyes and yarns during the late nineteenth century, the weaver's palette consisted of indigo dye, raveled red cloth, and various shades of natural white, black, and brown found in the wool itself.[10] Matthews' account indicates otherwise. Although he refers to the use of indigo and bayeta, he also discusses the native dyes he found in common use at the time: "yellow, reddish and black" (1884a:376). He continues with detailed recipes for the preparation of each dye. Thus Matthews provides documentation for the use of plant dyes well before the Wheelwright and McSparron experiments of the 1920s that are generally considered to have initiated the vegetal-dyed style.[11]

Unlike silversmithing, in which there have been dramatic technological advances in the last hundred years, Navajo weaving techniques have remained substantially the same since Matthews' time. However, there have been important changes in the function, style, and design of Navajo textiles. While Matthews' silversmithing report is, in part, significant because it was undertaken during the infancy of the art, his study of

Navajo weaving occurred at an equally critical time, coinciding with what has been commonly referred to as the "Transitional Period." By the late nineteenth century emphasis on handwoven garments for Indian use began to shift to a more commercial orientation.[12] This transition was the result of several factors: disrupted trade and market routes; the introduction of machine-loomed Pendleton blankets; and the establishment of Anglo-managed trading posts on the Reservation. The Transitional Period was characterized by the use of merino wool and the incorporation of commercial, aniline dyes as well as commercially processed yarns known generically as Germantowns.[13]

In the overview of Navajo craft arts contained in the introduction to *Navaho Legends*, Matthews provides some interesting comments on these introduced materials.

> [My] treatise on Navaho weaving . . . describes their art as it existed some thirteen years ago. But since [that time] the art has changed. . . . It has deteriorated in [one] respect: fugitive aniline dyes purchased from the traders have taken the place of permanent native dyes formerly used. In finer blankets, however, [Germantown] yarn obtained from white traders has supplemented the yarn laboriously twilled on the old distaff. (1897a:20)

In this same discourse, written thirteen years after the publication of his original report on Navajo weaving, Matthews makes one of his most notable contributions to our understanding of the socioeconomic and aesthetic realities of Navajo weaving. "It is not only for gain that the Navajo woman weaves," he observes. ". . . At best, the labor brings low wages. The work is done, to no small extent, for artistic recreation" (1897a:21). Thus we perceive, through Matthews' eyes, the importance of the creative impulse that is inherent in the weaving process.

Matthews provides one additional and revelatory piece of information in *Navaho Legends*. He recounts: "An important new invention has been made or introduced—a way of weaving blankets with different designs on opposite sides" (1897a:20f). This is the first account we have of the appearance of the two-face textile, thus providing an approximate date for its development.[14] Moreover, Matthews corresponded with his friend, the trader Thomas V. Keam, in order to date this invention. Keam replies in a letter of 27 January 1897:

> As you supposed it [has been] only about three years since I first saw this work and to date there are only a few who understand this weaving. . . . The diamond or twill weave is undoubtedly copied from the Moqui [Hopi], but the double or reversible weaving I believe to be their own invention as I know of no other tribe who does such weaving. (Guide:45, Correspondence, Roll 1, f. 467–68)

Even though these textiles are made with the typical Navajo weft-face tapestry weave, the process requires a complicated manipulation of sheds. In a subsequent publication, "A Two-Face Navaho Blanket," Matthews confesses, "I should have to see the weaver at work and even then might find it difficult to analyze the process. . . . I know of no fabric made by civilized man that is quite like this" (1900b:641).

Although Matthews' studies were well received by the prominent academic journals of the time, during the course of his career he made several attempts to have his monographs on Navajo "industrial arts" published by a popular press. It proved to be an exercise in futility. A letter from The Burrows Bros. Co. typifies the reasons for rejection:

> We have been working very carefully with your manuscript of 'Indian Blankets'. . . . We did not wish to put [it] on the market without having it in a form . . . saleable and catching . . . [therefore] it will be impossible for us to handle it (15 January 1903: Guide:48, Correspondence, Roll 1, f. 764)

To this Matthews responds with some acerbity:

> I regret greatly that you feel unable to publish the work. . . . What I want is to instruct the public [and] to dissipate error. . . . Is [my] work too scientific? Is it not sufficiently popular? In short, should I make it more trashy in order to make it more saleable? (1 February 1903: *ibid.*)

Matthews' urge to make his studies accessible to the public was, in part, a reaction to the publication of U. S. Hollister's *The Navajo and His Blanket.* This book was greeted with outrage by Matthews and some of his colleagues—and with justification, for it represents the antithesis of Matthews' careful research. To compound Hollister's ineptitude, he makes no reference to Matthews' pioneering work, and indeed, based on the numerous mistakes and misinformation contained in the book, it seems clear that he was unaware of Matthews' studies. Hodge writes to Matthews in 1904; "My Lord! My Lord! Have you seen Hollister's [book]? It takes the cake—except for the illustrations, which are excellent. . . . I have commenced to review it, but words fail" (2/23/1904, Guide:44, Correspondence, Roll 1, f. 416). Matthews' reply reveals that he had a lively sense of humor.

> My Lord! My Lord! Yes, I have seen Mr. Hollister's work. . . . When publishers will not handle a decent book . . . some fake comes in and captures the field . . . I have been in bed for several days . . . [and] I see now what is the matter with me—it is Hollisteritis—perhaps your review will cure me. (24 February 1904: Guide: 44; Correspondence, Roll 1, f. 419–420)

Although today scholars of Navajo weaving view Hollister's book as an amusing curiosity, many consider Amsden's *Navaho Weaving, Its Technic and History*, published at the late date of 1934, as the first definitive work on the subject. Ironically, Amsden frequently cites Matthews in the first few chapters of his book. As Kate Peck Kent, one of the foremost authorities on Navajo weaving, observes:

> Some consider Amsden to be the Bible, but Matthews really is. He remains the primary source. He had such a great feel for process and communicated it so well. Most often you can't tell what's really going on in other ethnographic accounts." (1986: personal communication)

Ceremonial Arts[15]

BASKETRY Early Spanish chronicles suggest that Navajos were making and trading baskets as early as about 1600 (Joe Ben Wheat 1985: personal correspondence.) Archeological collections in the Laboratory of Anthropology (Museum of New Mexico), the Maxwell Museum of Anthropology (University of New Mexico), and the National Park Service provide examples of both twined and coiled baskets dating from about 1700–1750. Based on Navajo baskets found in museum collections, coiling seems have become the preferred technique for basketry production sometime during the nineteenth century.

By 1884 Matthews had turned his protean intellectual energies to the study of Navajo myth and ritual. One interesting byproduct that emerged from this research was the first ethnographic account of the *ts'aa'*, the coiled basketry tray. Since these baskets are chronicled in the creation story and have important functions in Navajo ceremonials, they are considered sacred.[16] Hence, they were of intrinsic value to Matthews' investigations. He discusses baskets in his monographs of *The Mountain Chant* (1887a), *Navaho Legends* (1897a), and *The Night Chant* (1902a), and in two smaller, but highly significant articles, "The Basket Drum" (1894a) and "Some Sacred Objects of the Navajo Rites" (1898d—reproduced in Part Two under the heading "Papers Published in Hard-to-Find Journals"). Cumulatively, these accounts provide critical information concerning several important aspects of Navajo coiled basketry trays. Matthews' description of technique reveals that the baskets are made "of twigs of aromatic sumac [*Rhus trilobata*] . . . wound in the form of a helix."[17] He goes on to observe that "the fabricator must always put the butt end of the twig toward the center . . . and the tip toward the periphery" (1894a:202). In an earlier study, Matthews analyzes the pervasive importance in Navajo symbolism of distinguishing the "butt and tip end of things . . . the butt end always having precedence over the tip" (1892b:345).

Matthews also collected an interesting story, "which is perhaps not wholly mythical" (1894:205), concerning the origin of the distinctive false braid (herringbone) rim finish:

> In the ancient days a Navajo woman was seated under a juniper tree finishing a basket in the style of the other tribes, . . . and while so engaged she was intently thinking if some stronger and more beautiful margin could not be devised. As she thus sat in thought the god Qastceyelci tore from the overhanging juniper tree a small spray and cast it into her basket. It immediately occurred to her to imitate [it] in her work. (1894:205)

Matthews describes and provides illustrations of two basic designs commonly found on coiled basketry trays: "A band of red and black, with zigzag edges" (1894a:202) and "four crosses [with] zigzag lines" (1902a:61). The first pattern conforms to the style that is generically known as the "wedding basket"; the second to the so-called "spider woman" or "rain" cross motif. While Matthews recognizes that trays with wedding basket designs are used to hold a variety of ritual paraphernalia, he asserts:

> The most important use of [this] basket is as a drum. . . . The Navajos say, 'We turn down the basket' when they refer to the commencement of songs in which the basket-drum is used, and 'We turn up the basket' when they refer to the ending of the songs for the night.[18] (1894a:203, 204)

Matthews also ascribes a function to the ceremonial break. "The line is put there to assist in the [east-facing] orientation of the basket at night in the medicine lodge" (1894a:202).[19] He refers to baskets having the cross design as "meal" baskets and contends that while they can be used for various purposes, the "chief use is for holding [sacred corn] meal" (1902a:61).[20] An additional informative observation concerns the fact that "The basket is given to the shaman when the rites are done" (1902a:59). It is interesting to note that baskets continue to constitute an important part of the medicine man's payment.

Additionally, Matthews notes a significant circumstance concerning basketry production:

> The art of basket-making is today little cultivated among the Navajos. . . . They buy most of their baskets from other tribes; but having generally let the art of basketry fall into disuse, they still continue to make this [wedding basket] form for the reason that it is essential to their sacred rites and must be supplied by women of the tribe who know what is required. (1894a:202)

Although subsequent studies by Tschopik (1938), Kluckhohn, Hill and Kluckhohn (1971), and others corroborate a decrease in Navajo-made baskets, more recent research suggests that this was not the case everywhere. There probably has always been regional variation in basketry production; thus while basket making may have indeed declined in the eastern and southern portions of the reservation, it continued to thrive in the more remote western region—the Navajo Mountain–Oljeto area (see McGreevy 1985, 1986, 1989).

Matthews also pays close attention to the fabrication of the yucca drum stick used in conjunction with the basketry drum. He not only describes in detail the gathering of the plant material used, he also relates that his knowledge of construction technique was based on firsthand experience: "I learned how to make it," he reports (1898d:232). Given the close intellectual and social intercourse between Matthews and Cushing, it seems possible that Cushing's extensive experience with artifact production as an empirical tool for understanding "how the objects . . . had actually been made and used by their originators" (Green 1990:5) encouraged Matthews' own experiments. To ensure the accuracy of his efforts, Matthews worked under the tutelage of the Nightway practitioner Laughing Singer (Faris 1990:49).

OFFERINGS One of the most important functions of Navajo ceremonies is to summon the participation of the *Diné Diyinii* (Holy People). The production of ceremonial offerings for them is thus integral to ritual procedure. Matthews' early articles on sacred objects (1892b, 1894a, 1898d) are thus significant for providing the first detailed description of the preparation and use of ritual offerings: cigarettes and wooden *k'eet'áán* (including prayer sticks, which Matthews calls "plumed wands").

As with his production of the drum stick, Matthews collaborated with Laughing Singer to gain intimate knowledge of all aspects of the manufacture and function of ritual offerings, thus establishing a precedent for what would later become known in anthropological circles as "participant observation." Some of the objects made by Matthews now reside in museum collections where they are catalogued as Navajo (also see Faris this volume). While Matthews was apparently permitted to produce a number of ceremonial objects, this hands-on empiricism did not extend to basket making, even though the *ts'aa'* was clearly of great interest to his research. In the absence of evidence to the contrary, we can assume that this omission was due to the fact that basket making was a ritually sanctioned woman's art.[21]

"Some Sacred Objects of Navajo Rites" cogently integrates the information contained in Matthews' previous studies of butts and tips (1892b) and the basket drum (1894a) with his descriptions of the preparation of other ritual paraphernalia. The article is particularly noteworthy, not only for its abundant detail, but also for Matthews' keen insights concerning the ways in which ceremonial arts "refer to, reinforce and reify" (Brody 1991:63) Navajo epistemology. For example, he observes that the cardinal directions and their associated colors are integral to each offering: from gathering the requisite organic materials, to ceremonial function, to ritual disposal after use. He also understands the importance of male and female symbolism to the fabrication process. Harmonious male-female relationships are integral to the achievement of *hózhǫ́*; a graphically explicit segment of the Creation Story is devoted to the dire consequences resulting from discord between the sexes. Thus Matthews' trenchant observation that the "shamans connect the custom of cutting of these [prayer] sticks on the San Juan [river]—the female sticks on the south and the male sticks on the north bank with this ancient [Creation] myth" (1893b:235), reveals how the realization of *hózhǫ́* pervades every aspect of ceremonial preparation. Although some diligent excavation is needed to uncover the richness of the subtext implicit in Matthews' observations, this essay (reprinted in Part Two under the heading "Papers Published in Hard-to-Find Journals") greatly enriches our understanding of Navajo world view.

In conclusion, Matthews was not only physician, scientist, and ethnologist, he was a consummate humanist as well. His studies illuminate the historical and cultural contexts of Navajo "industrial" and ceremonial arts and provide an invaluable perspective for contemporary research. Since the art of the Navajos is an inherent expression of internal values as well as a measure of adaptation to external influences, Matthews' pioneering research has provided a data-rich resource for subsequent generations of scholars. Although our knowledge of Navajo arts has expanded considerably since Matthews' time, the depth and dimension contained in current studies have been fabricated from the building blocks of his legacy.

Notes

1 *Diné*, meaning "the People" is the Navajo word for themselves.

2. Matthews' daily and monthly reports to the army are comprised of medical reports and descriptions of post conditions, contacts with Indians, leaves for attendance at ceremonies, visitors from Washington, etc. These military records from the National Archives (Guide:72–77, Roll 9, f. 1–1481; Appendix, f. 1–100; Roll 10, f. 1–392) are rich in factual details and provide much colorful information about daily life on an army post as well.

3. Matthews' struggled throughout his career to devise a coherent Navajo orthography.

4. Matthews' concern for detail is well exemplified in the following comment to F. W. Hodge, "I never do slovenly work, I always take the greatest pains . . . my signature to an article always bears accuracy . . . if nothing more" (Guide: 44, 26 January 1905, Roll 1, f. 437).

5. Listed as: Plate XVI.—Objects in silver
XVII.—Navajo workshop
XVIII.—Crucible and sandstone molds . . .
XIX.—Objects in silver
XX.—Navajo Indian with silver ornaments

Some of these objects are in the collections of the National Museum of Natural History, Smithsonian Institution.

6. The original sheep brought to the Southwest were the churros. This breed was well adapted to the environment and had the further advantage of fleece that was relatively easy to hand-wash and process. After Bosque Redondo, the U.S. government issued merino sheep, a breed that is a better meat producer but has fleece with a high lanolin content that makes it difficult to hand-process.

7. Listed as figures 49–55, Navajo blankets. Some of these textiles are in the collections of the National Museum of Natural History, Smithsonian Institution.

8. This omission may be due to the status of Matthews' mythology research at the time. Since the male role in loom construction is derived from the creation story, it seems likely that Matthews would have included it in his discussion had this knowledge been available during his study of Navajo weaving.

9. Matthews' study of native dyes was related to his larger interest in ethnobotanical classifications. (See Halpern this volume and "Natural Naturalists" reproduced in Part Two under the heading "Unpublished Papers").

10. Indigo dye, traded from Mexico, was available by the mid-eighteenth century if not earlier. Manufactured red trade cloth for raveling also appeared by the mid-1700s. Known generically as "bayeta" in the literature, the earliest cloth available was dyed with lac. Later examples are cochineal-dyed. From 1850 on, Mexican-woven bayeta, and from 1858 on, English baize were issued by the U.S. government (Wheat 1981:7).

11. Mary Cabot Wheelwright worked with Cozy McSparron, the trader at Chinle, Arizona, to encourage Navajo weavers in the area to revive classic-style, borderless, striped textiles using vegetal dyes. The vegetal style later was adapted at Wide Ruins (1936) and Crystal (ca. 1940) (Rodee:1987:99).

12. According to Jonathan Batkin (personal communication, December 1993), one of the earliest examples of a trader using Matthews for commercial promotion appears in an eight-page pamphlet published by Jake Gold of Santa Fe, ca. 1887, titled *Gold's Free Museum*. The pamphlet includes a description of Navajo weavings selectively plagiarized from portions of the text of Matthews' Navajo Weavers (1887a). In addition to the text, Gold included two engravings based on originals in Matthews paper. One is of a weaver seated at an upright loom with a batten inserted in the warps; the other is of a man's wearing blanket in Matthews' own collection.

Gold's text and illustrations were modified further by W. G. Walz of El Paso, Texas for his

1888 publication, *Illustrated Catalogue of Mexican Art Goods and Curiosities*. Walz altered the text slightly, and included an engraving of the Navajo weaver, further simplified from Matthews' original.

13. The name derives from their place of manufacture in Germantown, Pennsylvania. These yarns were first issued to the Navajos at Bosque Redondo. Joe Ben Wheat estimates that over 75,000 pounds of Germantown yarns were issued between 1864 and 1878 (1980: personal communication). While many textiles declined in quality as a result of the introduction of aniline dyes, Germantown yarns were used to weave the so-called "eye-dazzlers."

14. Today there are still only a few weavers who understand this technique. The best-known was Mabel Burnside (Myers), who died in 1987. In 1986 she told me that she feared that the two-face rug may soon become extinct "since young weavers do not have the patience to learn it."

15. Matthews' studies of sandpaintings are discussed by Parezo, this volume.

16. Basketry trays serve as containers for religious paraphernalia, sacred corn meal, medicinal herbs, and yucca suds and also as drums or resonance chambers and as portions of certain masks. They also constitute part of the payment given to the singer who conducts the ceremony. Matthews also makes passing reference to "wicker water-jars [that are] the proper receptacles of the sacred water" (1902a:45). In addition, he occasionally mentions the use of Navajo-made pottery vessels as ceremonial containers, but the brevity of his remarks suggests that the subject was of less interest to him than the more pervasive use of basketry trays.

17. However, Matthews does not discuss coil direction or work surface. Most of the basket weavers I have interviewed acknowledge that "a long time ago baskets had to be made in a sunwise direction." An analysis of Navajo baskets in several museums indicates that this ceremonially imposed coil direction fell into disuse by the early twentieth century. For a right-handed weaver using an interior work surface, a right-to-left coil direction is more natural. The transition to this technique may be a reflection of the gradual relaxation of ritual rules connected with basket making. Matthews also neglects foundation construction, a curious omission given his penchant for detail. In view of the much reported diagnostic trait of 2-rod and bundle for older Navajo baskets (versus 3-rod stack for Paiute and Ute), this would have been valuable information.

18. However, as Faris comments (1990:55), Matthews was in error concerning the specific nights that the drum is used in the Nightway.

19. According to contemporary basket makers, the *'atiin* (ceremonial break, road, or pathway) symbolizes the People's emergence and serves both as an entrance for the Holy People and an exit for the basket maker's creative energies. There also are several interpretations of other design elements: the white center is said to portray either the earth mother or the beginning of life; the stepped-terraces are clouds and/or mountains; and the red circular band represents either the sun's ray, or a rainbow.

20. A medicine man from Tuba City claims that these cross-design baskets were used in a rain ceremony that has been obsolete for about one hundred years (William Beaver 1986, personal communication). Late-nineteenth century Navajo baskets found in museum collections exhibit several additional designs. Contemporary Navajo basket makers have told me that baskets with these other designs were made for utilitarian, rather than ritual, purposes.

21. This is no longer the case. Due to the relaxation of a number of ritual restrictions (see Parezo 1983) and monetary incentives generated by the current Indian art market, today there are a number of successful male basket makers. Not only is there an "equal opportunity" collector's market for male-produced baskets, but medicine men find them acceptable for ceremonial use.

Washington Matthews' Contributions to the Study of Navajo Ceremonialism and Mythology[1]

CHARLOTTE J. FRISBIE

Ceremonialism and myth were the major focus of Matthews' ethnographic work with the Navajos. He conducted his fieldwork during two tours of duty at Fort Wingate (1880–84, 1890–94), and on two short trips (winter of 1884–85 and fall of 1887) while he was stationed at the Army Medical Museum (1884–89), and also by bringing Tall Chanter to Washington, D.C. (fall 1885). Matthews first witnessed the last night of a Night Chant on 19 December 1880. After seeing the Fire Dance from the Mountain Chant in November 1882, he attended a Mountainway at Hard Earth, New Mexico, on 21 October 1884, and thus witnessed sandpainting for the first time. Matthews' field work resulted in twenty-nine articles on ceremonialism and myth as well as three major works: *Mountain Chant* (1887a), which introduced the public to an extensive Navajo myth and expanded his 1885d work on drypaintings; *Navaho Legends* (1897a); and the *Night Chant* (1902a), a ceremony which Matthews studied for twenty-one years (1902a:v) and viewed as the most important and most ancient ceremony then in existence (1894b:247). The ceremonial and myth publications emerged between 1883 and 1910[2] and were based on work with at least five collaborators: Laughing Singer and Tall Chanter, both Nightway singers; Old Torlino, a Beautyway singer; Jake, a Windway singer; and Chee.[3]

Working at a time when public misunderstanding of Navajos was rampant, Matthews was able to dispel earlier ideas promulgated by Letherman (1856) and others that the People lacked symbolic art, religion, symbolism, and logic, that they had disagreeable music, believed in monogenesis (1886f:842), attributed all disease to demoniac origins (1897a:247 n. 224), and that all their ceremonies were dances (1887a:386). Being interested in other areas of anthropology, Matthews was well read and frequently commented on others' ideas, be they Fewkes' on "ceremoniology" (1897b) or the ceremonial circuit (1892d); Holmes' on stepped figures (1894e); Morgan's on gens (1897a), archaeology (1889c), myth and archaeology (1900c), snake symbolism in Mayan culture (1898c), and so forth. His published and unpublished works show that he enjoyed warm friendships with Cushing, Stephen, and Lummis, and also appreciated Mooney, Bandelier, Bourke, and Mindeleff; however, he had little respect for George Wharton James, Jesse Walter Fewkes, or either of the Stevensons (Halpern and McGreevy 1986:10). They also show that he was interested in a number of larger issues, including studies of the following: general ethnography (1897a, 1897b, 1899b, and Handbook articles 1907 and 1910); ceremonialism (for which Matthews wanted a different term and a special department of study) (1897b); secret societies and initiation rites (1897b, 1901c); Navajo and Pueblo similarities and dissimilarities (1892d, 1894c, 1898c, 1902a); symbolism (1885d, 1896a, 1898c, and elsewhere); cross-cultural comparisons (1897b, 1901c, 1902b, plus Pueblo above)[4]; oral transmission (1899b and elsewhere)[5]; Navajo borrowings (1894c, 1897a, 1902a); culture change, especially in religion (1894c, 1896a, 1897b, 1902a, 1907:28)[6]; comparative mythology (emergence myths [1902b], sacred brothers [1886f, 1897a:55])[7]; the relation of myth and ceremony (1894c, 1896a); and the relation of myth and song (1889b, 1894b).

Setting his own meticulous standards for fieldwork, and frequently paying collaborators and other field expenses from personal funds (Mooney 1905:516; Newell 1905: 246; Halpern and McGreevy 1986:14), Matthews made detailed, painstaking, hour-by-hour records while participating in ceremonial events; painted and sketched; and after 1890 (when Fewkes first used the Edison phonograph at Hopi and Zuni [Frisbie 1977: 11]), recorded songs and prayers on cylinders. His concern for complete records is captured in comments about arising during the fifth and sixth nights of Mountainway to make sure nothing was happening in the ceremonial hogan (1887a). On another occasion, the ever-watchful Matthews heard a prayer being intoned and located the event, thereby giving us "The Prayer of a Navajo Shaman" (1888a). He also received private instruction (1902a:v), which even included having a demonstration of a variant kind of Nightway dance (1901a). He was also interested in having ritual paraphernalia assembled and disassembled so he could better understand their construction, and in trying to make ritual items himself under the watchful eyes of medicine men (1894a). These interests led to some collecting for the National Museum and acquisition of things he could use in his own public lectures,[8] often illustrated by ritual items and later, cylinder recordings (1898d). In noting songs and prayers, his procedure was to record the Navajo and then provide both interlinear and free translations. In noting myths and legends, however, he evidently opted for English-only records except in the case of "The Origin of the Utes" (reproduced in this volume, Part Two, under the heading "Unpublished Papers"). In his publications, he used his own data to discuss issues, was careful to give others credit, and to recommend appropriate scholarly studies in cross-references and notes.[9] He never claimed to have produced definitive studies; instead, he noted doubts, undetermined etymologies, unidentified bird species, and things unwitnessed and thus only known through shamans' descriptions.[10] It was his own decision to censor descriptions of sexual activities of Fire Dancers from the Mountainway reports (1887a) and to publish them privately later, in response to criticism (1892c).[11]

An energetic participant observer, Matthews was flexible and adaptable. Only occasionally did he refer to the clash of two cultures he experienced while working on Navajo ceremonialism. For examples, see his remarks about the need to forget about bacteriology while eating from a communal bowl into which were dipped fingers "innocent of soap" (1896a:53–54), or his several comments about how the amount of repetition and use of the number four in recitations of rite-myths brought about "weariness [to] civilized hearers" (1897a:243–44 n. 202; 1902b:739). Using the language of his day, which today may seem ethnocentric and burdened with concerns for evolutionary schemes, he made such remarks as "A comparative study of worship will show that the same principles control the forms of worship among the lowest and highest" (1897b:263); elaborate and logical symbolism does exist among "this crude people" (1898d:247); Navajos have a religion—"an elaborate pagan cult" (1897a:33). He referred to the "heathen origin" of prayer (1888a), and called Navajo prayers "purely pagan compositions" (1897a:50). One also finds the terms "zoölatry and zoölaters," and "accoucheurs."

Despite such language, however, it is clear that Matthews understood shamans well, respected them, and won their confidence. Using interchangeable terms—shaman, medicine man, singer, *hataałii*, chanter, priest, and doctor—he knew they must be paid for their information and services. Comprehending that they spent a long time learning countless ceremonial details by oral transmission, he understood that they never told all, that different "schools" or "orders" existed among medicine men and thus differences of opinion (1885d, 1887a), and that lengths of myths could vary according to each medicine man's knowledge and personality characteristics and the recitation context. He believed that most chanters knew one big ceremony and some minor ones, and that with liberal fees, they could make a living as ceremonialists (1902a). He believed that medicine men operated by a code of professional ethics grounded in myth (1899b), acted as brothers without jealousy or boasting, helping each other out, visiting each other's ceremonies to assist and relieve tired singers (1896a), borrowing each other's equipment, and interfering little with tribal politics (1897a: 56–59; 1899b; cf. also Frisbie 1986). While references to their "ordination" are brief (1892b: 350), he understood that they acquired their equipment through construction, gift, and loan (1887a, 1892b, 1894a, 1902a). Chanters were viewed as "accoucheurs" (1897a:231 n. 100), while those who "pretend to suck out disease" were considered "charlatans and cheats" (1897a:56). Finally, Matthews understood that medicine men were not men of leisure, that personalities differed, and that work on esoteric materials could bring about fatigue, worry, and the need for protection (1888a, 1897a).

Ceremonialism

Since Matthews' publications can speak for themselves in their rich details, and since other essays in this volume address music, sandpainting, and poetry, I decided to identify what I believe to be Matthews' contributions to the study of Navajo ceremonialism and myth on a general level. What follows is based on a rereading of all of his published works in these two areas, itself always a humbling experience.

In the area of ceremonies, in addition to specifics on the Mountain Chant and Night Chant, the following should be noted:

1. Matthews used the term "ceremony" for the whole and "rite" for the minor divisions or acts within ceremonies. He contributed the terms "sacred buckskin" (1897a:214 n. 13), "sandpaintings" (1885d), and "rite-myths" to Navajo studies.

2. Matthews discovered that Navajos believed in a variety of deities and that there were some parallels between these beliefs and social democracy within Navajo culture. They did not believe in monogenesis but they were zoölaters, worshipping lower animals and zoomorphic gods (1886f:849). Some deities were more important than others (Sun, First Man and First Woman, Coyote the Trickster, Wind Gods, Sea Monster, Changing Woman, and the Twins), and most demons had already been removed (1886f).

3. Matthews realized that Navajo ceremonies could be studied only with great difficulty (1887a, 1888a, 1897a, 1897b). While considering why this should be so (1897b), as well as specific problems encountered when noting and translating songs (1887a:456) and prayers (1888a), he urged making these studies within the context of Navajo daily life and social intercourse, and doing so *now*, in view of missionaries' and government attempts to deny religious freedom to Indians (1897b).

4. Matthews believed that all of the great Navajo ceremonies were for healing; many were nine days in length, but some were only a few hours or a day in duration. There were also minor ceremonies for planting, harvesting, building, war, nubility, marriage, travel, and other life occasions, as well as those for special occasions, such as for bringing rain (1897a:41). He believed that there were seventeen great healing ceremonies (see Part Two this volume)[12] which used on the average four drypaintings each (1885d:934). Navajo ceremonies and rites may have derived from the cliff-dwellers, Utes, *or others*. These changed through time because of borrowing, abandoning, and modifications; thus, when studying them, one should expect both variation and change (1894c, 1896a, 1897b, 1902a, 1907).

5. All ceremonies included myths, prayers, songs, rituals, and other elements. However, in the great ceremonies, six elements of worship were especially important in Matthews' (1897a:42) opinion: sacrifice (or offering), drypainting, masquerade, dance,[13] prayer (see below), and song[14] (see McAllester, this volume). There was also much symbolism to be uncovered in the ceremonies, including color, directional, sexual, locality, and ritual action (1885d, 1896a). Matthews found symbolism difficult to study but believed that with enough years of

minute observations and detailed records by many, a data base would emerge from which better understandings of symbolism could be derived.

6. Ceremonial knowledge was transmitted orally. Different "schools" or "orders" existed among medicine men who had differences of opinion about rites and other matters (1885d, 1887a).

7. Navajo religion used many sacred objects, including a basket drum and drumstick (1894a), plumed wands, and two kinds of *K'eet'áán* (hollow cane "cigarettes" and straight or circular sticks) for making sacrifices or offerings to the deities and carrying messages to them. Rules and rituals surrounded everything in Navajo religion, from the preparing of offerings, use of pollen, preparing and eating of archaic food, smoking and sprinkling of masks, preparing of dance masks and costumes, and the making of drypaintings and unraveling cords. Rules surrounded the preparation, decoration, position, placement, use, and disposition of sacred objects, as well as the singing of songs, intoning of prayers, reciting of myths, and everyone's participation during ceremonies. Taboos also existed to be observed by the patient after the ceremony ended (1896a). (See also McGreevy, this volume.)

8. Ritual actions were based on definite theories or doctrines that had consistency (1892b). In addition to the "butt to tip" rule (1892b), events might be timed according to the sky and stars (1896a, 1901c), activities occurring both inside and outside the "medicine lodge" (1902a), and differences in procedures when patients were female rather than male (1892b, 1896a, 1901c). Other variations occurred because of decisions by medicine men, requests by the patient and that person's relatives, and extra fees paid for additional rites (1885d).

9. There were at least four types of prayers: silent, mental prayers, or prayers that are thought by either shamans or lay people; monologue prayers by shamans for their own benefit (either extemporaneous or formulated and set); short devotional expressions (formulated or extemporaneous) of a benedictory nature; and litany (or "dialogue") prayers. Prayers had structure; ending words, "Qojini quasle" or "hozóna hastlé" (Matthews' orthography), were comparable to "Amen." Prayers were iterative, might include obsolete terms, should be studied in ceremonial and mythological context, and could be rendered in Navajo, with interlinear and free translations.[15]

Myth

Besides contributing many myths and legends recorded mainly in English,[16] Matthews used myths or extracts thereof to discuss many topics. See, for example, his work on the significance of Mount Taylor (1895a), ethics (1899b), snake symbolism (1898c), context for sandpaintings (1885d), demons and deities (1886f), preparation of plumed wands and K'eet'áán in the Night Chant (1898d), and male and female symbolism (1896a). The major ideas he had about myth can be summarized as follows:

1. Myths must be understood in order to comprehend the spirit of Navajo religion (1902a). There are many great myths and numerous minor ones accounting for rites, origin of song groups, origins of divine personages, and so forth. One could never reasonably hope to collect and translate all of these (1907).

2. Ceremonies were connected with a myth or many myths, and many ceremonial acts were illustrative of mythic events (1896a). Myths provided prototypes: they might sanction or condemn customary behavior (1899b). In myths, men could become gods and gods could become men (1898c).

3. "Rite-myths" were those which accounted for the work of the ceremony, its origin, its introduction to the Navajos, or for all of these. Rite-myths never fully explained all of the foundation symbolism, although the creation and migration myths or other early legends sometimes did a better job of explaining such matters (1894c, 1897a, 1901b).

4. A tale that is unmythical was properly called a legend (1897a).

5. Myths were carried in the oral tradition. Tellers, who never told all, embellished them or not, according to their knowledge, memory, intelligence, age, and other characteristics (1899b, 1901b). Myth detail was never one-tenth of performance detail (1901b).

6. Some myths had great antiquity, demonstrated by the archaic character of the language and references to obsolete customs (1887a).[17]

7. Many versions of myths existed. (Matthews' approach was to select one version as the most complete, most extensive, and most consistent.)

8. When translating myths, the result must be readable and must capture the spirit of the original, even though such things as pantomime and vocal modulations could not be conveyed in print (1897a).

9. The connections between myth and ceremony were variable, in the numbers of myths which were relevant, how systematic their explanations were of the ceremony, and whether or not they detailed ritual acts in any kind of consecutive order. Myths had a narrative part known to many and an esoteric part known only to shamans (1894c).

10. The relationship among myth, legends, and song was variable. Myths might be very important or they might serve as "trifling memory aids," or as a means of explaining, giving interest to the songs (1894b:186), or making their significance apparent. Sometimes, however, additional cultural information was needed so that a myth could be more fully understood (as in the case of the Moccasin Game, 1889b).

> In the words of a contemporary, W. W. Newell (1905:246), Matthews' writings represent the new method in the study of aboriginal mythology, according to which legends are treated, no longer as mere curious tales, but as an essential part of the racial life illustrated and interpreted by abundant notes and illustrations. It has been said that 'Navaho Legends' was the best tribal study of the sort made. . . .

Despite these plaudits, it must be noted that while Matthews' work on myth, legend, and tales left us copious texts, it also left us some headaches. Sometimes myths were published with no reference to context (1883b, 1885c, 1889c) and often without reference to source.[18] Even more problematical was his decision not to record these materials in both Navajo and English, despite his care to do so with songs and prayers. Commenting (1897a:54) that neither he nor shamans were men of unlimited leisure, he explains that it was not practical to record the original texts of all stories. Thus, when forced "to choose between copious texts and copious tales, he chose the latter" (1897a:54). Such procedures, of course, make it impossible for others to cross-check information and rethink translations. The magnitude of the problem surfaced when Zolbrod set out to recast Matthews' *Navaho Legends* into *Diné Bahane': The Navajo Creation Story* (1984). Zolbrod's work with the Matthews notes, notebooks, and manuscripts housed at the Wheelwright Museum suggested to him that *Navaho Legends* is really

> a retrospective compilation of notes and recollections collated as a unified text and edited intentionally or unintentionally to demonstrate to an English-speaking audience that Navajos did indeed have literary traditions comparable to those of the Greeks (Zolbrod 1984:8).

Summary

When trying to evaluate Matthews' contributions to the study of Navajo ceremony and myth, it is important not to get entrapped by facile criticisms based on the advantage of hindsight. Matthews left us an enormous amount of published information about two ceremonies, Mountainway and Nightway, as well as some data on the Beautyway, Feather Chant, Apache Windway, and the Bead Chant. His papers, now available on microfilm (Wheelwright Museum 1985), provide information about ten other ceremonies. He also left copious texts of myths and legends recorded in English. All of this was made possible by the exacting standards he set for his own field work and publications, standards which continue to be worth emulating today. I wish he had told us more about "minor ceremonies," had recognized the importance of divination in determining what ceremony is needed (a decision he attributed to the patient and friends [1887a:387]), or had made some statements about Blessingway. Reichard (n.d.:32) faults him for not commenting on Shootingway and Enemyway, especially since she believes both were popular in his day, and since his "The Treatment of Ailing Gods" (1901b) myth seems to be from Enemyway. However, such criticisms and unmet expectations are really irrelevant, given the wealth of information he left behind in published form as well as the gold mine awaiting those able to work with the unpublished materials.

Equally inappropriate are evaluations of Matthews' contributions by comparisons between them and today's approaches, issues of concern, and standards. Yes, since his time, people in Navajo studies have become interested in psychoanalytic interpretations, male and female branches and ritual modes of ceremonies, relationship and classification of ceremonies, catalogs and classifications of themes and motifs in myths and sandpaintings and comparative analyses thereof, and prose that is not "impacted or unrepresentative." In some cases, there are glimmers of interest in these issues in Matthews' work. (See, for example, the major themes printed as page headers in the Mountain Chant [1887a]; his interest in Emergence myths and those concerned with Twins or sacred brothers; his recognition of male and female Mountainway, Shootingway, and Flintway; and his comments about connections between beliefs about deities and Navajo social organization.) Others have followed, building on his solid base, with further work on Mountainway and Nightway,[19] work on other ceremonies, and further discussion of his and newer issues of concern. There *are* obvious threads running from his work through that of many of us.[20] In the course of it, his ideas about a Navajo serpent cult (1898c) have been shifted through a thorough study of Beautyway, his comments about songless Navajo women (1896b, 1897a) are being corrected (Frisbie 1989), and it has become quite clear that bilingual texts need to be both recorded and published.[21] As the work continues to unfold, what seems most worth contemplating is just where any of us would be in our understanding of Navajo myth and ceremonies, and how to study and report them, without his thorough, tireless efforts at documentation, his astute powers of observation, his inquiring mind, and his energetic, prolific publication records. As Mooney (1905:517) said, Matthews "awakened the scientific world to the possibilities of Indian myth and ritual, and created an interest in the subject which has never slackened."

Notes

1. A shorter version of this essay was originally prepared for presentation in the symposium, "Washington Matthews and the Beginning of Navajo Studies: A Centennial Retrospective of His Contributions to American Anthropology," at the 85th annual meeting of the American Anthropological Association in Philadelphia, 2–7 December 1986. Since then, it has been expanded and revised several times to incorporate further data provided by Katherine Spencer Halpern and to take into account the helpful critiques of earlier versions offered by her, Susan McGreevy, and James Faris.

2. The ceremonial and myth publications were distributed as follows: two (1883b, 1884b) occurred during his first tour at Fort Wingate; seven, including *The Mountain Chant* (1887a), were published during Matthews' time at the Army Medical Museum (1885c, 1885d, 1886f, 1887a, 1888a, 1889b, 1889c); six were published during the second field-work period (1892b, 1892c, 1892d, 1894a, 1894b, 1894c); thirteen were published after ill health forced his retirement on 26 September 1895 and before his death on 29 April 1905 (1895a, 1896a, 1896b, *Navaho Leg-*

ends [1897a], 1897b, 1898c, 1898d, 1899b, 1901a, 1901b, 1901c, *Night Chant* [1902a], 1902b); and six were published posthumously (1907 with Goddard, and the five of his six articles for the *Handbook of American Indians* [1907 and 1910] which dealt with ceremonial and myth topics). References in this essay match those in the *Guide to the Microfilm Edition of the Washington Matthews Papers* (Guide:15–33) in the use of *a*'s, *b*'s, etc. on years.

3. Jake, also known as Biolzog, the Silversmith, and Náltsos Nigéhani, contributed Version B of the Origin Legend and also gave Matthews an account of his Windway ceremony and its *jish* (see 1883b; 1897a:50–51; Guide:54–55; Frisbie 1987). Whether he led the Apache Windway that Matthews witnessed on 6 February 1891 (Guide:51) is unknown. Jake died in 1896 (Halpern 1985:47). Chee (of unknown profession) gave Matthews a list of "dances" on 3 June 1890 (Guide: 50). Old Torlino, a Beautyway singer, provided Version A of the Origin Legend, which Matthews recorded in English, during October and November 1893 and first thought to be Beautyway (Schevill Link 1960). Hatali Nez (Tall Chanter), a Nightway singer with whom Matthews began to work in November 1884, contributed "the" Origin Legend (1897a), "The Visionary," and "So, A Variant of the Visionary" (1902a:159–71, 197–212). He made *K'eet'áán* for exhibits and helped Matthews check field data during a trip to Washington, D.C. in the fall of 1885. Known for his irritable temper in later years (1897a:57), it is also possible that he was the reciter of "The Prayer of a Navajo Shaman" (1888a). Hatali Natloi (Laughing Singer or Smiling Chanter), a Nightway singer, worked with Matthews between December 1891 and March 1892, between December 1892 and April 1894, and also with Goddard in 1906 after Matthews' death (see Matthews with Goddard 1907). He provided information on Nightway myths, prayers, texts, and ceremonial procedures, as well as the myth of "The Whirling Logs, a sequel to the Visionary" (1902a:171–97). Matthews helped him make ceremonial equipment during Nightways (December–January 1891–92; March 1892). He also credits him with understanding pathology (1897a:247 n. 224) and the following personal characteristics: keen sense of humor, kindness, honesty, self-respect, courtesy, and dignity (1897a:57). Faris' (1990) work on the Nightway suggests that Tall Chanter is better remembered and genealogically more significant than Laughing Singer; for further information on both men, as well as on Ben Damon, another important collaborator, see Faris, this volume and 1990.

4. Besides general Pueblo comparisons, he specifically was interested in those with Moki (Hopi), Zuni, Mandan, and Arikara peoples. He also contemplated groups that had accepted the Ghost Dance. See also note 7 below.

5. Matthews was interested in oral transmission and the amount of stability it ensured or undermined. He initially doubted that sandpainting designs could remain accurate through time (1887a:445).

6. Matthews was interested in noting difficulties in getting sacred buckskin, how parts of rituals might be omitted if sacred buckskin was not available, how it was getting more difficult to obtain buffalo robes and proper rattles for ceremonial use (and the subsequent changes these conditions precipitated), and also in addressing the responsibilities of the U.S. government as well as missionaries for changes in Navajo religion.

7. Even though he carefully kept rein on his thoughts about comparative mythology in *Navaho Legends* (1897a:56), Matthews was interested in similarities with Hindu, Greek, Roman, and Norse tales of sacred brothers (1886f), as well as in the worldwide distribution of emergence myths, including ascent from lower worlds through a vine, reed, or tree, and a deluge (1902b). Although I found no published comments by Matthews on the "stages of mythic philosophy," J. W. Powell's (1887a:xliv) introduction to the *Mountain Chant* says that the "myth exhibits the state in mythic philosophy in which zootheism and physitheism are both represented" and animal gods "are becoming anthropomorphic."

8. He was allowed to keep a yucca drumstick intact, which had never been used ceremonially (1894a:207). He did buy *kethawns*, among other things, for the National Museum, but he

never was allowed to keep any yucca masks (1897a:214–15 n. 14; see also Faris, and McGreevy, this volume).

9. Thus, Mountain Chant information can be found in 1884b, 1885d, 1886f, 1894c, 1897a, 1898c, as well as in 1887a, 1892c, and an article published in German in *Der Westen* on 8 April 1883 by Sgt. Christian Barthelmess, a friend of Matthews, also stationed at Fort Wingate. Night Chant information can be found in 1885d, 1886f, 1892b, 1894a, 1894b, 1894c, 1896a, 1897a, 1898a, 1898c, 1901a, 1901c, as well as in 1902a and the posthumous 1907 edited by Goddard. The latter expanded the 1902a study with "A Tale of Kininaékai [White House]" (including six songs and six prayers), "The Story of Bekotsidi" (with one song), two prayers, and a Protection Song, all from Laughing Singer.

Some of the concern for proper credit came about because George Wharton James used Matthews' information on the Fire Dance in a 1900 publication without acknowledging him. Matthews first wrote a ten-page scathing review, but settled for Lummis' review and a brief comment of his own (1901e). Among studies he cross-referenced were Mooney's work on the Ghost Dance, Mindeleff's on "Navajo Houses," Stephen's "The Navajo," Catlin's work on Indian games, and a variety of studies by Cushing. It is also clear that Matthews believed that Fewkes had not given Stephen credit for sharing his Hopi knowledge, and that James Stevenson had failed to credit Stephen for his assistance and sharing of Navajo knowledge (Halpern and McGreevy 1986:10). Whether he felt bitterness toward Stevenson for not acknowledging his own work and for being the first to publish Nightway data in 1891 on the basis of one observation in 1885 near Keams Canyon is not clear in the published materials, but see Faris (1990:41) and Faris this volume.

10. See, for example, the comments about the version of Nightway which does not include a public exhibition on the final night. Matthews collected "The Stricken Twins," (a myth of "*To'nastsihégo hatál*") in conjunction with this version, but never witnessed it (1902a:212–65). Faris (1990:32) notes that this is a Big Godway myth and later (1990:66–67 n. 11) discusses the problematic relationship of Nightway and Big Godway. Matthews also never witnessed the making of Nightway masks.

11. It is interesting that Haile (1946:16–17) noted that such activities were objectionable to white "sensibilities" and to the U.S. government. Zolbrod (1984:10–11) suggests that Matthews also deleted explicit sexuality from *Navaho Legends* (1897a).

12. The "List of Navajo Healing Dances" (see this volume, Part Two) obtained from an unidentified male, enumerates seventeen (actually sixteen different) ceremonies with their Navajo names and, in most cases, their translations. It also provides comments about the kinds of illnesses the ceremonies "are good for," and says that while all of these have associated drypaintings, the lack of public exhibits in most make them unknown to whites. The second list (also this volume, Part Two) was "obtained from Chee, Tuesday, June 3rd, 1890."

My work with these two lists shows that Matthews identified sixteen ceremonies, the names of two of which are not given in English translation. One of the latter is associated with ghosts, and the other with paralysis. Male and Female "kinds" were recognized for Mountainway and Shootingway; Flintway is entered as Flintway and Male Flintway. Also of interest are the recognition of what are now called "etiological factors": the multiple names for Beadway/Eagleway, Feather Dance/Deer Dance, and Shootingway/Lightningway; and the combined Mountainway/Shootingway ceremony. Matthews identified five kinds of Nightway and four kinds of Mountainway (two of which were Male and two Female), and also commented on the decline of Hailway.

The published materials also give indications that Matthews' knowledge of ceremonialism extended beyond Nightway and Mountainway. It is clear that he knew something about Beautyway from working with Old Torlino (1898c). It is also clear that he knew something about the Feather Chant (Plumeway), having recorded its Hollow Log story, Natinesthani, in English in January 1894. He suggests (1897a:250 n. 249) that the Feather Chant had only four living priests, was a nine-day ceremony associated with the deer disease, that a Deer Dance was formerly part of it, and that it had "more stories, songs, and acts than any other Navaho ceremony." It is also clear that he saw an Apache Windway on 6 February 1891 and recorded an account of Jake's Windway and the contents of his Windway bundle (see Guide:54–55; Frisbie 1987). Finally, he knew something about the Bead Chant, having published one of its rite-myths in 1894c which he called "the most ingenious and poetic rite-myth" he had obtained (1894c:250), and having recorded a Song of the Eagles (published in 1897a:267 n. 86). Additional comments on the fragment-myth of the Great Shell of Kintyél (18972:53, 250 n. 250) tell us that the nine-day healing ceremony, the Bead Chant, was becoming obsolete, having only one singer left. Also (1897a:251 n. 263), he remarks that the myths of the Great Shell and the Mountain Chant corroborate each other.

13. Like many others, Matthews was fascinated by the public dance exhibitions that might occur on the final nights of the Mountain Chant and the Night Chant. Known as the Dark Circle of Branches, or more commonly the Fire Dance or Corral Dance in the Mountainway, Matthews found these shows, acts, or dances much more varied than those in the Nightway. In describing the Fire Dance, which Wyman (1975:13) terms a "sacred vaudeville show," Matthews (1887a) uses his observations of 5 November 1882 and 28 October 1884 as bases, adding information from other performances where appropriate. In his major work on the Night Chant (1902a), Matthews carefully notes costuming, masking, and movements of the *Yéii Bicheii* dancers, the "undress rehearsals" of the dancers and singers on the sixth, seventh, and eighth nights, and the careful rehearsing of the First Dancers under the critical eyes of shaman experts throughout the afternoon and early evening of the ninth night. Despite his identification of masquerade and dance among the six important elements in ceremonies, Matthews believed that dance existed mainly to attract and entertain spectators.

He also noted the white national prejudice of viewing all Indian ceremonies as "dances" (1887a:386) (a habit he himself also had, as shown in his list of Healing Dances), and recognized that variation occurred in dance just as it did in song, myth, and prayer. Matthews believed that dance could be described; that personages, including the possible clown, must be understood; and that care should be taken to note connections between music and dance, such as in the *Yé'ii Bicheii* performances wherein dancers got cues from singers' vocables.

14. Matthews recognized that songs could be improvised or set, depending on context. They were sequenced, and some were more "special" than others. He also discussed the relationship between myth and song (1889b, 1894b, 1896b). For works specifically on song, see 1889b, 1894b, 1896b, and Fillmore's contributions to *Navaho Legends* (1897a). Matthews also incorporated songs in other works: 1886f, 1887a, 1888a, 1894a, 1896a, 1897a, 1898d, 1901a, 1901c, 1902a, 1907.

15. Prayers are incorporated in the three big works (1887a, 1897a, 1902a) as well as in Matthews 1894a, 1896a, 1898d, and the 1907 posthumous publications; that of 1888a, "The Prayer of a Navajo Shaman," is solely concerned with prayer. Finding this prayer to be a narrative rather than a supplication, Matthews deemed it a "composition unique in form and bearing internal evidence of a purely heathen origin" (1888a:149). He also indicated its context, wherein the unidentified shaman (probably Hatali Nez) felt the need to counteract witchcraft possibilities after completing his recitation of the Lower Worlds portion of the Origin Legend. While Matthews used the term "litany prayer" in most of his work, in *The Night Chant* (1902a:296) he shifted to "dialogue prayer" which he came to prefer because the patient was repeating the shaman's exact words rather than giving a response, and because there was no congregational response. He also recognized that such prayers sometimes needed to be rehearsed (1887a:420). Matthews was concerned with producing intelligible, smooth English translations of prayers (1888a:151). Of all of those he ever documented, he was particularly interested in the Prayer of the Navajo Shaman (1888a) and that of the First Dancers in the Night Chant, which he found to be the most interesting prayer of the entire ceremony (1902a:296). His work on prayer left a solid base on which others, especially Reichard (1944) and Gill (1981), have built.

16. Only "The Origin of the Utes" (see Part Two) occurs in the Notebooks in both Navajo

and English (Guide: 55). Two versions, collected from the same unidentified person at different times, are presented in Navajo, and then, in interlinear and free translation; another version, again from an unidentified source, for which texts were not recorded is presented in 1885c; Matthews refers to it as a "very free translation" (Guide: 55).

17. See Matthews' decision that one of the versions of the origin of Changing Woman was the "most ancient and purest" (1886f:845).

18. While it is clear in *Navaho Legends* that the major version is from Hatali Nez (with Version A, from Old Torlino, and Version B, from Jake, being used in the Notes for augmentation), I have not been able to discern from the published materials who authored the myth of the Mountain Chant (1887a:387–417), the Great Shell of Kintyél (1897a:195–208 from the Bead Chant), or "Natinesthani" (1897a:160–94, the Hollow Log story from the Feather Chant). Since Matthews (1897a:35) says the latter was told by a Nightway singer, and Notebook #674 contains it recorded in English dated January 1894 (Guide:55), it is possible, if not probable in this last case, that Laughing Singer was the author. Faris (1990:26, 37) suggests that the authorship of both "The Visionary" and "Whirling Logs" is also problematic and cannot be securely attributed to either Tall Chanter or Laughing Singer.

19. Since Matthews' 1887a study (reprinted in 1952 and 1970), our knowledge of the Mountain Chant, Mountainway, or Mountaintopway has been expanded by English versions of Mountainway myths published by Coolidge and Coolidge (1930), Wheelwright (1951), and O'Bryan (1956); Haile's (1946) work on the Fire or Corral Dance; Reagan's (1934) documentation of a Fire Dance at Steamboat, Arizona on 5 November 1923; and, of course, by Wyman (1975). Both Haile (1946:introduction) and Wyman (1975:14, 127) suggest that Matthews' (1887a:387–417) myth is from Male Mountainway, a fact Matthews recorded (see Part Two of this volume, Unpublished Paper No. 1, "The Great Navajo Healing Dances," item #69, where Matthews says "Dzilkidji-bakadji, this is the one I've got"). Wyman's study presents Haile's 1935 work with Yucca Patch Man, thereby giving us the only Mountainway myth recorded in both Navajo and English, namely one of Female Mountainway. Wyman further discusses the Fire or Corral Dance (pp. 25–29), and explores the connections among Mountainway, Beautyway, and the Jicarilla Holiness rite. Yucca Patch Man's data add information on 142 songs from the final night (eight sets), and prayersticks (pp. 46–56, with prayers). Wyman, of course, covers sandpaintings, reviewing the sixty-eight extant Mountainway ones (p. 64), showing locations (Table 1, p. 63), and then discussing major symbols and designs in all. (The four originally published by Matthews are included in the sixty-eight.) Likewise, Matthews' myth is included in Wyman's review of the eight available Mountainway myths (p. 123) and discussions of major mythic motifs (pp. 122–56). Herein, The Pueblo War and the myth of Female Mountaintopway are treated separately.

Other Mountainway information can be found. Musically, a few songs from the Corral Dance are available commercially (see Frisbie 1975; Canyon Record 6117; Thunderbird Records TR 1943, Side 2, Band 6; Laura Boulton's album, "Indian Music of the Southwest," Victor Records P494, 91B; Feather Dance). A transcription of a Feather Dance song occurs in McAllester and Mitchell (1983:622) and further comments on the Fire Dance and one photo of a Fire Dancer occur in McAllester (1979). The four Mountainway sandpaintings of Sam Tilden, two of which are included in the Wyman (1975) discussion, receive further attention in Olin (1982: 45–57). Finally, the Mountain Chant as well as the Night Chant are known through photographic records (see below).

Since the 1902a and the posthumous 1907 addition to it, Nightway information did not increase significantly until Faris (1990). In the intervening period, general information appeared in Curtis (1907); Tozzer (1908, 1909); Franciscan Fathers (1910); Coolidge and Coolidge (1930); and Kluckhohn and Wyman (1940). Kluckhohn (1923) documents one witnessed in Thoreau, New Mexico, 9–18 November 1923. There were also some studies of specific aspects of Nightway; see, for example, the Franciscan Fathers' 1910 and Haile's 1947 work on masks; Nightway myths in Wheelwright (1938) and Sapir and Hoijer (1942); and discussion of sandpaintings in Tozzer (1909) and Koenig (1982).

Musically, because Yeibichei teams travel and compete for prizes at fairs and ceremonials, that part of Nightway music has been available commercially since 1941, after first being discussed by Helen H. Roberts in 1936 (see McAllester [1968, 1971]; Frisbie [1975]; Canyon Record ARP 6069, 1970; Indian House record 1502; and the transcription in McAllester and Mitchell [1983:621–22]). Faris (1990:59–63, 72–74 nn. 43–50, and elsewhere) provides extensive additional discussion, and notes other musical resources.

While we have no comparable advancements in our understanding of *Yé'ii Bicheii* dancing, linguistically, vocables as calls of deities (among other things) have received further discussion, most recently by Frisbie (1980:350–92). Masks and other sacred paraphernalia of Nightway and other ceremonies are considered in Frisbie (1987), and of course are considered in depth in Faris' (1990) work on the history of Nightway and its documentation (see also Faris 1986a). Faris (1990) also presents the extensive, previously unpublished Hastiin Klah Nightway narrative, as well as twenty-two previously unpublished sandpainting reproductions in color.

According to Wyman (1983:546), Nightway and Mountainway remain the ceremonies best known to non-Navajos because of their spectacular public dances on the final night, the public performances of dancers outside ceremonial contexts, and because of the very early, detailed discussion they received from Matthews and a few others. It should not be surprising, then, that both the Nightway and Mountainway have been filmed in part or in whole. The references known to me at present include E. S. Curtis' 1904 film of Yeibichei dancers, filmed during the day and used in "The Shadow Catcher," but with errors (Lyon 1986:25 n. 16); Emery Kolb's short film of parts of the Nightway, made in the daytime c. 1911; and Laura Armer's film of sixth-day activities of a Mountainway, February 1928 near Ganado, held with the help of Roman Hubbell. A copy of Armer's film is at the Southwest Museum and at the Wheelwright Museum; the latter also has many of Armer's photographs (Lyon 1986). For additional discussion and resources, see Faris (1990:11, 22 n. 13, 110–11, 133 n. 5, 248).

Additionally, both the Mountainway and Nightway were among ceremonies filmed and recorded in 1963 by the American Indian Films Group from the University of California, Berkeley, under the direction of Dr. Samuel Barrett. Both were filmed and recorded at Totso Trading Post, Lukachukai, Arizona, the Mountainway in October, and the Nightway in December. While the unedited footage and tapes are housed at the Lowie Museum (where a transfer to the Smithsonian is being planned [Faris 1986b]), some stills taken during each have been used in publications. William R. Heick supplied both Nightway and Mountainway photographs for use in Wyman (1983); although the printed captions indicate six as Nightway and one as Mountainway, Faris (1990:119) notes that the top picture on page 554 (in Wyman 1983) is most likely from Mountainway. His correspondence with Heick indicates that some mislabelling did occur at the Smithsonian. Gill (1979) chose to use sixteen Mountainway and sixty-three Nightway photos from those taken and made available to him by David Peri. Both Wyman and Gill also used one Nightway photograph each taken by Kenneth Foster (and/or Max Lair [Faris 1986b]), who accompanied the American Indian Films Groups.

Finally, the Mountain Chant, or specifically portions of the Fire Dance, Plumed Arrow Dance (with arrow swallowing), and the Feather Dance, are included in the Navajo Night Dances film by Coronet, produced by Lewin (Culture Heritage Series, 1957). Then, too, both the Mountainway and Nightway were among topics of discussion during "Interview with American Indian Musicians" by Charlotte Heth (see the two Navajo videotapes, IIIA and IIIB, and the *Unedited* typescripts; Frisbie 1981:365–81).

20. Rather than trying to document all the threads, let me just identify various topics and some of those who have continued Matthews' interests in them:

recording entire ceremonies: Haile, Reichard, Wheelwright, Wyman, Luckert, McAllester, and Frisbie

prayer: Reichard and Gill

sandpaintings: Newcomb, Wheelwright, Tozzer, Armer, Reichard, Haile, Wetherill, Olin, Dutton, Oakes, Koenig, Wyman, Parezo, and Faris

music: McAllester and Frisbie

vocables: Reichard, McAllester, and Frisbie

translation problems: Haile, Wyman, McAllester, and Witherspoon

myths: Wheelwright, Astrov, O'Bryan, Reichard, Luckert, Stephen, Spencer [Halpern], Wyman, Zolbrod, and Faris

singers: Reichard, Newcomb, Olin, McAllester, Frisbie, Chiao, and Faris

symbolism: Fishler, Newcomb, Wheelwright, Reichard, and Sandner

culture change in religion: Many, with Aberle (1982), Frisbie (1985, 1987, 1992), and Frisbie with Tso (1993) among the latest

dance: no definite threads yet apparent in published works, but data available in unpublished papers of Luke Lyon (Faris 1991)

aspects of religious philosophy: Reichard, Witherspoon, Luckert, McNeley, Farella, and Faris

21. I am in no position to evaluate the extent of Matthews' deafness and its impact on both his Navajo and English notations. As Oswald Werner remarked, both during the AAA symposium in 1986, and at the 5th annual Navajo Studies Conference in 1990, we still need to develop a consistent, acceptable way of deciphering Matthews' Navajo orthography.

Washington Matthews And Navajo Music

DAVID P. McALLESTER

In the mid-nineteenth century the following opinion of Navajo culture was published by the Smithsonian Institution:

> Of their religion little or nothing is known, as indeed all inquiries tend to show they have none. . . . The lack of traditions is a source of surprise. They have no knowledge of their origin or of the history of the tribe. . . . Their singing is but a succession of grunts and is anything but agreeable.

This was in a letter from Jonathan Letherman, an army doctor who had lived for three years at Fort Defiance on the Navajo reservation, and it appeared in "Sketch of the Navahoe Tribe of Indians, Territory of New Mexico," in the Smithsonian's tenth annual report in 1856. It must have caused tremors in that Institution even then. From the time it was founded in 1846, it had included the study of Indian tribes in its mandate. Lewis H. Morgan's monumental and appreciative *League of the Ho-dé-no-sau-nee, or Iro-quois* had been published in Rochester, New York, in 1851. Letherman's colonial obtuseness was already out of step with what was known about Native American culture.

John Wesley Powell's explorations, both geologic and ethnographic, began in 1870 and he became director of the Smithsonian's Bureau of [American] Ethnology in 1879. He was influential in getting Washington Matthews, an army surgeon who had already distinguished himself with linguistic work among the Hidatsas, posted to Fort Wingate on the Navajo Reservation. During eight years of field study, conducted while he also fulfilled his army duties, in 1880–1884 and 1890–1894, there began the refutation of Letherman, chapter and verse.

Matthews' general description of Navajo culture could hardly be improved upon today. He pointed out that their myths and pantheon of gods and heroes compare favorably with those of the ancient Greeks. He noted that in addition to the narrative literature,

> . . . besides improvised songs, in which the Navahoes are adepts, they have knowledge of thousands of significant songs—or poems, as they might be called—which have been composed with care and handed down, for centuries perhaps, from teacher to pupil, from father to son, as a precious heritage, throughout the wide Navaho nation. They have songs of travelling, appropriate to every stage of the journey, from the time the wanderer leaves his home until he returns. They have farming songs, which refer to every stage of their simple agriculture, from the first view of the planting/ground in the spring to the "harvest home." They have building songs, which celebrate every act in the structure of the hut, from "thinking about it" to moving into it and lighting the first fire.[1] They have songs for hunting, for war, for gambling, in short for every important occasion in life, from birth to death, not to speak of prenatal and *post-mortem* songs. And these songs are composed according to established (often rigid) rules, and abound in poetic figures of speech. (Matthews 1897a:24)

He speaks of the songs as poems and it is almost exclusively in their literary aspect that he studied them. His analysis of the song texts surpasses that of most of the scholars who followed him.

> <u>Figures of Speech.</u>—It is probable that all rhetorical figures of speech known to our poets may be found in these simple compositions of the Navahoes. But in many cases the allusions are to such recondite matters of symbolism, or incidents in their myths, that they could be made plain, if at all, only by a tedious recital. Thus it would not be easy to make clear in a few words why, when the goddess 'Asdzáá Nádleehé [Changing Woman], in one of the songs to her honor, is spoken of as climbing a wand of turquoise, we know the poet means to say she is ascending San Mateo Mountain, in New Mexico, or why, when he speaks of her as climbing a wand of haliotis shell, he is endeavoring to tell us that she is ascending the peak of San Francisco in Arizona. Yet we may gain some idea of the meaning by referring to the myth.
>
> But some of the metaphors and similes are not so hard to understand. Here is a translation of the Dove Song, one of the gambling songs sung in the game of *késhjéé'*:
>
> *Wosh Wosh picks them up* (seeds),
> *Wosh Wosh picks them up,*
> *Glossy Locks picks them up,*
> *Red Moccasin picks them up,*
> *Wosh Wosh picks them up.*

> Here Wosh Wosh is an onomatope for the dove, equivalent to our "coo coo"; but it is used as a noun. Glossy Locks and Red Moccasin are figurative expressions for the dove, of obvious significance. Metaphor and synecdoche are here combined. (Matthews 1897a:27).

Matthews goes on to discuss other figures of speech in Navajo poetry: antithesis, climax, repetition, and rhyme (ibid.:27–28). In the case of rhyme, he points out examples of rhyming lines in the European sense of the word, "but they more often produce this by the repetition of significant meaningless syllables. . . . "(Ibid.:28–29).

Matthews was the first scholar to give serious attention to the "meaningless syllables," or vocables, which are a highly significant, and by no means "meaningless," feature of most Native American music. In *The Night Chant* (1902a:271) he discusses the role of vocables in the structure of Navajo songs.

> Usually a Navajo sacred song has a prelude to each stanza and two kinds of reiterated endings, one for the verse and one for the stanza. For convenience in this work, the former is called the burden and the latter the refrain. Preludes, burdens, and refrains are often meaningless, or of doubtful meaning.

To help the reader visualize these features, I give a translation of the House Building song referred to above, with the different structural parts indicated in parentheses; the italics indicate vocables:

Leaders' House Song: *Construction Song Number 1*
(McAllester and McAllester 1987:25–26)

(Prelude)

He ne yana,
About this, he* is thinking, *'e-ye,* about this, he is thinking, *'e-ye,*
About this, he is thinking, *'e-ye,* about this, he is thinking, *'e-ye,*
About this, he is thinking, *'e-ye,* about this, he is thinking, *'e-ye,*
About this, he is thinking, *'e-ye,* about this, he is thinking, *holaghei;*

(Stanza no. 1)

Neye, Earth Women, *'iye bila,* her roof beam to be, *ye,* *(1st verse)*
About this, he is thinking, *'e-ye,* *(burden)*
Wood Woman, *'iya,* the roof beam to be, *ye,* *(2nd verse)*
About this, he is thinking, *'e-ye,* *(burden)*
Now, Long-life-returning, now Creating-blessing-everywhere, *ye,* *(3rd verse)*
The roof beam to be, *ye,* *(refrain, the much*
About this, he is thinking, *holaghei;* *reduced end of prelude)*

(Stanza no. 2)

Niyi, Mountain Woman, 'iye bila, her roof beam to be, *ye,* *(1st verse)*
About this, he is thinking, *'e-ye,* *(burden)*
Wood Woman, 'iya, the roof beam to be, *ye,* *(2nd verse)*

About this, he is thinking, *'e-ye,* *(burden)*
etc. . . .

(At the end of the song, Stanza no. 4, about Corn Plant Woman, the refrain is longer, made up of the second half of the prelude):

About this he is thinking, *'e-ye,* about this he is thinking, *'e-ye,*
About this he is thinking, *'e-ye,* about this he is thinking, *holaghane!*

---

* one of the leaders

In *The Mountain Chant: A Navajo Ceremony,* his first full-scale work on Navajo ceremonialism, Matthews has this to say about vocables and the meaning of song texts:

> In some cases a number of songs in the same set are nearly alike; the addition or substitution of one verse, or even one word, may be the only difference. Such songs usually follow one another in immediate succession; often, on the other hand, we find a great variety in subject and in style.
>
> Some songs are self explanatory or readily understood, but the greater number cannot be comprehended without a full knowledge of the mythology and of the symbolism to which they refer; they merely hint at mythic conceptions. Many contain archaic expressions, for which the shaman can assign a meaning, but whose etymology cannot now be learned; and some embody obsolete words whose meaning is lost even to the priesthood. There are many vocables known to be meaningless and recited merely to fill out the rhythm or to give a dignified length to the song. For the same reasons a meaningless syllable is often added or a significant syllable duplicated.
>
> Other poetical licenses are taken, such as the omission of a syllable, the change of accent, the substitution of one vowel for another. The most familiar words are often distorted beyond recognition. For these various reasons the task of noting and translating these songs is one of considerable difficulty. (Matthews 1887a:456)

Matthews' pioneer observations on Navajo poetics and the extensive use of vocables in song texts has been followed by a wide interest in the subject of vocables in general. A roundtable, "The Use of Vocables in the Music of American Indians," was organized by Norma McLeod at the 1979 annual meeting of the Society for Ethnomusicology. Charlotte J. Frisbie surveyed the studies of vocables in Native American music and in Navajo music in particular in "Vocables in Navajo Ceremonial Music" (1980:347–92). Her earlier discussion of the music of the girl's puberty rite yielded a set of twenty-three tentative "rules," or regularities, observed in the changes in spoken Navajo when it was set to music (1967:177–79).

It is notable that Matthews, the first scholar to make extensive translations of Navajo song texts, remains one of the most outstanding in his insistence on recording the *ipsissima verba* so that subsequent students can make, from the originals, comparative observations or, if needed, retranslations. Where some ethnomusicologists, even today, publish transcriptions of melodies with no notation of the text at all, Matthews provides the original with both interlinear and free translations.

In the best ethnomusicological sense of the term, "music" includes the entire cultural matrix in which musical sound occurs. It is here that Matthews' contribution to the study of Navajo music is at its richest. His two great compendiums on major ceremonials, *The Mountain Chant, A Navajo Ceremony* (1887a) and *The Night Chant, a Navaho Ceremony* (1902a), bring out the ways in which the myths are reflected in the songs. He also provides much of the esoteric knowledge required in order to comprehend the meaning and the function of the songs. He gives us extensive background on the social and/or religious context, the costumes, the graphic art in drypaintings, body paint, and decorated religious paraphernalia.

The relationship of song to story is brought out with particular clarity in his two papers, "Navajo Gambling Songs" (1889b) and "Songs of Sequence of the Navajos" (1894b). In the former, Matthews tells the tale of the contest between the night animals and the day animals: the outcome of a moccasin game was to decide whether there would always be night (as preferred by the "noctivagant beasts") or always be day. The incidents of this legendary, prototypical game provided the texts for the brief songs that are sung over and over today as the game progresses. The outwitted *Yé'ittsoh* weeps, the Owl is discovered cheating, the Bear puts his moccasins on the wrong feet when he leaves hurriedly (and so his big toes seem to be on the wrong side, today), and so on. For each song there is a story that explains a text that might otherwise be baffling (1889b:1–19).

In "Songs of Sequence of the Navajos" Matthews presented the series of songs related to the farm, or garden, of Hashch'éé'ooghaan[2] and told the story of how the deity prepared a planting stick and, with "his people," broke the ground, planted the corn, watched it grow and ripen, admired its beauty, explained to his son how it was nourished, and harvested it along with the beans and squash in the same field. Rain, lightning, rainbow, and associated deities all figure in the story and for each step in the story there is a closely related song.

> Such is a Navajo song myth. It reminds one of certain plays which have recently come into vogue, in which the plot, if plot can be found, serves no higher purpose than to hold together a few songs and dances. (Matthews 1894b:194)

Which Came First, Song or Story?

In the above quotation one might wonder if the songs and dances had served to create the plot. Elsewhere Matthews says:

> In some instances we are impressed with the idea that the myth-maker composed his story first, and introduced his songs afterwards as embellishments, but in more cases the myth is a trifling element, and seems devised merely as an aid to memory, or as a means of explaining or giving interest to the songs. (1902a:186)

In *Navaho Legends* Matthews refers to "rite-myths" as those versions which are told by a practitioner of a ceremony, and points out that they contain "minute and often tedious particulars concerning the rite, its work, symbolism, and sacrifices," but that when the same story is told by a layman, "these esoteric parts are altogether omitted, or only briefly alluded to." (1897a:51).

Gladys Reichard has noted instances where the singer did not even know the story but still commanded all the songs and ceremonial sequences and was a respected practitioner. She cites one singer who depended on his songs to help him recall parts of the Hail Chant myth (1950:276, 283). In the 1940s Mary Wheelwright told me of instances where she went to some trouble to visit singers from whom she hoped to record myths only to find that they "did not know the story."

Our own Western conception of story as basic and music as an embellishment, from ballad to opera, seems so "natural" to us that we may project the same creative sequence on the Navajos. I would like to suggest here that the Navajos show us another possibility: that the myth, especially in the case of the "rite-myths," may be based on the order of ceremonial procedures including song sequences.

"If the slightest error is made . . ."

Matthews laid the groundwork for the belief, still generally held, that any mistake in procedure, especially in the rendition of songs, will invalidate a ceremony.

> These songs must be known to the priest of the rite and his assistants in a most exact manner; for an error made in singing a song may be fatal to the efficacy of a ceremony. In no case is an important mistake tolerated and, sometimes, the error of a single syllable works irreparable injury. . . . not a single vocable may be omitted, mispronounced or misplaced. A score or more of critics who know the song by heart are listening with strained attention. If the slighest error is made, it is at once proclaimed; the fruitless ceremony terminates abruptly and the disappointed multitude disperses. (1896:198)
>
> The accomplished Navajo shaman must be a man of superior memory and of great intellectual industry. For one thing, he must commit to memory many hundreds of songs, and some of these songs are so sacred that not the slightest mistake can be made in repeating them without rendering void an elaborate and costly ceremonial. (Matthews 1894b:185)

Reichard also comments on the seriousness of mistakes in ceremonial procedure, but her emphasis is not on mistakes as cause for invalidation and termination of ceremonies but rather the various ways of correcting the error itself or the effects of the error.

> RP ascribed her trouble to mistakes made by a singer of the Shooting Chant when he had sung over T's wife twelve years before. RP believed that singing the

same chant now, without error would "straighten everything out." (Reichard 1950:96)

I have often heard songs started wrong and corrected simply by a new start as soon as the mistake was realized (ibid.:283).

She speaks of ritually formalized means of coping with the danger:

> . . . (the function of) the Fire Dance branch of the Shooting Chant . . . (was) to restore power to a chanter who had made mistakes. (ibid.:235)
>
> . . . a song called the "twelve-word song of blessing," sung when War Ceremony rattlestick is deposited, generally for correcting possible mistakes . . . (ibid.:274)

My own impression, also, is that Matthews' dictum is too absolute. I have observed special prayers near the end of a ceremony pleading that any mistakes made were inadvertent and should be overlooked. I have also seen numerous instances of errors in ceremonial details, including the order of songs and the content of songs, that were corrected by stopping and going over the same material correctly. As with the epic singers interviewed by Albert Lord, the definition of "exact repetition" may be quite different in an oral tradition from what it means in a tradition with written documentation (Lord 1971).

The Melodic Aspect of the Music

We have seen that Matthews' contribution to the study of Navajo music is a formidable one, especially if our definition of "music" includes texts and context, as well as melody. Where the musical sound itself was concerned, he saw the futility of relying on words to describe the subtleties of pitch, timbre, rhythm, and the way melody moves. He left us 196 carefully documented wax cylinder recordings. This treasure provides the scholar of today with the material for diachronic comparisons hardly available in any of the world's other musics.

Matthews felt unequal, however, to the transcription and analytical study of these recordings and turned to an accredited music scholar of his day, Professor John C. Fillmore, who notated twenty-eight of the songs. He described, accurately, several of the sonic features of Navajo music: the rhythmic freedom, the powerful melodic weight on the tonic or base note of most songs, and the robust vocal dynamics. He also remarked that the tone system was prevailingly made up of the notes of the major or minor tonic triad (do–mi–sol, or 1–3–5) and concluded that, even though they did not use chords, a "harmonic sense" was implicit in the melodies. He also noted this in other non-Western musics he had heard and felt that he had found a universal human trait linking "primitive" music with the harmonic music achieved by civilized nations (Matthews 1897a:255–56).

Matthews himself was far ahead of his time in his avoidance of simplistic developmental theories and found Navajo religious and artistic life quite on a par with our own. He did make some astute observations of his own on melody as well as text. In discussing the "songs of sequence," for instance, he pointed out how one song might follow another with almost identical text but sung to a different tune and beginning with different vocables. "It is a common thing, in these songs of sequence, to have several songs in succession repeat the same ideas and differ from each other only in the music, or in the refrain or the prelude" (Matthews 1894b:193).

Future Harvests

Because of the mass of unpublished material and, in the case of the music, the sound recordings, the harvest is by no means all in from Washington Matthews' labors. The phonograph cylinders are there in the Library of Congress. The Federal Cylinder Project is trying to find responsible ways of returning such material to the people from whom it was collected and to formulate standards of confidentiality with respect to sacred and, often, secret information.

Those of us who are not ceremonial practitioners may have to face the possibility that the further study of certain kinds of Navajo music may be none of our business. But if the material remains accessible, what are some of the research problems we might address, using the music preserved by Matthews, the later cylinders of Hoijer and Herzog, the discs of Laura Boulton, and the comparatively recent tapes of Barrett, Frisbie, Luckert, myself, and others?

Correcting Texts and Translations

A very large work lies ahead in correcting texts in Navajo to the present standardized orthography. A correlary necessity is the preservation of the wide variety of recording media now in existence. Wax cylinders have shown remarkable durability, but they can crack or be attacked by mold. Aluminum discs wear out; the signal can fade from magnetic tape. Digital technology shows promise for very long-lasting recordings.

In the case of Matthews' texts a good deal of missing material could be restored by consulting the sound recordings. The concept of vocables as "meaningless syllables" became obsolete with the publication of Hymes' "Some North Pacific Coast Poems: A Problem in Anthropological Philology" (Hymes 1965). Here, the important relationship of vocables to the lexical text was clearly demonstrated. I have shown it to be equally true in Navajo music (McAllester 1980a, 1980b). A few examples from Matthews' song texts will show the kind of reconstruction that would be possible, thanks to his recordings.

In the final chapter of *The Night Chant, A Navajo Ceremony,* the song texts are presented. The first example is the first song on the opening night of the ceremony. From the point of view of musical analysis and Navajo poetics, it would be valuable to know whether this is as stripped down as it seems. In most Navajo ceremonial music there is a carryover from the prelude, both melodically and textually, into the final phrases of each verse of the stanzas—aptly labeled by Matthews the "burden." Is that really missing in this song? Usually a larger carryover from the prelude is found at the end of each stanza in what Matthews called the "refrain." Whatever the number of stanzas, the refrain at the end of the last one concludes with an extended formula indicating the end of the song (see example, pp. 44–45). Matthew's cryptic notation, "repeat," suggests that the formula is missing. This would be a significant difference from contemporary practice, worth checking against the sound recording (Matthews 1902a:272).

On the next page is the text of the first song accompanying the preparation of the *k'eet'áán* (prayer offerings) on the morning of the second day. In this case, it is not clear whether the prelude and refrain are identical, so one is not sure what comes at the end of each stanza. Fortunately, when the time comes for a closer study of the formal structure of song and text, the recording will resolve the question.

Another kind of problem is found in example three, the fifth song accompanying the making of the *k'eet'áán*. Two lines of vocables are presented as prelude, but the second line, as published, ends with "etc.," that nemesis of scholars. There is no way of telling, without resorting to the sound recording, what has been left out. Again we are told that the song ends as in stanza 1, and we have the same question as in the first example as to whether this is an omission or a significant difference between song style today and one hundred years ago.

We all have to resort to shorthand in publishing extended and repetitious ethnographic material, and we are especially likely to do so with repetitions of "meaningless" text. *The Night Chant* is a large volume of 340 pages, measuring 11 inches by 14 inches. It is full of illustrations, including color plates of drypaintings. The publication was made possible by a generous patron of anthropological research, F. E. Hyde, Jr. Certainly the ethnomusicological world would rejoice if all the songs of Nightway had been published in musical notation, without abbreviations, but there are a great many. Matthews recorded or listed 324 of them and mentioned other whole categories of song that could also be used at various points in the ceremony. Most of these songs would require at least a full page, perhaps half of them might require two or three pages, for a full transcription. Each might need at least one more page of analytical commentary. One can imagine the additional funding and scholarly labor required for 1,200 more pages.

In Navajo studies sheer volume of material is one cogent reason why only relatively small amounts of the song literature have ever been published. I cite Leland C. Wyman's decision regarding the publication of Fr. Berard Haile's voluminous Navajo texts of three versions of the Blessingway myth:

> In order to reduce this mass of material to make a book which would be convenient both physically and financially. . . I decided to omit the Navajo text and interlinear translations. . . . The few linguists who would use the native text may see it or obtain copies of it by applying to one of three repositories. . . ." (Wyman 1970:xxvii)

Given preservation, correction, and completion, a valuable area of future research would be the comparison of song sets from different performances of any given ceremony. This is a study that Navajo practitioners themselves have been engaged in for generations. In some cases, the early recordings could give the research a time depth of from fifty to one hundred years. This is a perspective rarely available in ethnomusicology or any musicology. Building on Matthews' work, much could be learned about change and stability in this oral tradition.

The mass of recorded material makes possible the comparison of song sets with similar functions but from different ceremonies. There are fire songs, emetic songs, songs for the making of *K'eet'áán*, bathing songs, dawn songs, and many others that occur in most ceremonials. Are they the same, or similar, in Shootingway, and, to name a closely related ceremony, Red Antway? What about the case of two ceremonies as dissimilar as Enemyway and Blessingway? Would such comparisons be helpful in our efforts to distinguish what makes a male version of a given ceremony different from the female version?

The uniquely long time span of recorded material might yield information on the saliency of certain stylistic features in Navajo music. The wide use of tone systems limited to the 1st, 3rd, and 5th degrees of the scale, noted in Navajo, Apache, and Northern Athabascan music, would seem even more significant if it really is as strong a feature in the Matthews material as Fillmore suggests.

Another stylistic feature is a preponderance of binary note values: it is rare to find long-held notes. The somewhat rapid, flowing quality of the songs is due, in part, to the almost exclusive use of only two values. These could be represented as quarter notes and eighth notes (♩and ♪). Such features as these, along with other complementary pairs—male and female stanzas, verses and refrains, pairings in vocables and texts—if they seem well established by comparative study and the time depth afforded by Matthews' work, might be more confidently related to the dualities that seem to run through much of the Navajos' concept of themselves and their universe. They might also be of interest in historic reconstructions looking northward to the northern Athabascans, and even on west into Siberia.

We owe much to the past and will owe much in the future to Washington Matthews' work. If we find errors of interpretation and omission in the great corpus he has left to us, this is something that he understood well himself. As we have seen, the Navajo practitioners understood this inevitability also, and were well prepared with corrective strategies to cope with it. We can let Matthews speak to the subject:

> Those songs which pertain to their rites and mythology are so numerous that I have no hope of ever making a collection that will approximate completeness. (Matthews 1889b:1)

> The best poets in the English tongue may not make their meaning clear to the most intelligent English readers. Our scholars differ as to the interpretation of many passages in Shakespeare. Recognizing these facts it must not be supposed that the translations from an unwritten savage language, which follow, are perfect. . . . He (the author) simply offers the work as the best he can do. But here stand the texts. (Matthews 1902a:269)

Notes

1. See Hogan songs in Frisbie 1967:112–209 and McAllester and McAllester 1987.

2. Young and Morgan agree with others that "House God," or "Hogan God," is an incorrect translation of this deity's name. They suggest the possibility of "Growling God," but leave the translation in question.

Matthews and the Discovery of Navajo Drypaintings[1]

The excellence to which the Navahoes have carried the art of drypaintings is as remarkable as that to which they brought the art of weaving.

Washington Matthews, *The Night Chant,* p. 34

NANCY J. PAREZO

"The Indians make figures of all their devils, sir," Jesus Arviso told Washington Matthews soon after his arrival at Fort Wingate, New Mexico, on 29 October 1880.[2] Arviso, a Mexican from Sonora, had been captured in his youth by Apaches around 1850. He had been traded to Black Shirt and raised as a Navajo by his family (Loh 1971:126). Arviso had served as an interpreter for several army officers, including General Sherman, because of his command of Navajo and Spanish. He began to assist Matthews in this capacity soon after his arrival and helped teach him Navajo. But unfortunately this did not last long. Arviso was discharged on January 1 and "since then I have had no teacher, but have employed myself in putting into shape the material gleaned from him" (NAA: WM to JWP, 2/7/1881), which unfortunately contained no more information on their "devil" figures.

Matthews' assignment to Fort Wingate, made at the request of John W. Powell,[3] was to learn as much about the Navajos as possible in all their aspects in order to help with the Bureau of Ethnology's classification of tribes. To understand the religion, mythology, and symbolic arts of native peoples were priorities of Powell's research agenda; the Navajos were seen as a crucial group with whom to work because so little was known about them. Needless to say, Matthews was intrigued by the idea that the Navajos made "devil figures." He began to search for visual evidence of the sacred figures. Arviso's statement was fascinating because it was the first ethnographic indication of any Navajo religious art.[4] Matthews reported (1902a:35) that "white men (some of whom had lived fifteen years or more among the Navahoes) with whom the author conversed when first he went to the Navaho country, and . . . all ethnographers before his time" held that the Navajos lacked sacred art and symbolic representations of any kind. To find that they produced symbolic art used in ceremonial contexts would be a significant discovery.

The First Sight of Navajo Drypaintings

It was several years before Matthews actually saw "the illustrated visions of the prophets" (Matthews 1886f:841) even though he witnessed parts of several Navajo ceremonies.[5] After completing his first tour of duty in the Southwest, he returned to Washington, D.C., in the spring of 1884 to work at the Army Medical Museum. During that fall, however, he returned to the Southwest for a brief resumption of his scientific investigations as part of a three-month expedition sponsored jointly by the Bureau of Ethnology and the U.S. Geological Survey.

The months of September and October 1884 were very frustrating for Matthews, who was eager to return to New Mexico, as his correspondence with Powell demonstrates (NAA: WM to JWP, 9/6/1884). He told Powell that he found the time spent in Washington waiting for the trip to begin time-consuming and costly; there were problems receiving back pay and advances. Next there were delays on the railroad at every point; his army and scientific passes for free transportation were lost by railroad officials. Promised scientific assistants were delayed, and unexpected military duties kept him busy.

Matthews was able to locate Christian Barthelmess (Band, 13th Infantry), a musician and photographer who had previously been his assistant, for this fall research trip. Again Powell proved instrumental by using his influence to have Barthelmess detailed to accompany him. Barthelmess arrived several days after Matthews. They immediately made plans to travel north to see one of the sacred mountains of the Navajos only to discover that they could not find their interpreter (possibly Ben Damon). After several days' delay, Matthews, Barthelmess, and their Navajo interpreter (name unknown) finally left. As they were climbing Mt. Taylor they learned of a "great Navajo festival." Matthews decided to stop at this Navajo ceremony, which was being held at Nihotlizi (or Hard Earth), twenty-five miles north of Fort Wingate. Arriving on October 19 in the company of Ocario Candalario and a Mexican guide Julas Varela (Guide: 54, Notebook #214), Matthews and Barthelmess were able to observe a nine-night Mountain Chant. As Matthews' monthly report to Powell notes, they stayed at the Navajo ceremonial encampment until the end of the month. For the first time, Matthews could see an entire ceremonial, one that was "most interesting to the Caucasian spectator" and that "the white man is rarely the first to leave at dawn" (Matthews 1887a:385)—the Mountain Chant.[6]

As often happens in ethnographic fieldwork, Matthews' luck held. During the course of the ceremonial, he was able to obtain "the most valuable and original information that I have yet collected in the Navajo country" (NAA: WM to JWP, 10/1884; see this letter reproduced in Part Two of this volume):

> At Nihotlizi, I saw large and beautiful sketches in five different colors, drawn on the sanded floor of the medicine lodge to represent different cosmogonic and reli-

gious conceptions. The labor of drawing these designs occupied several hours and a dozen operators, all working under the exacting eye of the chief shaman who allowed not a line of the unalterable hieratic figures to be done awry. There were four different designs—each made on a different day and each covering the great part of the floor of the medicine lodge. . . .

Matthews described the drypainting process in great detail in his field notebook (Guide: 54, Notebook #214):

Presently Manuelito enters with a lot of dry sand which he dumps into the middle of the cleared space. It is spread out a little. The old medicine man leaves and all operations are suspended for a while.

At 12:55 the old man returns [the door is always to the east.] At 5 minutes to 1 he makes a pile of the earth on the floor about 6 inches high to represent the mountain of the west and covers it with dry sand.

At 1 the hole in the center is begun. He digs it with care. Manuelito brings to order white and black earth. The hole in center 6 to 8" in diam, 2 in depth, nearly concave. Center hole, but the rings around are not more that ¼ inch thick and made as finely as they can be by sprinkling earth through the fingers.

Line 2 is made by two assistants while the old man covers the western mountain with black, first making a ring around it near the base, then making a straight mark up one side working into a wedge.

Then the assistants make the other line like "2" at the south, west, while the old man puts blue line to San Francisco and then proceeds to work the other colors. . . .

The red is about the color of light red. The blue is a distinct and proper grey. All the colors are subdued and the effect very pleasant.

Matthews' notes continue to describe when each line of color and each figure is drawn, who draws it, the value or tone of each color, the detail in the sequencing in which designs were laid down, and the exactness of the proceedings. His diagrams were made while in the *hooghan* with the Navajo name for each figure inscribed next to it and colored in later. These drawing were interspersed with his textual notations.

The first picture, Home of the Bear and Snake, seen on the fifth night (published in Matthews 1887a: Plate XV), was a full-size painting used in the shock rite, an accessory ceremony, in which a person dressed as a bear accompanied by a Yé'ii, springs from behind a screen to frighten the patient, who sits on the drypainting. If the patient faints or trembles, it confirms that the correct chant has been diagnosed (Wyman 1973, 1983).[7] As Matthews described the rite:

At 7 we were recalled to the lodge. [I] Find a circle ranged nearly round the lodge. I am given a place in the extreme west. The Cantador and other singers are in the north. Women in the south. The sick woman is made to sit on the figures on the ground at the junction of the two east wind serpents. Her feet facing the east. Song and noises proceed. After a while a man previously well hidden, dressed in pinon jumps out from behind the medicine man, rushes towards the woman but all yell

> and he retreats. This is done four times at due intervals. The Cantador tips him a signal when to appear.
>
> Some time after the last appearance, Old Man walks chanting into the arena and with his rattle demolished the mountain in the west. Then the bear's tracks, then the figures in the central hole, then one by one the various other figures ending with the outside serpents. Then the sand spread on the floor is gathered, put in a blanket and taken out doors. (Guide: 54, Notebook #214)

In the next few days Matthews observed other paintings and continued his detailed descriptions in his field notes. Page after page of his notebooks was devoted to describing the figures in detail, noting how they were similar to or how they varied from those of previous days. He described the techniques of overpainting and how mistakes were corrected. On the second day, he took particular care to describe the rainbow figure that "extends around ¾ of the picture from the middle of the corn to the middle of the tobacco." He documented the paintings in use. For example, the following day he noted:

> The woman is placed sitting legs extended on the east god, her feet toward the door. There is a bowl of some decoction in the east with a peculiar brush made of feathers with a yarn handle about 10" long. Old man dips brush in solution and then sprinkles plentifully over picture. Then he goes round and touches each of the four gods in three places—brow, lips, and breast, dips brush in decoction. In the meantime the other woman has squatted on the corn stalk, facing the east.
>
> The bowl is given alternately to the sick woman and her companion to drink twice each. Then he drinks the rest himself giving the solid dregs to Jake and his companions to finish.
>
> Now the female companion gets off the picture and sits near the door. Each is supplied with some red coals on the ground beside her—the coals are sprinkled with a powder which emits a strong but disagreeable fume. The women move the smoke toward them and breathe it in. Coals are extinguished. Then the old man moistens his hands and presses them on the feet of the gods, some of the colored dust of each adhering to his palms. Then presses these soiled palms on the feet of the women. So he goes up the gods and the woman at different parts consecutively ending with the heads. Strong massage is used in each case.
>
> The woman is then removed and the old man proceeds to demolish the picture beginning with the east god. Coming round to the tobacco plant and ending with the rainbow (foot to head). Meanwhile he sings one of the most musical songs I have yet heard among them while others rattle. He knocks down the planted arrows rather fiercely while he demolishes (with pointed stick—one of the arrows perhaps) the rainbow. Just after he removes this west god he destroys the center, digging up a round buried cup I didn't know before was there. (Guide: 54, Notebook #214)

Thus Matthews began to document his "most valuable information," even though he was quick to point out that "Navajos regard the song as the chief part of the ceremony" (Matthews 1887a:386). The existence of symbolic art in the form of ephemeral paintings—drypaintings—was a momentous discovery for Matthews, as he related to Powell in his monthly report. Until this trip he had questioned the existence of sacred art: "As the Navajos have neither the ornamental robes, painted lodges, decorated pottery, carved images or rock inscriptions of other tribes, it is generally supposed that they have no pictorial mythic symbols and such was my impression until I made this excursion" (NAA: WM to JWP, 10/1884). This lack of religious art and paraphernalia had been confusing for nineteenth-century scholars like Powell, who adhered to an evolutionary paradigm: Navajos should have produced and used symbolic art, given their location in the evolutionary hierarchy. This discovery and documentation of drypaintings would support Powell's evolutionist theories (see example, pp. 221–28).

Matthews' excitement and relief is evident in a letter to Frank Hamilton Cushing. He jokingly states: "The rascals who have neither ornamented robes, skins or pottery, or craven idols, have nevertheless a complete system of pictographic mythic symbolism. . . . Have you ever heard of such an art? . . . I have seen things I never dreamt of" (Guide: 81, 11/4/1884). Matthews immediately thought about sharing his new knowledge with the scientific community; he wrote Powell: "I think of writing a brief description of the mere technicalities of the work, for some scientific periodical in order to elicit comment and later to embody all in a monograph on the whole ceremony for the publication of your office. . . . The entire ceremony is one of great interest and deserving of an extensive description" (NAA: WM to JWP, 10/1884). Powell, of course, was supportive, because he felt religion was crucial for understanding native peoples and he had urged Matthews to pursue this subject. He quickly reported Matthews' discovery in his introduction to the Sixth Annual Report of the Bureau of Ethnology for 1884–1885: "His most interesting discovery on this occasion was that of their system of mythic drypaintings by which they represent various legends or traditions with dry pigments on the sanded floor of the medicine lodge" (Powell 1888:xiv–xv).

Continued Research and First Publications

Continuing his field trip to the Fort Defiance, Arizona, area, Matthews was able to observe more drypaintings in use. In November 1884 he observed a Night Chant ceremony and again "gained full access at all times to the medicine lodge, and obtained a number of sketches, photographs and important notes." As before, "a number of symbolic pictures were drawn with dry colors on a surface of sand" (NAA: WM to JWP, 11/1884).

Upon returning to Washington, Matthews began to work on his lectures, articles, and the proposed monograph. A short, technical article, "Mythic Dry-paintings of the Navajos," was presented as a two-part lantern slide lecture to the Philosophical Society of Washington in March and April 1885[8] and published in the American Naturalist, a widely read scientific journal edited by Frederick Putnam, in October (Matthews 1885d). A similar but expanded lecture was given to the Anthropological Society of Washington that summer; and another, called "The Gods of the Navajos," also illustrated with slides of drypainting drawings, was given at the Smithsonian's National Museum of Natural History in April, 1886.[9] In these articles and lectures, Matthews discussed how the paintings were made, their purpose, the symbols and thematic content of seven paintings from the Mountain and Night Chants, and the ephemeral nature of the art form and the difficulties of studying these "most transitory pictures in the history of art" (Matthews 1887a:423).

Over the next several years Matthews recorded the designs of many more drypaintings, although it is difficult to tell from his field notes exactly what these were, which designs, how many, and when they were observed. For example, he witnessed a Night Chant in the late fall of 1887 during his return journey to Washington from the Hemenway Expedition. He saw others during his second extended tour of duty at Fort Wingate between 1890 and 1894, when he was conducting much of his work on the Night Chant, and at that time,[10] he notes that he knows of seventeen ceremonials which use sixty-eight drypaintings (Matthews 1898c).

Recording and subsequently writing about drypaintings (or Navajo religion, in general, for that matter) was no easy task. While Matthews was given "unrestricted access to the medicine-lodge, saw the hieratic figures drawn, and was given permission to sketch them," this task was undertaken much to the consternation of some of the Navajos attending the ceremony (Matthews 1885d:931). Matthews persisted in his meticulous recording of ritual detail until he was asked by singers to put away his notebook. As Halpern and McGreevy (1986:11) have noted: "His early field notes reveal that he persisted, even in the face of occasional Navajo disapproval, in seeing as much of the ritual as he could, and it appears that he put away his notebook only when overruled." During an 1890 Night Chant for a woman patient, he recorded: "Now we go out to see sweating. Jake says I can't go, but I do all the same" (Guide: 53, Notebook #589). Persistence and disregard for community resistance or apprehension were not uncommon in the research measures used by his anthropological contemporaries—James and Matilda Coxe Stevenson, Bourke, Cushing, Bandelier, Fewkes—so that they could continue recording their observations until all but forcibly asked to leave.[11] This is not to say that Matthews did not develop cordial relations with singers and laity. Navajo *hataatii* are the intellectuals of the Navajo nation. As historians, doctors, and ritual practitioners they could appreciate Matthews' intellectual curiosity. Matthews, as has been shown throughout this volume, had a deep respect for the Navajos; and as Frisbie and Faris have shown, he was able to convey his sincerity in seeking knowledge about ceremonialism and religious concepts. But his work presented a dilemma for *hataałii* and for him when it came to recording and analyzing drypaintings. To understand this ethnographic recording dilemma and how Matthews circumvented it, we must first discuss the nature of Navajo drypaintings.

Navajo Drypainting

Navajo drypaintings (or sandpaintings) are found in most, but by no means all, Navajo curing ceremonies (Parezo 1983a; Wyman 1983). Made of pulverized sandstone, charcoals, and other dry materials, the pigments are strewn onto a sand background on the floor of the ceremonial hogan, without the aid of an adhesive or template. Drypaintings are sacred; they are impermanent pictures of "the gods with their hieratic belongings" (Matthews 1897a:33). Drypaintings, or *'iikááh* (which means "the place where the gods come and go") are pictures of: the protagonist of the myth that explains the ceremony and provides its rationale; the Holy People whom he encounters in his mythological adventures; supernatural beings and forces that need to be brought under control; and subsidiary beings.

Drypaintings are designed to attract the Holy People, powerful supernaturals who are invoked to cure and bless, thereby promoting holiness. They serve as the temporary altars where ritual actions can take place during Holyway rituals (which emphasize the attraction of good and the restoration of the patient to health). The goal of these ceremonies is to restore beauty (or *hózhǫ́*) within the individual as well as in the external world, so that peacefulness, mental and physical fitness, and a state of harmonious being is attained.

Dramatic and ephemeral, beautiful in that it attracts holiness actively, a drypainting exists in time and space only for the duration of a ceremony; when its use is fulfilled, it is ritually erased. The drypainting is sanctified upon completion by sprinkling sacred pollen or cornmeal on it; it becomes a transitory moment of holiness. Holy and powerful, full of the Holy People themselves, the singer uses the drypainting to transfer the illness out of the patient and the health and perfection of the Holy People into the patient. This sickness goes into the painting, through the medium of the singer. The patient is then identified with the Holy People, and he or she is made strong like those being portrayed.

The supernatural power contained within a drypainting is considered dangerous, especially to the uninitiated, that is, those who have not been sung over. They can be used safely only in the proper controlled context, at the correct time and under the supervision of one who has the knowledge to direct the use of potentially dangerous interactions. According to Reichard (1963:112–13) drypaintings should be conceived of as the ceremonial membrane that allows for ritual transference.

Thus, the paintings made of dry pulverized materials are "drawn according to an exact system" (Matthews 1902a:36). Drypaintings are the gifts of the Holy People and "the shamans declare that these pictures are transmitted unaltered from year to year and from generation to generation" (ibid.). The Holy People have indicated proper methods of construction and use.

> We will give you white earth and black coals which you will grind together to make black paint, and we will give you white sand, yellow sand, and red sand, and for the blue paint you will take white sands and black coals with a very little red and yellow sand. These together will give you blue. (Stevenson 1891:278)

In their proper setting, if ritual rules are followed exactly as prescribed by the Holy People, drypaintings are the exact pictorial representations of supernaturals who, called by their likenesses, are compelled to cure under the rules of the universe. Only in some minor details, such as the depiction of pouches suspended from the waists of the Holy People, are the painters allowed artistic creativity.

Deviations from this transmitted wisdom could cause mistakes; therefore, aesthetic or symbolic innovation is frowned upon. Exactness was always an issue with the Navajos and before each painting was used, the men present in the ceremonial hogan would discuss its accuracy and a covering prayer from Blessingway would be intoned to correct for unintentional errors.[12]

Thus, the use of drypaintings was strictly prescribed, as Matthews soon learned. As he (1902a:36) recounts:

> No permanent design is anywhere preserved by them and there is no final authority in the tribe. The pictures are carried from winter to winter in the fallible memories of men. They may not be drawn in the summer. The custom of destroying these pictures at the close of the ceremonies and preserving no permanent copies of them arose, no doubt, largely from a desire to preserve the secrets of the lodge from the uninitiated; but it had also perhaps a more practical reason for its existence. The Navahoes had no way of drawing permanent designs in color.

In addition, supernaturally sanctioned rules, postulated in the origin myths accompanying the ceremonies, prohibited the construction of drypaintings outside the ceremonial context. When the Holy People gave the pictures to the mythological protagonists and instructed them in their production, they were kept rolled up on clouds. The myth of the Mountain Chant recounts: "They drew from one corner of the cave a great sheet of clouds, which they unrolled, and on it were painted the forms of the yays of the cultivated plants" (Matthews 1887a:404). The Holy People forbade the reproduction in permanent form lest the paintings be soiled, damaged, used up, or misused by evil. For example:

> The yei who unfolded it [drypainting designs on clouds] to show the prophet said: "We will not give you this picture; men are not as good as we; they might quarrel over the picture and tear it, and that would bring misfortune; the black cloud would not come again, the rain would not fall, the corn would not grow, but you may paint it on the ground with colors of the earth." (Matthews 1902a:165)

Navajos believe that to misuse a drypainting would cause serious consequences: drought and destruction to the society; blindness, illness and even death for the individual. If permanent copies were made, evil forces and beings (i.e., witches) could find them and turn that which brings blessing into that which brings illness. The efficacy of the paintings could be used up and they would no longer be useful for curing (Parezo 1983a). Drypaintings were to be treated with respect to ensure the safety of all. For these reasons, Navajos have been opposed to photographing or copying drypaintings in any permanent medium.

It was difficult to study drypaintings.[13] Matthews had to learn a great deal about Navajo religious prescriptions and values before he could reproduce Navajo drypaintings.

In addition, he had to analyze Navajo concepts in order to understand the problems involved. At times this must have been bewildering. For example, most Navajos were afraid to disobey the prohibitions of the Holy People and possibly incur negative sanctions, and thus did not produce drypaintings in any permanent medium. Many lay Navajos were upset if Matthews recorded the drypaintings in his notebook during a ceremony for fear that this deviation from established practice might anger the Holy People who could then not be compelled to cure. This could negate the ceremony, or even worse, reverse it and bring additional sickness to all present. Even talking about the religious symbolism contained within the paintings could be dangerous if done outside the ceremonial context, as Matthews repeatedly noted. For example, he once described talking with his "very liberal minded" Navajo guide and informant Juan [last name unknown] in the late summer about *Estsanatlehi* [Changing Woman], the goddess of the West.

> . . . neither of us had noted a heavy storm coming over the crest of the Zuni Mountains . . . when the house was shaken by a terrific peal of thunder. He [Juan] rose at once, pale and evidently agitated, and, whispering hoarsely, "Wait till Christmas; they are angry," he hurried away. I have seen many such evidences of the deep influences of this superstition on them. (Matthews 1887a:386–387)

Time and place were thus crucial. Working on drypaintings could not be a year-round activity, for the importance of seasonality was a central concern for singers. Matthews states that singers were more concerned that the reproductions would be exposed at the wrong season and seen by the uninitiated than they were that the designs would be kept on paper.

This does not mean that capturing the design on paper was not without its problems. To record a drypainting meant to produce it outside the ceremonial context, which was all but inconceivable. As Reichard (1939:2) has shown in her discussion of Miguelito's production of drypainting reproductions:

> There can be no doubt that he had to overcome genuine fear of breaking a Navajo rule. . . . Furthermore, it is a difficult thing for a Navajo chanter to paint or to give any part of his ritual without a patient. . . . A chanter cannot understand having it [a ceremony] cut up in the way a white man demands.

In addition, recording on paper made a drypainting an object, and drypainting is essentially an act for the Navajo rather than a thing. While it is visual and has texture, it should not exist after the action of making and using it has ceased. This would turn it into thing, which is inappropriate.

There was also a delicate balance in the use of drypaintings, as in the use of other ceremonial paraphernalia. To use something too often was to use it up, thereby rendering it no longer efficacious. This is one reason there were so many types of drypaintings; there were variations based on gender of the patient, frequency of recent use, seasonality, local preference, preference of the family, and the like, although the extent of the repertoire was not known to Matthews. "Overdoing" is a cause of disharmony for the Navajo. To continually talk about a painting, to look at it constantly, to make numerous reproductions would have used up that by which the singer could cure. This could leave the people in a perilous situation.

Personal safety was another key concern. Singers were concerned for Matthews' health, even if he did not consider his health in jeopardy. Unprotected from continual contact with such concentrated power and not knowing all the symbolic regulations, Matthews could unintentionally make errors. Violations of drypainting restrictions could bring imbalance and danger to the recorder and viewer; only the singer and his senior apprentices had some safety because they were used to being near and controlling concentrated power.

In short, Matthews was asking his interpreters and singers to perform an exceptionally difficult task. Some refused altogether. Matthews speaks often in his letters of his frustration in securing help for his research on religion, especially with regard to the meaning of drypaintings. Obviously, since Matthews published drawings and descriptions of drypaintings from two ceremonials, he did convince a few individuals to work with him. Matthews had to develop a research strategy and a methodology that met Navajo religious rules, as well as find liberal-minded singers with whom to work. While Matthews "does not describe self-consciously and systematically his methods of observing and recording" (Halpern and McGreevy 1986:4) in his publications, his field notes and correspondence show how he went about this most difficult task.[14]

Developing a Rationale for the Recording of Drypaintings

Navajo culture has a tenet that while there are proper ways to act, knowledge held by an individual can be used as he or she sees fit. As would be expected, some individuals could be persuaded to serve as anthropological consultants and use their knowledge in a new manner, while others could not. It depended on how the individual felt about his or her knowledge, how they interpreted the novel situation, and on their abilities to rectify problems, if necessary. To break a rule was to disrupt harmonious relationships and would *probably* (but not necessarily) cause trouble. Given the flexibility in interpretation of proper behavior in novel situations, a scholar could persuade some individuals to use their knowledge in novel contexts and in ways that had not been tested previously.

Tall Chanter and Laughing Singer (Hatali Natloi) eventually felt confident enough of their own abilities to work with Matthews. Rather than reiterate what has already been said in this volume about these remarkable men, here I would like to outline Matthews' process of obtaining information on drypaintings. This took trial and error and a great deal of searching and argument. As Matthews reported to Powell (NAA: WM to JWP, 11/1884; see this letter reproduced in Part Two of this volume):

> . . . I opened negotians [*sic*] with three different medicine men offering them as liberal terms for their services as I could afford but only to meet with the most positive refusal. I was on the point of abandoning these plans and devoting my time to

> obtaining the myths of locality and minor legends of the people known to the laity, when I heard of an old shaman living beyond Nutria, about 70 miles distant, who it was thought would be found less scrupulous that [*sic*] the others had proved. I dispatched a messenger for him at once, and on the evening of the 15th he came. With some trouble I concluded a bargain with him and he began his narration on the morning of the 16th. I have been engaged with him ever since and do not believe I will be through with him until it is time for me to leave Defiance. . . .

This individual was presumably Tall Chanter.

Matthews succeeded in obtaining the cooperation of medicine men by several means. First, he offered adequate financial compensation. Matthews paid singers for their time and information. In fact, financial compensation was crucial in Matthews' ability to witness and record his first drypaintings. Through the "judicious use of money, and by good management," Matthews told Powell, he was given access to the ceremonial hogan and permission to "note and paint *ad libitum,* except for two brief occasions where I was obliged to put up brush and pencil" (NAA:WM to JWP, 10/1884). This payment was in line with that given to singers whenever they imparted their knowledge during a ceremony or by instructing an apprentice (Aberle 1967); "the price of learning the craft, according to Chee, is 2 horses and the first fee received by the young practitioner" (Guide: 54, Notebook #468). In many cases, the amount was substantial, especially given that the Navajos were moving into a cash economy. As Matthews wrote anthropologist Pliny Goddard in 1904, he paid $1.00 per day in cash and an equivalent in dry goods and groceries to singers who would help him with the paintings, songs, myths, and other ceremonial knowledge (Guide: 45–46, see his letter of 1/16/1904 in Part Two of this volume).

Second, Matthews developed two recording methods, based on the reactions of the singers and the community attending the ceremony. If there was support or tolerance for his work, Matthews would sketch in the *hooghan* as the painting was being made or before the patient entered and sat on it.[15]

> I had obtained accurate watercolor paintings of these sacred pictures and accurate descriptions of the process of forming them (and this is a material and significant part). Soon after each picture was finished it was with interesting, significant and consistent ceremonies erased, and the very sand on which it was drawn removed from the lodge. (NAA:WM to JWP, 10/1884; see this letter in Part Two of this volume)

As already stated, however, some lay people were apprehensive and viewed with "horror" Matthews' recording or sketching during a ceremony for fear that the painting would become less powerful as some of its essence was being taken away for mundane purposes (Matthews 1885d:931). If this reaction was too vocal, the singer would ask Matthews to stop sketching because discord could cause the negation of the ceremony, even if he, the singer, was not opposed to Matthews' recording technique. Then Matthews would quietly watch, commit the painting to memory, and draw it in his notebook when the drypainting ceremony was over. Matthews felt that this was not a problem, for he easily carried out his observations "in memory for record outside of the lodge" (NAA:WM to JWP, 10/1884).

Matthews never convinced singers to make drawings of their own, as did later collectors of drypaintings. He always produced his own drawings (Matthews 1897a:45). In effect, he persuaded the singers to supervise and correct errors. This was very much in the mode of how Navajos teach and convey knowledge to students, as mentioned below. In this way, he as the anthropologist was taking responsibility for the possible transgression rather than the singers. There was always the idea that being non-Navajo made a difference in terms of a person's relationship to the Holy People.

Third, Matthews developed a line of argument that proved so successful that other anthropologists have used it to this day. He persuaded singers that it was their duty to future generations of Navajos to record oral traditions and knowledge in new media—pencil, brush, and paper (Parezo 1983a, 1983b). Although Navajo religion could not be said to be dying, the number of different ceremonials was decreasing by the turn of the century; sometimes shorter versions of chants were conducted. The Long Walk and periodic epidemic diseases had taken their toll on singers as well as the laity. In addition, as outside forces impinged on the Navajo, fewer young men were undertaking the many years of training necessary to memorize a complete nine-night chant. Schools pulled potential pupils away during their formative learning years. The result was that some singers had no apprentices. In their debates with Matthews these men decided that permanent recording and risking supernatural displeasure was preferable to losing the knowledge altogether. This argument was similar to that used by proponents of "salvage ethnography"; this was the idea that the scientific study of primitive peoples was necessary because they were doomed to vanish on the disappearing frontier of an advanced civilization. Matthews was not as great a proponent of this view as Stevenson or Cushing, but it was a commonly accepted argument used by most Bureau of Ethnology anthropologists when working with native peoples (Parezo 1987).

Fourth, singers, expressing anxiety for the safety of the individuals with whom they worked, feared that the Anglo-American recorder could not withstand being in constant contact with concentrated supernatural power, just as a Navajo apprentice could not. It was thought that they had to be ritually prepared, that is, to have been initiated and sung over (been the patient in a ceremony). There is no positive indication that Matthews was sung over or initiated, but there are hints that prayers were said over him to ensure his safety.

Matthews recognized that initiation and being sung over were important in order for him to be allowed to learn. This would have been necessary if he were to be allowed to produce ceremonial equipment for actual use or help produce a drypainting. As he wrote to Cushing:

> I have gained a position among the shamans that I have never hoped to get. Now they *urge* information and opportunities on me—nothing is withheld; I have been baptized and confirmed and have partaken of the Lord's supper (or its undoubted analogue) with them, and they urge on me a final ceremony of consecration,

> which I doubt if my constitution will withstand." (Guide: 82, WM to FHC, 4/5/1892)

How hard the singers pushed for Matthew's ritual preparation is unknown. There may have been some uncertainty as to whether an Anglo-American or any other non-Navajo needed to be so ritually prepared. By the time Gladys Reichard studied Navajo religion in the 1930s, being sung over before studying Navajo religion was seen by Miguelito, the singer with whom she worked, to be a necessity.

With time, fewer singers were opposed to reproducing drypaintings, especially when they found that the new media could prove useful. As Matthews notes (1887a: 45–46):

> After the writer made copies of these pictures, and it became known to the medicine men that he had copies in his possession, it was not uncommon for the shamans, pending the performance of a ceremony to bring young men who were to assist in their lodge, ask to see the paintings, and lecture on them to their pupils, pointing out the various important points and thus, no doubt, saving mistakes and corrections in the medicine-lodge.

Fifth, Matthews also took care to follow Navajo restrictions with regard to viewing and discussing the paintings in the correct season and only with those who were ritually prepared, at least while he was in Navajo territory. For example, "The water color copies were always (as the shamans knew) kept hidden at the forbidden season, and never shown to the uninitiated of the tribe" (Matthews 1887a:46). For Mountainway and Nightway, this meant that the paintings were not to be shown during the summer when lighting, bears, and snakes were active. In this way, Matthews demonstrated to the singers that he was sincere and understood their restrictions on use in the new situation.

Years later, Navajo singers developed a rationalization for producing drypainings outside the ceremonial context which eased their consciences and offset possible negative reaction by the community and the Holy People (Parezo 1983b). This involved the readjustment of rules by which drypaintings could be made by developing a new category of non-consecrated drypaintings. Singers and later artists made the non-ceremonial reproductions incomplete and eventually began to conceptualize them as "not the same thing." They separated the sacred from the profane in this distinction. They did this by intentionally leaving the reproductions incomplete. The germ of this idea can be found in Matthews' notes:

> Chee says that they always purposely omit some part of a picture [in a ceremony] which on another occasion is inserted to the exclusion of some other part. They think death would follow the completion of a picture. For this same reasoning when a student is to learn the medicine man will not teach him all the songs but will make him learn some of them from another person. (Guide: 54, Notebook #468)

By the mid-twentieth century, this was amended to making them intentionally incorrect. There is no evidence that Matthews and the singers he worked with used this later measure. Indeed, given Matthews' desire for detail and accuracy, this would have been difficult for him.

Incompleteness was an easy extension of the idea of how Navajo singers train their apprentices. Whenever a singer trains an individual, he does not give the neophyte all of his information. If he did this, the knowledge would no longer belong to the singer and would mean that the established singer was retiring. Instead, he deliberately does not relate a portion of a prayer, myth, or drypainting symbol, as a "life line" to preserve continuity from the past to the present, as a way for both individuals to use the knowledge in the future (Reichard 1939:6–7). Thus, singers always reserved a part of their knowledge, and the apprentice went to another singer to obtain the last piece of information on a painting or prayer in order for all to use the ritual knowledge in the future. Leaving something out was thus an accepted educational device and meant that Matthews would have had to consult at least two singers on each painting in order to obtain all the symbols and their meanings.

In a sense, Matthews became an apprentice and surrogate singer himself; he learned much as an apprentice learned. It was appropriate for Matthews to undertake this role because it conformed to Navajo conceptions of learning and was, therefore, understandable. In addition, Matthews was a healer himself who would naturally want to know how others heal; like many other scholars, Hinsley (1983:211) has attributed Matthews' success to his standing as a healer, "which permitted a cross-cultural exchange of privileged information." As a result of this cultural sensitivity and adaptability, Matthews could, with time, begin to work with singers as equal health practitioners.

The fact that Matthews was a physician like the singers was a consideration in his success in obtaining information from and working with Navajo religious practitioners. They worked together as two professionals and friends who valued each other's wisdom, knowledge, advice, and access to resources. Matthews convinced singers of his interest and sincerity, that his work was done out of respect, not for simple curiosity. He worked with men who believed in their own power and in him. But ultimately it was the Holy People who decided on the appropriateness of the activity. The visible test was whether the individual became sick and there is no time limit on this test.

Tall Chanter and Matthews did become sick. According to a story told to Dane and Mary Roberts Coolidge (1930:105), "Washington Matthews, the first white man to make copies of Yeibitchai sandpaintings, is cited as a particular instance, since he and his medicine man became stricken with deafness and later both died of paralysis." These illnesses constitute "yeibichai sickness" and are both symptomatic of the need for the Night Chant. This was evident to the Navajos on Matthews' second major stay in the 1890s. Several authorities have attributed Matthews' increasing deafness and disabilities to a stroke in 1892. However, a careful reading of his papers and military records is not fully clear on this point (see Halpern's introductory paper in this volume). Poor (1975:51) states that it did not strike the Navajos as unusual that Matthews should suffer physical complaints for his unintended errors. This explanation was also noted by Mooney (1905:518) and Reichard (1950:82, 95), who says that many Navajos attributed Matthews' physical disabilities to learning the powerful ceremonies. Mary Cabot

Wheelwright (1942:10–12) states that Klah warned her of this occupational risk in her own work, relating to her Matthews' and Tall Chanter's illnesses, and I was told the same thing by several Navajos in the early 1980s.[16]

Presentation to the Scientific Community

After his first article and lecture, Matthews appears to have rarely presented a paper solely on Navajo drypainting. However, at the end of his career he did write a brief article, "Dry-painting," for Hodge's *Handbook of American Indians* (1907). This summary article contains a cross-cultural comparison of the ephemeral art found throughout the Americas, with emphasis on the Navajos. Other groups, like the Hopis and Zunis, are implicitly and explicitly compared to them. The comparative focus on drypaintings was unusual, however. Matthews' discussions of drypaintings are more commonly embedded in his books on religion, especially his monographs *The Mountain Chant* (1887a), *Navajo Legends* (1897a), and *The Night Chant* (1902a). This does not diminish the importance Matthews gave to the sandpainting art. Even in his short articles, such as "Serpent Worship among the Navajos" (1898c), he describes specific drypaintings in detail. But, in every case, the information is presented in relation to the ceremonial; drypaintings are never portrayed as isolated entities to be admired for their decontextualized or abstract beauty.[17] For Matthews, the beauty of the painting was in its symbolism.

Drypaintings, of course, received full-scale publication and explanation in Matthews' monographs *The Night Chant* (1902a) and *The Mountain Chant* (1887a). The Mountain Chant "also has the distinction of containing the first color reproductions of Navajo drypaintings" (Wyman 1975:1). Shown in these works are several major paintings: Home of Bear and Snake, Bear's Den, First Dancers, Great Plumed Arrows, and Long Bodies for Mountainway,[18] and Mountains and Pollen Figures, Fringed Mouths (in linear form), First Dancers (in linear form), and Whirling Logs for Nightway, as well as examples of paintings that would be made on top of the sweat lodge for purification. Here as elsewhere Matthews "set an early standard for thorough and exact ethnographic observation and description" (Halpern and McGreevy 1986:11). Naming and categorization were crucial. Presentation in both is concerned with sequence and order. For example, the Home of the Bear and Snake was the first Mountainway drypainting seen by Matthews between one and three o'clock on the fifth day and used in the evening for a shock rite followed by a restoration rite (Matthews 1887a:422–24).

Matthews had no specific theory of religious or artistic symbolism that he used the drypaintings to illustrate. He felt that the paintings should be described precisely as they were used. But he did try to decode the symbols by ascertaining which Holy People were being portrayed and therefore summoned; which symbols were crucial for the painting; and which details could be varied. From this he tried to draw some limited descriptive generalizations regarding symbolism. For example, he noted that the heads of male Holy People were round and female Holy People rectangular. He developed the law of contrasting colors, that is, colors are paired and one color will outline its contrasting mate (Matthews 1902a). He slowly worked toward the formulation of Navajo-specific rules, which, as all scholars of Navajo drypainting have pointed out, is exceptionally difficult.

Matthews was concerned with accurately identifying which Holy People could appear in each drypainting and when they could be used. He did not provide the entire repertoire of all the paintings that could be used in Mountainway or Nightway, for at the time he was working this information was unavailable (and we can even question if any anthropologist, no matter how thoroughly he has researched a single chant, knows the complete drypainting repertoire). Nor does it appear that he published copies of all the paintings that he saw. Besides running into the problem of editors who would not or could not foot the bill for color plates, Matthews was trying to find representative paintings—those that were to be shown on their appropriate day in the ceremonials. In a way, the plates given are typological paintings. The drypaintings he depicts in *The Night Chant* are composites of what he learned from Tall Chanter and Laughing Singer (Faris 1990), as one would expect given the manner in which the paintings were gathered and checked for accuracy.

Matthews tried to place each painting in mythological time and space by relating each to the ceremonial and to the origin myths that accompany it. This was done either to demonstrate how the painting could serve as a mnemonic device for singers or to illustrate how the Holy People gave the drypainting to the protagonist of the myth who, in turn, gave it to Earth People.

While concerned with typological construction in order to bring an array of confusing information under intellectual control, Matthews was very interested in variability in two senses. One, he wanted to know when a painting was used and under what circumstances. As he states of Laughing Singer: "He changes purposely his rites, so that one is never exactly the same as the one that just preceded it. Some of the pictures are changed, but two are never substituted [Whirling Logs and First Dancers]" (Guide: 53, Notebook #632). During a Nightway ceremonial no more than four major and two small paintings are used. For Mountainway, only four major and one small are used during any one ceremonial.

Second, Matthews was interested in internal variation in a painting. Did two painters make it the same? What details were consistent or variable? What changed over time? This has been a major concern for anthropologists since and has been studied most critically by Leland Wyman (1983). But Matthews noted that some of the pictures published in James Stevenson (1891) differed from his. ("Pictures of the same subjects, differing somewhat from these in detail, have previously appeared . . ." Matthews 1902a: 316ff.). Unfortunately, he does not analyze the difference, feeling possibly that Stevenson should have done this. But neither, for that matter, do Stevenson (1891) or Tozzer (1909).

Wyman (1975, 1983) and Faris (1990) view Matthews' identification schemes and analyses of the meanings and contextualization of drypaintings with favor, although Faris notes that Matthews was in error in some details, based on his lack of available data on variation and the like.[19] Some of his branch identifications were inaccurate and this affected his classification of drypaintings, but not enough to negate or invalidate his work.

Faris (1990) is critical of Matthews for producing composite paintings rather than exact renditions of what he actually saw in each observation session, a charge he levels against all "rationalists." But Matthews, like other anthropologists of his day, was working under a natural science paradigm. The goal of research was to produce accurate descriptions of ideal types from which variation could later be analyzed. This could be done in two ways, either producing a description of the first X seen as the ideal type or talking to several informants to obtain agreement on the ideal type. This later methodology was actually the preferred Bureau of Ethnology methodology (Parezo 1987). The goal was to develop a categorization scheme, to bring the wealth of new data and information under some form of intellectual control so that it could be dealt with in a "logical" manner. Thus, potential chaos was to be brought under control.

Given Matthews' far-reaching influence in the matter of how drypaintings are studied and published, it is legitimate to ask how much his commitment to natural science and its paradigm imposed his culture's own conceptual schemes on the data. The fact that Matthews tried to convey information about drypaintings within a conceptual framework that was "Navajo" and not defined by evolutionist preconceptions demonstrates that he would only take the schematization of positivist anthropology so far. Yet he remained concerned with facts and variation from the "norm" much more than did Frank Hamilton Cushing or Alexander Stephen in their works on Zunis and Hopis respectively.

This perspective can be demonstrated in Matthews' classification efforts. Matthews classifies drypaintings based on their place within the Navajo ceremonial context rather than by design, layout, or any formalistic or stylistic scheme that would be used by an art historian. First, he distinguishes between those used for purification rites and those used to attract holiness. From this overarching placement, he works downward, in a manner similar to a tree-diagram, based on use and then theme. On the next level, he categorizes drypaintings on the day of the ceremonial in which they were used; then by dominant symbolic motif. He sees this classification scheme as a search for symbolic orderliness as defined in Navajo terms. In this way, Matthews' categorization efforts combined the efforts of the natural historian and scientist with the field worker trying to describe to a middle-class, educated, Anglo-American audience a foreign world view in terms that would be understood by the audience yet which faithfully and accurately described what he had seen and learned through interviews. His work is thus not a romantic presentation like that of many later scholars; it does not contain the "feel" or the "poetry" of the religion. Matthews was trying to advance scholarly knowledge of native peoples and their religion as objectively and as dispassionately as he could.

Conclusion

Given their compelling nature, their artistic fascination to non-Navajos, and their importance to Navajo religion, it is paradoxical that research on Navajo drypaintings was sporadic until the 1920s. This, of course, reflects the nature and history of research on Navajo religion in general. At first, the ceremonials studied were the large, spectacular ones that included God Impersonator dances and other impressive public ceremonies; Matthews (1902a), James and Matilda Coxe Stevenson (1891), Edward Curtis (1907), and Alfred Tozzer (1902, 1909) witnessed and recorded Nightway and Mountainway ceremonies after Matthews reported their existence to the East Coast scientific community. Comparisons to Puebloan kachina dances, which many of these scholars had already witnessed and described, were inevitable and became an implicit focus of research, as did the search for the origins of the masked dances. Given this focus, drypaintings became useful for illustrations but were not the cornerstone of research on Navajo religion. This finding makes sense when one realizes that the ceremonies focused on are not those which necessarily contain the most intricate nor the greatest number of drypaintings.

This does not mean that drypaintings did not fascinate Anglo-American scholars and lay people. Sporadic attempts were made by traders and amateur anthropologists to collect drypaintings, but these were rarely published in the early 1900s (Parezo 1983a). The Franciscan Fathers (1910) were collecting the origin myths and legends with references to drypaintings, searching for the etiological origins of the phenomenon. Drypaintings became illustrations—drawn to accompany articles dealing with Navajo religion. This, of course, carried on a tradition that Matthews himself had begun.

Scholars agree that Matthews' work was the beginning of professional studies on the Navajo, and all subsequent ethnographers have continued to take into account his activity, his research rationale, and his methods. When drypaintings later became the focus of study for their own intrinsic interest, they had become collectors' items and the object of study by both avocational and professional anthropologists—Laura Armer, Flora Bailey, Bertha Dutton, James Faris, Kenneth Foster, Charlotte Frisbie, Berard Haile, W. W. Hill, Clyde Kluckhohn, Karl Luckert, Franc Newcomb, Maude Oakes, Caroline Olin, Gladys Reichard, Margaret Schevill, Louisa Wetherill, Mary Cabot Wheelwright, and, of course, Leland Wyman. As a result of their combined efforts (and those of other collectors who did not publish on their activities), more than 1,600 drypainting reproductions can be found in museums and archives throughout the United States. These men and women used Matthews' research techniques, arguments, and methodologies as well as his basic presentational style.

Matthews was both innovator and preserver of a long-standing tradition of research. Simultaneously, Matthews affected Navajo society by his research efforts. This was the beginning of the formation of new cultural ideas about the nature of drypaintings which has had ramifications for studies of Navajo material culture, aesthetics, ideas about the universe, categorization schemes, values, and their conceptions of the relations of Earth People with Holy People.

Notes

1. Information for this paper was collected during several projects and thus funded indirectly by several agencies. I would like to thank the School of American Research, the National Endowment for the Humanities, and the Wenner-Gren Foundation for Anthropological Research. I would especially like to thank the Smithsonian Institution for funding a postdoctoral fellow-

ship during which I began to study the influence of anthropologists and their research methodologies on Native Americans, especially in relation to the development of art. This project began with my realization of the unintended side effects of Matthews' discussions with singers during his research projects and how subsequent Navajo artists had utilized his and Tall Chanter's ideas and rationalizations.

Information for this paper was collected in the National Anthropological Archives (cited as NAA), the Museum of Northern Arizona, the Wheelwright Museum, Tulane University, and the Southwest Museum. In addition I have made extensive use of the Microfilm Edition of Matthews' papers and documents. A copy of this microfilm is at the University of Arizona Library. I have noted as from different archives those materials on Matthews which I obtained from archival sources before utilizing Halpern and McGreevy's microfilmed materials. It should be noted, however, that almost all of this material is contained in their microfilm. I would like to thank both Katherine Spencer Halpern and Susan Brown McGreevy for their excellent suggestions, editing, and patience.

2. "Los Indios hacen figuras de todos sus diablos, señor . . . it was this hint which led to the discovery of their drypaintings" (Matthews 1897a:39). As Matthews told James Pilling (17 December 1880), "I have found here a good Spanish speaking interpreter of the Navajo and am getting along well with him" (NAA: WM to Pilling 12/17/1880).

3. Matthews had a great deal of trouble getting transferred to Fort Wingate. The new posting required the intervention of both Major Powell and Col. James Stevenson with Generals Logan and Pope as well as with the Surgeon General (NAA: WM at JWP, 10/30/1880). Powell made Matthews an official Smithsonian Institution, Bureau of Ethnology collaborator when he embarked on the assignment. This unpaid position conferred scientific status and affiliation on holders. (Other well-known Smithsonian collaborators at a later period were Franz Boas and Frances Densmore.) Matthews was listed as a scientific collaborator in the Smithsonian Institution annual reports.

4. Jonathan Letherman, stationed at Fort Defiance, wrote in 1855: "Of their [Navojo] religion little or nothing is known, as indeed, all inquiries tend to show they have none" (Letherman 1856:294). Word lists had been collected by other army personnel but little was known about Navajo religion. (See also Frisbie in this volume.)

5. Navajo ceremonials can be performed with or without drypaintings, so Matthews could have easily attended versions where drypaintings were not used. It is also likely that he tended at first to observe only the last day and night of the Mountainway or Nightway, which do not use drypaintings. Navajos were also not likely to talk to a stranger about the activities within the medicine lodge until they had assessed his sincerity.

6. The Mountainway is a ceremonial that can be performed only during the winter months, after the first killing frost when the bears and snakes are hibernating and before the first thunderstorms of the spring. It is used to cure mountain sickness—that is, illnesses stemming from improper contact with mountain animals and forces, especially bears. This was manifested in arthritis, rheumatism, swollen limbs and joints, mental illness, fainting, temporary loss of mind, delirium, nervousness, violent irrationality or insanity, and occasionally in stomach trouble, constipation, kidney, bladder, or gall bladder disturbances (Wyman 1975).

7. Matthews also witnessed a shock rite with drypainting for Nightway later that same year (1902a: Plate II). This was a painting of Talking God, Male Yei and Female Yé'ii which is also used to frighten the patient.

8. James Stevenson attended these lectures. He later observed a Nightway at Keams Canyon in October 1885 while on a Bureau of Ethnology collecting trip, and as a good Bureau of Ethnology employee, he quickly wrote up a description of the experience, with the assistance of his wife. Powell published this in the next Annual Report of the Bureau (Stevenson 1891). Matthews was offended by Stevenson's lack of acknowledgment and the speed with which he published.

This can be seen in what was apparently a first-draft preface to the Night Chant, where Matthews wrote: "He [Stevenson] fails, in his work, to mention my previous labors and also his indebtedness to Mr. A. M. Stephen of Keam's Canyon who rendered him much assistance in his researches. . . . He had little previous knowledge of the Navahoes, understood nothing of their language and had an incompetent interpreter, Navajo John . . ." (Guide: 62, MS #535). Faris has made an extensive analysis of Matthews' and Stevenson's interactions and the value of Stevenson's work to our knowledge of Navajo religion (Faris 1990:40ff).

This incident reflects the intellectual and personal rivalries and factionalism of the Washington scientific community (see Hinsley 1983 and Parezo 1986). As Hinsley (1983:192) has noted, "The Indian cultures of the region apparently fostered unusual attachment and possessiveness, and under the exposure of public popularity anthropology in the Southwest became heavily infused with personal style." Matthews intensely disliked the Stevensons, as did his friend Cushing. They speak of their rivalries repeatedly in their correspondence (Guide: 81–82, 8/17/1886, 8/1/1881).

It turns out that Matilda Coxe Stevenson actually made the copies of the drypaintings: "Mrs. Stevenson was also able to secure a minute description of the celebrated dance, or medicine ceremony of the Navajos called the Yeibitcai. Mrs. Stevenson made complete sketches of the sand, altars, masks and other objects employed in this ceremonial" (Baird 1889:57).

9. Notice in the Washington Post, 11 April 1886, review of "The Gods of the Navahoes" (see Guide: 64, 68–69, #80). For a listing of the published abstracts of these lectures, see Matthews' bibliography item 1885d. The paper for the Anthropological Society of Washington was probably the same as that for the Philosophical Society of Washington. Mooney (1905:521) lists that an abstract of the talk was published in the Transactions of the Anthropological Society of Washington 3:139–140. I have not seen this abstract. In the Smithsonian Miscellaneous Collections, which always published abstracts and proceedings from scholarly and scientific meetings in the Washington area, Matthews published line drawings, at first without any explanation. Then, in the American Naturalist article, there were black-and-white line drawings of two paintings, Home of the Bear and Snake, and Long Bodies, with explanations (Matthews 1885d: Plates XXXII and XXXIII).

10. The drypainting described by Link (1960) was related to Matthews by Old Torlino on 25 November 1893.

11. See Parezo 1984 for an example of Cushing's use of this technique to obtain information at Zuni and Hopi.

12. Matthews felt that exactness might not be achieved because of the way in which the paintings were transmitted through oral tradition; however, he recognized this as an interesting anthropological problem. In fact, it is one that is still noted today. All scholars (with the exception of Faris 1990) have noted the remarkable stability of the drypainting designs over time and the breadth of the reservation.

13. Matthews, in his work with Navajo weavers and silversmiths, had encountered no strenuous opposition to his inquiries. From his letters to Cushing and Powell, his first ethnographic topics seem to have involved fairly easy field work; it had certainly not taken him four years to secure access and to record this information.

14. While Poor (1975:12) is correct in his assessment that Matthews left little information about his ethnographic methods in that he wrote no explicit statements beginning "my methods of obtaining and analyzing information were . . . ," one can still glean insights from correspondence and footnotes.

15. Matthews did have professional artists and illustrators reproduce the paintings in his publications. One artist was Delaney Gill, who worked for the Bureau of Ethnology. As a result of the publishing process, however, the color blue is more brilliant than it would have appeared in the ceremony.

16. Father Berard Haile suffered paralysis and has also been said to have contracted "Yé'ii

Bicheii sickness." Several Navajos also told me while I was conducting my fieldwork that the same was true for anthropologist and museum director Kenneth Foster. Aberle (1966:197) and Waters (1970:260) have also recounted the story of Matthews' and Tall Chanter's illnesses.

17. To do so would have been to present a false picture of Navajo drypaintings as disembodied art—to use the Anglo-American concept of art as divorced from the act of which it is a part. More interesting to Matthews was how drypaintings were used, how they formed an integral part of Navajo ceremonies, and what their symbols meant.

18. It should be noted that there is some problem with the numbering of these plates. The second drypainting described in the text (radial picture of four deities and Four Sacred Plants), on pages 447–450 is mislabeled in the colored plates as "Third Dry-Painting" (Plate XVII), and the third drypainting, a linear picture of the Long Bodies (pp. 450–451) is mislabeled in the colored plates as "Second Dry-Painting" (Plate XVI).

19. It should be noted that no two authorities agree on the classification of Navajo ceremonies.

Dr. Washington Matthews, Assistant Surgeon,
United States Army, ca. 1875–1880

(Photograph No. 7, William Wallace Wellborn Collection, Courtesy United States Army Military History Institute)

Officers' Quarters, Fort Wingate, ca. 1890
(Photography by [?] Waite, Courtesy Museum of New Mexico, Neg. No. 14529)

Fort Wingate, New Mexico, 1903 *(Photograph by Ben Wittick, Courtesy School of American Research, Collection in the Museum of New Mexic Neg. No. 15772)*

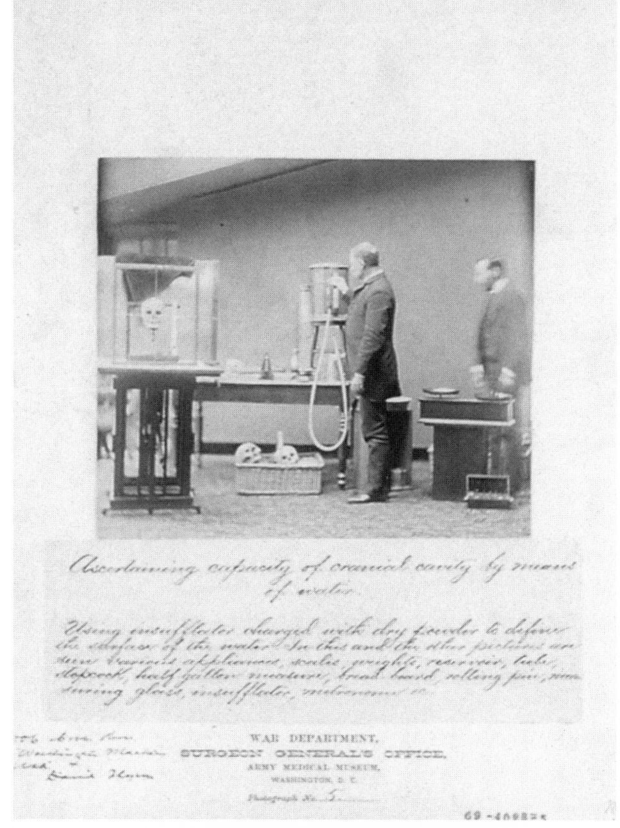

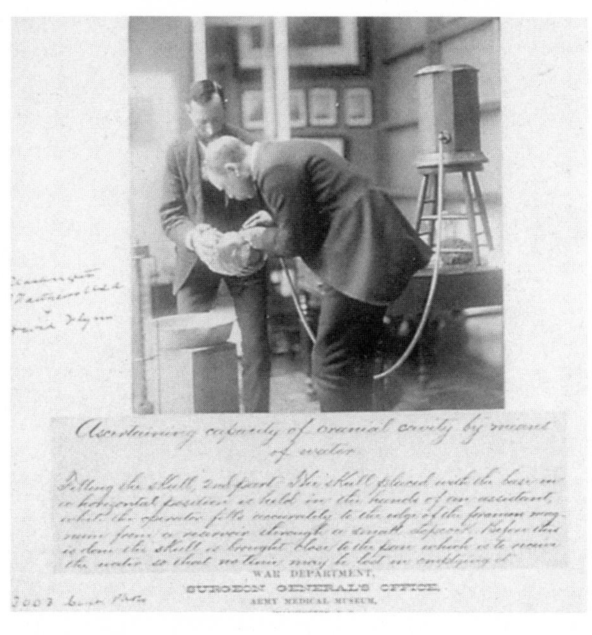

Washington Matthews and David Flynn Performing Measurements on the Crania. This photograph was taken at the Army Medical Museum, Washington, D.C., ca. 1885–1889. *(Otis Historical Archives, Armed Forces Institute of Pathology, Courtesy National Museum of Health and Medicine.)*

The Shaman,
Hatali Nez
(Tall Chanter)
(From Navajo Legends, Fig. 32)

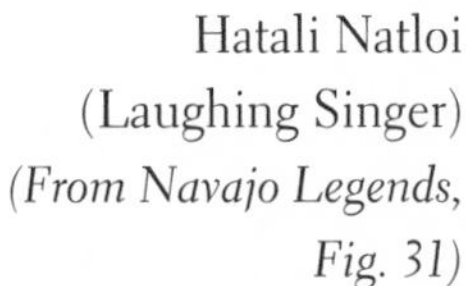

Hatali Natloi
(Laughing Singer)
(From Navajo Legends, Fig. 31)

Some Observations on the Ethical Integrity of Washington Matthews in Navajo Research

(with particular reference to his work with the Nightway)[1]

JAMES C. FARIS

As Washington Matthews was a medical doctor by profession, his ethical behavior while undertaking research amongst the Navajos was hardly due to received anthropological standards. Moreover, the ethical "shape" of anthropology in the United States during Matthews' period amongst the Navajos was in any case certainly poorly formed, or in flux or in debate, and thus not very imposing on him. This short paper will, however, argue that Matthews' ethical concerns during his work in Navajoland were (or should have been) of vital importance to the emergent discipline of anthropology in America. Matthews set standards in these directions only rarely again met, for he was something quite more than simply a man of his time—he was, in several significant ways in terms of personal integrity vis-á-vis the Navajos, a man ahead of his time. And it is my view that these are the ancestors most worth listening to (as opposed to disciplinary forefathers with far less foresight and ethical integrity, but who were nevertheless canonized for their place in the establishment of formal anthropological institutions).[2]

With regard to ethical integrity, I hope to discuss several of Matthews' attitudes and behaviors—his demeanor and deportment toward his Navajo collaborators, his perspectives and postures toward future scholarship, his ethical actions toward friends and enemies relevant to his research. My discussion will include what might today be covered under the category of field research methods by the more conscientious, but I will also examine Matthews' commitment to the integrity and shape of ethnographic accounts, and his solutions to issues of specific descriptions (as opposed to composite accounts),[3] as well as his allegiance to conventional anthropological wisdom of the day (particularly concerning the derivative character[4] of Navajo ceremonialism) and toward other prevailing notions about indigenous peoples.

It must be remembered that Matthews was in Navajoland as a physician—for the occupation army.[5] Reading his papers and journals through time, however, one gets the impression that Matthews became more and more influenced by—and sympathetic toward—the adequacy of local discourses and their logical cohesion, and by the integrity of Navajo healing systems. There is, nevertheless, no evidence of which I am aware that Matthews ever seriously considered Navajo healing efficacy *on its own terms*—that is, as would a Navajo believer, so his commitment to the integrity of indigenous discourse was from an anthropological—Western scientific and rationalist—point of view. The Nightway was not considered by Matthews, in other words, from a local or an ameliorative or rehabilitative view; it was not looked upon as a discourse for healing—which is, of course, its primary relevance for Navajos.

Matthews and His Navajo Collaborators[6]

Washington Matthews was very fortunate in having had relations with some strategically important and very accomplished Nightway medicine men. Indeed, the two principal informants for Matthews' Nightway research, commonly known in English as Laughing Singer and Tall Chanter, were among the most widely known and prestigious of Navajo medicine men at the time. Their collaboration with Matthews certainly enhanced their reputations with non-Navajos as well,[7] and at least Laughing Singer was recommended by Matthews to other researchers in the area.[8]

They were, moreover (and especially Laughing Singer), also used to dealing with Euro-Americans. There is evidence (Faris 1990:8, 20–21; see also note 6 herein) that Laughing Singer was the medicine man that Stevenson recorded in 1885 (Stevenson does not tell us his name—see Stevenson 1891), and certainly Laughing Singer was involved with other recorders,[9] photographers, and collectors—even to the point of selling a set of Nightway masks to Culin in 1903 that Matthews had tried unsuccessfully to buy earlier (Culin 1903:112). Stevenson listened to two of Matthews' lectures on the Nightway in Washington, D.C. in the spring of 1885 (Guide: 62, Manuscript #535:4ff, Roll 4) and then recorded a Nightway near Piñon in the fall of the same year. He published his account quickly (Stevenson 1891), with no acknowledgement of Matthews' lectures or his years of pioneering work, nor mention of A. M. Stephen, a researcher in Hopi country who had arranged for Stevenson to record the ceremony. But Matthews—certainly after this no friend of Stevenson—never acknowledges that Laughing Singer may have aided Stevenson.

Neither Laughing Singer nor Tall Chanter were proficient in English, though they could presumably make themselves understood to English speakers (cf. Culin 1903). Matthews thus relied on translators a great deal, particularly early in his research. He developed a rather acute "ear," however, and going through his papers, one can see his "ear" (his ability to phonologically record in more detail and with increasing accuracy), his linguistic abilities in Navajo, and his comprehension of spoken Navajo become better and more improved. This improvement was, unfortunately, accompanied by an advancing deafness. During the 1890s, Matthews probably came to rely less and less on translators,[10] but since his hearing was failing, he thus also probably took down fewer phonological materials.

Matthews seemed to get along very well with both medicine men, perhaps because as a physician he saw them as fellow professionals. He worked with Laughing Singer extensively in the mid-1890s (Guide: 53, Notebook #632, dated 1891–92, Roll 2)—and under Laughing Singer's tutelage, he actually made various disposable sacrificial materials, such as *k'eet'áán*, necessary to the Nightway. Some of these even found their way into museum collections as "authentic" Nightway artifacts.[11]

Matthews seemed to rely more on Laughing Singer for sequential detail, for material culture knowledge, for specific procedures or ceremony; and on Tall Chanter for songs, prayers, texts, and discursive materials, as well as for checking translations and materials, at least some of which he had gotten elsewhere.[12] Matthews employed each of these medicine men for a couple of months at a time, but there is no specific evidence that he used one to correct the other, though Tall Chanter was, as noted, used to correct Matthews' notes in general—certainly during his trip to Washington in the fall of 1885. In this case, however, there is no specific mention of the sources of the original notes that Tall Chanter was asked about. This inability to document the origin of the notes is of some concern since Laughing Singer and Tall Chanter had different apprenticeship histories (cf. Faris 1990:19) and practiced different "branches" of the Nightway (Newcomb 1964:112). Thus, corrections by one of the practices of the other could distort the legitimate differences between each branch. This potential problem is rarely acknowledged by Matthews. (For one rare exception, see Guide: 52, 53, Notebook #586, Roll 2, where Matthews' notes carry the annotation "the old man [Tall Chanter] prefers" when detailing names of *yé'ii* presumably gotten from another medicine man—possibly Laughing Singer.) Matthews was certainly aware of the notion of "branches," and of the somewhat different procedures appropriated to specific diagnostic etiologies (cf. Guide: 49, Notes #69, Roll 1); indeed, he introduced the concept into the Western classification of Navajo ceremonials.

Description, Explanation, Interpretation

In *The Night Chant* (Matthews 1902a), Matthews frequently notes materials from specific Nightways he has witnessed, but without any specific information as to the date, medicine man, place, cost, or outcome. As mentioned, occasionally there are notes with some comment that Laughing Singer did it this way or Tall Chanter preferred it that way, but we lack in this work precise identification of the sources of specific Nightway descriptions.[13] Matthews is certainly aware of the implications of publishing a composite account drawn from the many Nightways, he attended, or from which he gleaned information. In an unpublished manuscript labelled "Ceremonies" (Guide:60, Manuscript #516:3, Roll 4), Matthews justifies his composite approach. Since each Nightway will differ from every other in minute ways, writes Matthews, it would give the wrong impression to publish a specific description and claim it as generalizable to all Nightway practice.[14] Matthews thus publishes a composite account, but is nevertheless able to give specific details, as he witnessed these ceremonies time and time again. We are not told, however, what situational determinants surround each practice (some specific practices, for example, are negotiated each time between the medicine man and the family of the person sung over; some are specific to the diagnostic etiology; some are "branch" specific; and some are appropriate only to the practices of medicine men of a specific apprenticeship genealogy—adapted to secure rainfall, to stop snow, etc.). At points there will be a footnote in the great 1902 text qualifying details in one manner or another, and Matthews does state that to detail all the possible intricacies ("a complete account of the ceremony") would probably require two more volumes (1902a:v). But for the numbers of specific Nightways Matthews claims to have seen "in whole or in part a dozen times or more" (Guide:60, Manuscript #516, Roll 4), beginning in 1880 (Matthews, 1902a:v), and for occupying much of his spare time for twenty-one years, there are some conspicuous gaps and mistakes.[15]

Matthews does acknowledge the potential for determining etiological factors in the specifics of ceremonies (1902a:v), but he generally seems to think that complexity is a function of the medicine man's knowledge. He certainly related some practices to their specific "Indian mythic etiology" (1902a:v), but this is not detailed. He notes, for example, that some sandpaintings are appropriate to specific branches (1902a:316), which they are, but since he does not identify them, it is difficult to assess the claim.

Nevertheless, Matthews' rigor and care is everywhere evident, and his precise attention to Navajo logics is dramatic, particularly when compared with less careful accounts of the time. Several publications are based on his interpretive conclusions of such logics—in the proper construction of material culture items (Matthews 1892b) and in the organization of song materials (Matthews 1894b). But Matthews never examined the limits and precise shape of such local logics so as to comment on its ideological character and their relevance to the restoration of a specific orders in Navajo social relations.[16] It was sufficient for him to note that practices existed to restore order and heal, and he did not attempt to go further to query the exact contours and configurations and parameters of the order to be restored. He did not, for example, query the strictures on women so dramatic in Nightway practice, nor the clear specifications of authority relations (such as leader over led—cf. Faris and Walters 1990). Of course, neither did he critique its practice as contrary to Christian practices or inadequate to Western medical knowledge. Perhaps, in the latter case, this is implicit, however, for though he accepted Navajo belief to the extent that he did treat it as a specific local ideology, he did not accept it to the extent that he thought it adequate to its task. Matthews did not, for example, undergo a Nightway to address his advancing deafness—even though the Nightway addresses deafness among its specificities, and Matthews was probably aware that this type of malady might come to one as a consequence of an insufficiently pious attitude toward the Nightway, or simply having watched and participated in too many (yielding a condition known as "yeibichai sickness"—see Faris 1990:56, 79). Current Nightway medicine men, for example, may undergo Nightway (as the person sung over) periodically for precisely these reasons. Other non-Navajos have undergone Nightway—with mixed results. Roman Hubbell, the Ganado trader, troubled by advancing deafness, was one of the persons sung over in a Nightway in 1926. It is reported that his hearing improved subsequently (interview with Dorothy Hubbell, January 1987, Faris 1990:247).

Truth, Authenticity, Origins

The relationships with the Navajo medicine men with whom Matthews worked were such that they appeared to have commonly interceded for him against the wishes of others assembled for the ceremonies. Though he did not record reactions to his sketching in Nightway ceremonies, Matthews did record the horror with which his attempts to sketch Mountainway sandpaintings was met by congregations (Poor 1975:31 quoting from Matthews 1885d:61).[17]

Matthews did persuade Laughing Singer to instruct him in the manufacture of materials to be consumed in each Nightway, as noted. Moreover, he did purchase some items of permanent medicine bundles other than Nightway. Certainly, he was well aware of the sanctions against such purchases, especially of Nightway masks, for he quotes Tall Chanter:

> He does not want to sell [the] broken gourd, [and] says when any of the property of the yeibitcai is broken, it should be buried in the bed of a stream and dedicated to the Gods. Furthermore, if he were to sell Born for Water and Monster Slayer he would sell the properties of the greatest gods they have. They live in the mountains [a]round here and if they found the sacred masks gone they would visit the country of the white man with fire or a great flood and destroy them all. (Guide: 52–53, Notebook #538, Roll 2).

Matthews' conscience was not apparently distressed, for as noted above, he did attempt (unsuccessfully) to purchase such Nightway *jish* from Laughing Singer.

Matthews' concern with accuracy, with care, is a rather different sort of obsession than the notions of "authenticity" previously noted (see note 11). He carefully checked his materials, as he could, and changed materials as he became aware of problems, better data, more accurate accounts, etc. He never rested on what had appeared in print under his name, nor attempted to suppress data that contradicted what he had earlier published. His care was such that only occasionally did he publish materials that he later found to be wrong, but certainly his unpublished notes (as with all anthropologists) are filled with errors that were later corrected. Matthews usually corrects his errors in subsequent publications without comment on the earlier mistakes. What is most significant, ethically, however, is that he *did* publish the correct material. This is particularly evident in the errors concerning the important First Dancer's prayer on the final evening of the Nightway. In Matthews 1897a:275, he discusses the last night prayer, in error, to be corrected without comment in Matthews 1902a. Similarly, Matthews has a confusing and curious discussion of a "mythic thunderbird god" in Matthews 1897a: 275, not to be repeated in the more correct Matthews 1902a. And an early erroneous conclusion that the first four nights were accompanied by rattle, the last five nights accompanied by basket drum (1894a) is not repeated in Matthews 1902a.

These are not simply picky matters, for several of the earlier erroneous (or confused) materials were adopted and repeated (or further confused) by others (i.e., the "mythic thunderbird god" [Matthews 1897a:275]—see University of Arizona, Haile, MS UAZ:AZ/132/Box 13; see also Young and Morgan 1987:639). Indeed, Matthews—sometimes acknowledged, sometimes not—is probably the most frequently quoted and copied of sources by commentators and researchers on Navajo ceremonies in the first quarter of the twentieth century. His work was the measure that later scholars used—a fact that these scholars often acknowledged (cf. Tozzer 1909; Haile 1947). Tozzer actually specifically compares his own description (1909) to Matthews', and readers have the distinct impression that his research has less to do with accurately observing and describing what took place than with focusing upon what happened that Matthews didn't describe, or on how things happened differently from Matthews' accounts.[18]

In general, Matthews relied little on the accounts of others. Indeed, he ignored Stevenson altogether, and as noted, he corrected (but did so without reference to) some of his own earlier accounts. And he sometimes even ignored his earlier accounts (perhaps because they might contain error?). While Matthews commends Sgt. Barthelmess' "excellent account" (1902a:311)—a particularly interesting one, inasmuch as it describes the unique Fringed Mouth of the Water Holy Person Impersonator, with its blue/yellow face mask—he nevertheless does not make use of it. Indeed, Matthews' notes contain an error on the details of curvature of the right eye of the Fringed Mouth mask (Guide:58, Sketch #542/3, Roll 3), a mask Barthelmess describes in detail. Matthews also erroneously states that this account was published in the Chicago German newspaper *Der Westen* in January 1894; it only exists, so far as I have been able to determine, in Matthews' notes [Guide:60–61, Manuscript #361, Roll 3]).

Matthews sometimes reports only what he has been told, but usually qualifies this if it is not something he actually witnessed himself (1902a:27–28) or if his notes have been misplaced or lost (1902a:316). There are some puzzling problems in Matthews' notes (cf Guide: 58, Sketch #539–540, Roll 3) in that he says he never saw the masks of Monster Slayer or Born to Water finished nor worn, whereas in notes to a Nightway he saw in 1891, he states both were present, and that the "rites of succor" were administered by the War God (Guide: 60, Manuscript #483, Roll 3).

Matthews was no idle theorist—he learned by repeated asking and doing. He was a solid empiricist. Many queries he had about details were only satisfied after he "apprenticed" to Laughing Singer in the early 1890s—at least one spring, Matthews actually helped prepare the proper and ceremonial materials (drumstick, *k'eetáán*) under Laughing Singer's direction.[19]

Perhaps because Matthews was such a serious and careful empiricist, his research materials reveal an integrity not evident in the printed versions. For example, in the original manuscript of *The Night Chant,* Matthews labels one of the illustrations so the reader will be aware that the man illustrated is inserted for purposes of scale only (1902a: Plate 1, Figure C). This caption is ignored in the printed version, presumably by the publishers. Matthews' original sketches for the sandpainting reproductions are also less elongated and less dramatically contrasting in color (i.e., more like those actually relevant to Nightway) than those eventually printed.[20]

Conclusions

Matthews has been noted both as a man of his time, and in significant ways, as a man ahead of his time—particularly in his integrity and his ethical attitudes toward scholarship and toward other human beings. Most authors herein would undoubtedly agree. Let me end with a more controversial note, however, about another way in which I believe Matthews was ahead of his time (rather than simply being misinformed, misled, or insufficiently anthropological). This is in his attitude toward Navajo history. Though he erroneously thought the Nightway "the most important and ancient ceremony then in existence" (see Frisbie, herein; and see also Faris and Walters 1990 for the placement of the Nightway in Navajo sequences of chantway acquisition), he was willing to entertain a much greater time depth to the chantway, and to suggest that both Navajo and Pueblo belief systems had a common origin (Matthews 1892d: 335; 1894c: 247; 1902a:5). This suggests that Navajos may well have been in the Southwest during the time that the great Anasazi sites were still occupied. Navajos may have been instructed by these Anasazi [or vice versa, inasmuch as the Anasazi also lacked, classically, the "kachina cult" (see Schaafsma 1980; McGuire 1987)] and may have been a factor in the abandonment of the great Anasazi villages.[21] This is counter to the more contemporary conventional wisdom of the Pueblo-derived character of much Navajo ceremonialism, intact from the time of Tozzer (1909).

Free, then, of many of the conventions of anthropological rationalism, Matthews was able to speculate in interesting and unconventional directions. Washington Matthews thus pursued his own research interests carefully and thoroughly. With his character and integrity, he did so remarkably carefully and thoroughly. And he did so governed by an ethical and personal demeanor that still bears appreciation and attention.

Notes

1. Specific and general ethical appreciations of Matthews are found throughout the present volume, but most particularly in Halpern, Frisbie, and Zolbrod. I have tried not to overlap their commentaries. I am indebted to the editors for their help and expertise in the Matthews records.

2. Matthews was not, of course, totally beyond the general scientific character of the late nineteenth century, and throughout I will subject him to the most severe standards by holding his work hostage to the judgments of the present. He was clearly influenced by the predominant theoretical currents of the time. He was certainly an evolutionist (cf. Matthews 19012:13, 19022:5) and sometimes even worse (cf. his use of the term "savage", 19022:118), but he was also in tune with (or ahead of) the positive and progressive views of the turn of the century (i.e., the Teddy Roosevelt "Progressivism"), however benighted that may seem today. His ethical integrity—toward subject populations as well as toward scientific character, for example—is most instructively contrasted with an important and very influential anthropologist of the time (and also a specialist on Navajos), Alfred Tozzer, who falls far short, even exhibiting contempt for Navajo

belief in his published work. Matthews also contrasts well, in all dimensions, with Stevenson, Curtis, Culin, and even later, Reichard, and Kluckhohn. Indeed, of all those who worked in Navajoland, his integrity most resembles that of Fr. Berard Haile.

3. In his great monographs on specific Navajo healing practices (*The Mountain Chant: A Navajo Ceremony*, 1887a; *The Night Chant: A Navajo Ceremony*, 1902a), Matthews' descriptions are principally composite descriptions based upon and taken from several specific ceremonies he witnessed, and about which he asked questions; they do not usually contain specific descriptions of the particular healing ceremonials that he witnessed or that were described to him. (The Mountain Chant does contain somewhat more identifiable specific description than the Nightway.) Matthews was aware of the important distinction between specific and composite descriptions and he discussed this in his notes (cf. Guide: 60, Manuscript #516:3, Roll 3). The epistemological implications of specific vs. composite descriptions are discussed further in Faris 1990:40ff, 70).

4. This issue is discussed further later in this essay (see pp. 84–85), and see also the references in note 21.

5. There is no direct evidence that Matthews treated Navajos with Western medicines. However, his military diary for 1881–82 notes outbreaks of smallpox among neighboring Indians and that in June 1881 he was away at Zuni to vaccinate Indian children (Guide: 72, Military Diary, Roll 9, f. 1395–1432). Also in his military correspondence, Matthews requests rations for "citizens" in the post hospital—which may or may not have included Navajos (Guide: 73, Military Correspondence, Roll 10, f. 26–65). I am indebted to Halpern for tracking down this information.

6. I will use the current preferred spelling—"Navajo"—throughout, except in direct quotation. (Of course, this is the spelling preferred by English speakers—it is a foreign word for people who refer to themselves as Diné, or "people on the earth.") Certainly in his later publications, Matthews preferred the spelling "Navajo" and in his preface to *The Night Chant*, he engages in a sharp polemic over such spelling (see also Matthews, 1897a:55–56). This curious (and uncharacteristically unctuous) outburst at so important and significant a juncture is perhaps to be explained as an oblique criticism of Stevenson (who used the spelling "Navajo"). There exists a probable original preface (Guide: 62, Manuscript #535), which is a more direct critique of Stevenson, but Matthews chose not to publish this (see Faris 1990:41 for this text). Perhaps, then, this rather trivial issue of spelling came to be the most severe way in which this gentle man could criticize Stevenson.

Indeed, Matthews never refers to Stevenson in *The Night Chant*, except to acknowledge him in the very last note of the last page of the volume. Perhaps in subliminal pique, Matthews even errs in the title of Stevenson's work (1902a: 316):

> Pictures of the same subjects, differing somewhat from these in detail, have previously appeared in the following work:—"Ceremonial of Hasjelti Dailjis and mythicals [*sic*—mythical] and paintings [*sic*—sandpaintings] of the Navajo Indians," by James Stevenson. (Eighth Annual Report of the Bureau of Ethnology, pp. 229–85, Washington, 1891)

Faris (1990:68) argues, in fact, that Matthews knew Laughing Singer had been the medicine man Stevenson recorded and deliberately avoided mentioning it, especially since everything else about Stevenson's account was castigated in this unpublished preface, including even his translators—whom Matthews labeled "unreliable."

7. Also a factor, of course, is the extent to which various early traders were important in amplifying and augmenting reputations and in brokering relations between Navajos and researchers. Certainly J. L. Hubbell (Ganado), the Days (St. Michaels and Chinle), and J. Moore (Crystal) were important in introducing various medicine men to outsiders. Matthews was well acquainted with these traders, though I am unaware of the specific extent to which they may have helped him. But certainly he was aware of the close links between some of these traders—

especially the Days—and Navajos. In 1989 Matthews sent a copy of *The Mountain Chant* to the Franciscan Father Anselm Weber in Arizona, cautioning him to let no one see it but his trusted missionary associates. Matthews felt that he had violated the confidence of his Navajo associates in publishing this ceremonial knowledge, and he did not want them to see the publication. He did not trust "the ordinary white men" on the reservation to keep it from them (Poor 1975:31). I do not know of any such cautions over the publication of *The Night Chant.* Indeed, I have seen a warm greeting from Matthews to the Days traders in an autographed copy of the latter volume in the possession of Sam Day III.

8. Matthews (Guide: 53–54, Notebook #674:106, Roll 3) undoubtedly underestimates the numbers of active Nightway medicine men of the time, probably as a consequence of relying exclusively on Laughing Singer and Tall Chanter—and perhaps because they misinformed him about the availablity of others. Nevertheless, Nightway medicine men got around vast areas of Navajoland even in the late nineteenth century, and perhaps as many as seven or more were active at the time of Matthews' research (Faris 1988, 1990).

9. Matthews recommended Laughing Singer to Goddard in 1903 (Guide: 46, Correspondence, Matthews to Goddard, 12/26/1903, #347, Roll 1). In a letter to Culin the same year, he attempted to get Culin to share expenses to bring Laughing Singer, but not Tall Chanter, East—even though Matthews had brought Tall Chanter to Washington to work with him in 1885. Matthews does note that Tall Chanter had trouble with his reputation in later years (Matthews 1897a:58), and everywhere refers to Tall Chanter as an "old man," even though Tall Chanter and Laughing Singer were probably about the same age (Faris 1990:82).

10. I have been able to identify Ben Damon (Guide:53, Notebook #632, Roll 2; Manuscript #416, Roll 3) and Chee [Dodge?] (Guide: 49, 50, Notes #175, Roll 1; Notes #383:3, Roll 2, f. 87–101) as the principal translators involved with Matthews' Nightway research. The former was "a Navajo half-breed," educated at Carlyle (Guide:53, Manuscript #416, Roll 3), whom Matthews persuaded to go through a Nightway initiation (Matthews 1897b:260).

11. This, of course, raises the issue of the use of these materials outside Nightway, as they are designed to be consumed (sacrificed so as to invite Holy People to attend) at Nightway and are normally not made except during Nightway by medicine men, and/or by apprentices and assistants under the guidance of the medicine man. Thus, from this point of view, *any* Nightway consumables that exist outside Navajoland are "inauthentic."

Two collections contain Nightway sacred materials from Matthews—those of the Museum of the American Indian, New York City; and the Lowie Museum, University of California, Berkeley. As I have only examined the former, I cannot say which Nightway materials were indeed manufactured by Matthews. Of course, save the fact that Matthews was not Navajo and not a believer, their "authenticity" is unquestionable (but note caveat above), for he was making these materials with Laughing Singer's advice and under his guidance, just as would any apprentice. As noted previously, Matthews was unsuccessful in his attempts to purchase some of the permanent (non-consumed) materials of a Nightway medicine bundle, such as masks. We do not know, however, the circumstances that surrounded these attempts. Did he offer too little? Did Laughing Singer think it inappropriate to sell to Matthews? Or did Laughing Singer once refuse (Matthews) and subsequently change his mind on the ethics of such sale and later assent to the purchase of permanent Nightway materials (Culin)?

12. Matthews' notes are filled with marginal citations ("1885'd", "Old Manned", "OK, 1885"), indicating that he had checked materials with Tall Chanter, mostly during the medicine man's visit to Washington in the fall of 1885.

13. While some of the brief sketches contained in the manuscript notes of specific Nightway practices are attributed to the practices of individual medicine men, this is not the case with them all.

14. Notwithstanding this logic, Matthews does not seem to see the resulting contradiction that

could be argued of publishing a composite account as representative of any specific "Night Chant." See Faris 1990 for an argument that the only possible appropriate Nightway must be specific.

15. The gaps are conspicuous, but much more impressive is the wealth of detail that *does* occur. Indeed, the point here is that Matthews' problem is *too much* detail with little or no etiological reference or identification of specific practices, and thus the absence of breaks that would indicate the precise limits and boundaries of local discourse, and each distinctive convention.

Nevertheless, Matthews never did seem to get clear some details of Nightway masks (Black God, Red God, Fringed Mouth—cf. Matthews 1902a:25–27; Guide:58, Sketch #542/3, Roll 3), nor did he successfully distinguish the Nightway founding texts that he collected from specific practices in the Nightway ceremonial, and he erred on which Holy People Impersonators appeared in actual practices and in sandpaintings (Matthews 1902a:21, 24, 25). These are corrected in Faris 1990.

16. In current philosophical criticism, the specific ideological character, the specific rhetoric, or a construct, are best approached by a determination of its limits and boundaries and shape—to confine it rather than to allow it universal (and thus persuasive) application. In other words, by a statement of the concrete shape of a category, its metaphorical character can be examined. This technique is employed in Faris 1990, and Faris and Walters 1990, for Navajo constructs.

17. His sketching here was probably facilitated by the medicine man presiding, named Gordo (Guide: 52, 54, Notebook #468, Roll 2).

18. Tozzer's first report of this Nightway (Tozzer 1902) appeared prior to Matthews' (1902a), and thus differs from his later account of the same Nightway (Tozzer 1909) which he wrote after having read Matthews. This subsequent account is oriented around Matthews' 1902a description (Tozzer did, of course, always have access to Stevenson [1891]). Despite his having witnessed a rather dramatically distinct Nightway with some unique (and heretofore unrecorded) sandpaintings at a remote eastern location (Chaco Canyon, 1901), Tozzer (1909:328–29) continued to insist that Matthews was wrong to suggest that the Nightway changes, citing his own account as proof that the Nightway is unchanging in time and space!

19. The evidence in the Matthews' materials suggests that this "apprenticing" took place outside of an actual Nightway performance and was private tutoring. See also the previous discussion, pp. 81–82.

20. These materials today rest in the G. H. Pepper Papers of the collections of the Latin American Library of Tulane University. I am endebted to Dr. Caroline Olin for informing me of the location of the manuscript materials.

21. This speculation and the controversy surrounding it are discussed further in Faris 1990: 16ff. See also Faris and Walters 1990.

Washington Matthews' Folklore Studies

KATHERINE SPENCER HALPERN

The hero of the Mountain Chant story, as he embarked on his adventures, paused and looked north toward the San Juan River and the country of his people:

> *And he said to the land, "Aqalani!" (greeting), and a feeling of loneliness and homesickness came over him and he wept and sang this song:*
>
> *That flowing water! That flowing water!*
> *My mind wanders across it.*
> *That broad water! That flowing water!*
> *My mind wanders across it.*
> *That old age water! That flowing water!*
> *My mind wanders across it.*

Washington Matthews,
The Mountain Chant, *p.* 393

When Matthews came to Navajo country in 1881 the nature of Navajo religion was essentially unknown to western scholarship. In the quarter century of his Navajo studies from 1881 to his death in 1905, he succeeded in identifying the main elements of Navajo ceremonial practice and their basis in mythology. His detailed studies of two important Navajo curing ceremonies, the Mountain Chant and the Night Chant, demonstrated the integral connection between myth and ceremony in Navajo thought, with the myth describing the source and nature of ceremonial practices and justifying their curing effectiveness. In connection with these sacred stories, Matthews recorded songs and prayers, paying particular attention to their aesthetic and poetic qualities, that are essential to ceremonial performance. He also obtained several versions of the tribal origin myth, which embodies Navajo beliefs about how their world came into being, the behavior of their gods, or Holy People, and the relation between these Holy People and ordinary mortals. The origin story is the basic charter of Navajo history and philosophy. In addition, Matthews recorded a number of animal tales and other brief secular tales told for instruction or entertainment. Most of this body of myths is intimately related to ceremonials, and their esoteric details are known primarily to the medicine men who perform the ceremonies. But other stories, such as the highly regarded tribal origin story and the brief secular tales, are more widely known to the lay public, at least in their outlines. In the century since Matthews first brought to light this body of Navajo myth, numerous Navajo scholars, native as well as non-native, have contributed to the accumulation of an impressive native literature. In their work, Matthews remains a dominant figure whose legacy is appreciated and respected.

This chapter will briefly describe the types of Navajo folklore that Matthews collected and will show how his folklore studies developed over the approximately twenty years of his active work. It will attempt to pull together what we know of his field-work methods—the informants and assistants who worked with him and his means of translating and recording their data. Finally, it will comment on some of his own analysis and interpretation of the folklore materials that he collected.

Types of Navajo Folklore

ORIGIN MYTHS OF CEREMONIES There is a basic similarity in the narrative pattern of the chantway origin myths. They recount how a hero (or, more rarely, a heroine) becomes separated from his home and sets out on adventures, in the course of which he is overcome by misfortunes. The Holy People rescue him, protecting and restoring him with ceremonial procedures that he himself learns and then brings back to teach to his own people (Spencer 1957:18–30). Descriptions of these ritual acts of restoration occupy the major part of the account, especially if the myth is obtained from a practitioner of the rite. Matthews collected the origin stories of four major curing ceremonies. For two of these, the Mountain Chant (1887a) and the Night Chant (1902a), he described from his own observations the ceremonial procedures and presented their origin stories, songs, and prayers as recounted to him by a priest of the rite. In two other cases, the Feather Chant (1887a:160–94) and the Bead Chant (1897a: 195–208), he collected only the origin myths.[1]

SONGS AND PRAYERS Matthews devoted great attention to the ceremonial songs and prayers that originate in the mythical account and become embodied in the action of the ceremony. They carry the burden of the petition to the Holy People for cure. These songs and prayers tend to be more poetic in their expressions of feeling and thought than the story narratives that recount the hero's adventures and his instruction in ceremonial practice. Matthews published songs and prayers of the Mountain Chant and Night Chant in Navajo text with interlinear and free translations, and during his later field work he recorded many such songs using the newly available phonograph.

TRIBAL ORIGIN MYTH Matthews obtained several versions of the Navajo tribal origin story that describes the emergence from the lower worlds, the preparation of the present world for habitation, exploits of the Hero Twins and their encounters with monsters, and the creation and wanderings of people in the present world (1883b, 1890a, 1897a:89–110; Schevill Link 1960:317–25). This story forms a background for the whole body of Navajo folklore. While it is not the basis for a specific ceremony, elements from it appear in many ritual actions, and its outlines are generally known to the lay public. More recently some Navajo scholars have described the tribal origin myth as the central stalk of a plant, from which the origin myths of ceremonies branch off in a tree-like structure.[2]

BRIEF TALES In addition to these sacred traditions (but sometimes included within the priestly accounts), Matthews obtained a number of briefer tales that are told informally for education or entertainment—for example, coyote stories (1897a: 231–85) and the story of the Great Gambler (1897a:208–30; 1889c) that were told to him as parts of the tribal origin myth. Another story of Coyote's misbehavior accounts for the origin of the Utes (1885c; also see Guide: 1985:55). The moccasin game story and songs tell how the day animals and night animals gambled to determine whether light or darkness would prevail (1889b).

The Development of Matthews' Folklore Studies

From Matthews' papers (as described in the *Guide to the Microfilm Edition*, 1985), we can glean some information on the progress of his work on folklore. Powell had pressed his field investigators for the Bureau of [American] Ethnology to seek out information on religion and mythology, which he considered crucial for support of his own version of social evolutionary theory. However, Matthews was aware of how complex and sensitive such inquiry would be, and he recognized that it would take time for him to gain some linguistic facility in the Navajo language and to locate able and trusted informants.[3]

In December 1880, shortly after his arrival in New Mexico, Matthews caught his first glimpse of a Navajo ceremony, the last night of a Night Chant, and he continued to attend ceremonies whenever he could. However, he had been in Navajo country for over two years before he was able to obtain the tribal origin story. On 28 February 1883 he wrote enthusiastically to Cushing at Zuni: "Have got the Navajo Creation myth at last . . ." (Guide:81). This story was told to him by "Jake the Silversmith," who had already been instructing him in silversmithing, and it became his first publication on Navajo myths (1883b; later in 1897a:50–51, identified as "Jake's Version B"). Aside from this version of the origin myth and two brief popular tales (an early version of the coyote story that tells of the origin of the Utes, 1885c, and the animal stories of the moccasin game, 1889b), Matthews' papers during his first field-work period reveal little or no folklore data up to the time he left Wingate for Washington in the spring of 1884. The four field notebooks devoted to the Mountain Chant during this period (Guide:54) do not tell us how or when he obtained its origin story nor who was his informant.

However, in the fall of 1884, Matthews returned from his new post in Washington for a field trip to New Mexico. This trip proved to be a watershed, for it opened up new resources for his work on ceremony and myth. Matthews' papers contain drafts of two monthly reports to Powell: that for October recounts with great surprise and delight his first observation of sandpainting at a performance of the Mountain Chant (see Parezo's paper this volume), and the report for November tells with satisfaction of his final success in obtaining the services of an expert medicine man (Guide:46, Correspondence with Powell, #190, reproduced in Part Two of this volume):

> I have the honor to submit herewith a monthly report of my ethnological work during the month of November 1884. . . . The provisial [*sic*] plans for my season's work, on which I placed the greatest value were those for obtaining a full insight into the nature of these ceremonies. A medicine man, with whom I made a bargain two years ago could not now be found. On my return to Defiance I opened negotians [*sic*] with three different medicine men, offering them as liberal terms for their services as I could afford, but only to meet with the most positive refusal. I was on the point of abandoning these projects and devoting my time to obtain the myths of locality and minor legends of the people known to the laity, when I heard of an old shaman living beyond Nutria, about 70 miles distant, who it was thought would be found less scrupulous that [*sic*] the others had proved. I dispatched a messenger for him at once, and on the evening of the 15th he came. With some trouble I concluded a bargain, and he began his narration on the morning of the 16th. I have been engaged with him ever since, and do not believe I will be through with him until it is time for me to leave Defiance. No doubt I could profitably spend several months with him did circumstances permit. The information I am obtaining from him I consider of the highest value.

It may be assumed that this was Tall Chanter (Hatali Nez), who became one of Matthews' most trusted collaborators. Among Matthews' papers there is a manuscript (Guide:60, #290) of one of the origin stories of the Night Chant, "The Story of So," obtained from Tall Chanter and dated 16 November 1884. It seems that they must have set to work immediately on a myth that came to be at the heart of Matthews' interests. Matthews later states that Tall Chanter was the first medicine man to be persuaded to relate rite myths to him, and that he had perhaps "a better knowledge of the legends than any other man in the tribe" (1897a:58). Tall Chanter provided him with the most complete version of the tribal origin myth (1897a:50–51), certainly with much mythological data on the Night Chant, and perhaps also the myth of the Mountain Chant. In 1885 Matthews brought Tall Chanter to Washington, using funds furnished by Powell's

Bureau of [American] Ethnology, to spend a month checking over with him some of his field data.[4]

During the five years intervening between his two Navajo field assignments Matthews was stationed in Washington and found time to prepare much of his Navajo material for public lectures and publication. Among these publications were several on folklore: the early version of "The Origin of the Utes" (1885c); *The Mountain Chant* origin myth (1887a); "The Prayer of a Navajo Shaman" (1888a); the stories of the moccasin game (1889b); and the clan origin portion of the tribal origin myth (1890a).

On returning to New Mexico for field work in 1890, he focused his attention on the Night Chant. A second Navajo collaborator appears frequently in the field notes of this period. Laughing Singer (Natloi), like Tall Chanter, was a practitioner of the Night Chant. Overall, in the collection of Matthews' papers the Night Chant looms very large, but many of the loose field notes, notebooks, and manuscripts are not dated, and it is difficult to know where they belong in the development of his work. Fortunately, several notebooks of the Night Chant can be dated (Guide 1985:53–54). Two give hour-by-hour accounts of ceremonial performances (#589, November 1890; #632, December 1891–January 1892). An oversized notebook (#674) contains field notes dated from December 1892 through April 1894, in which Laughing Singer was the principal narrator; in it are found many songs and prayers, some with Navajo text and interlinear translation, and two chantway myths attributed to Laughing Singer—one the Night Chant story of "Cilneole" (The Whirling Logs) and the other the Feather Chant story of "Natinesthani."[5] A late notebook (#707) contains two stories of minor rites of the Night Chant (with Navajo text and interlinear translation) handwritten in ink and seems to be essentially the same as the posthumous publication by Matthews and Goddard (1907). The narrator was presumably Laughing Singer, to whom Matthews had sent Goddard when they began collaboration in 1903. Matthews must have obtained the origin story of the Bead Chant sometime between 1890 and 1894, but among his papers there is no evidence of its source, who recounted it, or the circumstances of its telling.

Matthews identifies three informants for his versions of the tribal origin story. The major version by Tall Chanter (1897a) must have been obtained in the 1880s (since portions of it were published separately in 1889c and in 1890a); it also contains interpolated brief coyote stories and the story of Changing Bear Maiden, who learned witchcraft from Coyote. An earlier version of the tribal origin story had been given by Jake the Silversmith in February 1883 (1883b, see above), and another, briefer version was told in 1893 by Old Torlino, a priest of the Hozoni ceremony (this was left unpublished [see 1897a:50–51, 53], but later published with some abridgment by Schevill Link 1960: 317–25).[6]

Matthews' papers contain undated notes (see Guide:50–51) on the moccasin game story of the gambling of night and day animals (1889b), and these seem to be early and from several different informants.[7] In addition to the coyote stories that appear in the major origin myth, Matthews recorded three versions of the story in which Coyote tricks his daughter into marriage and the offspring becomes the progenitor of the Utes.

The narrator is not specified in any of these. An early version, "The Origin of the Utes" (1885c), is in English only, but the two later, unpublished versions have Navajo text and interlinear translation.[8]

We know that Matthews' principal narrators were Tall Chanter and Laughing Singer, with Jake the Silversmith and Old Torlino contributing versions of the tribal origin myth. Although Matthews found Tall Chanter to be a most valuable informant, the only narratives attributed directly to him in unpublished and published sources are the Night Chant story already mentioned ("So, a Variant of the Visionary") and the principal version of the tribal origin story, together with its interpolated stories about Coyote and the Great Gambler (1897a:50–51, 57–58). Laughing Singer appears frequently in the 1890–94 fieldwork notes; the narratives attributed to him are in a notebook of 1894 (Guide: 54–55, #674, "Story of Cilneole" and "Natinesthani") and in a notebook (Guide:53–54, #704) and Notes (Guide:49, #335) that were published later (Matthews and Goddard 1907).[9] On the basis of data in Matthews' papers, Faris feels that he used Laughing Singer more for specific ceremonial procedures and Tall Chanter especially for "texts, songs, prayers, and assistance in translations," and that "he employed each medicine man occasionally for a couple of months at a time" (Faris 1990:49). Some notebooks show several hours of narration each day over a period of several days. The following chart shows Matthews' mythological narratives that were published or appear in his field notes, together with what identification we have been able to make of the narrator, date of narration, and source in field notes.

Recording Practices

Matthews tells us something about his procedures in collecting stories in the Introduction to his volume *Navaho Legends*. Regarding translation, he says (1897a:53–54):

> In rendering the Navaho tales into English, the author has not confined himself to a close literal translation. Such translation would often be difficult to understand. . . . He has believed it to be his duty to make a readable translation, giving the spirit of the original rather than the exact words. The tales were told in fluent Navaho, easy of comprehension, and of such literary perfection as to hold the hearer's attention. They should be translated into English of a similar character, even if words have to be added to make the sense clear. . . . Still the writer has taken pains to never exceed the metaphor or descriptive force of the original, and never to add a single thought of his own. . . .

For Matthews the circumstances of narration were quite different from sessions of native folk tales told around the fire with an audience of interested adults and children. Nevertheless, he notes that ". . . the original was often embellished with pantomime and vocal modulation which expressed more than mere words . . ." (ibid.).[10]

Regarding the Navajo texts, Matthews explains the time limits within which he worked, the pressures of his own medical duties, and the fact that his Navajo narrators could rarely "devote more than two or three hours out of twenty-four to the work of

Table 1. Matthews' Folklore Narratives

Story Title	Story Content	Date of Narration	Narrator	Source in Matthews' Papers	Matthew's Publication
Navajo Creation Myth—A Version by Biolzog	Progression upward through underworlds, separation of the sexes, emergence, twin war gods, and killing of monsters.	February 1883	Jake, the silver-smith (Version B, see 1897a:50ff.)	Guide: 49, Notes #193, pp. 18–42	1883b: 387–417
Nquoilpi, the Gambler	Pueblos bet against supernatural Great Gambler and lose; Gambler is punished by Sun for refusing him shell treasures, sent to rule over Mexicans	1880s	Tall Chanter	—	1889c; see also 1897a:82–87
Gentile System of the Navajo Indians	Story of clan origins and wanderings (abridged version of 1897a:135–59)	1880s	Tall Chanter	—	1890a: see also 1897a:135–59
The Navajo Origin Legend	Underworlds and separation of sexes; emergence; coyote stories and Great Gambler; twin war gods and killing of monsters; clan origins and wanderings	1884	Tall Chanter	—	1897a: 63–159
Another Version of the Origin Legend	(content similar to Tall Chanter's version but less complete)	Oct.–Nov. 1893	Old Torlino (Version A, see 1897a:50–51, 58–59	Guide: 55, Notebook #674, pp. 36–66	Schevill Link 1960: 317–25 (abridged)
Moccasin Game Stories	Day and night animals gamble to determine whether light or darkness will prevail	1880s	John Watchman and others	Guide: 51, Notes #5, 104 pp.; #24, 20 pp. 1889b	Ute Origin Story
Ute Origin Story	Coyote (or oldman) tricks his daughter into marriage; she abandons baby who is brought up by an owl and becomes dangerous to companions; he becomes progenitor of Utes	1880s	—	Guide: 51, Notes #5	1885c
	(two other recordings of same story)	—	—	{ Guide: 55, Notebook #588, pp. 99–131; #633, pp.0–27 }	unpublished
Other Coyote stories	Six stories in which Coyote is outwitted (contained in origin myth)	1880s	Tall Chanter	—	1897a:87–93
	Coyote and Changing Bear Maiden (a story of witchcraft contained in the origin myth)	1880s	Tall Chanter	—	1897a:93–104

Table 1. Matthews' Folklore Narratives *(continued)*

Story Title	Story Content	Date of Narration	Narrator	Source in Matthews' Papers	Matthew's Publication
Mountain Chant—Captured by Utes	Hero disobeys father's hunting instructions, is captured by Utes, then rescued by gods	1880s	Possibly Tall Chanter	—	1887a:387–417
Night Chant—"The Visionary"	Hero with visions is scorned by brothers for his vision claims, but rescued by gods	Possible 1880s	Possibly Tall Chanter	—	1902a:159–71
"Story of So"	A variant of "The Visionary"	11/16/1884	Tall Chanter	Guide:61, MS #290	1902a:192–212
"The Whirling Logs" (Cilneole)	Lonely hero seals self in hollow floating log, is protected by gods, at end of river journey learns to plant corn	4–13 Mar. 1894	Laughing Singer	Guide:53–54, notebook #674, pp. 69–99, 152–63	1902a:171–97
"The Stricken Twins"	Twin sons of supernatural father and Navajo mother are crippled in rock fall (one lame, one blind); they seek cure from gods; when finally successful they are given means to trick Pueblos and steal their valuables	—	Tall Chanter or Laughing Singer	—	1902a:212–65
Tale of White House and Story of Bekotsidi	How Dawn Boy is welcomed at White House in Canyon de Chelly, and how Bekotsidi and Sun Bearer made animals	—	Probably Laughing Singer	Guide:53–54, Notebook #707, pp. 3–87	Matthews and Goddard 1907
Feather Chant—"Natinesthani"	Hollow log trip (as in "The Whirling Logs); hero is subjected to further trials in which he outwits his witch father-in-law and gains power over game	1–10 Jan. 1894	Laughing Singer	Guide:55, Notebook #674, pp. 110–51	1897a:160–94
Bead Chant—"Great Shell of Kintyel"	Navajo beggar is tricked by Pueblo neighbors to climb to eagle's nest, where he is befriended by eagles, rescued by gods, and retaliates by stealing Pueblo treasures	1890s	—	—	1897a:195–208

ethnography. . . . For these reasons it was not practicable to record the original Indian Texts of all the stories. The author had to choose between copious texts and copious tales. He chose the latter" (ibid.). He goes on to explain that in the notes to this volume of legends he includes examples of recorded texts with interlinear translation to give the reader the opportunity to judge how closely his translations follow the original (he gives ten paragraphs of the origin legend and selected songs and prayers, 1897a: 258–79).

Matthews must have understood much of the Navajo language, but presumably he would also have needed the services of translators, at least for the narratives. We do not know who these translators were, but throughout the notes we find references to the presence of several Navajo assistants who could have served in this capacity—especially Jake "the Silversmith," Chee Dodge, and Ben Damon. The only complete narratives recorded in Navajo text with interlinear translation found among Matthews' papers are the brief coyote tale that accounts for the origin of the Utes (Notebooks #588 and #633) and two short stories of the Night Chant published with Goddard in 1907 (see notes 8 and 9). However, we are left without precise knowledge of how Matthews went about the English translation of much of his large body of Navajo stories.

The translation of songs and prayers was a different matter. Many of these Matthews did present in Navajo text with interlinear and free translations. Each of his major works—on the Mountain Chant, the Night Chant, and the volume of legends—contains separate sections of songs and prayers in Navajo with English translations. Also, a number of his articles contain prayers or songs with Navajo text and translation (1888a, 1889b, 1894b, and 1907). In 1892 the scope of his recording was greatly enlarged when he was able to acquire the mechanical recording device that had just appeared on the market. His correspondence with Cushing at this time (Guide 82) shows his eagerness to obtain this device, which would make possible a permanent record that could be checked with informants and would be available for future scholars. Matthews was among the first anthropologists to demonstrate the resulting wax cylinder recordings at scientific meetings.[11]

Matthews was sensitive to the artistic form and emotional content of these Navajo poetic expressions, and in translating the songs and prayers he made full use of his own poetic powers. Both McAllester (in this volume) and Zolbrod (1984) speak of Matthews as a pioneer in bringing Native American poetry to western audiences. Zolbrod comments that "when he recorded songs and prayers, he composed such material on the written page as verse . . . and the lyrics he transcribed stand today as some of the finest examples of Native American verse . . ." (1984:10). A number of these have been reprinted frequently in the century following their publication. What is not so well known to anthropological scholars is the large body of recorded songs (some 196 wax phonograph cylinders, now in the possession of the Archives of Traditional Music at Indiana University and of the Library of Congress), many of which Matthews did not have time to translate and analyze. McAllester describes at some length, in his essay in this volume, some of the ways in which these valuable materials may be put to use by contemporary scholars.[12]

Matthews' Analysis and Interpretation of Folklore

Matthews was, above all, a natural scientist who observed, studied, and reported. His field observations, in folklore as in other aspects of his Navajo studies, met the highest standards of accuracy and completeness of reporting. In order to use his field-work time most effectively, he had made a deliberate decision to take down his Navajo stories only in translation, but he had acquired sufficient linguistic skill to record songs and prayers in Navajo text with interlinear translation, and toward the end of his field work the introduction of mechanical reproduction represented a new step in this process. Beyond these scientific and technical abilities, Matthews also showed a sensitive appreciation of the aesthetic and poetical qualities that he found in Navajo folklore. He was himself a poet, and he applied this understanding especially in the analysis and interpretation of Navajo songs and prayers (in this regard, see the papers by MacAllester and by Zolbrod in this volume).

Although his recording of Navajo folklore stands on its own merits, Matthews went further to show something of the meaning of this folklore to the Navajos themselves and the ways in which it was related to everyday Navajo life and culture. A central theme apparent in all of his work is the intimate relation between myth and ceremony in Navajo religion. In his two great monographs of the Mountain Chant and Night Chant, the myth and the description of ceremonial performance are published together. In these myths, once the hero has been accepted by the Holy People, he is subjected to a continuing series of trials in which the curing procedures applied to restore him after mishap become the ceremony that he learns and brings home for the use of his people. The myth gives the instructions from the gods for performing the curing ceremony. Matthews fully demonstrates the important role that these narratives play in directing ceremonial practice and shows that the content of the myth has a very practical use for the medicine man in learning to conduct the ceremony. While this relationship of myth to ceremony was certainly not a new idea at the time, Matthews' data provided detailed empirical demonstration of it.[13]

In a brief paper called "Some Illustrations of the Connection between Myth and Ceremony" (1894c), Matthews spells out the nature of this connection, citing examples from the myths of three different ceremonies. Here he introduces some further ideas. He finds the connection between myth and ceremony variable: sometimes the myth may give an account of all the important acts in a ceremony; other times it may describe it in a less systematic manner. Although the myth gives an account of the acts of the ceremony, it never explains all of its symbolism.

> . . . A primitive and underlying symbolism, which probably existed previous to the establishment of the rite, remains unexplained by the myth, as though its existence were taken as a matter of course, and required no explanation. Some explanation of this foundation symbolism may be found in the creation and migration myth or in other early legends of the tribe; but something remains unexplained even by these. (1894c:246)

Matthews does not assume "that all rites have originated in myths, or at least in the myths with which we now find them connected." He speculates that some of the Navajo rites may have been derived from the ancient Pueblo inhabitants who are pictured in the stories as superior to the Navajos and likened to the gods. In any case, he thinks that some of the rites and myths may have been introduced recently from other tribes, a point that has been confirmed by later work.[14]

Matthews was also interested in another dimension of the relation of myth to everyday Navajo life—the way in which folklore can reflect the ethical and moral standards of a culture, a subject that later anthropologists continued to pursue.[15] In an article titled "The Study of Ethics among the Lower Races" (1899b), Matthews first points to the difficulty that Europeans have in examining without prejudice any ethical and moral standards different from their own. But he recognizes that, regardless of this barrier, there are difficulties in studying morality among primitive peoples where there seem to be no organized sanctions. He proposes the study of myths and tradition as "the safest way to discover the ethical notions of savages." If actions meet with the approval of the gods or are rewarded in the action of the story, they may be "regarded as virtuous" (1899b:2).

He draws examples from Navajo stories that reveal ethical standards different from our own. In one Night Chant story the gods conspire with the crippled twins to defraud the Pueblo people of their jewels so that they can pay these same gods for their cure. Similarly, in the hollow log journey of the Feather Chant, the hero's theft of valuables from his own family to pay for his cure is rewarded with success. Thus, Matthews concludes that Navajos do not frown on theft if it is from aliens or for a good purpose. The myths also show evidence of benevolence: the gods help men in trouble, take pity on them, and give good advice in adversity. On the other hand, incest in the stories meets with punishment or disgrace. Although falsehoods and prevarication occur frequently, if a direct question is repeated four times the responder must be truthful. While external sanctions seem to be minimal in Navajo culture, Matthews cites a convincing illustration of the internal sanction of conscience. With these words, his informant Old Torlino protests that he will be truthful in what he tells:

> Why should I lie to you? I am ashamed before the earth . . . [before the heavens, the dawn, the evening twilight, the blue sky, the darkness, the sun]. I am ashamed before that standing within me which speaks with me. Some of these things are always looking at me. I am never out of sight. Therefore I must tell the truth. That is why I always tell the truth. I hold my word tight to my breast. (1899b:7)

This article (despite its unfortunately worded title) shows Matthews' unusual capacity for openmindedness and acceptance of cultural differences as well as his appreciation for the sympathetic human qualities that he found in Navajo life.

Matthews must have been fully aware of the extent to which his Navajo narratives carried a broader cultural content than the ethical standards that he emphasized in this paper. These stories provide a native perspective on Navajo life and thought in general.

They give a picture of early Navajo existence as poor and humble. They begin with a hero living in rude conditions, subsisting on seeds and small animals. Hunting large game is an important undertaking in which success is prized. By contrast, their Pueblo neighbors are viewed as wealthy, living in well-built houses, able to raise corn and with plentiful food supplies. They scorn and exploit their Navajo neighbors, who on their part seek and are finally successful in appropriating Pueblo wealth and shell "valuables" by trickery and deceit. With these vivid images of Navajo-Pueblo relations, it is understandable that Matthews might speculate, as he did, that the Navajos may have had some role in Pueblo abandonment of the area (1902a:5; see also Faris 1990: 34–35).

Toward the end of his life, Matthews published a brief paper that presented some new and refreshing interpretations of his folklore data. In a brief article titled "Myths of Gestation and Parturition" (1902b), he discusses a type of myth common among American Indians, but not limited to them, in which the origin of human beings is portrayed as an emergence from an underworld to the earth's surface. Usually a body of water, or a flood, is associated with this emergence, and the people are helped to the surface by means of a reed or vine. The earth itself is personified as a woman or mother, and the sun or sky becomes the father. The Navajo tribal origin myth belongs to this type. As a physician, Matthews sees in this combination of symbols the similarity to actual human birth. In pointing out this common human basis for a mythological theme, he does not claim it as a universal theme, nor as indicating a necessary stage of social evolutionary development. In view of other more elaborate anthropological and psychological explanations, Matthews' interpretation has a disarming simplicity.

Matthews stayed aloof from the theoretical issues that influenced the folklore interests of some of his contemporaries. His folklore was entirely a fieldwork enterprise, grounded in Navajo data. He was not concerned with demonstrating evolutionary stages of mythological thought but rather with showing Navajo folklore as a native literature related to the thought and action of Navajo life.[16] When he offered interpretations of this literature, they were worthy of attention, and they have stood the test of time to remain credible and valuable today. His important accomplishment in the collection of Navajo folklore remains a testament to his scholarship and as a rich body of data still available to be mined by contemporary scholars.

Notes

1. Subsequent to Matthews' work our knowledge of the ceremonial origin myths has been greatly enlarged by the contributions of many Navajo specialists. Some of the most important contributors have been Fr. Berard Haile, Gladys A. Reichard, Leland C. Wyman, and Mary C. Wheelwright.

2. Luckert (1981:iv–xv), editor of Fr. Berard Haile's *Upward Moving and Emergence Way*, speaks of this reed or plantlike structure and presents a diagram found among Fr. Berard's notes that shows such a structure with the ceremonial origin stories branching off from the main stem. See also Spencer (1957:11) and Gill (1981:57).

3. Matthews' reluctance to undertake premature publication on mythology and religion is indicated in his correspondence with Pilling at the Bureau of [American] Ethnology. A letter to Pilling dated 3 May 1882 says: "However, if the major [Powell] must have myth and nothing else

for his next report, I will send him what I have . . ." (Guide: 77, National Anthropological Archives, Roll 10, f. 505, 566). Matthews offers instead his current work on silversmithing.

4. Matthews apparently misstates the timing of this visit as 1884 (1902a:42), but his correspondence with Powell places it a year later (Guide: 78–79; Poor 1975:36, 79).

5. The story of a hero's journey in a hollow log occurs in the Night Chant ("Cilneole," or Whirling Logs, Guide: 54, Notebook #674, pp. 69–99. 152–163) and, in a somewhat different version, in the Feather Chant ("Natinesthani," Guide: 55, Notebook #674, pp. 110–151). In both of these, Laughing Singer seems to be the narrator, as indicated by references to him throughout; see also 1897a:53, 57, 250 n. 249. However, both Faris (1990:26) and Frisbie (this volume) are uncertain whether Tall Chanter or Laughing Singer is the narrator.

6. Old Torlino's version of the origin story occurs in the large Notebook #674, pp. 36–66, with recording dates of October and November, 1893 (Guide:55).

7. Matthews' field notes for the stories and songs of the moccasin game mention the following assistants: Jake, John Watchman, Chee Dodge, Jesus, Sam, and (Old Man) Tsenagahi (see Guide: 50–51, notes #2–5, 24).

8. Toward the end of his life in 1904 Matthews was apparently working on these two versions of the "Ute Origin Story," which occur in Notebooks #588, pp. 99–131, and #633, pp. 0–27 (Guide:55). In the latter notebook Matthews comments:

> Two recitals of this text were obtained at different times from the same shaman. On comparing them many years later (1904) I find that my records are somewhat different for each. The later record is the text here written in full. The differences are given in notes on the opposite pages. . . . A very free translation of another version for which texts were not recorded was published in the *American Antiquarian*. (see 1885c)

The version from Notebook #588 is reproduced in Part Two of this volume with Navajo text and interlinear translation.

9. After the agreement in 1903 for Matthews to leave his papers to the University of California, the linguist Pliny Earle Goddard collaborated with him on the preparation of myths, songs, and prayers of a minor rite of the Night Chant. The instructions that Matthews gave in his correspondence with Goddard for obtaining the help of Smiling Chanter and Ben Damon in translating this Night Chant material supplement our knowledge of Matthews' relations with both of these collaborators. (See Guide: 45–46, Correspondence #347, 355, 357, 349 and the reproduction of this correspondence in Part Two of this volume.)

10. Although Matthews does not elaborate this idea, his brief comment does indicate his sensitivity to what modern folklorists would term the performance aspects of folklore.

11. At the International Folklore Congress organized by Fletcher S. Bassett for the 1893 Chicago World's Fair, Matthews gave a paper titled "Navajo Songs and Prayers, as recorded by the Edison Phonograph, with Sacred, Agricultural, Building, War, Gambling and Love Songs." Matthews, who was a friend of Bassett, was at this time vice-president of the Chicago Folklore Society. (See Zumwalt 1988:20–28 and McNeil 1985 for a discussion of the factional differences between Bassett's Folklore Congress and the folklore section organized by Daniel G. Brinton under the Congress of Anthropology at this 1893 World's Fair.)

12. An "Inventory of Matthews' Wax Cylinder Song Recordings" is reproduced in Part Two of this volume. See Guide: 89–90 for a detailed description of these recordings in the Archives of Traditional Music at the University of Indiana and in the Federal Cylinder Project of the Library of Congress.

13. In his analysis of Night Chant materials, Faris emphasizes this function of chant origin stories as mnemonic aids to the ceremonial practitioner for the conduct of the ceremony (1990:25ff.).

14. See, for example, Wyman's discussion of the origin of Chiricahua Windway (1962:214-16).

15. The idea of cultural reflection in myth has been implicit, if not stated, in the Native

American work of other anthropologists. Boas focused directly on it in his Northwest Coast studies (1935), as did a number of his students (Benedict 1935; Ehrlich 1937; Wittfogel and Goldfrank 1943); and my own publications on Navajo cultural reflection and values owe a great debt to Matthews' ideas and work (Spencer 1947 and 1957).

16. Matthews' approach may be compared with the work of two of the best-known early scholars of American Indian folklore. H. R. Schoolcraft (1793–1864), an Indian Agent at Sault Ste. Marie married to a halfblood Ojibwa woman, had collected a large body of Objibwa folklore some forty years earlier. He had also sought to learn Ojibwa beliefs and to view their world through their tales, but he believed that Indians were not at an evolutionary stage to attain a fully developed literature, and in his translations he made some changes that reflected his own aesthetic standards (Clement 1990: 180 ff.). Daniel G. Brinton (1837–1899) published on a wide array of topics related to linguistics and the emerging discipline of anthropology (Darnell 1974). Like Matthews, he was a physician who held no academic appointment, but he played an important role in the newly emerging learned societies (such as the American Philosophical Society and the American Association for the Advancement of Science), and he had ties with Powell's Bureau of American Ethnology. His many publications on American Indian mythology were based primarily on literary and documentary evidence rather than on intensive field work, and his interpretations were dominated by the evolutionary views of his time.

Washington Matthews Writes a Ballad: The Anthropologist as Poet and Literary Scholar

PAUL G. ZOLBROD

Buried in Washington Matthews' papers is a poem—"The Eyes of Judah"—which he had apparently written in the 1890s and then revised in 1904, a year before he died. Published posthumously in *Out West* in 1905 (vol. 22:68), a magazine that ceased to exist soon thereafter, that work can all too easily be dismissed as a fanciful departure from Matthews' professional concerns. But it deserves attention. (The 1904 revision is reproduced in Appendix A to this essay (page 116), together with earlier versions of some stanzas.) It reveals more about him and his assumptions than we might otherwise realize; it adds to his stature as a pioneer ethnographer and a frontier intellectual; and it demonstrates what an important asset poetry can be in interpreting another culture, especially for those who do not confine it to the printed page.[1]

Easier to describe than to summarize, "The Eyes of Judah" purportedly deals with Judaism and its Old Testament roots. At the same time, however, it conveys a broodingly implicit desire to speak out against the treatment of Indians—a desire that Matthews might not otherwise have expressed. It opens with a first-stanza image of "a living tide" of worshippers leaving a synagogue. As they emerge, the speaker—presumably a gentile—reads in their eyes "the story of a race." Each subsequent stanza then identifies a different expression seen in those faces, ranging from "the sordid eyes of Judah" and "the noble eyes . . ." to "cruel eyes" and "tender" ones—each implying a different aspect of prejudice.

A work of some merit, "The Eyes of Judah" shows that Matthews possessed substantial poetic gifts. He employs sharp, functional images; his allusions—sometimes erudite but never obtrusive—add meaningful depth; his clear, sonorous diction produces a distinctly lyrical quality; and, as I hope to argue, the poem has an inner dimension that results in more by far than simple or whimsical verse. I find myself wishing that he had written more poetry, not least of all because a careful reading of "The Eyes of Judah" prompts further speculation about how effectively literary knowledge and ethnography can complement each other.[2]

Matthews obviously commanded such knowledge—an impression strengthened by statements he makes elsewhere, as well as in his translations of Navajo stories, songs, and prayers. In his introduction to *Navajo Legends*, for example, he writes that the tribe's ceremonials "might vie in allegory, symbolism, and intricacy of ritual with the ceremonies of any people, ancient or modern"; and he goes on to say that their "lengthy myths and traditions" contained "a pantheon as well stocked with gods and heroes as that of the ancient Greeks" (1897a:23). It would have been reckless for Matthews to have made such an assertion unless he knew classical literature. And he demonstrates his broad familiarity with Old World poets and literary traditions when he writes that the Navajo warrior twins resemble "Castor and Pollux and the Asvinau of India . . . or even Romulus and Remus." Such literary pronouncements lie scattered throughout his published and unpublished works.[3] In various places he mentions classical Greek and Roman poetic traditions (1886f:847; 1897a:23); he cites Shakespeare (1902a:269); and he invokes Norse and Germanic epic material (1886f:847). Obviously, he knew mainstream literature well and relied on it to guide him through the Navajo chants and stories whose intrinsic worth he also came to appreciate. He could also apply that knowledge to the work of his own colleagues and contemporaries. It is on display, for example, in a review he published (Matthews 1893e) in an early issue of *American Anthropologist* of *The Song of the Ancient People*, a poem about the Anglo-European intrusion into the Southwest written by Edna Dean Proctor. While brief, that piece exhibits not only Matthews' receptivity to poetry about American Indians, but also a well-developed literary taste and a critic's eye for distinctive poetic features both good and bad.

His literary sophistication clearly shows in "The Eyes of Judah," and it assumes an unusual dimension. Consider, for example, his technique of employing the ballad stanza, a form with deep folk origins.[4] In England ballads emerge from the songs and stories of farmers and yeomen who dwelled far from royalty, even though many specimens related courtly events. Or where ballads originated with nobility, they did so in courts such as those of early Scotland, where oral tradition was slow to disappear. In utilizing the ballad form, Matthews also tapped a genre recovered by authors like Wordsworth and Coleridge, who composed in print but who wanted their poetry to be associated with an unlettered peasant class. And he drew from a source which in nineteenth-century America was adopted by the Protestant church for its hymns; by loggers, sailors, miners, and cowboys for their popular expression at work or at leisure; and by poets like Longfellow, Whittier, and Emily Dickinson in their effort to forge a democratic, egalitarian American identity distinct from Europe. Ballads were ubiquitous during Matthews' lifetime; they were as likely to have been sung as to have been in print. Which helps to explain why, as a literary critic, he recognized poetry in what he heard as well as in what he read.

For the most part, ballads bear common properties—a heavy repetitious beat, usually iambic; a pervasive rhyme scheme; stanzas of fixed length; diction and syntax alike fairly simple; and usually a straightforward story to tell, often ending grimly or tragically. Also, a good ballad may display small variations both metrically and syntactically within a broader uniform pattern, producing an intricacy more readily felt than observed. When examined closely, though, those irregularities somehow correspond with the action, and the experienced reader or listener soon learns to appreciate such skillful use of language in so seemingly simple a poem.[5] "The Eyes of Judah" is a case in point. With the exception of the initial stanza, for instance, which does not mention eyes until the next to last line, each stanza opens with a play on the poem's title: "The sordid eyes of Judah . . ." "The warlike eyes of Judah . . ." "The noble eyes of Judah . . ." and so forth. The first verse is the lone exception. Meanwhile, in stanza 2, which introduces the recursive pattern, the word "eyes" is reiterated in the second line, as if to make up for omission in stanza 1.

Such finely chiselled variation also occurs in the poem's structure. The ballad stanza normally consists of four lines alternating between lengths of four feet and three (a foot being a unit of at least two syllables, one of which is accented, in some combination repeated to provide rhythm). Or it is possible to speak of a single seven-foot line. Exceptions may occur, but never conspicuously or to extremes. Instead of alternating, for example, all lines in a given ballad might be three feet long or else they might all contain four. Sometimes a stanza might consist of two quatrains, with the second four lines mirroring the first, as they do in "The Eyes of Judah." Lines generally rhyme alternately rather than successively, and the rhyming is as markedly fixed as the metrical pattern seems to be. But ballads display less formal rigidity by far than certain other kinds of verse, say like sonnets, allowing for interesting variations that produce distinctive if subtle effects. To recognize them, however, requires a quantifying scrutiny more readily associated with science than literary criticism.[6]

In "The Eyes of Judah," for example, the number of feet each line contains varies. The poem overall consists of nine octets, which are in effect twin quatrains or four-line stanzas, a form common enough both in traditional ballads like "Barbara Allen" and "Edward," or in authored ballads like those that Emily Dickinson wrote. Line length shifts subtly in this poem, though, so that while each at first seems identical in its number of syllables, the stanzas do not uniformly match in feet per line, except that the second stanza duplicates the next to last in having three feet in all but the next to last line, which contains four; and the third matches the third from last in having three feet per line in all but the third of those eight lines, which likewise has four. Thus, the second and third stanzas from the top match the second and third from the last metrically and in line length, injecting a narrow element of symmetry in a broader field of incremental irregularities, somewhat the way a Navajo sandpainting does in its graphic effects, as I will explain later.

A critic who wanted to could determine what this fairly small technical feature adds to the poem conceptually. I am tempted to do that myself, but my point just now is merely this. In patterning his ballad so finely, Matthews the careful observer is at work creating poetry of his own. What calls for attention is the way he has apparently noticed small details common to lyric—a poetic form once as likely to be sung in actual performance as audiences now presume to encounter it in print. Furthermore, he here displays control over his language commensurate with his ability to master "the semantic categories of [the Hidatsa] language and the patterns of Hidatsa thought" that Halpern refers to (this volume, quoting from Wedel 1969:176); with his success in learning the complex Navajo verb system; with his appreciation of the artistic intricacy of Navajo weaving and silverwork; and with his broad mastery of the verbal, musical, and material intricacy of Navajo chantway procedure. In other words, a poet's power and a literary critic's perceptiveness overlap considerably with the skill of the ethnographer. More specifically, in the array of its minute components, this poem shows how Matthews could apply careful observation to produce sophisticated results throughout his career as an early anthropologist. It also heightens an appreciation for his capacity to *hear* poetry, where critics and writers as well as ordinary readers conventionally look for it only on the printed page (see Zolbrod 1984).

Successful ethnography calls for an awareness of aesthetic components whatever the medium. It can gain especially from a greater understanding of the way language is applied within a given culture in that special kind of verbal transaction we call poetry. It makes no difference whether that language is employed to amuse and entertain, to assure ceremonial success, to transmit important information, or to secure sacred expression. Poetic discourse matters as much as material culture does—even though its medium of the human voice, whether in speech or in song, is ultimately ephemeral and non-material, save when it is recorded graphically by way of glyphs, codices, wampum, or the like; or save when it is stored via printed texts the way Europeans had learned to preserve it by the time they began to arrive in the New World.[7] Their reliance on print as a means of storing poetry, in fact, had become secured by the time they established colonies in the Americas; they all too easily assumed that without a recognizable print technology Native Americans produced no poetry, preserved no historical records, maintained no viable sacred traditions, and were hence uncivilized by the Anglo-European way of determining levels of civilization.

This poem demonstrates how Matthews managed to overcome the limits of that point of view and could draw from sources beyond the printed page as well as from resources on it. It is arguable whether ethnographic field work requires a thorough understanding of poetics to be successful today. Yet for Matthews poetic awareness and effective field work went hand in hand because he knew literature well and could listen as carefully as he could read and could observe. In a number of ways, the literary skill manifest in "The Eyes of Judah" reflects what he learned first about the Hidatsas and then about the Navajos. The poem matches his achievement in transmitting Navajo chants, stories, and prayers in written English, for example. His ear for the lyrical properties of English parallels his recognition that Navajo has lyrical properties, too.[8] His English version of the prayer from the fourth day of the Night Chant—one of the earliest efforts to register poetic qualities in Native American verbal discourse, and still one of the most successful—sets a high standard of translation to this day, not only because of its technical quality, but because it subsumes an understanding of the culture producing it.[9] It has been anthologized in the most enduring collections of Native

American poetry[10]; it won the recognition of critics as well as anthropologists in the early twentieth century (see, e.g., Walton and Waterman 1925); it has been quoted in popular works like *The Family of Man* photographic exhibit assembled during the fifties (Steichen 1955:60); and it has been recognized by mainstream literary scholars whose interest extends beyond ethnography (see, e.g., Welsh 1978:162–71). It is exemplary because in it ethnography and poetic skill merge fully and gain broad visibility well beyond the academic realm.

"Tse'gihi," it begins, invoking the Navajo name for Canyon de Chelly, the dwelling place of the supernaturals. Then it proceeds (Matthews 1902a:97; 1907:54; or Astrov 1946:85):

2. Hayoolkáál beehoghán	House made of the dawn.
3. Nahotsoí beehooghán	House made of evening light.
4. K'osaiilhil beehooghán	House made of dark cloud.
5. Níltsábika beehogán	House made of male rain. . . .

Picking up the pattern of variation within repetition so patently Navajo and yet so keenly analogous to the repetitious structure found in ballads, Matthews recreates this poem in an English idiom that looks simple, in the same way that a ballad is deceptive in its apparent simplicity, or that the treatment of a patient by a medicine man seems crude or simplistic to an outsider. Passages of incremental repetition, like lines two through five above, contrast strikingly with corresponding passages, like ten through fourteen below, which contain little or no repetition:

10. K'osdilhil dáádinílá	Dark cloud is at the door.
11. K'ósdilhil bits'a dzétiin	The trail out of it is dark cloud.
12. Atsiniltl'ísh yík'i dah siziní	The zigzag lightning stands high up on it.
13. Hashch'é baka	Male deity!
14. Na'na'ílyá	Your offering I make.

Meanwhile, the contrast between passages of rigid syntax, like two through five, and those of freer, less repetitive phrasing, like ten through fourteen, stands in subtle counterpoise against passages wherein the increments of variation consist only of a single syllable or occasionally two, as when a passage that sounds like this:

16. Shikee' sháánidíílííl	Restore my feet for me.
17. Shijáád sháánidíílííl	Restore my legs for me.
18. Shats'íís sháánidíílííl	Restore my body for me.
19. Shíni' sháánidíílííl	Restore my mind for me.
20. Shiinéé sháánidíílííl	Restore my voice for me.

alternates with one containing variants of several syllables, which sounds like this:

29. Doo shaah tééhgó naasháadoo	No longer sore, may I walk.
30. Doo shee hodíílníigo naasháadoo	Impervious to pain, may I walk.

31. Chanah nishlíingo naasháadoo	With lively feelings may I walk.
32. Da'al'kidáági át'éego naasháadoo	As it used to be long ago may I walk.

As do similarly translated passages which Matthews includes in his monumental volume *The Night Chant,* these lines recreate the impression of the carefully reiterated gestures and activities that go into producing a ceremony. On a slightly more abstract plane, the verbal phenomenon at work here is not all that different from what occurs in ballads, where sharp contrast such as that between rhyming consonants is played off against more subtle kinds of contrast where strikingly ritualized action is being described. In a Navajo chant such as this one, syllabic length may vary more among lines or among clusters of lines. Meter works far differently, as it must with a language as different from Germanic English as Athabascan Navajo is. Furthermore, syllabic repetition occurs within lines and does so far more abundantly in a Navajo verse such as this one, whereas it occurs exclusively at the end of a line in a ballad, corresponding with a terminal sound two lines away. Hence, what we call rhyme gives way to incremental repetition, creating the semblance of stark differentiation. It goes virtually without saying that Navajo poetry differs so drastically that the term verse itself might well not apply. Yet subtle patterns of variation and repetition are similarly employed in the poetry of both languages.

One analogy which comes to mind in either case is how a single note may vary by as little as half a tone when it concludes the final bar in a repeated or closely parallel line of a score by Bach or Mozart, in contrast with the concluding bar one or two lines later that repeats the same note in two halves and then in four quarters. A more appropriate analogy may be found in Navajo sandpaintings, where smaller details vary minutely while larger ones are more symmetrically arrayed. Take plate 6 in Wyman (1983:94), "Talking God and Calling God with Sunflower People," for example, where the two deities flank the four sunflower people to the north and south. Identical to one another in things like height, shape, and headdress, the former wears a white robe with no markings and holds a white fox, while the latter appears in black marked with an array of four stars holding a black staff. Meanwhile, the four sunflower people are even more closely identical, wearing precisely the same earrings and headdresses and similarly possessing two branches on the north side and three facing the south. Yet each stands on a pedestal of a different color, which becomes all the less obvious because that particular set of details is so small in so manifestly symmetrical a design.

Matthews apparently recognized comparable features in English ballads and Navajo poetry alike, just as he recognized comparable features of patient artistry in Navajo weaving and silverwork, and as he learned to identify complex patterns of all kinds intrinsic to Navajo ceremonies. Such awareness is effectively displayed in the language of his own ballad, as well as in the poems he translated from Navajo. It is as much a tribute to his ear that he could discern those varying particles of sound in the Navajo prayers and songs as it is to his eye in discerning commensurate patterns of variation in other kinds of Navajo art, whether sandpaintings, weavings, or silverwork. Beyond that, as a pioneer ethnographer, he sets an important example in demonstrating such artistic astuteness, especially in the realm of poetics.

His achievement becomes all the more remarkable when we consider that he produced translations like this from Native American chants. For most whites, Indians were, as Hobbes had said, a race with "no place for industry . . . no culture of the earth . . . no arts; no letters; no society . . ." (1983:186); or as Locke had as dismissively declared, a people "who never yet heard of a syllogism" (*Essay*, IV, xvii, 4, 1975:389). And, of course, with the complaint that among the tribes there were "no letters" or no syllogisms, the fundamental assumption was that without print technology and with no tradition of literacy, Native Americans could not reason or produce poetry, and in fact had little or nothing to contribute to what was already being considered high culture. Jonathan Letherman, who preceeded Matthews into Navajo country by a quarter century, wrote that those people had no known religion, no tradition, and "no knowledge of their origin or of the history of the tribe." Their singing, he continued, was nothing more than "a succession of grunts . . . anything but agreeable" (Letherman 1856:297).

Obviously, Letherman's attitude belongs to an established tradition, beginning with the earliest European entry into the North America. At least as far back as the eighteenth century children were formally schooled on such assumptions. Textbooks attributed to Indians such traits as "stupidity and insensibility; want of knowledge and reflection" (Morse 1784:107), or described them as "akin to all that is rude, savage and unreclaimable. . . ." (see Edwards 1832:166–170).[11]

Fundamental to such an attitude, therefore, is the bias of the literate against the illiterate, which perpetuates the notion that without print there can be no literature: nothing equivalent to Homer, no Chaucer, no Shakespeare, no Bible, and hence no religion and no culture, in the European manner of determining what that was. One interesting postulate (among many) growing out of this assumption is that words not written down do not exist.[12] Summarizing Samuel Johnson's criteria for making entries in his dictionary, Kernan explains, "A word was real enough to be included in his dictionary only if it appeared in print" (1990:155). Analogously, we assume that a poetic work is not legitimately a poem unless it exists in written form. All the more reason, then, to deny that poetry ever existed among Native Americans. Oral tradition did not yet count, or it was reduced to folklore or legend or even myth in that hackneyed sense of its being some kind of rudimentary falsehood—all less worthy than literature as it is still conventionally defined, however tacitly.

The attitude of the print-oriented European towards the so-called illiterate native is so salient and so deeply pervasive that it becomes difficult to pinpoint, just as it would now be awkward to document in any precise way how television has reshaped consciousness today. I wish we were more sharply aware of that outlook and had a better grasp of its implications. It accrues almost insidiously beginning soon after Gutenberg's invention of the printing press and gains status as a confident assertion by Samuel Johnson, who did as much as any individual to shape the middle-class outlook on literacy and illiteracy. Books, he wrote in *Rambler* 52, take on a permanence which makes the poetry they contain "objective," as Kernan suggests (1987:8) and virtually a part of our own material culture. In the hands of ordinary people those texts permitted "the vulgar" to "rise above their humble sphere." On the other hand, Johnson wrote, without print "the mass of every people must be barbarous" (*Rambler* 52, quoted in Kernan 1987:19). Accordingly, the people that Europeans encountered in the New World were "barbarous" in their nonliteracy and their lack of poetry because it was nowhere manifest in print, or at least in the kind of print that Europe knew and could understand.[13]

Hence, Europeans brought with them certain underpinnings of what Alvin Kernan calls "Gutenberg society." The skill of literacy is a central premise among participants in that society: "To be acknowledged as able to read is an initiation rite, as it were, into the human condition. . . . It is from writing and reading that Gutenberg people not only get information but find out who and where they are" (Kernan 1990:131–32). It follows, then, that nonliterate people remain uninitiated into the human condition and do not fully know "who and where they are." Therein resides the unarticulated license to enslave them, to slaughter them, to usurp their land, or appropriate their resources the way rational humans feel entitled to consume the flesh of unreasoning beasts.

People like Henry Rowe Schoolcraft who had made an effort to harvest literary material from Indian tribes belonged to a very small minority during the earlier 1900s merely because he attributed to the Indians a certain poetry-making power. Even then, he relied on Algonquin narratives more to examine the savage mind, so-called, than to explore the way Indians applied language poetically (see Clements 1990; Pearce 1965: 120–28). After all, they did not read and write. I do not believe that he worked as carefully to appreciate the poetic texture of what he heard Ojibways or Chippewas recite as Matthews has done with Navajo verbal artifacts. Therefore, he was unable to overcome entirely the print bias which prevented Europeans from seeing the relevance of poetry to culture in tribal America—which adds an unappreciated dimension to the latter's significance as a pioneer in the emerging field of anthropology.

While Matthews could recognize poetry, not just in print but in what he heard, his literary awareness was not confined to formalistic details like meter and versification, either, or to incremental repetition and sound differentiation. As I have already suggested, an intellectual depth accompanied his technical sophistication, which helped to make him both a better critic and a more alert anthropologist, just as it made "The Eyes of Judah" a richer, fuller poem—to focus attention on it again. For example, he applies his thorough Biblical knowledge uniquely to express a sympathetic understanding. From stanza to stanza, the poem reverberates with facts and details as pertinent to Navajos or Hidatsas and other tribes as to Scriptures.

Hence, the harsh treatment of Native Americans by whites virtually assumes a Biblical dimension. The "living tide" passing through the "portals of the synagogue" in stanza 1 provides a framework for the "Long Walk" of the Navajos to and from Fort Sumner following their defeat in 1864, as does the image of Judah's "sordid eyes . . . cast down." And Judah's "execrated name" in stanza 2 evokes the overall disregard for Indians among whites which was to intensify as hostility increased between them on the Western frontier. Likewise, "the martial eyes of Judah" which "seldom shine today" could easily be a response to the demise of tribe after tribe, especially if Matthews first composed the poem in the early 1890s, not long after the Wounded Knee massacre. Meanwhile, the reference to David's victory in stanza 4 over Goliath could very well parallel the defeat of Yé'iitsoh, the Big Giant, by the Warrior Twins in the Navajo emergence story, which contradicts the notion that Indians had no traditions, and which makes all the more poignant the images of downcast eyes or eyes no longer shining. And, on a personal level, in the way he mentions Jacob and Laban he invokes the constant intrigue that inevitably went on between Indians and whites. And the reference to Esther in stanza 7 could be an oblique allusion to his own interracial relationship with the Indian woman whose child he allegedly fathered (Poor 1975:13; Link 1960:318).

Apparently, Matthews sometimes referred to Indians in the hackneyed way, as when he calls them "savage[s] vanishing on the disappearing frontier of an advancing civilization" (Gruber 1970:1299). However, the term *savage* did not always necessarily bear the negative force then we associate with it today. To him the threatened demise of these aboriginal people was more poignant than their being savages, whatever that may have connoted. He produced an earlier poem on that topic, "The Pagan Martyrs" (also reproduced in Appendix A to this essay see Baxter 1882), which reveals a prolonged concern over the fate of Native cultures. That work boldly contrasts the perverted mistreatment of tribes by the Spaniards with the Bible's alleged idealism. In it he writes of "the terrors/ Wrought in the honor of the peaceful Christ," and admires the Zunis for persisting against Spanish assaults to sing again "the old-time gods . . . no more in trembling, but with voice uproarious." But he concludes by doubting that his own contemporaries could really grasp the depth of earlier Zuni suffering or appreciate the intricacy of their own culture.

"The Pagan Martyrs" concludes with a recognition uncanny for its time. In the next to last stanza it acknowledges the pity its Anglo readers would no doubt express for Zunis and the contempt they would feel toward the Spanish oppressors. But the final stanza poses the question of sincerity. "Oh, Christian sage! Oh, maiden tender-hearted," it asks, "Whose eyes are streaming in the silent room," over that "sad page" of history which tells of Zuni martyrdom; "Have ye but scornful glances for the plaint/Of him who sings the pagan martyr's glory,/ Who sings the sorrows of the savage saint?" In other words, Matthews wonders out loud whether those who profess sympathy for tribes like the Zuni would listen seriously to someone able to understand their culture, raising a likelihood that prevails today: fawning, overstated sympathy for a subdued race merely disguises a covert unwillingness to examine a mythic past that leaves no written record. How many people today speaking in behalf of Indians would trouble to harvest a narrative like the Navajo Plumeway, which tells of a banished hero's clash with his father-in-law (see Matthews, 1897a:163–94); would then compare it, say, with the ambiguous story of Jacob's exile to the household of his deceiving uncle and father-in-law Laban; and would do so without declaring that the culture which produced the one account was necessarily superior to that which produced the other? It is easier to feel sorry for Navajos or Sioux than it is to apply the rigors of objective biblical scholarship to their sacred stories.[14]

Such perceptiveness aside, however, "The Pagan Martyrs" is written with considerably less poetic skill than "The Eyes of Judah." Composed in the fall of 1882, perhaps in haste, to celebrate his friend Frank Cushing's returning to Zuni from the East with a new bride (Green 1990:240 and note 11), it lacks the economy and the subtlety of the latter poem, and its language seems more stilted and self-consciously composed. It suffers, too, because its sense of outrage overshadows the irony promised in the title and identified in its conclusion. Where the latter poem rests firmly on a deep foundation of long-standing knowledge and understanding of Navajo culture, "The Pagan Martyrs" bears the shrill self-righteousness that might easily accompany an initial revelation that injustice has occurred. Matthews squanders his emotional fervor on explicit assertions in "The Pagan Martyrs," whereas in "The Eyes of Judah" he understates the links between Navajo culture and Biblical tradition by implying them, unpresumptuously transmitting indignation to the reader instead of brandishing it self-indulgently. Between them, the two poems mark a difference between the newcomer to the craft of versemaking and a skilled, seasoned poet. The usefulness of the first and lesser poem is that it demonstrates an early concern which finally gains effective expression in the later, superior one.

Because "The Pagan Martyrs" displays less poetic skill than "The Eyes of Judah" does, however, it gives us a raw glimpse of a subjective outlook which Matthews the seasoned objective investigator would never reveal outright in his more strictly ethnographic writings, and which he merely implies in the latter poem. For the most part, he and his fellow researchers strove to assemble data on Indians in the name of disinterested truth rather than for the sake of a deeper, more personal sympathy that might accompany broad understanding. Nonscientists, meanwhile, either belittled Indians by way of unabashed prejudice, or trivialized their cultures with the kind of "streaming" tears invoked in Matthews' first poem. On neither side, though, was poetic implication effectively used to reconcile objective discovery with liberal conviction. It was inconceivable that through poetic expression the Bible might be coordinated with observation to argue in behalf of Indians both subjectively and objectively. In that regard, Matthews may have broken new ground as a poet-ethnographer. He employed poetic implication in "The Eyes of Judah" to confirm his personal convictions by applying the Bible as literature rather than as religious doctrine in something of a juggling act where two levels of reality are invoked, one explicitly and one implicitly. It takes literary sophistication to do that.

Hence Matthews' overall literary knowledge adds in yet another way to the poem's depth what his meter and diction add to its texture. With unusual poetic acumen he manages to overlay strong poetic sympathy upon what he observed in the field without compromising his objectivity as an ethnographer, superimposing the intangible and the verifiable through the use of an old literary device—allegory. In asserting as he does in *Navaho Legends* (p. 27) that Navajo stories might match the works of any race for their allegorical quality, he did not speak casually; he evidently had a feel for allegory. "The Eyes of Judah" does indeed function on separate levels the way traditional allegory does. Literally, the poem speaks of antisemitism traceable to its Old Testament roots. But while Indians are never mentioned in the poem, they are really its subject, and its thrust is toward a revelation that they as much as the Jews have been martyred to a civilization which misunderstood them. In that regard, the poem might well have something profound to say worth considering a century after Matthews wrote and revised it.

Used loosely when used at all nowadays, the term allegory is no longer understood as it formerly was. So it is all too easy to overlook what Matthews implies when he links Navajo stories with allegory, or what he likewise implies when he creates allegory of his own by speaking implicitly of the Navajos while refering explicitly to the Bible. Today allegory is generally defined in terms of "symbolic functional figures and actions of truths or generalizations" *(Webster's Third International Dictionary)*. The *Columbia Encyclopedia* likewise treats it principally as a symbolic story. As a more strictly applied literary term, it is described in a characteristic textbook anthology as "an extended metaphorical narrative in which a figure stands for a specific quality" (Abrams 1986: 2559). In the fuller, more technical language of contemporary criticism and literary scholarship, it is seen as a set of techniques employed by the critic on the one hand and the poet on the other, but it is still represented largely as an extended application of symbolism (see, e.g., Preminger 1974:12–15). Reviving the concept in discussing ways of writing about culture, anthropologists today tend to use allegory still more broadly. James Clifford, for example, cites the definition from *Webster's New Twentieth Century Dictionary*—another standard desk dictionary—and adds that allegory "usually denotes a practice in which a narrative fiction continuously refers to another pattern of ideas or events. It is a representation that reinterprets itself" (1984:99–100).

Nearly a century ago, however, allegory was defined in the *Century Dictionary and Cyclopedia*—once a standard lexicon—more traditionally and more strictly as "figurative treatment of a subject not expressly mentioned, under the guise of another having analogous properties or circumstances; usually a sentence, discourse, or narrative ostensibly relating to material things or circumstances, but intended as an exposition of others of a more *spiritual or recondite* nature bearing some perceptible analogy or figurative resemblance to the former" (the italics are mine). The two ways of defining the term bear contrasting denotations. The more recent one associates allegory with symbolism, while the older one does not. Furthermore, the newer one speaks somewhat more simplistically of "truths or generalizations," as one dictionary definition puts it, or of the presence of "an abstract plane of similarity," as Clifford says (1984:101), while the older one specifies more restrictively that allegory entails an analogy between something figurative or palpable on the one hand and something more spiritual or recondite on the other.[15]

The older understanding of allegory that binds the real and the sacred analogously—as opposed to the recent tendency to think of allegory as a series of symbolic links—seems to have receded as the twentieth century progressed. That makes it more difficult now to appreciate what Matthews was doing in composing his poem, or what he fully meant when he associated Navajo ceremonies and their concommitant stories with allegory in *Navaho Legends*. Navajo "ceremonials might vie in allegory, symbolism, and intricacy of ritual" with those of "any people, ancient or modern," he said

(1897a:23), acknowledging that symbolism exists in such material, but as something *separate* from allegory, not part of it. Nowhere in what he has written, however, does he convey the impression that the narratives he harvested from Navajo culture functioned only as ideas or generalizations. He seems instead to have accepted them on their own terms as figurative expressions of something legitimately sacred to the culture which produced them, just as he implies in "The Eyes of Judah" that Navajo religion is analogous to Judaeo-Christian tradition in its sacred dimensions rather than an inferior religion not worthy of recognition.

As an elaborately religious literary mechanism, allegory dates at least as far back as Dante, who used it to describe *The Divine Comedy* to his patron Can Grande della Scala. There he specifies that it includes not just two but four levels of meaning working all at once: the literal, which merely tells a story; the allegorical, which places the narrative on a more recondite or abstract level; the moral, which establishes the ethical link between the literal and the allegorical; and the anagogical, which transmits a culminating spiritual revelation shared in an almost mystical union of reader or audience and story (Dante, in Latham 1892:193; see also Latham's footnote, p. 194). Not easily summarized or explained, the anagogical quality becomes the hardest to grasp, especially for secular twentieth-century readers who do not embrace the orthodox belief system growing out of the Bible with the fullness it once demanded of Medieval and Renaissance audiences.

In attempting to explain the anagogical property in allegory, Dante aligns it with "the departure of the sanctified soul from the slavery of this corruption to the liberty of everlasting glory . . ." (in Latham 1892:193). Elsewhere, he explains it by equating the literal description in *Exodus* with the transcendently analogous liberation of the baptized soul from bodily captivity at death. Thus occurs a kind of quantum leap, from a tangible story on one level about the Biblical escape from slavery, to a mystical understanding on another about resurrection and the "escape" of the Christian soul from this finite earthly life to an infinite heavenly existence.[16]

As the deeply religious poetic method Dante described and employed, allegory survived primarily through Edmund Spenser's *The Faerie Queene* and later through Bunyan's *Pilgrim's Progress*. Together those three works serve as the primary examples of Christian allegory in Western tradition. There is no direct evidence that Matthews knew any of them, but someone with his apparent literary background would have to have at least been familiar with the first two; and virtually everyone who grew up in nineteenth-century America certainly would have read Bunyan, which was standard fare for every schoolchild throughout the 1800s and well into this century.[17]

I do not necessarily suggest that Matthews applied the allegorical principle in writing "The Eyes of Judah" as strictly as Dante described it in his letter to Can Grande, or as he employed it in *The Divine Comedy*. But I would argue that he at least apprehends a relationship between something literal and something more deeply spiritual in the Navajo poetry he gathered and put into print. To him, the stories he heard were not what Chippewa tales were to someone like Schoolcraft: stories "characterized by habits of sloth," which testified to an inferior polytheism whose principal god was "more a monstrosity than a deity" (1839:31–35). Rather, the Navajo stories described gods who had a "poetic side"; who "like [Navajo men] stand much on a level of equality" with one another; and who were "kind—like Indians, to their kindred; usually cruel, yet often merciful and magnanimous, to their foes" (Matthews 1897a:33). In recognizing as much, Matthews equates so-called savages whose grunts meant nothing to people like Letherman with Israel's oldest tribe. Their history is as intricate; their origins and spiritual moorings as deeply based; their traditions likewise as sacred. They are capable of artistic creativity equal to that of a Homer or a Shakespeare. They are also capable of Dantesque spirituality in their poetry. And they are no more savage than the Biblical Jews were.

All of which adds significance to what Matthews achieved. Having studied cultures like the Hidatsa and the Navajo, he recognized therein the same depth and human complexity that the Bible's best narratives project, and saw in allegedly pagan societies spiritual conditions which were the same in essence if different in kind. When matched with the final stanza of "The Eyes of Judah," that perception adds special power to the poem's last line: "Oh Father mine forgive them./ They know not what they do." Thus he aligns Jesus' final words on the cross with an outcry which he himself very well might have wanted to make following what he called "the woeful butchery of Wounded Knee Creek" in a review he wrote of James Mooney's *Ghost-Dance Religion* (Matthews 1897c:248–49). That is an emphatic assertion, even for someone as reliant on plain-spoken understatement as Matthews was. Not given to expressing emotion in his clear, detailed, dispassionate prose, Matthews nonetheless puts it on display in this assertion he makes about the Wounded Knee massacre: "When we have finished this chapter, we cannot but feel that the many centuries of Aryan civilization have laid but a thin varnish of respectability over a white-skinned savage, as wild as any savage on earth" (1897c:249). Those responsible for that massacre failed themselves to recognize that "the Ghost-dance religion" was as common "among the Aryan and Semitic races" as it was to "our Indians," and that it "is founded on a universal idea as old as humanity,—regret at decay in men and nation; a yearning for old-time friends and conditions."

While more direct, the language Matthews uses here in his book review is starkly consonant with the ideas he expresses in "The Eyes of Judah," and with what he achieves in the poem beneath the veneer of its diction. It is "varnished" by the polished features of an old-style ballad with formal roots in a European oral tradition easy to dismiss because it does not originate in the alphabetically recorded Old World past. It also cites an explicit Biblical story acceptable to Western readers. But at the same time it employs the more implicit techniques of classical allegory to invoke the sacred dimensions of less acceptable Navajo thought. Thus, it bears the deep truth that the Indians are as capable as any people of a sacred vision commensurate with that of the Bible. Furthermore, in its capacity to establish relationships which ordinary empirical observation by itself does not allow, the statement represents the language of the poet every bit as much as it functions as the language of the ethnographer in its capacity to establish what can be observed with dispassionate objectivity. For if it identifies something that can ultimately be verified, it also conveys a passionate moral truth not easily quantified—a truth which Scripture itself can be seen to yield when we accept it as poetry rather than as doctrine. Matthews apparently was able to do that, whether working with our own sacred texts or those of the Navajos. For that reason, I consider him the complete field observer, saying something that still needs to be heard a century after he first expressed it.

Appendix A to Zolbrod Essay

The Eyes of Judah

by Washington Matthews

1904 Revision	Earlier Version
1. The portals of the synagogue Before me open wide And slowly through them from within There pours a living tide. I stand beside the steps and gaze Upon each passing face, And in the eyes of Judah read The story of a race.	
2. The sordid eyes of Judah The eyes to earth cast down While all unseen above them An angel holds a crown. The eyes of Judah, fallen From sainthood and from fame, To gain with his poor silver dole An execrated (?) name.	The warlike eyes of Judah That rarely shine today Anon the night where Gideon bade Three hundred trumpets play The eyes of David where he smote Goliath with a stone Of Joshua when he stopped the — — — In fateful Ajalon (?)
3. The noble eyes of Judah Of men whose great name throng The pages of our history, Whose deed inspire our song. O field of Judah, fruitful Throughout the vanished years O Statesmen, bards and martyrs, In rages and in seers!	The patient eyes of Judah That for two thousand years Have lifted to Jehovah Their glances dimmed with tears In ghetto and in Judenstrass In fetters and in fame Have watched for a messiah For such as never came.

4.
The martial eyes of Judah
That seldom shine today
As on the night when Gideon bade
Three hundred trumpets play,
The eyes of David when he smote
Goliath with a stone,
Of Joshua when he stopped the moon
In fateful Ajalon (?)

5.
The patient eyes of Judah!
Through many hundred years
They've lifted to Jehovah
Their glances dimmed with tears,
In ghetto and in Judenstrass,
In dungeon and in flame.
They've watched for a messiah,
For such as never came.

6.
The crafty eyes of Judah
With searching glance and wise
O, Leah the forsaken!
Had Laban not such eyes?
Was such the glance of Jacob
When, speaking filial words,
He practiced cunning arts and robbed
The father of his herds?

7.
The love-lit eyes of Judah
That conquered hearts of stone,
That was Ahasuerus' love
And guided Persia's throne.
Today, O glorious Esther!
The lights of Purim shine
In memory of the conquest
Of those brave eyes of thine Of those bright eyes of thine.

8.
The cruel eyes of Judah,
That saw the thorny crown
Upon his bleeding temples Upon his bleeding forehead
By heavy hands pressed down,

And shone where scornful laughter
   With mocking shouts did blend:
"If thou art truly son of God,
   Now from the cross descend."

With mocking voices blend

9.
The tender eyes of Judah,
   Such eyes as lit the face
Of dying Jesus when he prayed
   For mercy on his race
His palate parched with thirst
   His brow damp with the mortal dew—
"O, Father mine! forgive them,
   They know not what they do."

For many of his race
His palate parched with thirst, his brow
   Damp with the mortal dew

The Pagan Martyrs

by Washington Matthews

I.
Down from the shady pines of Zuñi Mountains,
   By lower hills where stunted cedars grow,
Across the sunny vale where Nutria's fountains
   Make green the fields that toiling Indians sow,
And on, o'er sage-grown waste, through gloomy cañyons,
   Past ruined towns that fell when Rome was young,
I travelled all the day with my companions
   Till length'ning shadows o'er our path were flung.

II.
At length arose to view the lofty mesa
   Whereon the ruins of Old Zuñi stand;
Along its beetling front you still may trace a
   Pathway to the summit of the table land;
With reeling head and trembling limbs you'll scale it,
   And gasping at the top you'll ask in dread,
If once the Spanish soldier dared assail it
   'Mid deadly missiles rained upon his head.

III.
"Is this some vast dun rock of lava lifting
   Its rugged mass above the withered plain,
Unchanged where restless sands are ever drifting
   And restless winds assault its front in vain,

Or is it some enormous ant-hill builded
   By giant insects of the mythic days
The Indians tell of, that we now see gilded
   By the last touches of the sunset rays?"

IV.
"'T is the strange home where dwells the race of Zuñi,
   As we approach it, mark its walls that rise
In terraced heights; its bristling ladders soon ye
   Will see revealed against the evening skies."
Our guide thus answered. Daylight waned. We entered
   And soon were mingled with the dusky throng
That toward a low and mystic chamber centered
   To hear the pagan priests intone their song.

V.
Yes, solemn priests who pray in tongue archaic
   The laymen know not: learned priests who hold
A law as ancient as the code Mosaic,
   A cult, as that of Baal of Indra, old,
Here in these days when timid adoration
   To one far God, with silent doubt contends
And spoken unbelief—in this wise nation—
   The pagan priest his blazing altar tends.

VI.
And oh! Have none, with valiant Paul's devotion,
   The joyful Tidings hither dared to bring,
In all these ages since, across the ocean,
   Came the first vessels of the Spanish king?
Aye, long ere Plymouth's forests heard the singing
   Of Pilgrim voices lifted to the Lord,
The Spaniard sought the "Seven Cities" bringing
   The Cross; but bringing, too, alas! the Sword.

VII.
Then came the sorrowful and weary ages.
   Though History hold his Vandal deed a crime,
'T is well, perhaps, the Gringo burned the pages
   That bore the annals of that fearful time.
Though still so many records of the errors
   Of Spanish rule remain, they've not sufficed
To tell an hundredth part of all the terrors
   Wrought in the honor of the peaceful Christ.

VIII.
Scourged to the portals of the gloomy mission,
   Whose slanting walls now crumble for decay,
Came these reluctant children of Perdition,
   With sullen hearts to kneel but not to pray;
For what, to them, the Deity supernal,
   Who loved, they heard, their cruel masters well—
Shared with such monsters for a life eternal,
   His promised Paradise were worse than Hell.

IX.
So, not for images with pallid faces
   Would Zuñi's sons their swarthy gods despite
Nor take the proffered bargain which replaces,
   With feast of saint, a day of pagan rite—
(Such saint as they of Acomà believe in;
   For there the Indian sings his song of praise,
Where the fair statue of the Royal Stephen
   Supplants the war god of the ancient days).

X.
Though well they knew the doom of death was meted
   To him who in idolatry was found,
They oft, in stealth, to deserts far retreated,
   Or met in nature's temples underground;
And there they taught their children tales of wonder
   And all the secrets of the priestly line;
On high Toyálani, the Mount of Thunder,
   They laid the gifts at Ahayùta's shrine.

XI.
But Faith, long-suffering, is at last victorious;
   And praise, to-day, the old time gods they sing,
No more in trembling, but with voice uproarious,
   Safe 'neath the shelter of the Eagle's wing.
Bright are the fires in the *estufas* lowly,
   Quenched are the tapers in the Christian fane,
Where now the stranger spoils the altar holy,
   No longer guarded by the arms of Spain.

XII.
"Thou stiff-neck'd generation, self-deceiving.
   May Heav'n enlighten thee!"—my reader prays.
"Punish their obstinacy, unbelieving"—
   Thus ran the orders of viceregal days.

Ah, had the persecutor been the heathen
   And he who died for faith the Christian been,
In lauding orders of that time had we then,
   Some other word than "obstinacy" seen!

XIII.
Oh, Christian sage! Oh, maiden tender-hearted,
   Whose eyes are streaming in the silent room,
O'er the sad page that tells of saints departed—
   Oh Alban's fate—Lorenzo's fiery doom!
Have ye but words of doubting for the story,
   Have ye but scornful glances for the plaint
Of him who sings the pagan martyr's glory,
   Who sings the sorrows of the savage saint?

Notes

1. At the outset, let me clarify what I mean when I use the term poetry, which has become all too mercurial. Simply stated, I define poetry as that art form whose primary medium is language, whether spoken, sung, or written, and whether performed before a live audience or stored on tape or on the screen. In other words, poetry is not limited to what is written down and stored by way of print technology. The term literature can be used to designate that. Novels and the scripts of plays, then, along with essays become a subcategory of poetry. Without much circumspection, we tend to use the word poetry to designate what I would identify as verse: poetry more clearly lyrical (i.e., possessing the more artificial properties employed by the singing voice, such as meter or rhythm, rhyme, etc.), and limit it to verse which is arranged carefully on the printed page, so that its lines do not extend from margin to margin both down and across as they do with prose, which is a printed format generally reserved for what I would specify as colloquial poetry (i.e., possessing the more natural properties of the conversatonal voice). See Zolbrod (1984) for a more elaborate discussion.

2. It seems that Matthews wrote a handful of poems that can be recovered. Those published in *Out West* (some posthumously) were "Sturnella's Song" (1903b), "The Eyes of Judah" (1905a), "The Contrast" (1905b), "Three Short Words" (1906). "The Pagan Martyrs" was included in an article by Sylvester Baxter ("The Tenacity of Indian Customs," *American Architect and Building News*, 21 October 1882). Cushing's journal for 20 October 1882 (Green 1990:240 and note 11) tells that Cushing sent the manuscript of this poem to Baxter. Matthews had composed it to celebrate Cushing's return from the East with his new bride. Among Matthews' papers there are six copies of the *Portland (Me.) Transcript* for 6 December 1899, containing a poem on America as the hope of Europe, signed W. M. Gamble, which may be a pseudonym for Matthews (Guide:64). While "The Eyes of Judah" is clearly the best, all five show enough merit to suggest that had Matthews wanted to he could have become an accomplished poet. The interfacing of poetry and ethnography is now receiving attention, although I would like to see the definition of that tired old term updated. See Clifford and Marcus (1984).

3. See Zolbrod (1984:398, 399) for a fuller set of references. For additional statements, see Poor, p. 34, note 8, where he refers to Matthews 1886f.

4. Material on the ballad is abundant, and a newcomer to the term must be selective in consulting sources. In my judgment, older, more comprehensive studies are as useful as recent ones, if not more so. That depends, however, on the biases of the reader and his or her purposes in

consulting material. I still like Ker (reprinted 1957), not necessarily because I subscribe to his values, but because he remains a rich source of information about how ballads overlap with classical epic and early romance. For a good thumbnail sketch of the ballad as a literary concept, complete with a basic working bibliography, see the entry in Preminger. Any reputable edition of Child will yield interesting and valuable information, to say nothing of the realization that reading ballads and studying them becomes a rewarding treat. Two basic sources useful to me as I renewed my acquaintence with the ballad genre while writing this essay were Leach (1955) and Leach and Coffin (1961). For one good thumbnail sketch of the ballad in a broad cultural context, see Toelken (1986).

5. In the Old Scottish popular ballad "Edward," for example, the last line of nearly every stanza contains an extra syllable, but not in corresponding feet. The poem consists of a dialogue between the protagonist Edward, who has killed his father, and his mother, who begins the poem by asking him why his sword is bloody. That slight element of metrical inconsistency is highlighted in the last line of the final stanza when Edward reveals that he committed the murder at his mother's suggestion. Meanwhile, the ballad "Barbara Allen" twice contains the line, "O slowly, slowly rase [rose] she up." It is used the first time to indicate that Barbara made her slow way up the hill where her lover Sir John Graeme lay dying; and it is repeated to describe how she rises slowly from his side once he is dead. In this case, then, meaning varies while words match, perhaps adding slightly to the irony that in all likelihood it was she herself who had ordered him slain.

6. Emily Dickinson's poems, abundant in their application of traditional ballad structure and brilliant in the way they are varied, provide a wealth of examples. To cite one almost at random, Number 520 ("I Started Early—Took My Dog—") opens on a stanza beginning with a four-foot line followed by three successive lines of three feet. The five subsequent stanzas then adhere to the more standard pattern of four-three, four-three, although the rhyme scheme breaks down in the last two stanzas. It is generally a mistake to assume that such "irregularities" exist only because Dickinson could not avoid them.

7. The difference between what I call alphabetical poetry—poetry composed and/or stored in print—and oral or performed poetry remains to be investigated more than it has so far been. Kernan (1987), however, makes several observations that could help point the way. Following the adoption of movable type throughout Europe, he points out that "Print . . . made literature objectively real for the first time, and therefore subjectively conceivable as a universal fact." Using the term literature to designate written poetry, he goes on to say that it "reveals the culture-making activity more overtly" than oral poetry could, at least to Europeans accustomed to using written records to validate a culture's institutions. "Inescapable conditions of the kind of socially constructed realities that make up culture, conditions that are more successfully hidden in such monumental cultural 'realities' as, say, language, or the state, are more obvious in letters than they are elsewhere," he continues (p. 5).

8. Notice this statement by Matthews, for example: "Such is a Navajo song myth. It remains one of certain plays which have recently come into vogue, in which the plot, if a plot can be found, serves no higher purpose than to hold together a few songs and dances" (1894a:194). Disarmingly unassuming, this is a remarkably astute literary observation. With no established critical vocabulary, Matthews here differentiates not only between the language employed in "a few songs and dances" and a more prosaic language more common to conversational speech than to song; but he also registers an ability to discern that in order to work effectively, the highly stylized language of song sequences sometimes requires verbal interludes made up of more ordinary speech. What he does here is akin to recognizing that, say, the lyrics in a musical review require expository of some kind to hold the songs together.

9. One possible rival to Matthews for the first to attempt to recognize Native American poetic discourse in North America is Henry Rowe Schoolcraft (1793–1864), who gathered and

translated material from the Chippewas and other Upper Great Lakes tribes and whose reputation has undergone some curious ups and downs (see Clements 1990). Another possibility is Daniel Brinton (1837–1899), who assembled material from all regions and made an effort to do so somewhat more objectively. An updated survey of translations of Native American poetry is badly needed, as is a detailed historical study of poetic encounters between Europeans and Indians. All that is available for now is Day (1951).

10. Matthews' English translation of this prayer was first published under his name in 1907:54–58. It has subsequently appeared in Astrov (1946:185–86), Bierhorst (1974:307–308; see also 325–30), Cronyn (1918:93–97), Levitas, Vivelo and Vivelo (1974:102–105), and elsewhere. In addition to many of the selections included in anthologies like Cronyn and Astrov, see Day (1961), which is a veritible catalog of clumsy translations but a bold attempt nonetheless for its time to produce a survey of Native American poetic material in something of a cultural setting. In spite of its now quaintly archaic style and patronizing touch, Barnes (1921) produced an early examination of Native American poetics still worth consulting. For discussions which define new approaches to translating from traditional Native American sources, see Hymes (1981), Tedlock (1982), and Sherzer and Woodbury (1987).

11. For a comprehensive yet compact survey of white attitudes towards Indians reflected in standard textbooks and readers from 1785 to 1900, see Elson 1964:71–87.

12. Characteristic of postmodern attitudes, which are as apt to generate unbalanced bias against Western traditions as print technology itself stimulated distorted biases against nonliterate peoples, Jacques Derrida (1976:124) summarizes this presumption in a clever epigram that becomes a wry joke: ". . . writing, the letter, the sensible inscription, has always been considered by the Western tradition as the body and matter external to the spirit, to breath, to speech, and to the logos. And the problem of soul and body is no doubt derived from the problem of writing from which it seems—conversely—to borrow its metaphors."

13. See Brotherston (1979), for a comprehensively assembled argument that the North American tribes were successful in producing, maintaining, and circulating records graphically, if nonalphabetically.

14. The Biblical allusion to Jacob, Leah, and Laban's stolen herds in stanza 6 of "The Eyes of Judah" has always fascinated me, because the story of Jacob parallels in certain ways the Plumeway story of the exiled Natinesthani, who manages to win a bride and then trick her father out of cornseeds, which he can then bring back to his people to win redemption. Matthews' reference to Jacob is very brief, but taken in the context the poem fully provides, it invites consideration as a cogent parallel to the Plumeway narrative which Matthews translated and included in Navaho Legends (160–94). Given his apparent intimate familiarity with the Bible and his thorough knowledge of a story after translating it, I have no trouble presuming that such a consideration occurred to Matthews himself.

15. Coleridge, whom Clifford quotes (1984:101), produced a definition that could for its time almost be called courageously secular, calling allegory "the employment of one set of agents and images with actions and accompaniments correspondent . . . to convey . . . either moral qualities or conceptions of the mind" or other transcendent sensations. Bold in its efforts to avoid a more strictly limiting Christian conception of allegory, this definition still surpasses twentieth-century attempts in remaining focused spiritually because it insists on a kind of transcendence no longer as appealing to us as it was a century and a half or so ago. That transcendence can be inferred from Coleridge's definition through his use of the term "moral," whose denotation differed from the way the word is used now, and from his appeal to organic theory, evident when he says that the likeness between the two levels of meaning "combine" in their parts "to form a consistent whole" (1936:30, cited in Clifford: 1984:101). Such transcendence does not seem to matter in Clifford's characteristically late-twentieth-century understanding, which sees the allegorical property working to produce—at least in such feminist ethnography as Mar-

jorie Shostack's—"conditions of meaningless" (1984:99), "a crucial moment of feminist politics and epistemology: consciousness raising and the sharing of experiences by women," or the recognition "of a common estate" with someone from another culture (107). Such insights might represent the transcendent overcoming of self to identify with another, but remain far from the kind of sacramental transcendence common to traditional allegory, where inspired insight apprehends a movement from the material world to a fully spiritual one.

16. Such a movement from the more palpable to the less so is more easily grasped by a standard dictionary definition of the term *anagogy*, such as the entry in *The American Heritage Dictionary*, where it is defined as "a mythical interpretation of the word, passage or text: specifically, scriptural exegesis that detects allusions to heaven or the afterlife." Dante's comments on allegory are actually scattered and incomplete. The fact remains, though, that his statements on the subject are the appropriate starting point for someone wishing to understand the concept fully. See Singleton (1986, especially p. 11), for example. His translation of Dante's statements in the *Convivio* is more revealing than Latham's and yields a clearer sense of what Dante understood allegory to be.

17. See, for example, Earle (1904:255): "*Pilgrim's Progress* was the first *light reading* [italics mine] of Benjamin Franklin"; and "Abraham Lincoln—learning little but the primer at school, read slowly and absorbed into his brain, his heart, and his everyday speech The Bible, *Pilgrim's Progress*, Aesop's *Fables* and Plutarch's *Lives*. . . ." Or see Heininger (1984:6), where we learn that "*Pilgrim's Progress* [circa 1850] was one of the few early [board] games manufactured for children."

Afterword

GLORIA EMERSON

I was invited to write an afterword to this collection of papers, all dedicated to Washington Matthews, the early Navajo scholar who produced the first trustworthy ethnographic records of Navajo culture. Over a hundred years ago, Washington Matthews began his work among the Navajo people, and his publications and papers hold a treasure trove of tribal knowledge of the late 1800s. With the help of our own Navajo intellectual giants, the ceremonial practitioners Tall Chanter, Laughing Singer, and others, Matthews set forth a body of daunting knowledge that still dazzles the mind.

In this year of 1994, this knowledge is being lost in many families throughout Navajo country, due to heavy external influences bearing upon us via white America's alien forms of education, Christianization and, most recently, television. After Matthews' initial work, we Navajos have not always liked what has been written about us, but we can appreciate the high standards of some Navajo scholars, those who have attained high levels of maturity, sophistication, and sensitivity in working with tribal societies. Such sensitivity has sometimes been lacking in western scholarship—we can list a number of scholars who have exploited us to get their dissertations published, who worked with inaccurate information, and so on. In spite of my own general distrust of "Eurocentric" scholarship, I have over the years, come to value the writings of several unsung hero-scholars, who have set for themselves high standards of research and writing and who continue quietly to add to Navajo scholarship. Several of them have become personal acquaintances and friends (Katherine Spencer Halpern, Susan Brown McGreevy, Oswald Werner, and Paul G. Zolbrod).

A group of these distinguished scholars decided in the late 1980s to join together in publishing this memorial volume on Matthews' original Navajo work. These contributors have examined various aspects of Matthews' legacy through the lens of their own disciplines and interests. These essays represent the fields of visual arts, religion and ceremonialism, folklore, literature, poetics, musicology, and ethics. In each case the author has revisited Matthews' late-nineteenth-century writings in the light of contemporary issues—to see whether his work has stood the test of time in meeting today's ethical and research criteria, whether his contributions are still outstanding, and whether they are still useful for the Navajos today.

I began by reviewing Katherine Spencer Halpern's biographical sketch of Matthews' life. In it she searches for the influences that drove this frontier intellectual. Matthews did not come directly to Navajo country but began his researches while stationed with the Mandans and Hidatsas of the upper Missouri region at about the same time that we Navajos were losing our war with the United States in the 1860s. (It would be interesting to learn what the Hidatsas have thought of his work, researched in the 1860s and 1870s, on their language.) In the Southwest Matthews was well respected by the other pioneers of Indian cultural studies—Cushing at Zuni, Stephen at Hopi, Bourke with the Apaches and western Pueblos, and Bandelier, the first southwestern historian. I was intrigued that Matthews had suffered symptoms of stroke, following the dire predictions of the medicinemen who had worked with him and who had forewarned this dedicated scholar that "too much medicine knowledge was not good for him." But the white doctor did not take heed. In her conclusions Halpern notes that Matthews enforced high standards for thorough and exact ethnographic observation and description and that he was unusual for his time in his understanding of and respect for the native viewpoint. She notes also his use of such common terms of the time as *savage* and *pagan*—and it could be expected that I flinched each time I read this choice of terms.

Susan Brown McGreevy discusses Matthews' studies of "industrial arts" (silversmithing and weaving) and examines his subsequent work with ceremonial objects. She is particularly impressed with "Matthews' respect and appreciation for the intellectual integrity of indigenous belief systems and the calibre of native artistic accomplishments. . . ." She comments on the "wealth of detailed information about silversmithing technology" in the post-Bosque Redondo period and considers the importance of his 1884 monograph on Navajo weaving, especially his observations on the use of plant dyes. She also notes the importance of Matthews' documentation of the development of the "two-faced" weave. McGreevy underscores how Matthews' awareness of the symbolic attributes of ceremonial objects enhances our knowledge of early Navajo aesthetics, and because of her own research on Navajo arts, she understands the historical significance of Matthews' work in this field.

Charlotte J. Frisbie credits Matthews with at least nine contributions to the study of Navajo ceremonies, based primarily on Mountainway and Nightway. Frisbie also enumerates ten major concepts that Matthews contributed to illustrate the complex body of Navajo mythology (which I prefer to call Navajo oral tradition). Although he left a prodigious number of accounts, there are referencing problems. His decision not to preserve the actual texts in both languages, due to the pressures of time, has created problems for contemporary scholars, as in the effort to cross-check information and to render meaningful translations of his recordings.

From David McAllester comes the delightful bit of news that Matthews fully refutes claims made by Letherman, an army doctor stationed at Fort Defiance, in a publication of 1856, that Navajos had "no knowledge of their origin or of the history of the tribe. . . . Their singing is but a succession of grunts and is anything but agreeable." To the contrary, Matthews wrote, " . . . they have knowledge of thousands of significant songs—or poems, as they might be called—which have been composed with care and handed down, for centuries. . . ." Among Matthews' many gifts to ethnomusicology are his collection of 196 wax cylinder recordings, his collaboration with the music scholar John C. Fillmore, and his recognition that "vocables" were more than Letherman's meaningless "grunts." McAllester points out problems and possibilities for future scholars in working through Matthews' monumental legacy: the problem of correcting texts in Navajo to present standardized orthography and the preservation of a wide variety of recording media (wax cylinders, aluminum discs, etc.). He notes the enormous amount of work left for future scholars to analyze the hundreds of pages; "One can imagine the additional funding and scholarly labor required for 1200 more pages!" Furthermore, these "early recordings could give the research a time depth of from fifty to one hundred years . . . a perspective rarely available in ethnomusicology or any musicology. Building on Matthews' work, much could be learned about change and stability in this oral tradition." McAllester, thus, credits Matthews with laying a solid foundation of Navajo musicology for current and future scholars to savor, as well as for Navajo singers and the Navajo people themselves.

From one of Matthews' field notebooks, Nancy J. Parezo presents in rich detail his "discovery" of drypaintings; this occurred in October of 1884, during a Mountainway ceremony at Nihotlizi some twenty-five miles north of Fort Wingate. (The medicineman was named Manuelito, and I asked myself: Who is this medicineman? That was also the name of a prominent medicineman, a maternal relative of our family from the same area, about whom I had heard many stories.) Parezo notes Matthews' excitement at this discovery in a letter to Frank Cushing: "' . . . The rascals who have neither ornamented robes, skins or pottery, or craven idols, have nevertheless a complete system of pictographic mythic symbolism. . . . Have you ever heard of such an art? . . . I have seen things I never dreamt of.'" That excitement still titillates both the Navajo people and the countless scholars who have diligently recorded and assessed the great body of drypaintings from Navajo ceremonies. Parezo reviews Matthews' work as preserver of the drypainting tradition and its impact on the subsequent studies of such scholars as Berard Haile, Faris, Frisbie, W. W. Hill, Clyde Kluckhohn, and many more, who continue to work in this century using Matthews' own research techniques and methodologies.

James Faris reviews the ethical standards that Washington Matthews used and finds that Matthews did establish and in general met and surpassed these ethical expectations. He says that it would have been useful if Matthews had noted the dates, the medicineman narrators, place, cost, and outcome in his recordings. Instead he tended to give "composite" accounts; "We are not told, however, what situational determinants surround each practice. . . ." In spite of these omissions, Faris maintains: "Matthews' rigor and care is everywhere evident, and his precise attention to Navajo logics is dramatic in the face of less careful accounts of the time." Finally, Faris notes one intriguing concept; that is Matthews' suggestion that the Navajos "may well have been in the Southwest when the great Anasazi sites were still occupied" and that Navajos may have been instructed by these Anasazis (or vice versa).

Halpern's second paper reviews the body of Navajo folklore that Matthews collected, the stories and traditions that lie behind the ceremonies. She includes a much appreciated description of Matthews' principal narrators: Tall Chanter and Laughing Singer. Behind Matthews' mental genius loom these two mysterious shadows. Not a lot is known about Tall Chanter and Laughing Singer; they were not fully personalized or characterized by Matthews (except in brief descriptions in the introduction to his volume on Navajo legends, 1897a:58–59). To my mind, they should be credited for ably guiding the edification of Matthews. Tall Chanter checked and corrected Matthews' field notes. It was only the protocol of the day that did not require Matthews to cite them as his editors! Tall Chanter and Laughing Singer may have played a major role in changing Matthews' Victorian attitudes. I can only surmise that they helped to diminish Matthews' own ethnocentricism, which seems to lessen as his understanding of Navajo culture matured. Lamentably, such is often the case of the invisible "cultural informants" behind the scenes. They lack "personas," and I think that, in itself, speaks to our bitter truths—"We are all alike to many non-Indians" and are useful mainly as "cultural informants." All the scholars who contributed to this compendium of papers seem to understand this dilemma.

In the final paper of this volume, Paul Zolbrod examines Matthews' own capabilities as a poet. In an analysis of one of Matthews' poems, he demonstrates Matthews' poetic and aesthetic sensibilities. He argues that because Matthews had a high appreciation of European classical literature, he was able to appreciate fully the power of Navajo ceremonial poetry. Matthews' appreciation for our tribal poetics far exceeded the banal treatment of Indians by the intellectuals of the late 1800s. Perhaps, until Zolbrod himself published a version of the Navajo creation story in his book *Diné Bahané*, no other white scholar has been as successful in illuminating, from a critical literary perspective, the genius imbedded within Navajo chants.

In conclusion, I would like to add that many years ago, it became clear that in order for me to understand my tribal history, I had to read what others had recorded, analyzed, and interpreted about Navajos. Some of us do not yet know how to draw on primary source material to conduct our own research, so as to develop our own body of studies. And we are finding that our most important primary sources of information, the elders in our own families are passing on and causing some of us to rely even more heavily upon historical and ethnographic accounts as our main sources of information.

Navajo educator Grace A. McNeley observes, and rightfully so, that modern Navajos are looking to the Matthews studies "as secondary sources of knowledge to supplement that of their fathers and grandfathers" (McNeley 1994:xiv, in her Foreword to a reprint of Matthews *Navajo Legends*). I would add, however, that many modern Navajos do not have the wisdom of grandparents as primary sources anymore, and that is a grave source of concern to many Navajo cultural educators. Therefore, this analysis of early Navajo ethnography is critical, appropriate and timely, and I am honored to have had the opportunity to review these papers.

PART TWO

Selections from the Papers of Washington Matthews

Part Two is comprised of two sections: "Unpublished Papers" and "Papers Published in Hard-To-Find Journals." In the first section, reproduced passages from the unpublished papers have been chosen not only for their intrinsic value to the history of Navajo studies, but also because of their relevance to the essays presented in this volume. Selections include excerpts from Matthews' field notes and correspondence with colleagues. The second section contains a selection of Matthews' early articles that were published in obscure or defunct journals and so are no longer readily accessible, as well as manuscript materials that never reached publication in formal scientific media. Collectively, these selections present important developments in Matthews' research and anthropological thinking.

UNPUBLISHED PAPERS

1. *List of Navajo Healing Dances*

(Guide: 49, 50, Notes #69 and #175, Roll 1, f. 832–38 and f. 1021)

A set of field notes made during Matthews' research of the early 1880s and 1890 lists seventeen (actually sixteen) ceremonies with identifications of their respective curing functions. These notes also contain a fragment of the myth concerning the "return of two skulls." See Frisbie note 12 for an informative discussion of this material.

~~no~~ Names of the great Navajo Healing Dances all of nearly equal in importance

1, Kledji qaçal, includ
~~2~~ Nauçi'gji " (rope bridge)
~~3~~ tke'nidji " (in a cave)
çal tlaïdji " (under water)
ço'içona " (across the water)
tciltsa " (~~drill team~~)

good for blind & deaf

all of which are a little different. it was the myths and songs of the last one that I got, which is the best of all the Kledji songs.

tcin lca = to the tree or not further than the tree for when the dance was in the Cañon the dancers danced up to a certain tree that grew there but danced no further

List of Navajo Healing Dances

Good for one who has been injured by a bear

2 Dzilkídjí {or 4 different dances
include
a – Dzilkĭdjí – baadjí,
b. " bakadjí this is the one Doc got,
c – ayajitcí
d – atsa-in qol djaʼdjí

3 qojóní – good for a man who has killed a snake or toad & becomes sick therefrom
4 Ntʼé. including
Tcĭlaqádjí – This is the kind they catch eagles with

good for a man who robs eagles nest or swallows an eagles feather and gets a sore in consequence

5 ātsóʼse {feather dance, good for a man that steps on a deer horn + becomes crippled
6 Niltcĭʼtcí, – wind dance –
7 qanilónéhe (no meaning
8 naqóʼe bakádjí, (
" baadjí
9 soíí water
10 intóʼí heat
11 pĕcí Iron, arrow head
12 Dzilkíj naqoí,

13 Holatci, ant
14 ɬeci bakadji
15 tcici binilitcidji, {wind of the southern apaches}
16 Dilnihi qaçal, (paralysis
17 Maidji qaçal (wolf)

6

if you get sick from sleeping on a windy hillside or from being thrown down by a strong wind or from burning twisted wood,

7

Good if you see a ghost, or sleep in a haunted House, This medicine originated from two man lovers who were killed. their friends lost them and two mens worked charms to see if they could hear anything of them, one night when trying their medicine they heard a distant whistle, four times repeated, nearer + nearer at last right near them, at last two skulls appeared in the fire-light. The men prayed to all their gods, the skulls came to life & give them an account of this medicine

8.

Good for broken bones, — the word signifies something about shooting

9

if you get sick from falling in the water or sleeping in an old arroyo

10

Is obsolete, all the doctors that knew it are dead and none of the rising generation have learned. It was practiced when he was a young man. Good for people who have been injured by lightning.

11

an immense song & story. ~~[illegible]~~ this is qobesoho qoŝĕjqw = fearful, none of its songs must be sung in fun; Behagkeg = we are afraid of it.

Good for wounds and injuries
falling against a rock, broken
bones &c

~~12~~,

12

~~Dzo~~ mountain shooting. Good for
witchcraft. if a rock is shot into
you &c,

13

If you spit or pees on the ant it
makes you sore, and this dance
is good for that,

14

bece bakáidgi, male pece
Good for injuries.

15

Good for wind injuries

16

Good for facial paralysis — mouth
twisted

17

Good if you get sick from drinking
from the same pond or sleeping in the
same ~~[illegible]~~ with a coyote

All these songs have a series of pictures; but as there ~~white m~~ are no public exhibits of most of them the Whites know nothing of them,

(175)

atsó ee-gagab. = Deer Dance. (Feather Dance)
Nil tci' dje gagab = wind Dance
Sö'i - gagab = Water Dance
nagö'i baká dje gagab = lightning Dance, male
Nagö'i baad dje " = " female
Chee only thinks it is lightning.
gojóni gagab = snake dance.
Tsói gagal (bead) Eagle Dance.
-Ilól gagal Hail dance, nearly died out.

chon = ugly (tcon)
So in tcon i = ugly. tcon is an abbreviation and such is the name of our "crow" boy.
(is the So-injoni- in another form)
~~Tcon~~

Obtained from Chee. Tuesday, June 3rd 1890

2. *Correspondence with Powell and Cushing Concerning the Discovery of Drypaintings,*

October and November 1884

(Guide:46, Correspondence #190 and Guide:81)

Matthews' enthusiasm over his discovery of Navajo sandpaintings is vividly articulated in his October report to Powell and his letter to Cushing. (The October and November reports to Powell occur as handwritten drafts among Matthews' papers; the letter to Cushing is in the Hodge-Cushing Collection in the Southwest Museum, reproduced in the microfilm of Matthews' papers.) Since Matthews was the first outsider to view this complex and rich iconography in the performance of a mountain chant, his observations mark a turning point in the study of Navajo culture. The last paragraph of the November report also contains the first reference to Tall Chanter.

DRAFT OF REPORT TO POWELL, OCTOBER 1884, TRANSCRIBED FROM HAND-WRITTEN MANUSCRIPT (GUIDE:46, CORRESPONDENCE #190)

In accordance with your letter of instructions bearing date of September 27th I have the honor to make the following report of the progress of my work during the month.

I left Washington on the 1st of October and arrived at Fort Wingate on the 15th. I was delayed at Kansas City and Albuquerque, in getting my railroad passes at these points. At Lamy Junction I left the direct line of travel and went to Santa Fe to obtain orders for Government transportation from the Commanding Officer of the District of New Mexico and to get the services of a soldier, who was skilled in photography. In the former purpose I succeede [*sic*], in the latter I failed. But I have since succeeded in obtaining a man at Fort Wingate, who claims to be acquainted with the dry plate process and has already taken a dozen negatives, how successfully I can not say, they will be forwarded tomorrow to Washington for development.

At Grants, N.M. I again left the Railroad and took wagon transportation to the town of San Mateo 25 miles to the north, with a view to learning something of the Indians of that section—perhaps the most eastern subtribe of the Navajo Nation—and to observe something of the topography of the sacred mountain of Tsotsil [Mt. Taylor]. Although I learned much that was of value to me on this expedition, it was on the whole, not as fruitful in results as I hoped it would be. I had heard of a famous Indian guide named "Buero [Abuelo?] Patolero" at San Mateo, a man eighty years of age, of great intelligence and well versed in all the tribal lore, whose services I had hoped to obtain. He is permanently employed on the ranch of Don Roman Baca, and I was assured I would not fail to find him there. But for once he had taken a leave and had gone to the Chusca, seventy miles distant to attend a great Navajo ceremony and would not return for a week. I had not time to remain. I ascended San Mateo with a younger and less intelligent guide and then came on to Wingate.

Arrived here and had determined to proceed at once to Fort Defiance, but I felt after my San Mateo experience that it would be well to enquire in advance if my special guide and interpreter were there. I sent a telegram to Manuelito Station, which was forwarded to Defiance and I learned that my interpreter and the Agent were both gone and would not return for a week or ten days.

At this juncture I heard that a great Navajo festival was to take place at a place called Nihotlizi—about 25 miles north of Fort Wingate and thither I proceeded on the day following receipt of this information. I took with me an Indian guide and general assistant and the soldier photographer. We built a brush shelter in the Navajo Camp and lived here, constantly until the close of the ceremonies on the 29th. During the period, of about 11 days, I obtained most valuable and original information that I have yet collected in the Navajo country. By the judicious use of money, and by good management, I succeeded in getting free access to the medicine-lodge with permission to note and paint ad libitum, except on one or two brief occasions when I was obliged to put up brush and pencil, but easily carried my observations in memory for record outside of the lodge.

As the Navajo have neither the ornamented robes, painted lodges, decorated pottery, carven images on rock inscriptions of other tribes, it is generally supposed that they have no pictorial mythic symbols, and such was my impression until I made this excursion. But at Nihotlizi I saw large and beautiful sketches in five different colors, drawn on the sanded floor of the medicine lodge to represent different cosmogonic and religious conceptions. The labor of drawing these designs occupied several hours and a dozen operators, all working under the exacting eye of the chief shaman, who allowed not a line of the unalterable hieratic figures to be done awry. There were four different designs, each made on a different day, and each covering the great part of the floor of the medicine lodge.

I had obtained accurate water color paintings of the sacred pictures and accurate descriptions of the process of forming them (and this is a material and significant part). Soon after each picture was finished it was with interesting significant and consistent ceremonies, erased, and the very sand on which it was drawn removed from the lodge.

In Col. Dodge's last book "Our Wild Indians" (I believe is the title) there is a passing reference (p. 15) to a similar art (not apparently in colors, however) practiced in the medicine lodges of some of the Indians of the Plains,—elsewhere I have seen no mention of an art akin to this. Have you met with anything of the kind in your experience, or description of such an art in the course of your reading? If you have not I think of writing a brief description of the mere technicalities of the work, for some scientific periodical in order to elicit comment and later to embody all in a monograph on the whole ceremonial for the publications of your office. The entire ceremony is one of great interest and deserving of an extensive description.

I returned from Nihotlizi on the afternoon of the 29th. Yesterday and today I have been busy in attending to a large accumulated correspondence and in developing some hastily taken notes. I hear my interpreter returns to Defiance tomorrow and I expect to arrive the following day.

Very respectfully your Obedient Servant,
W. Matthews

DRAFT OF REPORT TO POWELL, NOVEMBER 1884, TRANSCRIBED FROM HAND-WRITTEN MANUSCRIPT (GUIDE:46, CORRESPONDENCE #190)

I have the honor to submit herewith a monthly report of my ethnological work during the month of November 1884. On the 3rd, I left Fort Wingate, N.M. for Fort Defiance A.T. and arrived [there] the same day.

When I arrived . . . I heard that another important ceremony, that of the Kledjiqagal [*sic*], or night-song (called by the Whites the 'Yebitcai dance', from the fanciful characters of the public dance on the last night) was about to take place near 'The Haystacks' a point about 6 miles from here. I went to the dance of the 5th and remained there until the tenth, during which time I made observations almost constantly, night and day. I gained full access at all times to the medicine-lodge and obtained a number of sketches, photographs and important notes. Here again a number of symbolic pictures, such as I described [for the Mt. Chant] were drawn with dry colors on a surface of sand.

The provisial [*sic*] plans for my season's work, on which I placed the greatest value were those for obtaining a full insight into the nature of these ceremonies. A medicine man, with whom I made a bargain two years ago could not now be found. On my return to Defiance I opened negotians [*sic*] with three different medicine men, offering them as liberal terms for their services as I could afford, but only to meet with the most positive refusal. I was on the point of abandoning these projects and devoting my time to obtaining the myths of locality and minor legends of the people known to the laity, when I heard of an old shaman living beyond Nutria, about 70 miles distant, who it was thought would be found less scrupulous that [*sic*] the others had proved. I dispatched a messenger for him at once, and on the evening of the 15th he came. With some trouble I concluded a bargain, and he began his narration on the morning of the 16th. I have been engaged with him ever since and do not believe I will be through with him until it is time for me to leave Defiance. No doubt I could profitably spend several months with him did circumstances permit. The information I am obtaining from him I consider of the highest value.

EXCERPTS FROM LETTER TO CUSHING DATED NOVEMBER 4, 1884 FROM THE FORT DEFIANCE AGENCY (GUIDE:81)

My dear Frank,

. . . Have just finished ten days' visit to a hockan dance. Got into the medicine lodge and saw things that I never dreamt of. Would you imagine that the rascals, who have neither ornamental robes, skins, or pottery, or carven idols, have nevertheless a complete system of pictographic mythic symbolism? They draw immense hieratic figures in powdered colors on the sanded floor of the medicine lodge, and when done, erase them and carry the very sand out of the lodge. Each day a separate design of really artistic appearance. Did you ever hear of such an art? A slight mention is made of something like this in Col. Dodge's last book; but elsewhere I have seen no mention of it. I will see more of their mythic designs at the Yebitcai. One who had never entered their medicine lodge could not dream that they had such an art. I have written to Powell about it; but I presume no notice will be taken of it. Think I will send a description of it to the "Peat Bog" [American Naturalist]. . . . Please tell me what you know about the 'sand pictures.' . . .

3. Transcriptions of Matthews' Handwritten Correspondence with Goddard about His Proposed Trip to Navajo Country

(Guide:45-46, Correspondence #347, 355-a, 355-b, 357, 349-a, 349-b)

In 1903 and 1904 Matthews concluded an agreement with the University of California at Berkeley leaving his papers to them with the understanding that Pliny Earl Goddard would carry forward the preparation of some of Matthews' field materials. This correspondence from December 1903 to March 1904 (consisting of handwritten drafts of Matthews' letters and Goddard's typed replies) concerns preparation of myths, prayers, and songs of a minor rite of the Night Chant (published 1907). It was necessary to have a portion of Matthew's field notes translated by the shaman who originally gave them. In the correspondence, Goddard plans a trip to Navajo country and Matthews gives suggestions for engaging Smiling Chanter's services. Matthews also describes the pay he has given in the past. He recommends Ben Damon and Henry (Chee) Dodge as interpreters. After the trip, Goddard writes that he talked with Smiling Chanter and Ben Damon but couldn't complete the translation because Smiling Chanter was incapacitated by a wagon accident; he will try again in the early fall. Matthews suggests that Goddard invite the shaman and interpreter to San Francisco to do the work, but Goddard finally completes the work on a later trip to Navajo country. It is probable that Matthews' payment to collaborators were, in part, based on the fact that his research on Navajo ceremonialism placed him in a role similar to that of an apprentice.

[#347] Dec. 26, 1903

Dear Mr. Goddard,

I received yours of the 9th some days ago. I delayed an answer because I have been in worse health than usual of late; but am feeling better now.

I should much like to see my texts in print and to have the Univ. of Cal. print them; but not until the translations are more perfect than they are at present.

I have on hand two short myths with songs and prayers and some independent songs and prayers. There are altogether 8 good songs and 5 fine prayers. Four of the prayers much resemble some already published; but one is very different and is a precious discovery I made recently among my notes. The ¼ part which I have recorded has 74 verses. This would give for the entire prayer, with the two additional amens, 298 verses in all. The text was written in haste and no attempt was made to translate it on the spot. I translated some of it last summer in Gloucester; but much of it would have to be translated with the assistance of the shaman who gave it—Hatáli Natloí, the Smiling Chanter.

With the assistance of a good interpreter and the shaman, you might do this; but unless the shamans have become less superstitious than they were in my day, you can do it only in the winter.

I have only one copy now of each of these texts, but if you wish to go to Arizona or New Mexico this winter I shall prepare other copies. I must do this with my own hand.

You might get Hatáli Natloí and a good interpreter to come to Berkeley in the winter for about the same price that it would cost you to go to New Mexico. I am sure the old shaman would be delighted to make a visit to California. My favorite interpreters were Ben Damon and Henry Dodge (Chee); but I doubt if you could get either of them now. Mr. Tozzer found a splendid interpreter in the San Juan valley somewhere, a young graduate of Carlisle who has come up since my day.

I advised Prof. Culin to bring Smiling Chanter east with him this winter and promised to take a part of his time and share the expenses. Mr. Culin tried I believe, but did not succeed.

If you think you can work on the texts this winter, say the word and I shall begin to copy them at once, laying my dictionary work aside.

Berkeley, Cal. Jan. 2, 1904.

My dear Dr. Matthews,

I received today your letter. I make haste to say that I shall be glad to visit the Navaho during the month of February and complete the translation for you. I am sorry you will be obliged to copy the prayer. Please send me any suggestions which you think will aid me in the work. I may not be able to stay very long but will take time to complete the special work which will allow the printing of your paper.

I have been very busy with proof-reading and other work. I am very sorry to hear your health has not been so good as when I saw you.

With my very best wishes for you and Mrs. Matthews I am

very sincerely,

P. E. Goddard

Page one of Washington Matthews' letter to Pliny E. Goddard. *(From manuscript collection, Museum of Navajo Ceremonial Art, Santa Fe, New Mexico.)*

[#355] 1262 New Hampshire Ave.
Washington D.C.
Jan 8th 1904

My dear Mr. Goddard,

I am in receipt of yours of Jan 2nd and am glad to hear that there is a prospect of having my work completed. I shall proceed at once to copy my texts for you. I fear it will take nearly a month to do so, although I shall work as diligently as my health will permit. I shall give you copious notes for your guidance, along with the text.

[#357] Jan 16th 1904
1262 New Hampshire Ave.
Washington D.C.

Mr. Pliny E. Goddard
University of California

Dear Mr. Goddard,

I wrote to you some time ago; but I write to you now again, without waiting for a reply, for time presses & it is a long call from here to California.

I would recommend that you would go early in the season to Arizona, but I want to know as soon as possible when you intend to start.

I am now very busy in preparing that work which I promised you, if I do not get it all finished in time I will send you what I have done by express a week in advance of your departure from Berkeley; then I can forward the rest to you in Arizona.

I would recommend that you go to Fort Defiance and make that the base of your operations. Although Defiance Station is nearer to the Fort than Gallup, I would advise you to go to Gallup as that is a town of some size & you can get livery, hotel accommodations etc. there.

By all means employ Hatáli Natloí, or Smiling Chanter, for your informant if you can possibly obtain his services. It was he who gave me most of the material I send to you, so he can best explain it. Besides he is intelligent, accommodating and the least conservative of the Navaho priests that I know. He used to live at a place called Cottonwood Pass, not far from Fort Defiance, and probably lives there still.

I think you cannot fail to get a good room and board at Fort Defiance. Possibly Smiling Chanter may be busy at this season with his ceremonial work, but I would advise you to wait for him rather than get anyone else. Bring him in to Defiance if you can, and if you cannot do so, go out to his ranch. I think he probably has a good house now.

Ben Damon is an excellent interpreter, so is Chee (Henry Dodge) but Dodge is a rich man now and a trader and Ben is a stock-raiser. Perhaps you cannot obtain their services, but I have no doubt, that at this time, many good interpreters may be found. They were rare in my day. In 1880 when I began work, there were practically none.

The material I am going to send you I am writing in a book, and arranging it so that you will have abundance of room for your notes and comments. I thought a book would be more convenient than loose sheets to carry into the field.

[crossed out conclusion: "I hope to hear from you soon, yours truly." Text resumes.]

I think it well to give you information about prices. The Navahoes, as you are aware, are well to do, and used to good wages. "Strict" economy is not easily practiced among them. The Shamans particularly are accustomed to good pay.

I used to pay Smiling Chanter (and other priests) one dollar a day in cash and used to give them presents in dry goods, groceries etc. of about an equal value. I fed him well too when he visited me. He was always well satisfied, thanked me profusely and said prayers of benediction when he left me. But his gratitude was shown best by his readiness to return to me again when he had time to come. He had young children at that time to whom I used to send special presents of candies, nuts etc. and that pleased him very much; he was quite human. I used to pay the other Shamans in the same manner. He never made a bargain with me beforehand but left the matter to my generosity. Perhaps his "standards of value" have changed since my day.

The agent or some old resident of the Reservation will tell you better, now, than I can what you should pay your interpreter.

I hope to hear from you soon.

Yours truly.

[#349] Berkeley, Cal. March 3 1904.

My dear Dr. Matthews,

I have not written but I have been to Arizona. I left the letters that were to be written until the last and then had to turn the absolutely essential ones over to Mrs. Goddard to do for me. I got the book containing the manuscript on Thursday the 11th of Feb. It seemed best to wait until the following Tuesday on account of the large lecture course which comes on that day. I left at 8 P.M. on the 16th. and fortunately found the Asst. Supt. of the School at Gallup ready to drive to Ft. Defiance. I got there therefore on Thursday night. Friday I found Ben Damon and engaged him as intrpreter. On his advice I sent a messenger to *Hatál*i Natloí asking him to come to the fort. While the messenger was gone I visited the Franciscan Fathers who have a mission seven miles south of the school. I found them to be energetic and well-educated. They have made good progress with the language. They have many of the verbs tabulated. I had not expected anything nearly so good from them.

The messenger did not return until Saturday evening and reported the Smiling Doctor in a precarious condition from an accident which had be-fallen him a month before. He had started for Gallup to buy provisions in a big wagon with a span of horses. The horses ran away throwing him out. His coat or blanket caught in the spokes causing him to be whorled over and over. Monday, Ben and I started horseback to go to see him. We spent the night with Moore the trader and Tuesday morning found *Hatál*i Natloí. He was in a medicine lodge and was undergoing one of the lesser rites.

When told I was the friend and representative of *Hatal*iyitso he greeted me very cordially. He enquired for your health. I had hoped to find him in condition to help us with the few most essential words. He was evidently suffering from broken ribs next to the spine. The fact that he was being treated added to the difficulties. I did not ask him to give help. He told me how sorry he was that he could not do so, and expressed his willingness to help when he was better. He said he would come to San Francisco if I wished. He said he had a good house and I should come and stay with him when I came again. We talked for nearly an hour during which time we had breakfast. He says he expects to recover. Ben and I returned to the Fort that day. The Indians had let me a bucking horse to ride. I was not thrown but when I found how mean he was I changed with Ben who got some rather hard shakings up.

I had thought of asking *Hatál*i Natloí to recommend a brother chanter who could help me out, but after seeing the man I concluded it would be much better to wait until he was in condition to do the work. I am sorry the publishing must be delayed. I shall not be able to go again this spring but can attend to it early in the fall.

I went over the texts carefully with Ben and parts of them with other interpreters. They understood me when I read them and gave me the same or similar meanings to those you had written in most cases. The difficulty was with the words you had left blank or penciled in. For them a *hatal*i will be necessary. I spent Wednesday, Thursday, and Friday in this work and in getting verbs and other grammatical matterial for comparison with the Hupa. I was surprized at the closeness both phonetically and morphologically between the Navaho and the Athapascan dialects of California.

When I have a little leisure I shall copy some of the material and send it to you.

Very sincerely,

Pliny E. Goddard

[#349b] 1262 New Hampshire Avenue
Washington, D.C.
March 14th 1904

My dear Mr. Goddard,

Yours of March 3rd finds me down with a bad attack of grip. I have been confined to my bed most of the time for a month, and have a trained nurse. I am now a little on the mend; but have done no work for a month.

I regret to learn that your journey to Arizona was not more successful, but your time has not been altogether wasted. The trip has evidently been of some advantage to you.

I have given copies of all my works to the Franciscan missionaries at the Cienega, and have written them many letters to guide them in their work. I have taken much pains to help them. I am curious to know if in their conversation with you they acknowledged their indebtedness to me. Many people whom I have helped seem to take great pains to keep my name in the background. I wish to know if these reverend gentlemen belong to this class. I am pleased to learn that you approve of their work.

I think it would be well to have Smiling Chanter and Ben Damon come to Berkeley in September or October. It would not cost you much more than it would to go yourself to Arizona. You could continue your work at the University while you pursued your investigations with them. They would enjoy greatly a little sightseeing which you could give them without much cost; such as a journey to the Cliff House to see the sacred ocean of the west, a day in Golden Gate park, a view of the menagerie, a matinee at the variety theater, a run to the top of Mt. Tamalpais, etc.

I have a few more small songs to send you, but they are fully translated. They will add to the volume and interest of our work.

4. The Suppressed Part of the Mountain Chant (1892c)

(Guide:22, Printed Item #466)

Matthews had the small pamphlet, "The Suppressed Part of the Mountain Chant," printed privately at Fort Wingate in 1892. The Victorian attitudes present in Washington during the late nineteenth century had been evident in his expurgatory editing of the Mountain Chant (1887a). However, some members of the intellectual community were outraged by this censorship. For example, a letter dated 16 March 1889 from Louis Henri Ayme, a career diplomat and amateur ethnologist, to W. H. Holmes at the Bureau of Ethnology comments, ". . . such evidence of ridiculous prudery as is here displayed is supremely stupid" (Guide:44, Correspondence #424). In response, Matthews prepared a brief description of the sexual behavior imitated in the public dance around the fire on the final night of the ceremony. He also included a translation of the sexual joking that occurred in another part of this public dance that had been obtained by his friend A. M. Stephen. The pamphlet, containing both insertions, has since been available in the National Anthropological Archives of the Smithsonian Institution and in the Matthews microfilm. (Ed. note: *In the pamphlet, Matthews apparently made an error in the page numbers for these insertions, although his paragraph numbers are in accord with the text of 1887a. The text concerning sexual behavior should be inserted after paragraph 130, p. 441; the text concerning sexual joking should be inserted after paragraph 145, p. 443.)*

THE SUPPRESSED PART

OF

"The Mountain Chant:

A NAVAJO CEREMONY,

BY

DR. WASHINGTON MATTHEWS, U.S.A.

Extract from the Fifth Annual Report of the Bureau of Ethnology.

Washington, D.C., 1888

FORT WINGATE, NEW MEXICO.
1892

Notice.

In the paper entitled "THE MOUNTAIN CHANT: A NAVAJO CEREMONY," the following passage appears: (p. 441.)

"146. Many facts concerning not only the hackan inça, but other parts of the mountain chant, have not been allowed to appear in this essay. Recognized scientists may learn of them by addressing the author through the Director of the Bureau of Ethnology."

Suppressed Part of the Mountain Chant

The present pamphlet contains the information suppressed in the original. The author begs the pardon of his correspondents for having so long delayed the fulfillment of his promise.

W. M.

FORT WINGATE, NEW MEXICO,
FEBRUARY 26TH, 1892.

The Suppressed Part Of "The Mountain Chant."

After paragraph 130, p. 443, of "THE MOUNTAIN CHANT," read the following:

While the dancers are circling around the fire in the dance of Nahikai, if one is found in a stooping or kneeling attitude before the fire, trying to burn the down on his wand, another may come up behind him, mount him and imitate, without actual pederasty, the pederastic motions of an erotic dog. While thus engaged a third dancer may mount the second and a fourth may mount the third and enact a like play—just as a number of dogs are often seen engaged.

Sometimes one or more of the actors wear large imitation penes, made of rags or inflated sheep-gut; such may enact the part of dogs, feign to masturbate or to manipulate the part to produce erection.

Sometimes, when the down has been burned from the wand and before it has been restored, they treat the wand as if it were a penis; hold it erect or semi-erect between the thighs, rub it and manipulate it. This is done mostly by the last remaining dancers, who effect to have difficulty in restoring the down to the ends of their wands.

Their motions are of such a nature that many white spectators of this play have conjectured that the dance of Nahikai is symbolic of the sexual act; that the down on the wand represents the desire which is destroyed in the flame of gratification, and, with trouble, restored; and this seems not an unreasonable conjecture.

After paragraph 145, p. 441, of "THE MOUNTAIN CHANT," read the following:

That portion of the drama which succeeds the finding of the hoshkawn or yucca, I have seen enacted with varying detail and dialogue, but with the essential parts always similar. To preserve the unity, I will describe it as seen on the night of November 5th, 1882. (See "MOUNTAIN CHANT," par. 127).

DRAMATIS PERSONÆ:—The old hunter and the man dressed as a woman, who will be referred to as HE and SHE.

HE.—Come, my wife, I have found something good. This is what I have long looked for. Are you not glad I have found it?

SHE.—Yes, I am very glad, my sweet.

HE.—It tastes like you. *(He gives her a piece to eat).*

SHE.—It is sweet, but not as sweet as you.

(After this compliment he draws close to her and begins to dally, not over decently. One act is to put his hand under her clothes, withdraw it and smell it. At length he puts his hand in at the neck of her dress as if to feel her bosom and draws forth a handkerchief hidden there. He becomes furious).

HE *(Squealing in feeble wrath).*—Where did you get this?

SHE.—My aunt lost it at the spring and, when I went for water, I found it there.

HE.—I don't believe you! You have been cohabiting with some one else. This is your pay.

SHE.—No, truly, my aunt lost it.

HE *(Still in a jealous fury, lights a cigarette and tries to smoke, presently throws cigarette peevishly away).*—I will go away and never see you again.

SHE.—Don't leave! Don't leave! You are a fool!

HE.—Yes, I know it; but I will be one no longer. Now I go away. *(He moves off).*

SHE *(Pouts a moment, then takes a pinch of dust in her fingers, blows it toward him and says:).*—Thus do I blow away my regard for you. I will follow you no more.

(With head averted, and sitting, she watches him furtively till he shuffles off out of sight, among the crowd of spectators; then she runs after him and soon reappears dragging him back).

HE.—You were not strong enough to blow me away, I am so sweet. *(Again they sit side by side and indulge in dalliance and loud kisses).*

HE.—I don't like you to cohabit with others while I am away hunting. I find you food and sweet things to eat, but you are bad.

SHE.—Do not leave me. I will never touch another man again. *(They eat together of the yucca fruit).*

HE.—How sweet this fruit is! Let us see which is the sweeter, this or coition. *(Each puts a piece in the mouth and they proceed with the most complete realism of action, but without exposure, to imitate the sexual act. When through, he tumbles off with a groan as if completely exhausted).*

SHE *(Spitting the fruit from her mouth).*—The hoshkawn is sweet, but not half so sweet as what we have been doing. *(She rises, takes a handful of dust from the ground, and acts as if scattering it on the vulva. They put the fruit into the basket and depart).*

The spectators of this scene are persons of both sexes—married and unmarried—and of all ages; a most promiscuous audience.

The act of dusting the vulva I have heard of as done by Indian women of other tribes in the arid region after the act of coition *al fresco*.

The dialogue given above was obtained for me by Mr. A. M. STEPHEN of Keam's Canyon, Arizona, who witnessed with me the night ceremonies of November 5th, 1882, and next day, learned the words of the play from the man who enacted the part of the woman. I have since heard other versions of the dialogue, but none superior to this.

W. M.

5. *Inventory of Matthews' Wax Cylinder Song Recordings*

(Guide:53, 89–90, Notebook #633)

These wax cylinder song recordings were made during Matthews' second period of Navajo fieldwork in the early 1890s. His letters to Frank Cushing at that time mention repeated efforts to obtain the newly available phonograph recording machine (Guide:82). Matthews was among the first anthropologists to report on and demonstrate recordings of native American music—in 1893 at the Chicago World's Fair and again in 1894 at the annual meeting of the American Folklore Society. (In this volume, see Halpern's essays and the discussion of the continuing importance of the recordings for contemporary scholars in McAllister's essay).

Notebook #633, (pp. 1–33) contains a handwritten list of the 196 cylinders, with cylinder numbers and song titles listed on the odd numbered right hand pages; the opposite pages contain Matthews' notes and comments on the recordings. Since the notebook was judged to be too fragile and the writing too faint for satisfactory reproduction, we have prepared a printed version from his handwritten copy, a process that has required familiarity with the details of Matthews' handwriting and an understanding of the changes in his use of phonetic characters at different stages of his Navajo work. The list appears to be a working copy, one certainly not intended for publication as it stands. Some strikeouts are found in the list. Differences in spelling and in the use of phonetic characters occur in the repetition of many song titles, and the use of capitals and punctuation is not uniform. There are a few instances of raised phonetic characters. Variations such as these have been preserved in our copy. The list is written in ink, but comments and explanations appear to have been added in pencil. These pencil notations have been enclosed in brackets [ ]; comments by the editor are enclosed in second order brackets { }. The few parentheses that occur in ink in the original have been retained.

In 1994 the University of Utah Press reprinted Matthews' Navaho Legends

(1897a). In it Robert W. Young provides a "Note on Orthography" (pp. 301–303), comparing the phonetic characters used by Matthews in Navaho Legends *(1897a) and the* Night Chant *(1902a) with those used in Modern Standard Navajo. However, Matthews' earlier Navajo publications had used some different phonetic characters, particularly for a number of consonants, as specified in his* The Mountain Chant *(1887a: 382):*

> c for ch as in chin; ¢ for th as in this; ç for th as in think;
> j for z as in azure; q for ch as in German machen.
> Also l is usually aspirated, and an inverted quotation mark shows that a vowel is aspirated.

It is these earlier characters of the Mountain Chant that he used in the List of Phonograph Cylinders in Notebook #633.

(Note: *Matthews made a second list of his cylinders with texts and translations of some of the songs and with information on when he had exhibited them at lectures [see Guide:54, 89, Notebook #675, pp. 15–119]. The Indiana University Archives of Traditional Music hold 75 cylinders and the Library of Congress holds 91 cylinders [copies and/or originals]. For a fuller description of these holdings, as well as a third listing of cylinders by David McAllester, see Guide:89–90.)*

Cylinder Number	Contents of Cylinder
Page 1 of notebook	
1	"Hyĭ¢ezonà" Song of the vigil of the masks [very loud and distinct]
2	"Hyĭ¢ezonà" Continuation of same [good]
3	"Hyĭ¢ezonà" Conclusion of same [good]
4	Nagènezgani bigin war song, Protection song [injured?] {Opposite page says}: [4. Distinct, slightly incomplete]
5	Nagènezgani bigin Duplicate. [crackling]
6	Prayers to nagenezgani, Toba[d]jestcīni and qastceolgoi. one to each.
7	Aga 'hoàgisin or Summit Songs 1 and 2 {Opposite page says}: Have text and translation of no 1 in record of first Days ceremony, under title of "Yikal Agahoàgisin." [Nez says there are 26 of these songs.]
8	Atsa '´lēi bigin, or Song of the First Dancers. First part [fair]
9	Atsa '´lēi bigin, [second part] concludes [outside of lodge]
10	Tsĕńi-bigin nos 1 and 2
11	Cĭlnéòle bigin [akadièe] nos 1 and 2
12	Cĭlnéòle bigin nos 3 and 4
13	A 'saçinì bigin nos 1 and 2 [loud and good]
Page 3 of notebook	
14	Ăśaçĭni bigin Pumpkin Songs nos 3 & 4 [loud]

Cylinder Number — Contents of Cylinder

15 ~~Tehalheġl bigin~~ ~~Darkness Songs~~ nos 1 & 2 [very fair] {Note on opposite page says}: [15. Nillci bigin, so he says on hearing it again Mar 17th 93. Sung on the last night when the basket drum is down.]

16 ~~Teălhyèl bigin.~~ ~~Darkness Songs~~ nos 1 & 2 [very good] {Opposite page says}: [16. Nilcī bigin 3 & 4.]

17 Dsăhă¢oldjà bigin. Fringe Mouth Songs no.1 [flaw—not on record]

18 Dsăhă¢oldjà bigin. Fringe Mouth Songs no.2

19 Dsăhă¢oldjà bigin. Fringe Mouth Songs no.3

20 Dsăhă¢oldjà bigin. Fringe Mouth Songs no.4

21 Gàaskĭ¢i bigin. Nos 1 & 2

22 Gàaskĭ¢i bigin. Nos 3 & 4 [12 in set]

23 Ȼepè bigin. Mountain Sheep Songs Nos. 1 & 2 [clear]

24 Ȼepè bigin. Nos. 3, 4, 5, 6 [wrong for no 3]
[English Announcement] Nos. 3, 4, 5 & 6

25 Năńçi ‘gĭsĭn [Bridge Songs] 1 & 2 [also called Tcalhʸel bigin.] {Opposite page says}: 25. Bridge Songs or Darkness Songs. Two names. The first two are sung when making the ancole lather in the bath of the 4th Day.

26 Năńçi ‘gísin 3 and 4

Page 5 of notebook

27 Çàakē gisin Farm Songs nos 1 & 2

28 Çàakē gĭsĭn nos 3 & 4

29 Tse‘ bigin nos 1 & 2

30 Tse‘ bigin no 3

31 Ī¢·nī‘ bigin Thunder Songs nos 1 & 2

32 Ī¢·nī‘ bigin [15 altogether] nos 3 & 4

33 Qastceqogan bìgin [Faint] nos 1 & 2 {Opposite page says}: 33. No 1 was rather long. He sang no 2 quickly in order to get it all on the cylinder; but eventually failed to record the last few meaningless syllables.

34 Qastceqogan bigin nos 3 & 4

35 Qastceqogan bigin nos 9, 10, & 11 [Dup. 100] {Opposite page says}: 35. 9th song best. Also sung in Mountain Chant, when Qastceelçi and Qaaski¢i dance, or Qastceelçi and 2 baads. 11th song sung on Qastcee qogans farm when they were planting.

36 Qastcejiñi nos 1 & 2

37 Qastcejini nos 3 & 4

38 Nagenezgani bigin [dup. 98] nos 1 & 2 [good 2nd day p.69] {Opposite page says}: 38. Duplicated in 98. First song translated. 2nd day p.69. Loud and clear.

39 Nagenezgani bigin [dup 93] nos. 9 & 10 {Opposite page says}: 39. No. 10 Naço ‘li interesting. Repeated in 93.

Cylinder Number	Contents of Cylinder
Page 7 of notebook	
40	Yikàigin no. 1
41	Yikàigin nos. 11 & 12 [Renewed, very loud dup. 106] {Opposite page says}: 41. No. 12 the lively song of Bizaholò holi ani (in lodge) belongs to this set.
42	Atsa' 'lei bigin [Inside lodge] nos 1 & 2 [see 125, 126] sung by Qascin Gotcin.
43	Qastceqogan bigin nos 9 & 10 sung by Qasçin gotcin
44	Gambling Songs.
45	An Outside song of the last night. Èo nă¢o. one song
46	Last outside song of the last night. Ȼòla ăńe one song
47	Bènaqaça' li. Last songs in lodge nos 1 & 2 [Renewed very good]
48	Bènaqaça' li. no.3 [Renewed, very good 7th day p. 8] {Opposite page says}: 48. Fairly musical.
49	Bènaqaça' li. no. 4 [Renewed, very good. Dup 117] {Opposite page says}: 49. Very musical. Last song, in finishing which they turn up the basket.
50	Keçán bigin. Song sun in finishing cigarettes & tobacco song Kaçacanisçe 2 songs {Opposite page says}: 50. Two songs sung in preparing the cigarettes, "Kaç acànisçe," now it is finished, and naço biḡin or tobacco song.
51	The voices of the Gods
52	One of the Beyiçon songs of the Last night. sung by Jesus' son.
Page 9 of notebook	
53	Estsanatlehi Songs. As sung by Jake no. 1
54	Estsanatlehi Songs. Continuation of same
55	Rainbow Songs by Jake nos. 1, 2, 3 & 4
56	Bear Song. Sung by Jake no. 1 [weak, splutters]
57	Bear Songs. Sung by Jake no. 2 and part of 3, no.3
58	Bear Songs. Sung by Jake conclusion of no. 3 and no 4
59	a Beyiçon Song by Young Jesus
60	Eo Na¢o (Eo lŭlo) same as 45, as sung by Young Jesus.
61	no 60 repeated, louder, by young Jesus.
62	Song of last night. Composed by Tom Torlino. Sung by young Jesus. {Opposite page says}: [62 very fine Beyiçon]
63	Repetition of 62 {Opposite page says}: [63 very fine]
64	Foolish or Trivial Songs and Love. Sung by Young Jesus. Two sung by Young Jesus and Ben together.
Page 11 of Notebook	
65	Hyi¢ezna'. Vigil of the masks 1st part {Opposite page says}: 65, 66, & 67 are repetitions of nos. 1,2, & 3.
66	Hyi¢ezna'. Vigil of the masks 2nd part
67	Hyi¢ezna'. Vigil of the masks 3rd part

Cylinder Number	Contents of Cylinder
68	Kethan Bigin no 1 and part of no 2 "Kaç a¢anisçe." Painting Songs.
69	Keçan Bigin nos 3 & 4 dup. 124 {Opposite page says}: 69 or cigarette Songs. very musical.
70	Keçan Bigin no 5 and part of no. 6. {Opposite page says}: 70. No. 6 is sung when pollen is applied and symbolic lighting done.
71	Keçan Bigin Last part of no. 6 and no. 7. {Opposite page says}: 71. No 7 sung [immediately after] applying cigarettes to patient. Very loud & distinct.
72	Keçan Bigin, or Cigarette Song No. 8 {Opposite page says}: 72. Sung when the bearers leave the lodge.
73	Keçan Bigin no. 9 {Opposite page says}: 73. Contains also a part of no. 10 which was spoiled by interruption and begun on a new cylinder.
74	Keçan Bigin no. 10 {Opposite page says}: 74. has 3 flaws. Three cigarette songs appear first in record of 2nd days ceremony. Sung to all Yè keçan.
75	Bejiçon (last-night) Song. Sung by Natloi {Opposite page says}: 75 & 76. very loud and distinct
76	Last night song. sung by two voices.
77	Prayers to the War Gods: Cigarette Prayers {Opposite page says}: 77. very loud but rather rapid.

Page 13 of notebook

78	Prayers to the War Gods: Cigarette Prayers Repetition of 77 and 6
79	Three Gambling Songs. Wild-cat, blue-jay, bat. {Opposite page says}: 79 very musical and good particularly the last, naezni Tcogi. Tcapani.
80	Three Gambling Songs. Dove, yeitso, locust. [loud and harsh]
81	Repetition of 79
82	First House-Song. no. 1 Thinking about it.
83	Second House-Song. no. 2 Talking about it.
84	Rock-Songs. Tseniǧzin nos. 1 & 2 [second day p.37]
85	Rock-Songs. Tseniǧzin nos. 3 & 4 [loud]
86	Qastceelçi Song. "Benacoie" no. 6 [trans!, Second Day p.35]
87	Rock Songs. Tsenigisin no. 15 Last Song Ȼoliwan [p.39. 2nd day]
88	Repetition of 79 [very loud and good]
89	Thunder Song. "I¢ni' bigin" by Gordo. Hoshawn dance [loud]
90	Tsilke ¢iginu bigin. Holy Young Men Song. by Gordo from Hoshkawn dance [loud]
91	Songs of Bear Maidens. Tcike cac natlehi by Gordo from Hoshkawn [loud]

Page 15 of notebook

92	In¢ia' bigin or Plumed Wand Songs by Gordo from Hoshkawn.
93	Nagenezgani Bigin nos 9 & 10 Repetition of 39 [loud but harsh]
94	Dsil-bigin or mountain-Song Sung over patient on Anilçani picture {Opposite

Cylinder Number | Contents of Cylinder

page says}: 94. There are six of these songs altogether. Natloi says it makes him very happy to sing them.

95 Conclusion of 94 [fairly loud, 2nd day p.46]

96 In¢ia‘ bigin Songs of the Plumed Wands nos 1 & 2 [not musical]

97 In¢ia‘ bigin nos 31 & 32 {Opposite page says}: 97. Sung at the vigil of the masks, the last is Tcin yàn or food song.

98 Nagenezgani bigin no 1 & 2 Repetition of 38

99 Assaçini bigin or ~~Pumpkin~~ Songs nos. 8 & 12

100 Qastceqogan bigin nos. 9, 10, 11 Duplicate of 35.

101 Three gambling songs. Dove, Yeitso, Locust Duplicate of 80

102 Four gambling songs. Turkey, antelope magpie, Gopher.

103 Four gambling songs. Owl or chicken hawk, owl, badger, Rabbit.

104 Four gambling songs. Turkey no. 2, Lark (?), “Natsetligi,” Crow, and mouse, Natsosí.

Page 17 of notebook

105 Akan-benatsa bigin or Drying-with-meal Song {Opposite page says}: 105. Song sung when drying patient with meal after amole bath on the 4th day (p.9.b)

106 Yikaigin nos 11 & 12. Duplicate of 41—15 in all

107 }
108 } These three cylinders contain one song a Qastcelçi bigin sung in applying pollen. not one of the regular Qastcelçi set. Fourth day 9.b. much like 86
109 }

110 Tcalhyel bigin nos 2 & 3 [loud see 25 & 26]

111 Tcalhyel bigin or Nançi‘ gisin nos 1 & 2 Duplicate of 25 [loud]

112 Aga‘hoagisin no. 3 [Rec 4th Day. p. 14. important]

113 Qastcelçi qogan bigin no. 1 {Opposite page says}: 113. Twelve of these songs altogether.

114 Qojoni Yikagin no. 1 [rec. Fourth night p. 15]

115 Tsenitcenìçagin gisin no. 1 [see Fifth day p. 2] {Opposite page says}: 115. Ten of these in all.

116 Qo¢i/làç sin nos 1 & 2

117 Benaqaçàli no 4 Duplicate of 49.

Page 19 of notebook

118 Assaçini bigin nos 1 & 2 Duplicate of 13 [no 1 good No 2 harsh]

119 Benaqaça‘li no 3 [good record]

120 }
121 } Anilçani bigin. Grasshopper songs or Djic beqa¢ilne bigin. Songs to make masks with—5 in number no 1 [9th day p. 5]

122 Qastcelçi bigin—special. {Opposite page says}: 122. Not belonging to the series of (Cyl 86) qastceélço bigin. Sung by itself on the 9th day, when the masks etc. are finished.

Cylinder Number | Contents of Cylinder

123 Qastceelçi bigin—special concluded
124 Kethan bigin nos 3 & 4 Duplicate of 69
125 } atsa'lei bigin sung inside lodge no 1—Dup. cylinder 42
126 } atsa'lei bigin sung inside nos 2 & 3 [harsh] Duplicate part of 42.
127 } atsa'lei bigin sung outside of lodge Duplicate of 8 & 9
128 }
129 } qojodgisin or song of untying the yucca drumstick.
130 }

Page 21 of notebook
131 Qastcegogan bigin nos. 1 & 2 Duplicate of 33
132 Qastcegogan bigin nos. 3 & 4 Duplicate of 34 (metallic)
133 Qastcegogan bigin nos. 5 & 6
134 Qastcegogan bigin nos. 7 & 8
135 Qastcegogan bigin nos. 12 & 13
136 Qastcegogan bigin nos. 14 & 15
137 Qastcegogan bigin nos. 16 & 17
138 Qastcegogan bigin nos. 18 & 19
139 Qastcegogan bigin nos. 20 & 21
140 Qastcegogan bigin no. 22
141 Qastcegogan bigin no 23
142 Qastcegogan bigin no. 24
143 Qastcegogan bigin nos. 25 & 26
144 Qastcegogan bigin nos. 27, 28, & 29
145 Qastcegogan bigin nos. 30 & 31
146 Qastcegogan bigin nos. 32 & 33
147 Qastcegogan bigin nos. 34 & 35 {Opposite page says}: [147. Sung about meal-time.]
148 Qastcegogan bigin nos. 36 & 37
149 Qastcegogan bigin nos. 38 & 39 [good]
150 Qastcegogan bigin no. 40 & *last* (30)
151 Qastcegogan bigin nos. 36 & 37 Duplicate of 148
152 Gaas ki¢i bigin Nos 11–15
153 Assaçini bigin Nos 7 & 8 {Opposite page says}: 153. A long myth of Assaçini a log canoe and a pet turkey goes with this.
154 Mountain Chant. First songs of first dancers nos 1, 2 & 3—p. 456
155 Mountain Chant—pp. 457, 458 Mountain sheep songs nos. 1, 6 & 12 {Opposite page says}: 155. Order of first two called incorrectly on cylinder.

Page 25 of notebook {Top of page says}: (These are in the ? work "The Mountain Chant: a Navaho Ceremony")

Cylinder Number	Contents of Cylinder
156	Mountain Chant—pp 458, 459—Thunder Songs nos 1: 12 & ? One not in book
157	Mountain Chant Duplicate of 156
158	Mountain Chant—pp. 459, 460 Songs of the Holy Young Men nos. 1 and 6
159	Mountain Chant—pp. 460, 461 Songs of the Holy Young Men no. 12 Songs of the Young Women—Bears no. 8
160	Mountain Chant—pp. 461, 462 Tcìke cac Natlehi bigin ("Owl song" p. 146) Songs of the Exploding sticks. nos 1 & 2 [last song not in print]
161	Mountain Chant. Songs of the Exploding sticks Last and next to last—not printed
162	Mountain Chant Duplicate of 167, with order of songs reversed
163	Mountain Chant—p. 463 First Daylight song—not printed Mountain Chant—p. 463 4th Daylight song—printed as "1st" p. 463 Mountain Chant—p. 463 5th Daylight song—not printed {Opposite page says}: 163. Qaça'li Nez made a mistake in singing the 4th Daylight Song & had to begin anew.

Page 27 of notebook

164	Mountain Chant—pp. 463, 464 Daylight Song "Çahiz¢el."—"no.1" no.4 Daylight Song "soleyee" last Song of the Prophet to the San Juan River
165	Mountain Chant—pp. 464, 465 Song of Building the Dark Circle. Mountain Chant—pp. 464, 465 Song of Rising Sun Dance.
166	A Naakqaigin, outside song of the last night, sung by John Daw. {Opposite page says}: 166. First cylinder marked with water colors and in Arabic notation.
167	A second naakqaigin or outside song of the last night. Sung by John Daw "Loud and novel but rather harsh."
168	A third naakqaigin or outside song of the last night, sung by John Daw "Loud, clear, novel. not so harsh."
169	Naakqai bigin or outside song of the last night sung by Bitca Bige.

Page 29 of notebook

170	I¢ni' bigin or Thunder Songs niltsa bigin (storm songs) no. 1 Sung by Gordo. Mountain Chant
171	Naestca bigin, two owl-songs from the Mountain Chant. Sung by Gordo.
172	Two Tsilke ¢igini bigin or Songs of the Holy Young Men. from the Mountain Chant Sung by Gordo.
173	Assaçini bigin (from the Night Chant) no 8 Sung by Natloi. *Loud, musical, good.* "Sung when the turkey was running along the bank of the river."
174	Duplicate of 173 by natloi. not so good as 173. {Opposite page says}: 174. The words mean: "He floats down; the turkey runs on the bank."
175	Assaçini bigin no 1 sung by Natloi. Loud but harsh. {Opposite page says}: 175. The words mean: "It rains on the corn and the water runs down the corn."

Cylinder Number — Contents of Cylinder

176 Assaçini bigin no 2 By natloi. Loud, clear, musical but harsh in places. {Opposite page says}: 176. The words mean: “I walk among the corn—and melon—He holds his hands out to me, when I walk to him.”

Page 31 of notebook

177 Asaçini bigin by Natloi no 3 Loud, clear, but not very musical. {Opposite page says}: 177. meaning: “It rains upon my farm and the corn comes up.”

178 Asaçini bigin by Natloi no 4 Loud & clear. some harsh notes {Opposite page says}: 178. Meaning: “After the rain my corn ripens.”

179 Asaçini bigin by Natloi. no 5 Loud. clear. not musical. slow {Opposite page says}: 179. Meaning: “I am walking. I get presents where I am walking. It rains where I am walking. My corn gets ripe.”

180 Asaçini bigin. by Natloi no.6 loud. clear. slow. not harsh. not musical. obscure near end. {Opposite page says}: 180. Meaning: “There, up on the Mountain I walk from where the sun is now” & more perhaps.

181 Asaçini bigin by Natloi no 7 Loud. clear slow. musical satisfactory. {Opposite page says}: 181. Meaning: “I am walking on the river. The white—, blue—, yellow—, black river.” [It is white in the morning, blue in the day, yellow at sunset, black at night] Çonili ^{n}yé naca

182 Asaçini bigin. by Natloi no. 9 Loud, clear. {Opposite page says}: 182. çonolgecie (I am on) the moving water çolowucie “foaming”

183 Asaçini bigin by Natloi no 10 clear. fairly loud. no harshness. one slight hesitancy in delivery {Opposite page says}: 183. Çologeci yaani. The water is moving he said. qayaʻ to come out

Page 33 of notebook

184 Asaçini bigin, by Natloi no 11 Loud, clear, slow, harmonious. satisfactory. A few loud notes harsh. {Opposite page says}: 184. Hui iʻ inle tciniá: I have come to a glad place. colòlo, where the waters gurgle. niqolsid, said of water sinking back when he was thrown ashore. çologec & Çalawuc also appear.

185 Asaçini bigin by Natloi no 12 loud, clear, a few harsh notes {Opposite page says}: 185 “Upon the water the pumpkins are floating.” çalawac. esa skwona, put pumpkin in pot to boil

186 Atsosi gisin. by Natloi. First song about the pretty log {Opposite page says}: [186. See myth]

187 Song of the Vigil of the masks “Hyi¢ezna” by Natloi. Part 1st. {Opposite page says}: 187, 188, 189. Duplicate 1, 2, 3 and 65, 66, 67

188 Song of the vigil of the masks “Hyi¢ezna” by Natloi Part 2nd The singer interrupts himself.

189 Song of the Vigil of the Masks “Hyi¢ezna” by Natloi conclusion loud but harsh

190 Prayer to the Atsa'leì. by Natloi Part 1st From the night-chant. clear and moderately loud.

191 Prayer to the Atsa'lei conclusion From the Night-Chant by Natloi clear, loud toward the end {Opposite page says}: 191. Often interrupted to clear throat.

192 Qastceqogan bigin no 11 *Second* Farm Song. Kedìclej. {Opposite page says}: 192. "In beauty I am planting" second(?) Farm Song. [Runs irregularly owing to some changes in the electric current. To be renewed.]

193 Qastceqogan bigin no 12 Third (?) Farm song {Opposite page says}: [193. Rather harsh and changes time in the last few words, probably from change in current. To be renewed.]

194 Two Naakqai songs. Sung by elder son of Jesus. Fairly good. {Opposite page says}: 194. Record peculiar but apparently not finished.

195 Anyane bigin. Buffalo song belonging to an old Buffalo rite Sung by a man named Qasçlu {Opposite page says}: 195. Loud. harsh. interrupted. unfinished. not musical. [(?) perhaps to be rejected.]

196 [Atsa'çi qaçal song Sung by naço iaji] {Opposite page says}: [196. Very harsh and disagreeable. a pity. A good lively song. Perhaps to be rejected or renewed.]

6. *The Navaho Myth of the Origin of the Utes*

(Guide:55, Notebooks #588 and #633)

*This is a Navajo version of a widely known story, in which Coyote (in this version referred to simply as "he") marries his daughter by feigning death and giving instructions that his daughter is then to marry the first man she meets. After his presumed death, the daughter and mother depart together. The daughter marries the first stranger who accosts them. When his trickery is finally discovered, she throws away the resulting offspring who is raised by an owl. Arrows are made for him, and he becomes dangerous to other children, killing them with his arrows. The people try to trail him; each night they find evidence of chips from arrow making and an increasing number of tracks. By the ninth night they give up, realizing that his arrows have become a company of the fierce Arrow People (the Navajo name for Utes). In his discussion of the myth motifs in the Navajo Mountainway, Wyman identifies "Protagonist Feigns Death" and "Raised by Owl" as the concluding portion of the story of Male Mountainway and gives a summary of the versions known at the time (*Wyman 1975:148–56*).*

The story is one of the few myth narratives for which Matthews gave the Navajo text and interlinear translation. It exists in three versions in his papers, two with Navajo text and one in English only. The latter (published as 1885c) he describes as a "very free translation." The two Navajo versions with interlinear translation are handwritten manuscripts. One is in Notebook #633, pp. 0–17. (Ed. note: *In the notebook this is a second set of pages numbered from zero, separated from the first set by a block of blank pages.) The other, in Notebook #588, pp. 101–31, is the text given here. In this reproduction, we have not included the differences between the two texts; Matthews notes in his introduction that these differences are given on the "opposite (even) pages."* (Ed. note: *For ease in reading we have added a printed copy of the English text as it appears in the handwritten interlinear translation.)*

19a

99

Nóta̲ʼ Hodedé̲zlid̲o Ha̲ʼni.
Ute Origin Story.

The Navaho Myth of the Origin of the Utes.

Two recitals of the following text were obtained at diffrent times from the same shaman. On comparing these, many years later (1904) I find that my records are somewhat different for each. The later record is the text here written in full. The differences are given in notes on the opposite (even) pages. In some cases the words were differently recorded, for different parts of the same recital and such vari-ations are also noted.

A very free translation of ~~another~~ version for which the text was not recorded, was published in the American Antiquarian September 1885.

19c

Bitse yanteidikezgo. Binítea dakadilt
His daughter he began to think about. He became ill he acted as if.

Daeĭĭngo ĕlna. "Binĭteágo nii bakátse
A little bit he swallowed, "When I am dying a scaffold on top of it

haeiadoltel. Jákoi² dádĕsteal. Hátĭsa³
will take me up, There I shall die. Who

yosidoltel? Jákoi³ dasitili. Isteá
will carry me off? There I shall lie. You see

dáseteágo todenĭs nitado⁴. Joitsáta⁴
when I am dead I may groan no more. No noise

hazlingo dasĭstea dzĕnĭzĭnte. Dahoznĭz.
when there is I am dead you know. Decide for

ĭndzi das-diazle. Joiteásta⁴ hazlingo
yourselves where you two go together. No noise when there is

dasdiáz, tsĭní.
go you two together he said,

Haá[7] atsiáz ádo dzĭnaáz.[8] Dzoaz[9]
Over the hill they went together from there they went together. as they were walking together

ĭnté hadáte la[c] tsĭz niyágo hótsĭtsa.
there ahead one approaching they saw.

Ádo bagáu nádzotaz[9] áko tsigídi
From there further they walked together then nearer

dĕdzo-gál.[10] "Sitsé tákoi[c] dĭnestal. nĭla[c]
he walked. "my daughter here I shall rest. You alone

Tasáhadi bĭtsĭn dĭnaí, nĭnli. Háila
go go toward him, see him. Who is he

atĭnla[c]."
I wonder."

, Ádo adostiñya," haznija. "Hatédelaũ woaz?"

From there she started, she came to him, "Whence come ye two together?"

"Nilâte[13] yiáz."[13] Šizé yénaga daztea deáz.

"From yonder we come together. My father from us died at (the place) from which

yitaz."[14] "Ahaláni[15] šikis! Hatíla[16] kwöhyí?

we came together." "Greeting my friend! Of what did he die?

Dakatiš[17] ádzetiu? Hátisa[18] niyízdinidojo

Is he now no more? What did he tell ye

dádzištea?" "Kat taítee hatá yigáhagi

when he died?" "Now the first one whom you meet

bibahádzitaz[20] aína haésli. Níyi tsúniolani

with him you go together, that one stay with. To us he said that.

La áyízdonid. Ádo bamá yilnáholni; bamá

That they agreed to. From there her mother she told; her mother

da^c bidinid. Ádo ahaiłtaz. Bamá daandatsi
it agreed to. From then they were married. Her mother over there

sitá. Ádosa^c báni'yizdildzá, ákóhosa'
staid. From there for them he hunted, Then

yani'ziyegó dalá'zjiska^c.
he carried for them (game) every day.

Ákosa^c estsá[21] yiniłnága^c. ákosa^c
Then the woman was homesick. Then

tádahandiltsa da^cdiotsání[22] nahodíneełł nizingo
she went back where he pretended he died to see him again she wished

Aisa ánatsa. Ádosa^c[23] azdeiin. Ínstésa
(?) she got back.[23] From there she looked, There

ádzetin.[24] Todotá goyá. aidi atila nizinsa.
was nothing. she expected,[25] himself it was. she thought.

19g

Ádosa daindịtsa.
From there she waited back. [Dict. Dec. 6. 3 P.M.]

Ạísa natsa, ákogosa bitsé yílhọlnisa.
she got back,[23] then her daughter she told it to.

"Hategosá tosilhọ́lnita adzitégi? Ịnláti
Wherefore did you not tell me how he looks? Over there

dziztine[25] gaáteetin. Hazditégisa daidégo
that which lay is not there. His clothing how appear

hazdité?" "Naasteágí teya behazdite; hatsiga[26]
his clothes?" "Embroidery all with his clothes; his hair
? his clothes are made of.

ma'yinẹske; hanidzíga[27] dltó tsi bebikeéstsi."
is cut around; his face also red with is painted.

"Daaí adzitila! Ịnláti dziztinati ádzetin.
"Himself it is! Over there where he lay is nothing.

Indánaznosnigo.[28] Ĭntsé bigáhagi iżdilyála.[33]
He has taken a fancy to you. He has disguised himself to you[28]

Ĭndsĭtsago, adzĭbhasgo[39] śĭl ho-dĭlni.
When he gets home, when he sleeps tome tell.

Kat[30] dolzĭbhas[31] śididiníb; ákogo hádzeta
As soon as he sleeps let me know; then somewhere

adinab;[32] ákogo hátse deśáb, hodinĕśib.
go away; then to him I shall go I shall look at him.

, Aznijádo hoznĕlin ĭntésa, hóatsĭte.
When she arrived she looked at him there it was he.

Akó'gosa náhozdilte. "Dŭnĕdo, akó[33] táni daztsa.
Then she woke him, "You are a fine man, not surely dead.

Danásinĕtsago? Hósin sĭntye? Akosa[34] iznĭltsago[35]
Have you died again? Is that why you lie down? There enciente

Dict. Dec. 7. 3.25. P.M.

ha'hodelin. Akógosa' ahénataz ádosa' bitsé
the found herself, Then the two came together again when their daughter

tábini nïyidéya'.
went away by herself,
by herself went away?

, Ádosa' awé bidíináygo, daatsago yoinya'
When the child began to move, in the wilderness she wandered off

ádí' ástsin. Akógosa' awé tahyináygo nahastéet-an
there she bore, Then the child living a badger hole

góne ayídzilthal; ádosa yitsá dahándlitsa.
into she kicked it; from there leaving him she walked away.

, Akógosa' naéstsá bikéholid aísa
Then an owl arrived followed? ? "that is"

maidiltigo, yinésa' yánaldzégo akókosa'
picked it up, reared it hunted for it thereby

19j

yéyinésa.[36]
with he reared it,

formed arrows?, akógosa hadésin[37] ka bilya.. ádosa
Then some one arrows made for him. From that time

nizyidilgot tásapi[38] naldzé eilin. akógosa
he began to run around by himself to hunt was able. Then

altsíni indanédzi yitánalgo. akotíncle altsíni
children when they played among he ran! Then he was doing thus a child

ta yirjishyi. ádosa yóelgot. akógosa
one he killed. From there he ran off, then

tatobe'hosínda[39] ishyíni sa tatobe'hosínda[39]
they knew not whither the murderer him-self they knew not where

ádosa láti[40] ninárina ádisa altsíni áltso
thence elsewhere they moved there children all

19k

bitsąn yódsiškaigo ša yanánelgot ákoisa[42]
from them / They left — they wandered off — he — again ran among them — at that place

ła náyišyį. altšíni dątsa. Dayiláigosa[43]
one — again he killed. — the children — cried. — When it was done

banádsiškai. Ákoisa[42] altšíni indayįždeltįt.
they (parents) returned. — At that place — the children — they asked about it.

Akǫgosa altšíni holdahólni. "asikó tánińez
Then — the children — told them about. "A boy; — so big

le kwi[44] nagai ilgótgo niyinahí yenítyįltsa
There — he ran — our elder brother — one of us

comp hyi — ayiyįshyį ka yehwišyį. Ákoo niyį bitsąn
he killed — an arrow — he killed with. — Then — we — from him

yó-a hyelgot. Jádatsi tániltso naniyitsédo
ran off. — They thought — all of us — he might kill / took out for / na. & ni yo

The above Dictionaried. Dec 11. 1904. 3.10. P.M.
He ... again attacks

ìnté. 'Daitsáago, Yóahyelgot." "Ékógosa'"
there. We cried. He ran away." "Then

"Ha'dzégo dátílgot?" "Yúgwetsego elgót.
which way did he run?" "away off he ran

odzil bitzúngo." Ádosa' biké dasedíkai akóhosa'
the mountains toward." From there his trail they started there on

biké kédzokai. Sabígasa' dadzilkágo ìníha';
his trail they found. all day they trailed him till sunset;

da'biké dzúnéodzé.
behind him they camped.

Hosíngo biké názdíkai. Ìnté
at daylight behind him they started again. There

bis kálagi biké dzútkai ìnté tsúntléz índéstaad,
his camping place behind him they found there Tenolleria rupicola ~~shavings~~ chips.

19m

ĭn̲tcád̲o naki[6] tcĕ́bike. Ád̲os̲a nádadz̲ĭlkágo
from there two tracks. From there again they trailed him.

anáot̲a t̲as̲á́bike náznĕ́s̲dze.
till next night behind him they camped again.

The above Dictionaried Dec. 12th 1904. 3.20. P.M.

Hosíngo s̲ábike dan̲áz̲d̲ĭkai. Ĭ̆n̲té
at daylight behind him again they started. There

bĭ̆kála biké n̆ádz̲ĭ̆kai ákoi tcĕ́éskizi
his camping place behind again they found there ash

n̲ad̲est̲ád̲ ĭn̲tcád̲o t̲a tcĭnábĭ̆tĭn. Ád̲ós̲a
chips again from there three paths again. From there

biké d̲anáz̲d̲ĭkai aíg̲a t̲ábike náznĕ́s̲dze.
behind again they started they we behind again they camped.

Hosíngo biké náz̲dikai. Ĭ̆n̲té nel̲dzél̲aki
at daylight behind him again they started. There in their camp

Dict. Dec. 13. 1904. 3.25. P.M.

Look out for náznĕsdze / nádzĭkai (marginal note)

bike' nádzikai kintsilaki[46] nádestad, intcádo
behind them again they found aromatic sumac chips again, from there

tingo tsinábitin. Ádo biké dánázdikai
in four places paths again. From there behind they started again

tádo binádzilkai anáota, biké náznesdza.
before they found them again it was night, behind they camped again

Itoeingo. biké danázdikai inté nesdzélaki
at daylight behind they started again there in their camp

x bike nádzikai ákoiza tsilbtáteos[47] nádestad ádo
behind they found again there mountain mahogany chips from there

aslá. tsinábitin. Ádo bike tsokíko anáota
five paths again. From there behind they walked till again at night

biké náznesdza,
behind they camped again.

190 127

. Ḏosiṉgo ádo biké názdikai ṳṯé
at daylight from there behind they started again there

neẕdzélaki biké nádzǖkai tṣon[48] nádesṯaḏ ádo
in their camp behind they found again spruce[47] chips again from there

ẖasṯágo tṣináb̲iṯiṉ. Ádo biké tṣokágo anáoṯa
in six places trails again. From there behind they walked till again night

biké náẕnesdze
behind they camped again.

. Ḏosiṉgo biké da názḏǖkai ṳṯé nesdzé-
At daylight behind they started again there in their

laki biké nádzikai íkoi teéesṯáẕí 49
camp behind again they found there mountain mahogany

nádesṯaḏ. ádo tsostsēṯgo tṣǖnábǖṯiṉ. Ádo
chips from there in seven places trails again. From there

bikė́ tsokáko anáota biké náznesdze.
behind they walked till again night behind they camped again.

, Itosingo ádo biké dánázdikai inté'
At daylight from there behind they started again there

tcé'tsel[49] nádestad ádo teepi' tcináb̄itin.
oak again chips from there eight trails again

ádo biké natsokáko anáota biké naznesdze.
from there behind again they walked till again night behind they camped again

, Itosingo biké dánázdikai inté nesdzélaki
at daylight behind they started again there in their camp

biké nádzikai inté kat[50] nádestad ádo
behind they found again there juniper again chips. from there

nahastaigo tcináb̄itin. ádo dób̄itin. ákoisa'
in nine places trails again from there trails leading out there

19q 131

basadzilta dóbess dazdosída. Ádosa ta+

? They concealed something different they agreed. Thence back

Aesa nijédzokai aisa hodzobágo indzíkai.

They walked that is suffering needy they returned.

Tadíne'r ǎté; aíba haskéni daníli.

Arrow People tribe; therefore fierce brave, they are.

All the words in the above myth have been transferred to dictionary cards. The work was completed. Dec. 14th 1904 at 1. P.M.

TRANSCRIPTION OF "THE NAVAHO MYTH OF THE ORIGIN OF THE UTES"

Two recitals of the following text were obtained at different times from the same shaman. On comparing these many years later (1904) I find that my records are somewhat different for each. The differences are given in notes on the opposite (even) pages. In some cases the words were differently recorded for different parts of the same recital and such variations are also noted.

A very free translation of a version, for which the text was not recorded, was published in the American Antiquarian September 1885.

His daughter he began to think about. He became ill. He acted as if a little bit he swallowed. "When I am dying a scaffold on top of it will take me up. There I shall die. Who will carry me off? There I shall lie. You see when I am dead I may groan no more. No noise when there is I am dead you know. Decide for yourselves where you two go together. No noise when there is go you two together," he said.

Over the hill they went together from there they went together. As they were walking together there ahead one approaching they saw. From there further they walked together then nearer he walked. "My daughter here I shall rest. You alone go, go toward him, see him. Who is he I wonder."

From there she started, she came to him. "Whence come ye two together?" "From yonder we come together. My father from us died at (the place) from which we came together." "Greeting my friend! Of what did he die? Is he now no more? What did he tell ye when he died?" "'Now the first one whom you meet with him you go together, that one stay with.' To us he said that." That they agreed to. From there her mother she told; her mother it agreed to. From there they were married. Her mother over there staid. From there for them he hunted. Then he carried for them (game) every day.

Then the woman was homesick. Then she went back where he pretended he died to see him again she wished. She got back. From there she looked. There was nothing, she suspected, himself it was she thought. From there she started back.

She got back, then her daughter she told it to. "Wherefore did you not tell me how he looks? Over there that which lay is not there. His clothing how appear his clothes?" "Embroidery all with his clothes (are made of); his hair is cut around; his face also red with is painted." "Himself it is! Over there where he lay is nothing. He has taken a fancy to you. He has disguised himself to you. When he gets home, when he sleeps to me tell. As soon as he sleeps let me know; then somewhere go away; then to him I shall go. I shall look at him."

When she arrived she lookd at him there, it was he. Then she woke him. "You are a fine man, now surely dead. Have you died again? Is that why you lie down?" There enciente she found herself. Then the two came together again when their daughter went away by herself.

When the child began to move, in the wilderness she wandered off there she bore. Then the child living a badger hole into she kicked it; from there leaving him she walked away.

Then an owl arrived (followed?) "that is" picked it up, reared it hunted for it thereby with he reared it.

Then someone arrows made for him. From that time he began to run around, by himself to hunt was able. Then children when they played among he ran. When he was doing thus a child one he killed. From there he ran off. Then they knew not whither the murderer himself they know not where. Thence elsewhere they moved there children all from there they wandered off he again ran among them at that place one again he killed. The children cried. When it was done they (parents) returned. At that place the children they asked about it. Then the children told them about, "A boy, so big (?) there he ran our elder brother one of us he killed an arrow he killed with. Then we from him ran off. They thought all of us he might kill there. We cried. He ran away." "Then which way did he run?" "Away off he ran the mountains toward." From here his trail they started on their (sic) his trail they found. All day they trailed him till sunset; behind him they camped.

At daylight behind him they started again. There his camping place behind him they found there Fendleria rupicola chips, from there two tracks. From there again they trailed him till next night behind him they camped again.

At daylight behind him again they started. There his camping place behind again they found there ash chips again from there three paths again. From there behind again they started they are behind again they camped.

At daylight behind him again they started. There in their camp behind them again they found aromatic sumac chips again, from there in four places paths again. From there behind they started again before they found them again it was night, behind they camped again.

At daylight behind they started again there in their camp behind they found again there ~~mountain mahogany~~ [*sic*] chips from there five paths again. From there behind they walked till again at night behind they camped again.

At daylight from there behind they started again there in their camp behind they found again spruce chips again from there in six places trails again. From there behind they walked till again night behind they camped again.

At daylight behind they started again there in their camp behind again they found there mountain mahogany chips from there in seven places trails again. From there behind they walked till again night behind they camped again.

At daylight from there behind they started again there oak again chips from there eight trails again. From there behind again they walked till again night behind they camped again.

At daylight behind they started again. There in their camp behind they found again there juniper again chips. From there in nine places trails again from there trails leading on. There (?) they counseled something difficult they agreed. Thence back they walked that is suffering (needy) they returned. Arrow People tribe; therefore fierce (brave) they are.

7. *Barthelmess' Account of a Night Chant*

(Guide:60, Manuscript #361)

Christian Barthelmess was also stationed at Fort Wingate during the 1880s and occasionally served as Matthews' research assistant. Barthelmess subsequently wrote an article about a Nightway that he had attended. Matthews comments (1902a:310–11): "Barthelmess . . . wrote an excellent account of what he saw, which was published in a German paper of Chicago, Der Westen, in January 1884." No such publication was found among the Matthews Papers, nor in the search of the files of Der Westen *by Robert Poor (correspondence, 4 August 1983), but it seems probable that this manuscript is the original draft. Barthelmess' account is of particular significance because it is one of the few written descriptions of the initiation of women and children and of Fringed Mouth of the Water Holy Person Impersonator (also see Faris this volume).*

(Ed. note: *This typewritten account was copied from the original handwritten manuscript. Unclear words have been noted. The Navajo orthography is Barthelmess'.)*

YEBITCAI DANCE SERGEANT BARTHELMESS'S DESCRIPTION JAN. 1884

Among all dances in use among the Navajoes the 'Yeibitschai-cha-tchal' takes a first [unclear word] if not the first rank. [The Nightway is frequently called the Yé'ii Bicheii, referring to the Grandfather of the Yé'ii, who appears in the ceremony as a masked impersonator]. It unites with a religious medicine signification a thanksgiving for past harvests and prayers for abundant yields in the coming year. To the stranger ignorant of the medicine principles belonging to the dance, the thought would never occur that a sick man has a part in it [unreadable remark in parens] when and where this part in it is considered during the dance I could not find out, perhaps later on I may discover it when I shall have penetrated further into the mysteries of the dance. To describe with full justice this dance requires an exact knowledge of the customs and mythology of the Navajoes. A part of the mythology collected by Dr. Matthews I am well acquainted with, it was published some time ago in *Der Westen* [Barthelmess is no doubt referring to "A Part of the Navajo's Mythology," *American Antiquarian* 5: 207–24, 1883. A German translation of this was published in *Der Westen* 10/14/1883.] The Navajoes have not a very clear idea of their origin and the meaning of the Yeibetchai. From all I learned about the dance no two accounts were alike or agreed with what I saw. This much I know, he (I call *Yeibetchai* he because he is personified as a man in the dance) lives in the rocks of the Cañon de Chelly, and every one who sees him becomes blind, it seems to them they are enchanted. How to guard against this enchantment forms a part of the dance, and every Navajo undergoes it—three times in order not to be blinded by the *Yeibetchai.* I was told that a child who had seen him was made blind. The child was too young to understand what had occurred, and no one knew for a long time how it had become blind, finally a clever medicine man discovered that it was the work of the Yeibetchai. The child was placed in a newly built-hogan and the effects of different medicines were tried. At last the proper medicine was found; a tree of stalk grew out of the child's breast—which was trimmed (or lopped) towards the four winds, this restored the child's sight. The narrator did not know what became of the tree. Like all medicine dances this one required nine days of preparation. I would gladly have shared in the whole of these preparations, but leave was refused and by high authority, and the intercession of Dr. Matthews was required to get me a two days leave of absence.

After guard-mount, I set forth on horseback with an interpreter and his better half. The dance was said to be seven miles off, as usual Charley the interpreter had lied, and the distance turned out to be twelve or fourteen miles. Hardly a mile from the post, an Indian came rushing by on a foaming horse, saying the Yeibetchai procession was coming. I had already heard he had called with his company at the different hogans to collect what he could to defray the expenses of the dance. This time he had extended his visits as far as Wingate—hoping to glean a rich harvest from the soldiers. This hope was inspired by Christmas, which is usually a great festival among soldiers in whose luxurious feasts the Navajoes frequently have a share; the real meaning of Christmas is not known to them, they think it simply a day of feasting and present giving.

My companions said Yeibetchai was all [the] same [as] Christmas, this gave me the necessary inkling. Soon the cavalcade came by lengthened into a procession; as I had seen it once before. I refrain from giving a description, particularly as the same thing occurs in the dance. This much I will say, the procession was exceedingly pretty. I dismounted to wait for them, as soon as they saw me they also dismounted, threw off their blankets and approached me. I could not recognize one of them; no word was spoken, but I could see by their actions that I was well known to them. I gave them a trifle of money and they were off like the wind. After we had ridden ten miles further on, my companion became uneasy, turned often in the saddle and looked back, suddenly he alighted at a fallen hut, when I asked the reason, he said it was bad luck to get into camp before the Yeibetchai. In spite of my entreaties, he was not to be moved to continue our journey. As the dancing place was not known to me, I had to wait. In about two hours the cavalcade passed us and we followed it slowly.

Though the dance was not to take place till the morrow, on our arrival we found every one busy preparing things. Everywhere were enclosures of pine boughs for camping, sheep were roasting on spits, corn was being ground into meal. In another place fire was burning over Al Kan, beloved of the Navajoes. The following is the way Al Kan is prepared. Corn is first roasted, then rubbed to meal on three stones lying close together. On the first stone it is coarsely broken, on the other two rubbed to fine flour. The bran is not separated; this mass is cooked (boiled?) and laid in a hole in the ground lined with husks, it is covered with more husks, then a layer of earth, over this a fire is lighted and kept up until every trace of moisture has disappeared. The cover is then taken off, the contents, which are perfectly dry, cut in small pieces are now ready for use. This food lasts for months, and is very nourishing.

I had scarcely unsaddled and sent the ponies to pasture, when those present went towards an enclosure. I followed them. About forty five women and children sat in a semi-circle, their faces covered, their feet stretched out before them, their hands palms up laid on their knees. The men and boys, twelve in number, crouched on their left and were with the exception of breechcloth, perfectly nude. The Yeibetchai came out of the medicine lodge with two companions, Betchai and "Bezai" the first Yeibetchai in administering medicine to the men, the latter to the women. Yeibetchai wore a high white mask made of buckskin, small holes were cut for the eyes and nose, where the nose should be was painted a corn stalk with two ears on it which extended to the brown, over the forehead hung two deer's tails. The back of the head was covered with an eagle's tail spread out, at the base of which was a bunch of hawk's feathers; from ear to ear was a roll of red wool, around his neck he wore a thick wreath of pine twigs. His other clothing was that worn by all Navajoes except that he wore his blanket like a cloak. His companions were nude except the breechcloth, wore blue masks and their bodies were smeared with some white color. A blanket was spread out in the middle of the semi-circle on which those who were to be consecrated must be placed. The word consecrate may not exactly correspond to this ceremony, but when I think of the seriousness and devotion displayed by those who took part in it, the whole thing recalled the time when I took my first communion. The men and boys came first, and each one at a time placed himself on the blanket. The Yeibetchai took white medicine out of a bag, made with it a white mark on their knees, then on the right and left breasts. They then turned round and received a mark on each shoulder, again they turned and received one on each outstretched arm. At every mark the Yeibetchai uttered a cry like that of an owl, his companion Beitchai answered the cry and rubbed the mark with a leaf of the Spanish bayonet, as these leaves were sharp and rough a bloody remembrance (reminder?) always remained behind. Now it was the women and children's turn, who still had their faces covered so they should not be blinded by the sight of the Yeibetchai. The first marked with medicine the soles of their feet, then both open hands, right breast and left shoulder blade, then both shoulders and the crowns of their heads. At each mark, he cried twice, his helper Bezai had two corn ears bound together with which he rubbed the marks giving two answering shrieks. The masculine gender meanwhile cowered in their former position, but had on their blankets as it began to snow heavily. Beizai here took off his mask (whose mask?) and let every one who was protected against enchantment look at Yeibetchai. As soon as this happened, they all covered their faces. The two masks with the bag containing the medicine were laid on the blanket formerly used by the men, on which at a signal all uncovered their faces and stared around; beginning at the left of the half circle one after another arose and sprinkled the two masks with yellow medicine (atcha de din) which each carried in a little bag. First they sprinkled the Yeibetchai in the following manner, first from forehead to mouth, then on the right side from below upwards, next on the left from below upwards, in the same way they sprinkled the other masks. The two masks went back to the semicircle and placed the [unclear word] behind it. Great caution was used and it was sharply seen to that the sprinkling should be in the prescribed manner. If a mistake was made they must begin again to sprinkle until the Yeibetchai who now officiated without a mask was satisfied. As soon as one got through he was congratulated by his relatives, his clothes restored and then he joined the crowd. The women and children sprinkled the masks as the men had done and then retired. The last named medicine, atcha de din, seems highly appreciated by the Navajoes, for it was sparingly used and after the ceremony was carefully collected by the Yeibetchai.

Now they all ran to the medicine lodge, I with the rest. In front of it the snow was cleared away and a buffalo robe spread out so that its head lay to the north, the tail to the south. I mention this fact because the medicine man went into a fury because it was laid out east and west, and it was hastily turned north and south. A girl of twelve now came out of the hut holding in both hands a flat basket (Tzaan) containing corn meal. Yeibetchai had resumed his mask and with two new companions approached the girl springing forwards and backwards, giving a call from time to time. One companion was named Tacha dlo Aschuan [Water Fringe Mouth], and wore a mask half blue, half yellow, his whole body was colored in these two colors in two parts. The lower part of the mask was trimmed with fur, in his right hand he held a gourd (a chalch) in his left a feathered stick (alch thich) which he waved as he sprang to and fro. The other companion was a Navajo dressed as a woman, he carried with both hands a basket of corn meal, just as the girl did who stood on the buffalo robe. As they approached the girl, Yeibetchai sprang at the girl as if to frighten her, stopped however before he reached the robe, turned and sprang back to Tucha dlo Ashhuan, who then went through the same performance and sprang back to the woman. This was repeated three other directions. Every time they jumped at the girl, she scattered meal towards them each time over her shoulders, then she drew back. Great care was taken in springing not to touch the buffalo robe. When this episode was over the performers withdrew into the lodge, the child taking the lead, the woman coming last. I would willingly have followed but feared to be repulsed and also thought the ceremonies were over. I learned later that the lodge was full of nude men who had taken part in the previously described ceremonies. As I have already remarked the Navajoes must undergo consecration three times in order to be protected from the glance of the Yeibetchai. I have not found out up to date if the consecrations are all alike, but will do so in time.

[The manuscript here contains six *x* marks and continues.] Our pipes were hardly lighted, each of those present had helped himself from our store, when the Yeibetchai's call attracted me again into the open air. He was going from hut to hut collecting as already described, offerings in a bag, most of these were handed to him by small children whom he then frightened with loud cries and chased into the hut. Every kind of thing savory and unsavory went into the bag. Here bread, there meat with gravy, tobacco, money and what not. This time I went back with him to the lodge, where medicine man no.2 (whom I described to my readers in my last article) took the bag from him and shook the contents on a sheep skin, wooly side down. Those present were all Indians who had taken an actual part in the dance or had aided in building the lodge (an extraordinary large one about forty feet in diameter) or who had assisted in the preceding ceremonies. These persons were they who on the following day prepared and decorated the masks. All present pressed forward and seized what each could get in his hands. When everything was eaten or divided, two large fires were lighted and dance rehearsals were held for the next evening's performance. I staid [sic] a couple of hours and then went to bed.

[Manuscript here contains six *x* marks and continues.] After breakfast I went to the medicine lodge where they were just eating, the food was prepared by the visitors and brought in by squaws. In a short time all was cleared away. No.2 began to sing and the others set to work singing with him to paint the masks and make medicine. The latter cannot be used again in this dance but will be used in another Yeibetchai [Barthlemess' transcription of Navajo word not readable] where it will be employed in the nine day preparations. No.2 with the aid of an assistant made "Gledda", little pieces of wood about the size of a child's finger, which were pierced. Into this opening the sunbeams are concentrated by a piece of glass and sealed up in it with yellow medicine, acha de din. The little sticks were then laid in a basket full of corn meal. From time to time No.2 went to the groups who were painting the masks and instructed them in their work. I brought my camera and tried to photograph them, but they opposed it so strongly I was forced to give it up. I have already described the Yeibetchai mask, it therefore needs no further mention. The next most interesting masks were those of Nalie-nes-Channie [Naayéé' Neizghání: Monster Slayer] and Tho-ba-des-tchine [Tóbájíshchíní: Born for Water], the two brothers who according to the mythology killed the giants and demons who did so much evil to the Navajoes. Nalie-des-Channie was a completely black mask which had tiny mussel shells fastened near the eyes and mouth. Tho-ba-des-tchine's mask was red and was strewed over with small stars, near the eyes and mouth little mussel shells were also fastened and each one surrounded by a black half oval with a white border. I was sorry not to see these two masks in use, for they were used the evening before my arrival and were newly painted for the next Yeibetchai-cha-tchal. Other interesting masks were the Na-es-gite [Hump Back?] and the Tucha-dlo-Aschaa [Land Fringe Mouth]. The Na-es-gite was a blue with three cornered eyes and four corner mouth, had a crown made of a basket and over it two blue and white horns, on the edge of the crown were little red plumes [unclear word] who look like the tail feathers of the red bird. Tucha-dlo-Aschaa's mask was not remarkable, the face was divided in two parts one blue the other red, it also had the before mentioned crown but under it arose three eagle's feathers where the horns were in the other mask. Besides these there were six Yeibeka's and six Yeibead masks (everything that refers to the male or female sex is called by the Navajo beka or bead. A woman is a bead, a mare a horse-bead, a ram a sheep-beka). Every thing with Yei before it signifies something supernatural, as for instance Yeibetchai or Yeitzo. Who these Yeibekas and Yeibeads were and what part they play in the mythology I could not learn. The Yeibeka masks were blue with two eagle feathers on the left side, they wore wreaths of juniper twigs around their necks. The Bead masks were also blue and had on the sides white zigzag Stripes, were open behind so that the hair could hang free, on the lower edge hung a strip of red cloth which in some was ornamented with bead work. This work took nearly all day, all day the singing went on except when they were eating. The true Yeibetchai song was not sung in the lodge, but was heard in every nook and corner of the vicinity.

I tried several times to use my camera without success. If I found a suitable group they either refused to be photographed or asked such a monstrous price that I gave it up. Finally Mariana, the war chief offered to sit for two dollars. I accepted the offer and got an excellent picture. Then I photographed the hogan in which I was camping with the owners for another two dollars.

[Manuscript here contains six *x* marks and continues.] About seven o'clock in the evening the true dance began. It was opened with the same ceremonies that I described on the preceding day, but Yeibetchai was accompanied by two other demons, Tacha-dlo-Aschaa and Naestciti wore the mask with the horns, was wrapped in deer skin, and he had a row of feathers bound to his back. In both hands he carried a staff about three feet long. Again they rushed at the same girl who had already performed on the previous days and back again. Naestciti roared all the time. When the four points of the compass had been roared on and jumped at, the three retired to an enclosure, which was built a few hundred feet from the medicine lodge. The girl however went into the lodge. The call of the Yeibetchai resounded and the dancers led by no.2 made their appearance. The dancers consisted of six Yeibekas and six yeibeads who wore the masks I have already described, and were with the exception of the scarfs entirely naked. The whole body was smeared with white consisting of white clay and water, behind a fox skin was fastened to the scarf. Both of their wrists were decorated with feathers and silk ribbons, and each wore a silver belt. The Yeibekas had in the right hand a gourd full of small stones which they shook in the dance. In the left hand which was fastened by a string to the masks, probably to keep them from being moved, they held juniper twigs. The Beka wore juniper wreaths around their necks to represent hair. The Beads let their hair hang down their backs. These Beads were represented by men and boys. I was told that when there were women who understand the dances these were preferred. In the 24th repetition of the dance a real woman appears who dances with them the rest of the evening. The Beads carried juniper boughs in each hand. The Bekas had two eagle feathers fastened to their stockings, the Beads had none. On the opening of the dance all the dancers were led by no.2. They marched one behind the other in the following order: 1st no.2 Yeibetchai, the Bekas and Beads in such a way that a Bead was between Bekas. Last came the themselves into a line of their own on the right, and danced and sang with them, in certain passages when the music was soft the first Bead took the arm of the first Beka and danced forward and backward through the middle. The third time arrived at the lower end they loosened their arms and took the lowest place. The second pair did the same and so on till they had their former places; when the first pair again gave each other their arms and went the middle. All the others did the same and pressed closely together left the dance place. A little bit away they made a halt and took off their masks to refresh themselves. This performance resembles closely the well known Virginia reel. The Yeibetchai did not dance himself but jumped around the dancers, and sometimes jumped after those who went down the middle. On the second performance the dance was led by Yeibetchai and No.2 was not there. The file closer this time was Tonelili the bayadso. The girl this time came by herself and strewed her meal as before described, during the course of the dance. Tonelili's mask I have already mentioned. His other clothes were like those of the ordinary Navajo, and like Yeibetchai he had a sack made out of fawn skin. He tried by frantic jumps to amuse the bystanders; when the dancers retired he remained alone on the ground. First he tried to collect some presents, as this was unsuccessful he let his bag fall and jumped back again to hunt for it; and then he behaved as I have seen other Indians do who track game to their lairs. He made marks in the sand with two fingers which represented tracks made by game, the bag represented the game. Then he threw dust in the air to prognosticate the wind. When he got to the windward and where he had approached close enough to spring on his booty, he killed it by kicking it on the head. The performance though an imitation was heartily laughed at by the spectators, and was a faithful representation of the slyness and endurance which Indians employ in hunting. The carrying away of the bag gave great amusement for Toninili pretended to make great exertion. He often broke down with his burden before he finally succeeded in picking himself up and getting away. The different parts of the dance (I counted 48 only) were almost alike. When twelve had occurred there was a change of personnel. Every time new dancers appeared, they were led out and besprinkled by No.2; while in the intermediate dances the girl alone did the sprinkling. In two performances both sides were sprinkled by the girl. It was not done among the dancers, but [she] went up one side and down the other. Sometimes the dancers came without Yeibetchai and Thonenile, or they came after the dance had already begun. I did not know if this was the rule or only an accident. In all the figures of the dance the melody of the song remained the same, but I distinguished the words of ten different songs. During them there were various pauses in which the dancers paused on one leg. Frequently the word 'huppe' occurred. I could not get the meaning of it from anyone present. At first I followed the proceedings with great interest; but as it became late without any change, I lost my interest in the dance. My notes became smaller and smaller until I only wrote down the number of the performances.

I got on the track of one fact, of which I knew nothing until this date, which enlightened me on much that had hitherto been a riddle. I had remarked many times that when the Navajoes returned from a dance they related many stories a la Cazenova [*sic*] and squaws were mentioned whose husbands were present. As soon as there was a change of performers, those who were released made a fire near the squaws, soon one of the squaws retired from the others and went into the bushes on one side where she was followed by a dancer. The non-dancers also made these excursions. I watched a squaw who whispered something in her husband's ear. He got up and went into the bushes where I had shortly before seen a squaw disappear. She herself went in another direction, and was followed by a dancer. Nobody seemed to trouble themselves about these proceedings, and looked on it as a self-evident thing. In a five year's stay among the Apaches, I lost many of my romantic ideas about Indians, but I still had some about the Navajoes. After this occurrence they became fully realistic. I was disgusted and went to my hogan where worse awaited me. I had observed that the squaw of my host was among those who went several times 'into the bushes', finally I lost sight of her. I am satisfied that at the beginning of the dance she had not a cent, but when I came back to the hogan, she had a whole handful of silver dollars. She was playing cards with her husband by the firelight; he finally won from her evenings gains (?) after which they went to sleep. I too stretched myself under my blanket and slept until day break (about 4 A.M.). It was hardly dawn when my interpreter and his squaw waked me. I had paid him in advance but had not seen him the day before, or in fact at all during the dance. He was intoxicated with bad liquor and extremely desirous to tell me his evening adventures and his luck in love. He did not seem to pay the slightest attention to his own squaw. To judge from her appearance she was better off than he. I was raging and for want of a better missile threw my boot at his head and he departed.

(Manuscript here contains six *x* marks and continues.) The dance place where a few hours before hundreds of Navajoes had been sporting was entirely deserted, except by a few stragglers who had too much schnapps and were now dizzily hunting their ponies. A sharp three hours ride brought me to Fort Wingate.

8. Natural Naturalists

(Manuscript #421 of Matthews' paper read before the Philosophical Society of Washington, 25 October 1884; typed copy reproduced in Poor 1975:131–39)

Matthews' papers contain two manuscripts of this lecture (Guide:62, Manuscript #421, 16 pp.; and a shorter version #320, 10 pp.; for published abstracts of this lecture, see 1885a in Matthews' bibliography). Since Matthews was on a field trip to New Mexico in October of 1884, the paper was read for him by his colleague John S. Billings of the Army Medical Museum.

Matthews had collected data on ethnobotany during his early field work on Navajo vocabulary. Army medical personnel at frontier posts were expected to keep record of local flora and fauna, and medicinal plants would have been of special interest to him. He published a technical botanical article on "Navajo Plant Names" (1886e), and the 1884 lecture was a more informal presentation of some of the same material. This study of Navajo plants must have been among the earliest scientific studies of native ethnobotany. In 1941 Wyman and Harris comment that the "only considerable lists of Navajo names for plants, together with species identifications" were in Matthews' paper and in the work of the Franciscan Fathers at St. Michaels, Arizona (see Franciscan Fathers 1910).

In both of his papers Matthews emphasizes the accuracy of Navajo observation of the flora of their environment and the principles of classification and generalization used in their naming practices. Especially in this lecture he makes clear his respect for Navajo intellectual abilities and takes this opportunity to refute popular misconceptions of the time about the limitations of "savage" intelligence.

(Ed. note: *Poor's typescript of this manuscript has been edited for unclear spelling by reference to Matthews' published paper on the same subject, 1886e, and Poor's additions of proper names and dates have been put in brackets.)*

For us, "the heirs of all the ages," whose accumulated heritage of knowledge is stored in books, and who bequeathe this heritage from generation to generation through the medium of written characters, it is difficult to understand that a people having no knowledge of letters may accumulate and transmit to posterity a considerable amount of learning through the simple means of object teaching and oral instruction. We are accustomed to speak of an illiterate people as an uneducated people; but on close acquaintance with savage tribes we will find them in possession of a store of accumulated and inherited knowledge, a degree of education for their youth which at first we could not conceive to exist.

It is not a difficult matter for us to suppose that a savage may be well versed in knowledge and in arts which have a direct bearing on the sustenance of his individual life and the preservation of his kind under his own peculiar environment; that, when young, he should seek to learn from his elders the habits of various game animals, and the best mode of using this knowledge for the destruction of such animals; that as he grows older he should endeavor to increase his knowledge by personal experience and observation and that in time he should, through the natural sentiments of parental interest seek to impart his store of information to his offspring. But it is not easy to understand that he should with an equal care, acquire, transmit and disseminate information about creatures which he does not eat and which are of no economic use to him. If he is a member of a small and weak tribe, speaking a tongue which has no neighboring kindred we can readily comprehend why he should learn the language of the Alien races that surround him and, in time rival a [Giuseppe Gasparo] Mezzofauti in his linguistic attainments. But a practical reason for his burdening the mind and studying with assiduous care a host of rude myths, legends and songs is not so obvious.

It is a prevalent conception of savage life that the mind and body are only active when urged by physical necessity: that when not engaged in procuring inferior food, raiment, and a low degree of comfort, or in repelling the attacks of enemies the hours of the savage are spent in absolute idleness or in silly and vicious pastimes and meaningless pagan ceremonies. It is a prevalent conception of civilized life, that to it alone belongs the taste for arts and studies which have no immediate practical returns, and which merely embellish our existence or afford an outlet for an energy which will not be diverted into less worthy channels. That such conceptions are incorrect or correct only in a degree I trust I may convince some of my doubting hearers, if such I have, this evening.

"The horseleech hath two daughters crying give! give!" The horseleeches [*sic*] daughter begging for wisdom has cried in the heart of man since the infancy of the race. The human mind has ever sought two things, facts and the explanation of facts. Unfortunately from the beginning, in the latter quest it has been too easily satisfied with myth. It has asked for bread and it has been given a stone. Dissatisfaction with myth is not a thing that separates the civilized man from the savage, the white man from the red, it is, for the multitude, the dividing line between the very day in which we live and all the eternal past.

Whether it was our physical necessities or our inborn curiosity which first directed our race to the observation and investigation of all our surroundings it would be difficult to say. The latest writer on comparative psychology, Dr. [George John] Romanes, in giving a list of the products of emotional development, in the order of their appearance places curiosity high on the list. And, whether we agree or disagree with such formal classifications as he presents, we must admit that curiosity is an important characteristic of the lower animals. In the infant, curiosity is developed at the tenderest age. If in the history of our society it was not coeval with the manifestations of physical wants, it must have exerted, at a very early day, a great influence on the thoughts and acts of man. In the majority of modern scientific investigations, curiosity, no doubt, took the initiative, many branches of knowledge were well established and had grown to respectable proportions before their practical applications were thought of. We have always found among our ranks those who were willing to work without asking the question *Qui Bono?* We have had the vikings of science who, launched on unknown seas, let the winds drift them where they would, confident that they would land only to conquer. While giving our innate curiosity its due credit for the advancement of knowledge, we must not forget that, a science once recognized finds many notaries who seek chiefly distinction and approbation, while later on, when its practical applications have been discovered there are the further accessions to its ranks of those who desire only its substantial rewards.

What, amid all his varied surroundings, when the cravings of hunger and thirst were relieved, first attracted the attention of the investigating man we can only conjecture. Our doctors of the solar myth tell us it was the alternation of day and night—the most prominent facts in meteorology. Perchance they are right, but be that as it may there is no doubt that the organic life around him—The animals so much like himself in all their attributes, the plants apparently endowed with only a different form of life,—all possessing according to his conception a spiritual essence such as he imagined himself to have—excited, in the beginning his curiosity, caused him to observe their manifestations of life and ponder on the phenomena he witnessed.

Savage man is on terms of peculiar confidence and intimacy with the lower animals,—a confidence and an intimacy which perhaps even an Audubon could not feel. No metaphysical or theological barriers separated him from them. All are endowed with a similar soul. All have had a similar past and will have a similar eternal future. Immortality is, alike, the lot of all. The brutes are the kindred and friends of men. In the mythic days gone by they had the gift of language, they held council, waged war and did, all things even, as men did them. In many tribes the beasts are supposed to be the ancestors of men. In nearly all they receive a degree of worship. When the ghost returns from the other world, he assumes an animal form. When man was in his ignorance and infancy and struggled for existence with the demons, the lower animals were ever his friends. The coyote gave him counsel; the winged birds and insects were his messengers; the gopher dug the hole in which he might hide; the squirrel climbed the tree to spy for him; the horned toad lent him his scaly cap that he might conceal himself. And at a later day there was not such a wide difference between the one and the other as between civilized man and the brute. The coyote was more cunning than the Indian. The eagle flew where man could not follow, the deer was fleeter, the bear stronger, the beaver built a better house and felled a tree that the stone axe could not sever. Many had the power of killing man, he was but a weak combatant against them. The savage was not assured of his position as the Lord of Creation,—he never asserted it.

This feeling of community and confidence, this sense of equality with the lower animals, no doubt, was an important factor in directing the attention of man to the study of animated nature. The necessities of life constitute another easily recognized factor; but yet another is the fact that the savage having few arts and artificial interests his mind laid hold of that which was within its reach. There being little else to engage his attention he contemplated nature. Then again his out-door life, rendered nonetheless pleasant by contrast with the discomforts of his lodge, brought him in contact with the animal world and gave him opportunities for observation.

Everywhere in Indian folk-lore and in Indian Song the lower animals are characters of the greatest interest, and wherever they appear they always present themselves in proper shape. True they speak in the language of man and exhibit the possession of human reason, but apart from this their words and actions do no violence to the facts of natural history, on the contrary the Indian tales and songs show a close and discriminating study of nature on the part of the authors. The subject of a large part of Indian myths is the distinctive attributes and peculiarities of animals and the imaginary causation of these attributes. On one occasion, in order that he might reach home ere the sun rose the wood-rat had to run so far and so fast that he blistered the soles of his feet and this accounts for the callosities we see on the feet of the rat now. The black bear on the same occasion, running to his lair was belated; the rays of the rising sun shone on the tips of his hairs and thus it is that the coat of the bear is tipped with hairs of a ruddy hue. The badger, pioneer of the new race seeking to reach the surface of this world from below, emerged at the bottom of a lake, his feet were blackened with the mud, and therefore the feet of the badger are black to this day. There are like myths that seek to explain why a rabbit has a black spot on his neck, why the coyote has a black muzzle, why he buries his food, why the crow has a harsh voice, why the woodpecker has a red crest, why the mourning dove has its peculiar note, and thousands more of a similar character. My friend Mr. Cushing has given me a Havasupai myth which shows that this tribe have noted all the phases in the development of the cicada.

The Indian Adam did not lazily wait for the Lord to drive all the beasts of the field before him in order that he might give a name unto each according to its kind. He went forth into forest and desert and sought them in their homes. Knowing all the animals around him and observing their special characteristics he perhaps almost unconsciously, or unpremeditatedly found himself giving to each a name descriptive of something notable in their appearance or habits. I have never yet failed to get from an Indian a good and satisfactory name for any species of mammal, bird or reptile inhabiting his country and I have rarely failed to get a name for an insect which possessed any peculiarity of appearance. True all could not give me a name; but I never failed to find some old men or women who could. On entering a name, however, great care had always to be exercised not only that a wrong appelation might not be given me by the ignorant; but that a term might not be coined on the spur of the moment by some cunning youngster to satisfy my curiosity. The opinions of several had to be obtained and when possible the etymology and significance of the names.

As a general rule, when people find a new animal in a new land, if we can trace no resemblance between it and any animal with which we are familiar we adopt some paraphrase of the aboriginal name; but if we trace the slightest resemblance between it and some animal we formerly knew we bestow on it the name of the latter. Thus we have, the European names of partridge, pheasant, robin, buffalo, etc. transferred to totally different species on this continent. The Indian, on the contrary invents a name of his own for an exotic. The cat becomes round-face, round eyes, or the striped one. The horse is known as the strong, domestic animal or the wonderful domestic animal. The domestic cock is the crower and when, a resemblance is traced between the stranger and some old acquaintance of the animal kingdome, if the name of the latter is given to the former, they are careful to add some adjective which establishes a distinction. Thus we find in the American Bison, the "White-man's cow," and in the hog the "White-man's bear."

There is a chip from somebody's workshop which has done service to scientific men for many years. Who the wiseacre was that first set it floating down the stream of scientific literature I know not; but from time to time it comes to the surface in the dead eddy of some book makers pool. The last time I saw it (in Latham's Varieties of man) it appeared in this shape "The paucity of general terms.—What shall we say of a language where a term sufficiently *general* to denote an *oak tree* is exceptional, a language where the *white-oak* has one *specific name,* the *black-oak* another, the *red-oak* a third and so? yet such is the case with the Choctah. In another work Peschel's *Races of Man* [1876] it comes to light in this form: "A comparison of the languages of scantily developed races shows that the perception of specific differences arose much earlier than the recognition of generic characters." Having cited the Tasmanian language the author adds, "The same may be said of the North American Indians for in the Choctah language while there are names for white, red and black oak, there is none for the genus oak. Now according to my experience the Indian is just as good a generalizer and classifier as his caucasian brother and if he happens to be a better specializer than the unscientific white man, it is merely where he is a better observer. I might bring forward a thousand instances to prove this assertion had I the time tonight, but in a moment I will present some cases that will, I think make my position clear.

I have said that the Indians could name for me every mammal and bird in their country. How many well educated Caucasians even among those who live in the country and are fond of the chase yet who have not made a special study of zoology with the aid of books and specimens, can do this? Not one in a thousand I venture to assert. How many well educated white people, of this class, fond of roaming in the fields, of culling wild flowers and fostering cultivated plants; but who have not made a special study of botany by means of books and specimens, can name for you one wild plant in ten that they see every year of their lives. Not, I again venture to estimate one man in a thousand. Yet among intelligent adult Navajos I found very few who would fail once in ten times to tell the name and describe the habitat and properties of one of the wild plants of his country.

The extent of their plant-lore has been a cause of special surprise to me. Take as an instance the grasses. I have never seen an unbotanical white man, no matter if he was a stock-man or a farmer, or what his occupation or what his advantages for empirical study had been that could name and determine correctly half a dozen different wild grasses. Indeed I have seen numbers of excellent amateurs in botany who could do no better. I will tell you something which may serve to support this statement. Dr. [Asa] Gray has been assiduous in collecting popular names for plants and perhaps none of any extended use are omitted in his works yet he does not furnish ordinary English names for over one third the species of native grasses and some of these few names bear evidence of having been in part coined by the author, while others are repeated for widely different species. In New Mexico, I never found a non-scientific white man who could distinguish a single species of native grass. You will hear stock-men and travellers talk wisely of the virtues of Gama grass and gramma grass, not certain in their minds which is right. In the eighth issue of the fifth edition (not dated) of that standard work, "Grays Manual of Botany"—the latest issue I have seen—the name, gramma-grass, does not appear; but we find the term gramma-grass applied to the course broad-leaved tripsacum dactyloides which is found only in very moist soil in the older states, is not noted as observed west of Illinois and is quite unknown in the Arid Region of our continent. In order to simplify our discussion we will take it for granted that this trivial name is properly applied by Professor Gray, that there is no such thing as gama grass in New Mexico or elsewhere in the Rocky Mountain region and that when the frontiersman speaks of gama it is merely a slip of the tongue. Then we will endeavor to discover what this valuable and much lauded gramma-grass is. Mr. Sereno Watson, Professor Gray's assistant in the herbarium of Harvard College, tells us in the second volume of the "Botany of California" that all the species of the genus Bouteloua are collectively called gramma-grass; but his principal, Professor Gray assures us that the genus Bouteloua is the "Muskit" (*sic*) [Mesquit?] grass. Col. Cremony in his "Life Among the Apache" [1868] devotes several pages to describing gramma and ventures the extraordinary assertion that it has no stem bearing seed or flower. This statement shows not only how little this intrepid soldier knew of any grass; but that he could not have had *Bouteloua* in his mind when he wrote for the culms and spikes of this genus are very conspicuous. Another author, I think it is [Josiah] Gregg in his "Commerce of the praries" [1844] speaks of gramma as covering moist meadows and river-bottoms. Since *Bouteloua* has its home on the dry upland, this author also differs from Professor Watson. Other travellers, whose works I have not now the time or facilities for quoting are equally at variance as to what constitutes gramma-grass. I have induced several different gramma-grass specialists to point out their favorite plant to me and never more than two agreed on the same species.

In striking contrast with this wide-spread popular ignorance of the *Gramineae* is the knowledge of the Navajo Indians. Among them I failed in no instance to get a name for every species of this difficult family which I presented for their examination—a name with an obvious significance. Not only this; but I have had my attention called by them to species which, without their timely promptings, I would have overlooked.

I would take many pages to recount all the facts relative to the properties of plants I obtained from this people, but to illustrate the nature of their observations I will recount two instances. *Comandra pallida* is a small, low plant of unattractive appearance. It is rare in the Navajo Country, growing sparsely on the mountains among grasses and underwood [*sic*] which almost hide it from sight. An unpracticed eye might pass by this plant a hundred times without observing it. I once took a specimen of this Comandra to an Indian who was well versed in his aboriginal plant-lore, little supposing, however, that he knew anything of such an obscure rare and useless object. Without taking it into his hand or honoring it with more than a glance, he named it. I expressed some doubt of his knowledge when he replied, "I know it well, it has a blue root." Feeling now positive that he was wrong I exhibited the root which was a brilliant white. Without deigning a word in reply he took the specimen from my hand, scraped the root stock with his thumb-nail, handed it back to me and bade me observe it for a moment. In a few seconds to my great surprise, the denuded root changed from white to a delicate cerulean tint. He added that the plant was not of the slightest use to the Navajos.

On another occasion I met an Indian carrying in the fold of his blanket some specimens of the Pectis angustifolia, a plant which, on the dry mesas of New Mexico does not attain a height of more than two inches; but it has a delightful odor, like that of lemon verbena, and its infusion is used by the Navajos as a carminative. Their attention, therefore, has been drawn to it. The name which the Indian applied to this plant was so peculiar, signifying a breeze blowing through a rock, that I made no delay in getting a full explanation from him. He led me off a couple of miles to the top of an arid mesa where the plant grew fresh, here he picked up a piece of sedimentary sandstone about a foot square and three inches thick and held it up to my nose saying "Do you smell anything on that stone?" Of course the dry hard sandstone was unodorous. He then rubbed a little of the fragrant Pectis on one of the broad surfaces of the stone and applied the opposite surface to my nostrils. Three seconds had not elapsed from the time the plant was rubbed on until I was told to smell, yet the agreeable odor was at once distinctly perceptible through the rock. Later it could be detected in all parts of the petrous fragment but at first it was perceived only at a point directly opposite the point of application. He then repeated the experiment on a large slab of nearly two feet thick. The results were similar although the length of time which the highly volatile odor of the *pectis* took to penetrate the large rock was greater. "The fragrance," he said, "goes through the rock as if blown by the wind. Hence we call it *tse' ga' niltci*, the breeze through the rock."

The instances of their ability to generalize and classify in the vegetable kingdom are, literally, too numerous to be mentioned; but I must give my hearers a few. There are four kinds of Juniper growing on the Zuni Mountains, each has its appropriate name, yet the generic name for juniper, *Kas*, appears in all. As the Choctaw names for the oak seems to have particularly arrested the attention of the writers whom I have quoted, I must indicate how the Navajos have studied the genus Quercus. I observed but one species the Quercus Gambellii, in the region to which my observations were limited; but, in addition to the typical species there are two varieties, both of which are defined in the botanical reports of that locality. The Navajos apply to all, a common name, but when necessary the two varieties were distinguished from the typical species by the addition of qualifying words. The commonest kind of sunflower *helianthus annuus* bears the name of indigili. As with our scientific botanists the sunflower is taken as a type or foundation genus for a large number of plants which are included by us in the sub-order Heliontidae. So in the Navajo language we have names which signify tall sunflower, slender sunflower, rough sunflower, stinking sunflower, etc. It is easy to credit the existence among these Indians of such knowledge of a class of plants so rank and showy as the sunflower family; but it is difficult to realize that in the *Chenopodiaceae* or goose-foot family their observing faculties have guided them as safely. To this family belongs wormseed spinach, and the "lamb's-quarter" which is so eagerly sought as a pot-herb in western rural districts where cultivated greens are scarce in the spring. These constitute an unattractive family with an inflorescence so obscure that I have heard white people describe lambs-quarter as a plant without a blossom. In the section of the Navajo country where I resided there are three species of Chenopodium, so much alike that the whites do not differentiate them but call them all unqualifiedly *lamb's quarter* and there is another, so little like its congeners in its macroscopic characters that none but the scientific eye could trace the relationship. This is the Chenopodium cornutum. When burned it emits a fine aromatic odor; in autumn the whole plant changes to a fire rose-madder tint, and, as it grows abundantly, it lends a gorgeous coloring, in October, to the slopes of the Zuni Mountains. This plant too the Navajo class with perfect botanical propriety along with the *Chenopodiums*. Again, the ordinary pigweed or *Amaranthus retroflexus* is placed into the same category, yet the intimate relations of this plant to the Chenopodiums is among ourselves, I think, not known outside of the scientific circles. Upon what characters the Navajo have traced an affinity between these plants, I have not discovered; but some common character they undoubtedly have found, for to all are applied the name *tlo' táhi* while to all except *Chenopodium Fremonti,* which is the type species, is applied some limiting adjective, answering the same purpose in defining species as our specific names.

But it must not be supposed that in all cases we find the Navajo classification coincide so well with that of the most advanced scientists of the 19th Century. The instances I have cited show that these Indians study nature far more carefully than do the unscientific among ourselves; and that in some remarkable instances their observations agree with those of our trained naturalists. We classify according to one set of characters, The Indian according to another; therefore, at times, the two must vary widely. I will give a few cases in illustration of this: If an animal is observed to eat or frequent any particular plant, the latter is called the corn or food of that animal; thus we find names which we may translate butterfly corn, beetle's corn, coyote's corn, ant's corn, deer's corn, etc. Now some animals frequent or feed on more than one kind of plant and from this circumstance a similar name may be given to species which we place in widely different families. Thus Collomia aggregata, Pentstemon barbalus and Castilleja minor, three plants representing two very different families, are all known as humming-bird's corn. Again many plants are named for their supposed medicinal virtues. So, when herbs having no intimate relationship according to our classification, are employed in the treatment of the same disease they are apt to be designated by the same name, although qualifying terms may be added to distinguish them. The fact that they exude a milky juice unites the far removed species of Euphorbia and Asclepias.

But the time has arrived when I must close. If you will take my word for all I have related of my personal experience, I trust you will agree with me that I have described a people who are guided to the careful and discriminating study of nature by means of natural causes. In part to procure the necessaries of life, in part by innate inquisitiveness, by the natural interest which man feels in all his surroundings, but not by a desire to directly accumulate wealth, not by motives of ambition or an artificially stimulated emulation, not by means of a coercive education. In short, are they not natural naturalists?

9. *Paper on the Clan*

(Guide:62–63, Manuscript #358, abstract published as 1904b)

Sometime during the 1880s Matthews obtained Tall Chanter's version of the tribal creation myth (1897a) that concludes with a section giving an extended account of clan origins. This story of clan origins was first published separately, under the title "The Gentile System of Navajo Indians," in the Journal of American Folklore *(1890a). On two subsequent occasions Matthews discussed Navajo clans (or* gentes*) at meetings of the Anthropological Society of Washington. One was a program in 1890 that he and Bourke had arranged on the "gentile system" of the Navajos and Apaches (never published). The second was the paper here reproduced, which was read before the Anthropological Society of Washington on 29 November 1904, several months before Matthews' death.*

This paper seems to reveal something of Matthews' flexibility in dealing with social evolutionary ideas of the time. He says, in disagreement with Bourke, that he thinks it a mistake to apply "to all tribes a theory which seems to work well with one tribe or even many tribes," and he disagrees with Morgan on the formation of phratries.

Paper on the Clan for Tuesday Evg. Nov. 29, 1804 (*sic*)
of the Anthropological Society, Washington, D.C.
by Washington Matthews

I received the first notification of my selection to participate in this discussion so late that I felt I had not time to do justice to the subject and wrote, at once, declining to take a part; but on the following morning I got the card program in which my name appeared and I felt constrained to offer some remarks to the society, no matter how little I might be satisfied with them personally. They are at least correct in the statement of fact, if not elegant in form and if all too brief.

The title of our discussion is so worded that one might suppose each member was called on for a definition of "clan," but I cannot suppose that this is the intention. The paper of Dr. Thomas would seem from its title to cover this ground. I am called upon to speak of the Navaho.

I shall therefore make a few remarks on certain exogamic matriarchal hereditary groups among the Navaho—Remarks which may throw some light on the origin and nature of the Indian clan or gens.

I have obtained among the Navaho 51 names of clans, some of which are now extinct. And I have reason to believe that there are other clans, existent or extinct, whose names I have not discovered.

An elaborate legend, partly mythic and partly historic, is told, which accounts for the origin of these clans or for their adoption into the exceedingly composite Navaho nation. The evidence of the legend goes to show that they were originally for the most part local exogamous groups, simply settlements of Indians who were accustomed to seek wives in other settlements perhaps because the women of their own were too closely related to them.

But the legend is not our only evidence. The 51 names are mostly those of localities of tribes and bands. Some are names of springs and mountains; others of pueblos now in ruins and others of pueblos now inhabited; for instance, there is a clan of Zuni and a clan of Jemez.

Among the neighboring and allied Apache many of the clans have the same names as those of the Navaho and as Captain Bourke has shown, there are good reasons for believing that they originated in the same way.

Of tribes linguistically allied to the Navaho and Apache (i.e. Athapascan tribes) among the nearest, geographically, are those of the Siletz agency in Oregon. A few years ago their social organization was closely studied by the late Rev. J. Owen Dorsey. At that time they were (and perhaps they still are) collected on a reservation some distance from their original home on Rogue River. Yet they are now divided into a series of exogamous groups, each of which represents a different village in their old home and bears the name of that village. Here we have exogamous groups changed into clans or gentes within the memory of one generation.

The Navaho Origin Legend, to which I have referred, speaks of a large addition to the tribe, consisting of immigrants who came from the Pacific coast within a comparatively short period—within the last two or three centuries perhaps. These, when they came, were already divided into groups or clans. In a paper which I published in the *Journal of American Folk-Lore*, April–June 1890, I gave reasons for believing that these Indians had animal totems like those of our eastern tribes, and had originally totemic names. I have not time now to repeat all my arguments, so I refer you to this paper. But, in the course of time, I argued, that they gave their totemic names to localities where they sojourned and in turn, acquired from these places, local names in accordance with the prevailing custom of the Navaho. If I am correct in my conclusions, it would seem that the Navaho clans are not all of local origin.

Captain Bourke, in a paper published in connection with mine, in the same number of the Journal of American Folk Lore, argues forcibly, and almost conclusively in favor of the local origin of clans among the Apache; but he goes a step further and gives reasons for believing that such was the origin of the clans among all tribes. Here I do not agree with him. I think students make a mistake in applying to all tribes a theory which seems to work well with one tribe or even with many tribes.

As with other tribes, so among the Navahoes there are aggregations of clans, corresponding closely if not exactly to what Morgan defines as the phratry. Let us call them phratries. The Navaho phratry has no special name; but is usually known by the name of the most important component clan, and it seems not to be a very homogeneous organization. There are instances of clans having affinities with two different phratries. The legend mentions clans which in the course of time have changed their phratral affinities. Then there are what may be called sub-phratries; a clan may be more closely related to one group of clans in the phratry than to another group. Hence different authorities divide the tribe into different phratries. The number as given by different informants varies from 8 to 12 and some name independent clans which have no affinities. To marry within the phratry is as much forbidden as to marry within the clan and to marry within the father's clan or phratry is as bad as to marry within the mother's.

I said that I had found 51 names of clans; but this does not necessarily argue that there are 51 clans, for some have more than one name. A man whom I consider my best informant named but 43 clans in all.

Morgan, and others following him, maintain that the present clans, in tribes, are but divisions of parent clans which are now represented by the phratries; in other words that clans have come into existence by a process of segmentation. Some such segmentation seems to have taken place to a limited extent among the Navaho, but it is evident that in the majority of cases phratries were formed by the aggregation of clans, a process very different to that described by Morgan. The legend affords no abundant evidence of this; but if its testimony should be doubted we have other evidence on which to rely. We need have no doubt that clans derived from alien tribes and named from them are additions to the phratry from without. Morgan has found that among the tribes which he has studied, the phratry bears the name of one of its clans—that which is supposed to have been divided into the several component groups. The Navahoes, as I have before stated, give no formal names to a phratry yet they may refer to it by the name of one of its clans, usually the most ancient or most important one. It is easy to believe that this custom might in time lead to the permanent selection of a name for a phratry.

Series of Sandpainting Sketches

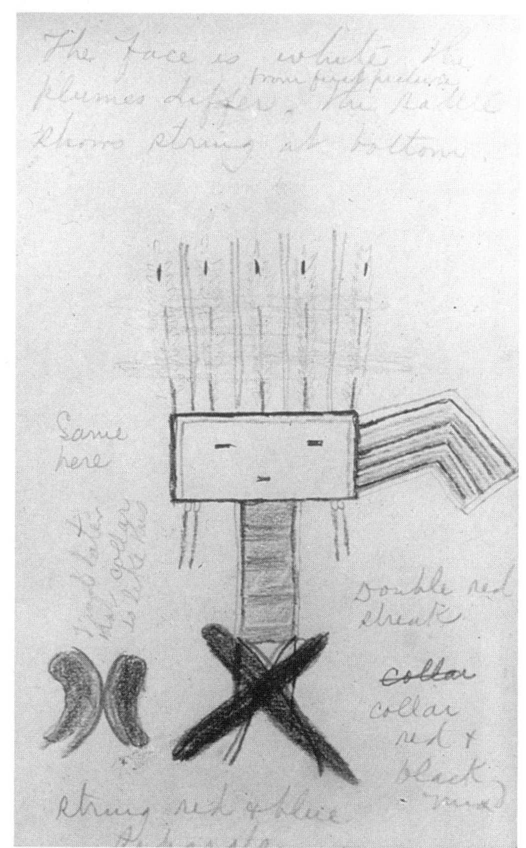

Sandpainting Detail,
Probably Mountain Chant
(Washington Matthews, Notebook 468, p. 19)

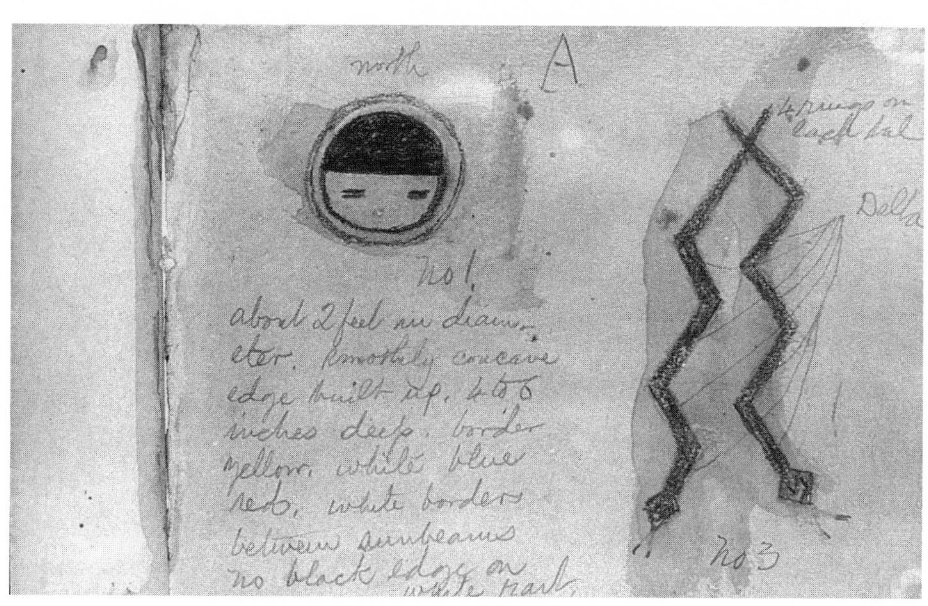

Sandpainting Sketch
(Washington Matthews, Notebook 469, p.3)

Yantcin of the western

dzil yantcin

white rings (3) about 1/4 in wide

Rings about an inch wide until after white was added

Mountain

the mountain about 14 inches in diam

Diagram of the central hole finished

The rays are of charcoal

Sandpainting Sketch, Mountain Chant

(Washington Matthews, Notebook 214)

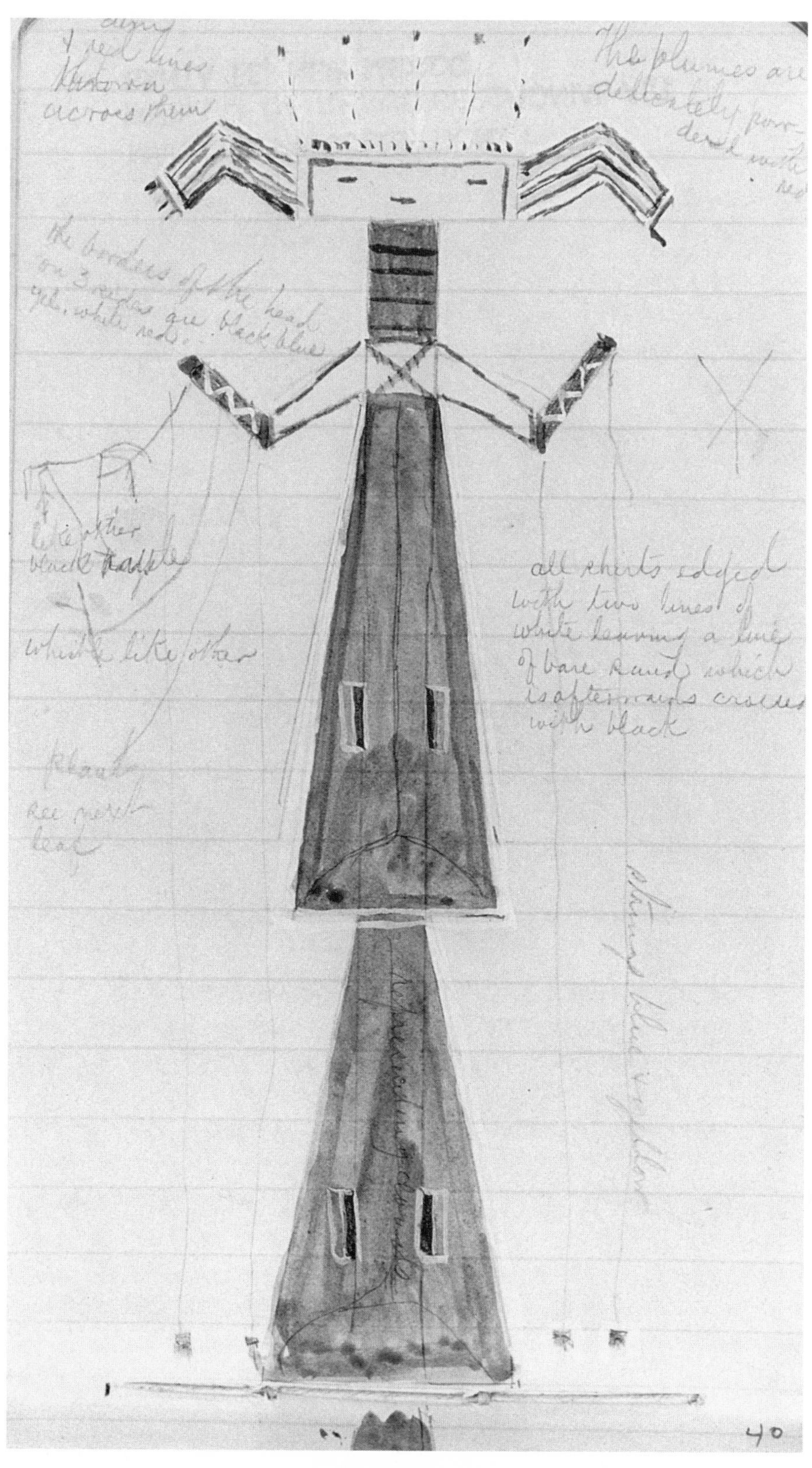

Sandpainting Sketch, "A Rain God," Mountain Chant
(Washington Matthews, Notebook 214, p.39)

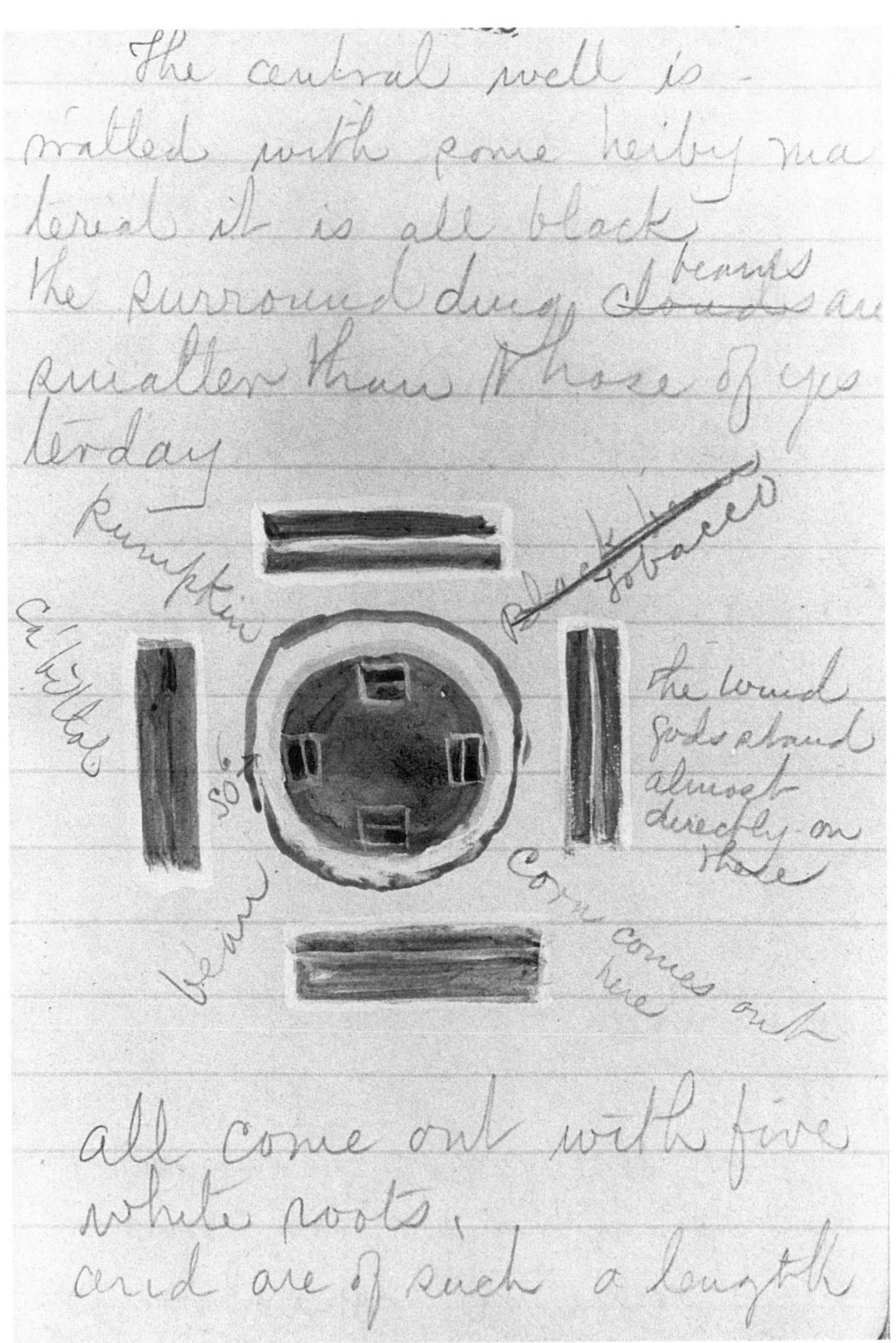
The central well is walled with some herby material it is all black
the surrounding ~~clouds~~ beans are smaller than those of yesterday

all come out with five white roots, and are of such a length

Sandpainting Sketch, Mountain Chant
(Washington Matthews, Notebook 214, p. 30)

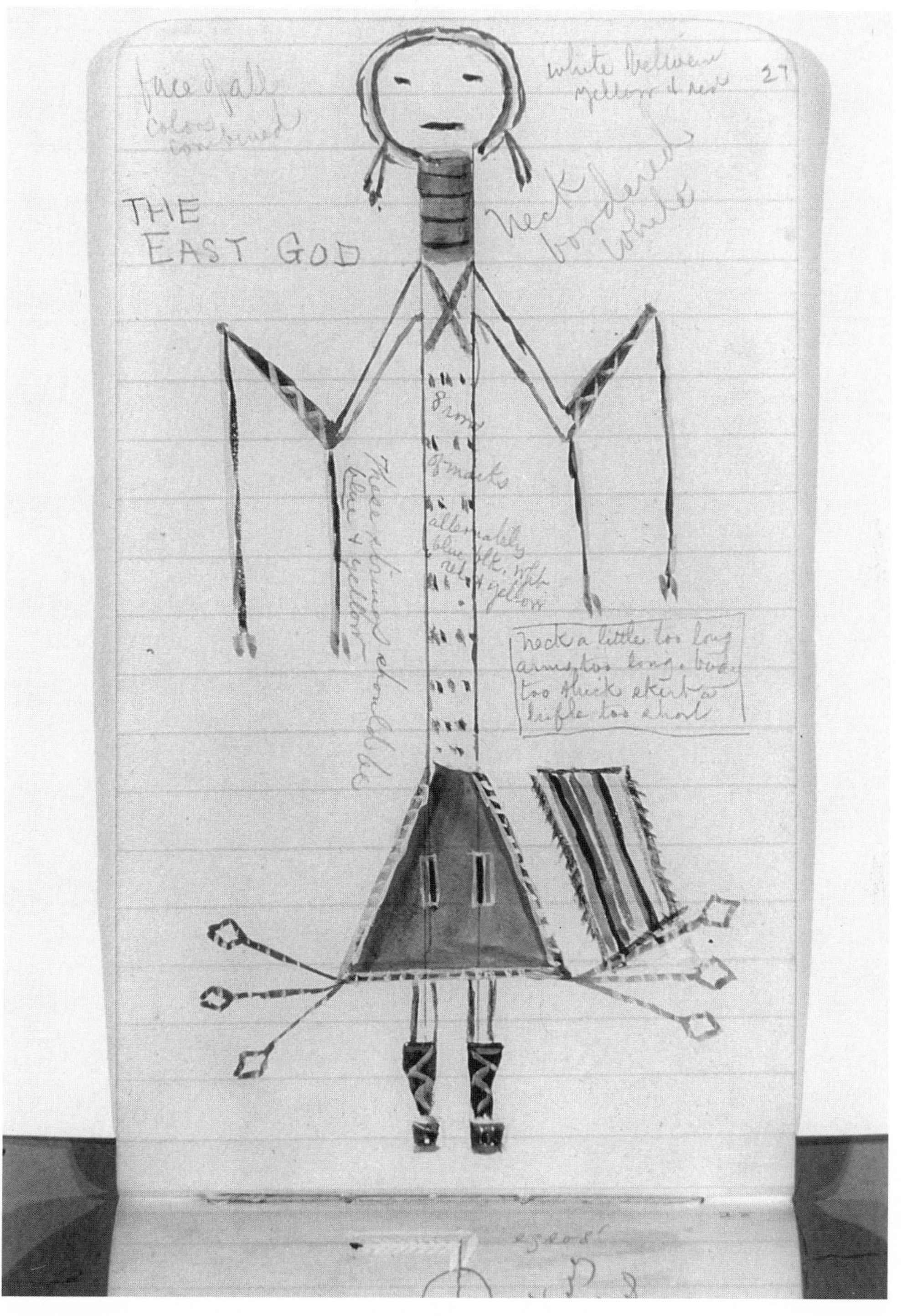

The East God

(From the Mountain Chant, notebook 214, p. 27; photograph by Herb Lotz)

Series of Mask Sketches

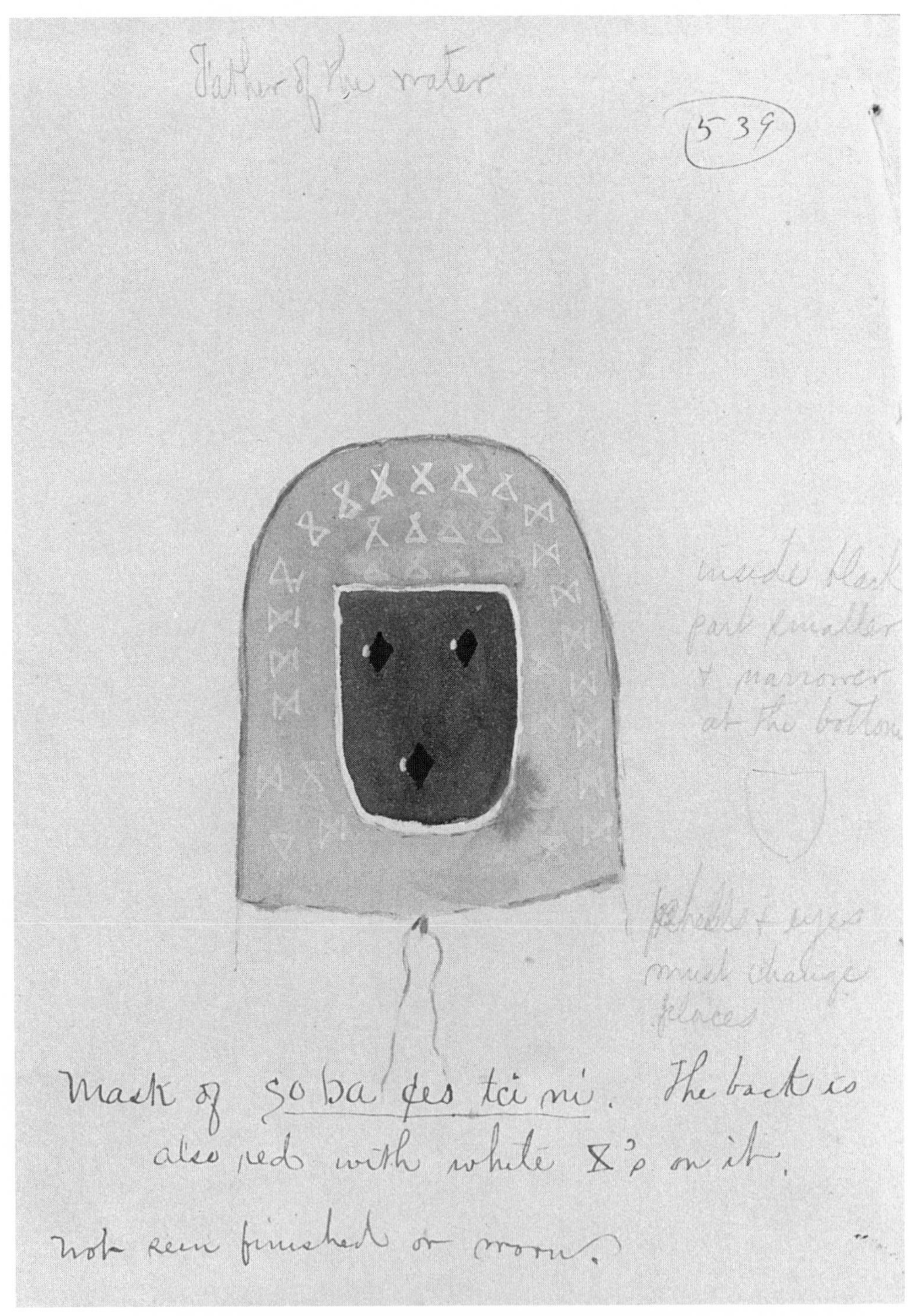

Mask of "Go Ba Des Tci Ni," Night Chant
(Washington Matthews, Sketch No. 539)

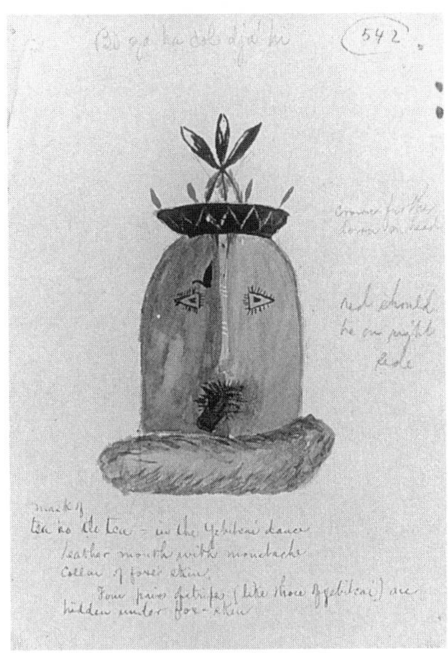

Mask of
"Tsa Ho Tlo Tcu,"
Night Chant
(Washington Matthews, Sketch No. 542)

Mask of
"Go Ne Mil I—
The Clown,"
Night Chant
(Washington Matthews, Sketch No. 544)

Mask of
"Na Es Kidi,"
Night Chant
(Washington Matthews, Sketch No. 545)

PAPERS PUBLISHED IN HARD-TO-FIND JOURNALS

Forest and Stream 23 *(November 6, 1884)*: 282–283

1. *A Night with the Navajos by Zay Elini (pseudonym)*

This is Matthews' first publication about the Mountain Chant. It is probable that he adopted a pseudonym because his research on this ceremonial was still in the formative stage. It also seems likely that he might have been reticent about associating his name with a popular publication, although this clearly was not true of his later contributions to the journals Land of Sunshine *and* Out West. *This article is introduced with the title "The Sportsman Tourist," and it is interesting to note that Matthews' language is lively and lyrical rather than pedantic, no doubt a concession to the general readership of* Forest and Stream. *In spite of its romantic overtones, the essay is nonetheless distinguished by a wealth of descriptive detail.*

NOVEMBER 6, 1884

In the Moon of Gentle Breezes the rattlesnakes go to sleep. Then at night, by the fire of his low hut, the Navajo may safely relate his mythic lore; then he may safely build his great brush corral and celebrate his most sacred rites, without fear of death from thunderbolt or venomed fang, until, in the Moon of the Falling Horns, the thunder is heard in the mountains and the serpents waken at the sound.

It is, therefore, only in the cold months that the ceremonies I am about to describe take place. They are collectively called by the Navajo *il-nas-tchin'-go ha thal,* or the Song of the Corral of Branches; but white men living in the Navajo country give to the whole night's entertainment the name of "Hoshkawn Dance," from the one dance of the evening which seems most to excite the Caucasian interest.

It was on the 5th of November, which fell in the Moon of Gentle Breezes in 1882, that I found myself at the trading post of Mr. Keam, in Keam Canyon, Arizona, whither

I had to come to witness an exhibition of the Hoshkawn Dance, which I was promised would be one of unusual interest and well performed.

Soon after nightfall, our party of eight white men set out from Keam's. A walk of about a mile took us out of the canyon, up the juniper-covered mesa, and to the locality where the dance was to be held. Here we found a large corral, or inclosure, of an irregularly circular form, about forty paces in diameter. Its fence, about eight feet high, was constructed of fresh juniper and pinon boughs. In the center was a conical pile of dry wood about twelve feet high, which was to make the great central fire. Around this, a few feet from the fence, a dozen smaller fires were burning for the comfort and convenience of the spectators, who numbered about 500 men, women and children, gathered here from various parts of the Navajo country. The majority were from the neighboring camps in Arizona and New Mexico; but many came from the distant borders of Utah and Colorado. The corral had but one opening, and this was in the east. All who wished to witness the ceremonies were obliged to assemble within the inclosure; none might peep through the fence or over the top of it, for the spirits of the bears and other ancestral animal-gods were supposed to be there, looking on at the sports of their children.

The weeds outside of the corral were illuminated by fires, in different places, and we determined to visit some of these before the ceremonies began. Some seemed to be merely the camp fires of parties who came from a distance, others were the ones around which different bands of dancers were preparing themselves. We entered one lodge or *hogan*, which stood close to the corral on the south, this was the principal medicine lodge (a sort of "green room" or place of preparation for the dancers). No objection was, at first, made to our presence; indeed, we were invited to enter by some of the liberal-minded Indians who stood at the door, but soon after we got inside an ill-natured conservative, sitting to the west of the fire which burned in the middle of the floor, made some grumbling remarks about the impropriety of admitting the "Bilikanos" (Spanish jargon for "Americans"). His words were approved by another grumbler in the north. Thus encouraged the man in the west motioned us to leave, which we did, notwithstanding that there seemed to be no other objectors in the house.

We next wended our way to where a brilliant light gleamed through the dark junipers, about three hundred paces west of the corral, and found a party seated around a fire in the open air. Two of the number were engaged in sewing some radiating eagle feathers to two circular wooden disks, covered with buckskin—properties which I afterward recognized in the dance of the Sun and Moon. They allowed us to observe their labors for a few minutes, when the man who was making the Sun looked up, saying, "The great fire will be lit very soon, the dance of the Wand will begin and if you do not hurry away you will miss it." Understanding this as a hint to leave, much more polite than the one given to us in the medicine lodge, we departed and visited some other camp fires, where, as no preparations for the dance were being made, no objections were urged to our presence.

He who comes among the Navajos with his notions of them formed by reading the reports of the explorations of thirty or forty years ago, the works of Pattee, Gregg, Hughes and Emory, or by the perusal of romances of the Mayne Reid school, can with difficulty realize that in these industrious, jolly, friendly groups around the fire, he beholds the former scourges of Northern Mexico, for these smooth-faced young men and laughing girls perhaps know of those days only from the tales they hear at night told by their elders in the smoky *hogan.* But see yon gray-haired, fierce-eyed old man, who warms his hands in the flame, and rubs with them his wrinkled chest. Many a tale could he tell you of his own exploits in the Rio Grande Valley, and on the distant plains of Sonora and Chihuahua. A whole library of dime novels might be written from his dictation.

Yet it is possible that we may not seek among the gray-heads for all the bloody raiders. When their cousins, the Apaches, are at war on the southern frontier, occasionally a Navajo youth is missing for a time, and when the war is over he turns up again; he has just been off on a visit to some friends of his. But he will not tell us of his adventures; he will find some other audience.

In this great Indian festival there was no vast supply of game brought in to feed the assembled multitude, nor deer and turkey from the neighboring forests of the Sierra de Chusca, nor from the great peak of San Francisco, whose snowy summit is visible from the neighborhood of our camp, but there is an inclosure of rocks and dead trees hard by, filled with fat, if prosaic, sheep. These are the gift of a sick man to the assembled dancers, who help themselves as they need.

When we returned to the corral we found an old man addressing the assembly. He congratulated them on the absence of liquor from the camp, exhorted them to temperance, begged them not to steal from one another, and declared that the heavens looked favorable for a calm and pleasant night.

At 8 o'clock a band of musicians—the orchestra, entered, sat down beside one of the fires in the west, and commenced to make various noises, vocal and instrumental, which were to them music. There were singers, there were rattlers, and there were those who scraped on notched sticks, laid on inverted baskets that answered the purpose of sounding-boards. From the moment it began until dawn when the dances ended, this music ceased not for a minute to delight the audience and drive away the evil spirits. At the moment the music began the great central fire was lit, and the conflagration spread so rapidly through the entire pile that in a few moments it was enveloped in great flames, throwing up a storm of sparks to a height of a hundred feet or more, and covered us with the descending ashes, which fell in the corral like a shower of snow. The heat was soon so intense that in the remotest part of the inclosure it was necessary for us to screen our faces when we looked in the direction of the fire. And now all was ready to test the endurance of the dancers, who must expose their naked breasts to the torrid glow.

When the fire gave forth its most intense heat, a warning whistle was heard in the outer darkness and a dozen forms, lithe and lean, dressed only in the narrow white cloth at the hips, and daubed with white earth until they looked like a group of marble statues into which the breath of life had suddenly been breathed, came bounding in at the entrance, yelping like wolves and slowly moving around the fire. As they advanced in single file they threw their bodies into diverse attitudes, some graceful, some strained and difficult, some menacing—attitudes that might have inspired the chisel of the sculptor. Now they faced the east, again the south, the west, the north, bearing aloft their slender wands, tipped with eagle down, holding and waving them with startling effect. Their course around the fire was to the left, *i.e.*, from the east to the west by way of the south and back to the east by way of the north; and this was the course taken by all the dancers of the night, the order never being reversed.

When they had encircled the fire twice, they began to thrust their wands toward it, and we soon saw that their object was to burn off the tips of eagle down; but owing to the intensity of the heat it seemed difficult to get near enough to the flame to accomplish this. One would dash wildly toward the fire and retreat; another would lie prone, as close to the ground as a frightened lizard, and endeavor to wriggle himself up to the fire; others sought to catch on their wands the sparks flying in the air. One approached the flaming mass, suddenly threw himself on his back, with his head to the fire, and swiftly thrust his wand into the flames. Many were the unsuccessful attempts, but at length one by one they all succeeded in burning the downy balls from the ends of their wands. As each accomplished this feat it became his next duty to restore, by a slight-of-hand trick (the mechanism of which I have since discovered), the ball of down to the end of the wand. He apparently did this waving his wand up and down as he continued to run around the fire. When he succeeded he held his wand up in triumph, yelped and rushed out of the corral. The last man feigned great difficulty in restoring the ball. When he at last gave his triumphant yell and departed my watch showed me that it was ten minutes to 9. The dance had lasted twenty minutes.

After an interval of three-quarters of an hour, the dance of the Great Plumed Arrow, a potent healing ceremony, began. There were but two performers; they wore broad sashes around the hips, silver-studded belts, long blue woolen stocking of Navajo make, moccasins and an ornament of plumes on each arm, otherwise they were nude, their skins painted white. Each bore a stone-headed arrow of great size, to the stem of which was attached tufts of feathers, not only for ornament, but also to conceal the mechanism by which the arrow was shortened telescopically when the bearer pretended to swallow it. While they were making the usual circuit around the fire, a sick man was placed sitting on a buffalo robe in front of the orchestra. They halted in front of the patient; each dancer seized his arrow between his thumb and forefinger about eight inches from the tip, held the arrow up to view, giving at the same time a yelp like a coyote, as if to say "so far will I swallow it," and appeared to thrust the arrow slowly and painfully down his throat as far as indicated. I doubt not that many of the audience actually believed that he accomplished the feat he feigned to perform. While the arrows seemed still to be stuck in their throats, they danced a *chassez*, right and left with short scuffling steps. Then they withdrew the arrows, held them up to view as before with triumphant yelps, as if to say "so far have I swallowed it," and sympathizers around yelped in response.

The next thing to be done was to apply the arrows. One of the dancers advanced to the patient, and to the soles of the feet of the latter, he pressed the shaft of the magic weapon with the point to the right; reversed it and pressed it again with the point to the left; and in similar manner he treated successively the knees, hands, abdomen, back, shoulders, crown and mouth, giving three coyote yelps after each application.

When the first dancer had completed this work the other took his place and went through exactly the same performance. This done, the sick man and the buffalo robe were removed; the bearers of the arrows danced once more around the fire and departed. All the rites of the night are to some extent intended for the benefit of the sick man who sits on the buffalo robe; but in the dance of the Great Arrow is performed the special healing act. It is this patient who gives the sorcerers rich presents for their efforts, and supplies all the sheep devoured by the whole multitude of visitors.

At 10 o'clock the sound of the whistle again called the spectators to attention, and a line of twenty-three dancers came in sight. The one who led the procession bore in his hands a whizzer—such as our schoolboys use—a little stick tied to the end of a string; this he constantly whirled, producing a sound like that of a rain storm. After him came one who enacted the *Yebitchai* of Navajo mythology; he wore a mask designed to represent an owl's face, and further to mock the doleful bird of night he hooted from time to time. Then there were eight wand-bearers, dressed, or rather decked, like the arrow-bearers in a previous dance; but instead of arrows having wands or grass, cactus, and eagle plumes. The rest of the band were men in ordinary dress, who were merely choristers or supernumeraries. When they had all gone around the fire a couple of times, they halted in the west, the choristers sat, and the wand-bearers formed a double row of four. Then while the owl hooted, the orchestra played, the choristers sang, and the whizzer made his mimic storm, the eight wand-bearers, keeping time with their feet, went through a series of figures not unlike those of a modern quadrille. The country fiddler would probably have called the dance in these terms: "Forward and back, *chassez* twice, face partners, forward and back, forward and bow, forward and embrace, forward and wave wands at partners," etc. When several of these evolutions had been performed in a graceful and orderly manner, the choristers rose and all went singing out at the east.

Three times more the same band returned. In the third and fourth acts, the wand-bearers bore great piñon poles, about twelve feet long, portions of which they pretended to swallow, as their predecessors had done with the arrows. The simple and devoted Indian of the unconverted pueblos, it is said, does actually, in dances of this character, thrust a stick far down his gullet, to the great danger of health and even of life but the wily Navajo attempts no such prodigies of deglutition. A careful observation of their movements convinced me that the sticks never passed below their tonsils.

In the fourth dance there were three interesting character dancers, all in fancy masks, who danced a lively and graceful jig, in perfect time to the music, with many bows, waving of wands, and other pretty motions which would not have looked ill in the spectacular drama of a metropolitan theater, but which, with the wild surroundings of an Indian camp were doubly attractive.

After the fourth dance there was an interval of nearly an hour, which passed slowly to those in the corral; some smoked and gossiped; some listened to the never-ceasing din of the orchestra or joined in the chant; some brought in wood and replenished the waning fires; some, wrapped in their serapes, stretched themselves on the ground to catch short naps.

It was after midnight when the blowing of a hoarse buffalo horn announced the approach of the group who were to perform in the fifth dance. There were but two character dancers in the party and these represented the sun and moon who in Navajo mythology are not male and female, as other nations have conceived them to be, but men and brothers. Like nearly all the character dancers so far seen they were arrayed in that cool and scant costume of which white paint formed the principal part. Their heads and arms were adorned with the plumes of the war eagle, their necks with rich necklaces of genuine coral, their waists with valuable silver covered belts, and their loins with bright sashes of crimson silk. The Sun bore upon his back a round disk about nine inches in diameter, decorated with radiating eagle plumes, to represent the orb of day; his companion carried a disk of six and a half inches diameter, similarly ornamented, as an image of the nocturnal luminary. While the whole party, including twenty-two choristers and a rattler were passing around the fire in the usual manner, they frequently bowed and waved their wands toward the flame. When they stopped in the west the choristers sat and sang; the rattler stood and rattled, and the Sun and Moon danced at a lively rate for just three minutes, when the choristers rose and all sang and danced themselves out of sight.

The sixth dance, that of the standing arcs, was both picturesque and ingenious. The principal performers were eight in number, as usual with scant clothing; their hair fell loose and long over backs and shoulders; and each bore in front of him, held by both hands, a wooden arc, ornamented with eagle plumes. The ends of the arc, which was a full semicircle, showed tufts of pinon twigs, and were evidently joined together by a delicate string which was invisible to the audience. Besides these eight there was a rattler, whizzer and a chorus. While the whole band was making the fourth circuit of the fire, frequent shouts of *Tho-he! Tho-he!* (stand! stand!) were heard, the significance of which soon became apparent. When it stopped in the west, the eight character dancers, having first gone through various quadrille-like figures, knelt in two rows, facing one another. At a word from the rattler, the man nearest to him, or No. 1 arose, advanced to the man who knelt opposite No. 2 with rapid shuffling steps and, amid a chorus of *Tho-he! Tho-he!* put his arc with caution on the head of the latter, where with its radiating plumes, lit by the flickering firelight and contrasting with the dark shadows behind, it looked like the halo around some saintly head on a medieval canvas. Although it was held in position by the friction of the pinon tufts at each ear, and by the pressure of the ends of the arc, now drawn closer by the subtending string, it had the appearance of standing on the head without material support and it is probable that some of the uninitiated believed the only the magic influence of the oft-repeated word *Tho-he* kept it in position. When the arc was secured in its place No. 1 retreated with shuffling steps to his former position and fell on his knees again, while No. 2 advanced and placed the arc which he held in his hands on the head of No. 1. Thus each in turn placed on his arc on the head of the one opposite until all were crowned. Then, holding their heads rigidly erect, lest their crowns should fall, the eight kneeling figures began a splendid, well-timed chant, which was accentuated by the clapping of hands and joined in by the chorus. When the chant was done, the rattler addressed the arc bearers, warning them to be careful, so they cautiously rose from their knees and shuffled with stiffened spines, out of the corral preceded by the choristers. This dance was repeated after a second performance of the fifth dance.

The seventh dance presented nothing worthy of special note, but its shortcomings were more than atoned for by the interest of the eighth dance. In this there were sixteen performers in ordinary Navajo dress. One of these was a whizzer who led the procession; another, who came about the center of the line, carried a hewn plank (puncheon) some twelve feet long and four inches broad, painted with spots and decorated with tufts of piñon, branchlets and eagle plumes. Immediately behind the bearer of the plank walked a man who had in a basket an effigy of the sun, formed of a small round mirror and a number of radiating scarlet plumes. Having walked around the fire as usual, the whole party gathered in the west in a close circle, which completely excluded from the sight of the audience the operations of the medicine man. Singing, rattling, and cries of *Thohe!* were heard. In a few minutes the circle opened and disclosed the plank standing upright on a small Navajo blanket without any apparent means of support, and at its base was the basket containing the figure of the sun. Singing was continued, and so were the uproarious cries of *Tho-he!*—cries anxious, cries appealing, cries commanding, while the bearer of the rattle stood facing the pole and rattling vigorously at it. At length, seemingly in obedience to all this clamor, the "sun" left the basket, and slowly, falteringly, totteringly ascended the plank to within a few inches of the top, stopped a moment, and descended in the same manner that it rose. Once more was it made to rise and set, when the circle of dancers again closed; the pole, sun and basket were taken in custody and the dancers departed. Taking into consideration the limited knowledge and rude implements of the originators, this was a good piece of leger demain. The man who pulled the sun up and down could not be detected. The dancers formed a semi-circle nearly ten feet distant from the pole, and the light of the great central fire shone brightly upon all.

It was in the "Wee sma' hours" when the real dance of Hosh-kawn' *(yucca baccata)* began. The ceremony was conducted in the first part by twenty-one persons in ordinary dress. One bore, exposed to view, a natural root of yucca, crowned with its cluster of root leaves, which remain green all winter. The rest bore in their hands wands of piñon; what other properties they may have had concealed about their persons, the reader will soon be able to conjecture. On their third journey around the fire they halted in the west and formed a close circle for the purpose of concealing their operations, such as we witnessed in the eighth dance. After a few moments spent in singing and many repetitions of *Tho-he!*, the circle opened, disclosing to our view the yucca root planted in the sand. Again the circle closed; again the song, the rattle and the chorus of *Tho-he!* was heard, and when the circle was opened the second time the small budding flower-stalk (or its excellent counterfeit rather) was seen amid the fascicle of root leaves. A third time the dancers formed their ring of occultation; after the song and din had continued a few seconds the circle parted for the third time; when lo! amid the frosts of November, the great panicle of creamy yucca flowers which, except in the mysteries of the Hosh kawn', never bloom on the high mesas of Arizona later than July. The previous transformations of the yucca had been greeted with approving shouts and laughter; but the blossoms were hailed with the greatest storms of applause. For the fourth and last time the circle closed, and when again it opened the blossoms had disappeared and the great dark-green fruit hung in abundance from the pedicels. When this act was completed the dancers departed, leaving the Hosh-kawn' behind them. Barely had they disappeared when the form of one personating an aged, short-sighted, decrepit man was seen to emerge slowly from among the crowd of spectators in the east. He was dressed in an old and horribly ragged suit; his face was whitened and he bore in his hands a short, crooked bow and a few crooked, ill-made arrows. His mere appearance provoked the "stoic" audience to scream of laughter, and his subsequent "low-comedy business," which excelled much that I have seen on the civilized stage, never failed to meet with uproarious demonstration of applause. Slowly advancing as he enacted his part, he in time reached the place where the yucca stood, and in his imbecile totterings he at length stumbled upon the plant and pretended to have his flesh lacerated by the sharp leaves. He gave a tremendous cry of pain and wined: "This must have been the yucca that cut me; where can it be." Standing directly over the plant he pretended, after much vain search, to find it, and rejoiced with querulous extravagance over his success. When he had marked the spot and the way back to it with an exaggerated burlesque of the Indian methods doing their things, he went off to find his "old woman" and bring her to pick the fruit. Soon he reappeared with a great, strapping Indian "buck," dressed to represent a hideous, absurd-looking old granny. The latter acted his part throughout the rest of the drama with a skill fully equal to that of his partner. But I cannot go further in describing this strange performance; many things that followed may not be told in the English tongue.

The night's entertainment fitly ended with the fire dance, which was the most picturesque and startling of all. Some time before the dancers entered we heard strange sounds mingled with the blowing of the buffalo horn. The sounds were much like the call of the sandhill crane, and may, perhaps, be properly called "trumpeting," and they were made by the dancers constantly during the exercises. The noises continued to grow louder and come nearer, until we heard them at the opening in the east, and in a moment after, ten men, having no more clothing on than the performers in the first dance, entered. Every man bore a long, thick bundle of shredded cedar bark in each hand except the leader, who carried four smaller fagots of the same material. Four times they all danced around the fire, waving their bundles of bark toward the flame, then they halted in the east; the leader advanced toward the central fire, lit one of his little fagots, and trumpeting loudly, threw it over the fence of the corral to the east. He performed a similar act at the south, the west, and the north, but before the northern brand was thrown, he lit with it the fagots of his comrades. As each brand disappeared over the fence, some of the spectators blew into their hands, and made a motion as if tossing some substance after the departing flame.

When the fagots were all lit, the whole band began a wild race around the fire. At first they kept close together and spat upon one another some substance of supposed medicinal virtue. Soon they scattered and ran apparently without concert, the rapid racing causing the brands to throw out long brilliant streamers of flame over the naked hands and arms of the dancers. They then proceeded to apply the brands to their own nude bodies, and the bodies of their comrades in front of them—no man ever once turning around. At times the dancer struck the victim vigorous blows with his flaming wand; again he seized the flame as if it were a sponge, and, keeping close to the one pursued, rubbed the back of the latter for several moments as if he were bathing him. In the mean time the sufferer would catch up with some one in front of him and, in turn, bathe him in flame. At times when a dancer found no one in front of him, he proceeded to "sponge" his own back and might keep this up while making two or three circuits around the fire, or until he overtook some one else. At each application of the blaze the loud trumpeting was heard, and it often seemed as if a flock of a hundred cranes were winging their way overhead, southward through the darkness. If a brand became extinguished it was lit again in the central fire; but when it was so far consumed as to be no longer held conveniently in the hand, the dancer dropped it and rushed trumpeting out of the corral. Thus one by one they all departed, and the spectators stepped into the arena, picked up fascicles of the fallen fragments of bark, lit them and bathed their hands in the flames as a charm against the evil effects of fire.

Did these dancers, next day, hide sore and blistered backs under their serapes? I think not. How then did they escape the effects of the flame? Did the medicine they spat upon one another save them? I doubt it. Does the cedar bark ignite at a low temperature, and is the coating of white earth with which their bodies were covered an excellent non-conductor? Such I believe to be the case. However, the thought that their bodies might have been ingeniously protected, lessened little, if any, the effect produced on the spectator. I have beheld many fire scenes on the stage, many acts of fire-eating and fire-handling by civilized jugglers, and many fire dances by other Indian tribes, but nothing quite comparable to this. The scenic accessories were unique. Demons scourging lost souls with the eternal fire could scarcely be pictured to look more awful.

A few unimportant closing ceremonies, and the labors of the night were done. The Indians began to stream out of the corral and we followed them with eyes sore from the bitter smoke and loss of sleep. When we stepped out of the glare and heat of the corral a frosty autumn morning and a cloudless sky greeted us. The morning star was high above the horizon; a faint hint of dawn was in the east. But although the last human votary of the Fire God had departed a celestial dancer still sped on his eternal round and held his blazing torch aloft—the great comet of Crull gleamed in the southern sky.

2. *Mythic Dry-Paintings of the Navajos*

American Naturalist 19 (*October* 1885): 932–939

This preliminary discussion of the sandpaintings associated with both the Mountainway and Nightway presages the attention to detail contained in Matthews' later publications (1897a and 1902a). This article weds Matthews' interest in the technique utilized in creating a drypainting with his broader concern with the symbolic content expressed within each representation.

I DESIRE, in this article, to call the attention of ethnographers to some pictures which are among the most transitory in the history of human art. They are the work of the Navajo Indians, a people who make no graven images of their gods, who do not decorate skins or robes, who place no symbols on their rude and rarely-made pottery, and may be said to have no rock inscriptions. A few slightly scratched sketches on the cliffs of Arizona and New Mexico may, perhaps, be attributed to them; but the vast majority of carvings on stone in their country, and all of the most permanent character, are the work of the sedentary races. Seeing no evidence of a symbolic art among them, one might readily be led to suppose that they possessed none. Such was my opinion for two years after I had come to reside near them. Such is the opinion of many white men, who have lived for periods of from ten to twenty years among them.

During my residence of nearly four years in New Mexico I had heard of these drawings through the less conservative Indians and through a Mexican who had been many years captive among them. But it was not until last November, when I made a special journey to the Navajo country under the auspices of the Bureau of Ethnology, that I obtained unrestricted access to the medicine-lodge, saw the hieratic figures drawn, and was given permission to sketch them, much to the horror of the large majority of the assembled multitude.

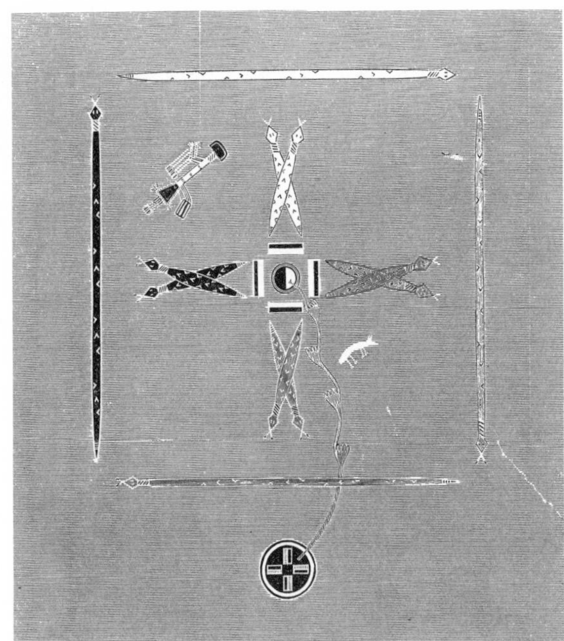

2.1
Navajo Dry-paintings: The Visit of the Prophet to the House of the Serpents.

The medicine-lodge, on the floor of which these pictures are made, is a simple conical structure of logs in the shape of an Indian skin tent. It is about twenty-five feet in diameter at the base, internally, and about eight feet high under the apex. The only apertures are a smoke-hole above and a door, communicating through a short passageway, in the east. The fire is built in the center of the floor except when the pictures are being made, then it is removed further to the east to make room for them. It is so dark in the lodge that on a brief winter day the artists must begin their work before sunrise if they would finish before night-fall and this it is essential they should do.

When the call is sounded in the morning, several young men go forth and bring in a quantity of dry sand in blankets; this is thrown on the floor and spread out over a surface twelve feet or more in diameter, to the depth of about three inches; it is leveled and made smooth by means of the broad oaken battens used in weaving.

The drawings are begun as much towards the center as the design will permit, due regard being paid to the precedence of the points of the compass; the figure in the east being begun first, that in the south, second, that in the west, third, that in the north, fourth. The figures in the periphery come after these. The reason for working from within outwards is a practical one; it is that the operators may not have to step over and thus risk the safety of their finished work.

While the work is in progress the chief shaman does little more than direct and criticise; a dozen or more young men perform the manual labor, each working on a different part. These assistants have had a certain ceremony of initiation performed over them before they are admitted to the lodge or allowed to help when these pictures are made; but they need not be skilled medicine-men or even aspirants to the craft of the shaman. They get nothing for their pains but their food, which, however, is abundant.

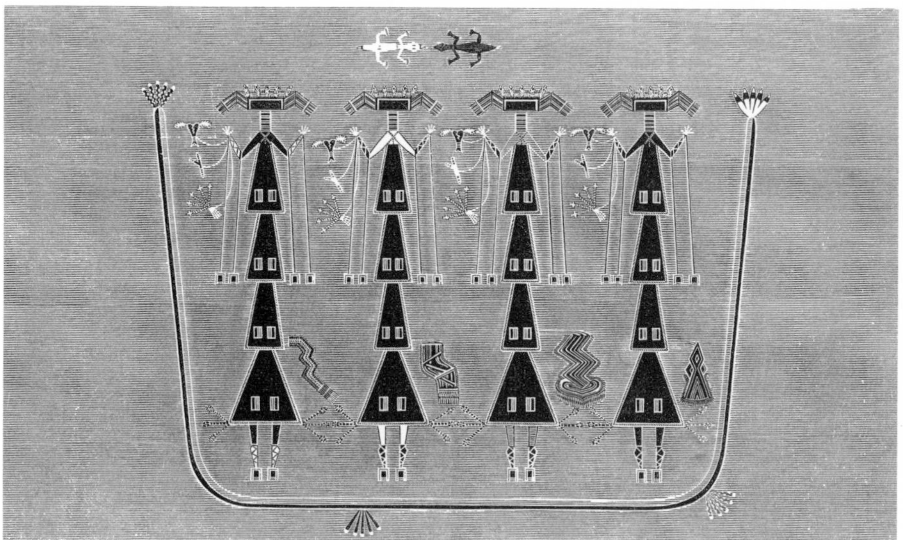

2.2 Navajo Dry-paintings: the Long Bodies

Three times a day the person, for whose benefit the dance is performed, sends in enough mush, corn-cake, soup and roasted mutton to satisfy to the utmost the appetites of all in the lodge. The shaman, or *hathàli* (chanter or singer), as the Navajos call him, gets a rich present for his services.

The pictures are drawn according to an exact system, except in certain well-defined cases, where the limner is allowed to indulge his fancy. This is the case with the embroidered pouches the gods carry at the waist (see Ill. 2.2). Within reasonable limits the artist may give his god as handsome a pouch as he wishes. On the other hand, some parts are measured by palms and spans, and not a line of the sacred design can be varied in them; straight and parallel lines are drawn on a tightened cord.

The pigments are five in number: they are black made of charcoal; white, of white sandstone; yellow, of yellow sandstone; red, of red sandstone, and "blue," of the black and white mixed in proper proportions; all ground into fine powder between two stones. The so-called blue is, of course, gray, but it is the only inexpensive representative of the cerulean tint they can obtain, and, combined with the other colors on the sandy floor, it looks like a real blue. These colored powders are kept on improvised trays of pine bark; to apply them, the artist grasps a little in his hand and allows it to flow out between the thumb and the opposed fingers. When he makes a mistake he does not brush away the color, he obliterates it by pouring sand on it and then draws the corrected design on the new surface.

The naked forms of the mythical figures are first drawn, and then the clothing is put on. Even in the representations of the *Bitses-ninez*, or long bodies, which are nine feet in length, the naked body of each is first made in its appropriate color—white for the east, blue for the south, yellow for the west, black for the north—and then the four shirts are painted on as shown in the picture (Ill. 2.2) from thigh to axilla.

It is the task of the shaman, when the work of painting is completed, to put the corn-pollen, emblem of fecundity, on the lips and breast of each divine form, and to set up the bounding plume-sticks around the picture. Then the one who gives the feast enters and is placed sitting on the form that belongs to the east—the white form—and looking eastward. Here the colored dust from various parts of the divine figures is taken and applied to corresponding parts of the patient, and many other ceremonies are performed, which it is not my purpose to relate here. When the patient has departed many of the spectators pick up the corn-pollen, now rendered doubly sacred, and put it in their medicine-bags. Some take dust from the figures on their moistened palms and apply it to their own bodies. If the devotee has disease in his legs, he takes powder from the legs of the figures; if in his head, he takes powder from the head, and so on.

By the time they are all done the picture is pretty badly marred. Then it becomes the duty of the shaman to completely obliterate it; this he does with a slender wand, while he sings the song appropriate to this part of the ceremony. He begins with the figure belonging to the east, the white figure, and proceeds in the same order as was observed in making the picture, i.e., in accordance with the apparent daily course of the sun. The figures at the margin are erased last, and when this is being done the bounding plume-sticks are knocked down. When no semblance of the picture is left the assistants gather the sand in their blankets, carry it to a little distance from the lodge and throw it away. Thus in half an hour after the completion of a large picture, ten or twelve feet in diameter, which has taken a dozen men, or more, eight or ten hours to construct, not a trace of it is left.

I have learned of seventeen great ceremonies of the Navajos, in which pictures of this character are drawn, and I have heard that there are, on an average, about four pictures to each dance. This would give us about sixty-eight such designs known to the medicine men of the tribe. But I learn that there are different schools or guilds among the medicine men who draw the pictures differently in some of the details, and that besides these seventeen great ceremonies there are many minor rites, with their appropriate pictures; so the number of designs in the possession of the tribe is probably much greater than that which I give.

The medicine-men aver that these pictures are transmitted from teacher to pupil, in each guild and for each ceremony, unaltered from year to year and from generation to generation. That such is strictly the case I cannot believe. No permanent design is preserved for reference, and there is no final authority in the tribe. The majority of the ceremonies can be performed only during the months when the snakes are dormant. The pictures are therefore carried over, from winter to winter, in the fallible memories of men. But I think it probable that innovations are unintentional, and that any changes which may occur are wrought slowly.

Out of this possible number of sixty-eight or more pictures I have seen seven, colored copies of which will, I hope, appear in some future report of the Bureau of Ethnology. The majority are too intricate to be reproduced in a satisfactory manner from a wood-cut on a page of this size, I therefore present illustrations of only two, and these of the simplest.

The first four pictures in my collection are those of the *Dsilyidje hathal*, or chant among the mountains. This ceremony is also called *ilnasjingo hathal*, or chant in the dark circle of branches, from the great corral of piñon boughs in which it is performed. As the public ceremonies of the last night are varied and interesting, it is best known to the whites of all Navajo dances, and by our people is commonly called the hoshkawn dance, from the particular performance of the night, which seems most to strike the Caucasian fancy.

The whole ceremony is propitiatory to the Yèï's, or gods of the mountains; but when the Navajo prophet, who learned these mysteries, was brought around by a friendly god from place to place to be taught them, he was, on one occasion, brought into the house of the serpents. Now the worship of the snakes and water animals constitutes a separate dance, that of the *hojoni hathal*, or chant of terrestrial beauty, with its own pictures and ceremonies; but to indicate that the prophet visited the snakes in his wanderings and saw a portion of their mysteries, this picture, representing the home of the serpents, is drawn (Ill. 2.1).

In the center of the picture is a circular concavity about six inches in diameter, intended to represent water. In all the other pictures where water was represented, a small bowl, I observed, was sunk in the ground and filled with water, which was afterwards sprinkled with powdered charcoal to give the appearance of a flat, dry surface. Closely surrounding the central depression are four parallelograms, each about four inches wide and ten inches long in the original pictures; the half nearer the center is red, the other half is blue; they are bordered with narrow lines of white. They appear in this and in some other pictures as something on which the gods seem to stand, and symbolize the *sha'bitlol*, or raft of sunbeams, the favorite vessels on which the divine ones navigate the upper deep. Red is the color proper to sunlight in their symbolism; but red and blue together represent sunbeams in the morning and evening skies when they show an alternation of red and blue. The sunbeam shafts, the halo and the rainbow are painted in the same colors, but they differ in form—the halo is a circle; the rainbow is curved and usually anthropomorphic, in Illustration 2.2, however, it is plumed. External to these sunbeam rafts, and represented as standing on them, are the figures of eight serpents—two in the east, white; two in the south, blue; two in the west, yellow, and two in the north, black. They cross one another in pairs, forming four figures like the letter X. In each X the snake which appears to be beneath is made first, complete in every respect, and then the other snake is drawn over it in conformity with their realistic laws of art before referred to. The neck in all cases is blue, crossed with four bands of red, which, in the snake-like forms run diagonally, but in the man-like forms to be seen in other pictures, run transversely. The V-shaped marks on the backs of the snakes represent mottlings; the four marks at the end of each tail are for rattles. External to these eight snakes are four more of much greater length but colored to correspond with those already described. They seem to follow one another around the picture in the direction of the sun's apparent course, and form a frame or boundary. In the north-east is seen one of the *Yeï's*, who accompanied the Navajo prophet to the home of the snakes. In the extreme west is a black circular figure representing the mountain of *Dsilya-ithin,* whence they descended to visit the snakes. In the original picture the mountain was in relief—which I have not attempted to convey in my copy—a little mound of sand about ten or twelve inches high. From the summit of the mountain to the middle of the central waters is drawn a wide line in corn meal with four footprints depicted at intervals; this represents the track of the bear. Immediately south of the track is the figure of an animal drawn in the gray pigment, this is the grizzly himself, symbolizing the prophet.

During the journeys of the Navajo prophet before referred to, he came one night in the Carrizo mountains to the home of the four bear-gods (so runs the legend). They took from one corner of their cave a great sheet of cloud, unrolled it and exhibited to his view a picture. They told him that this picture must be drawn by the Navajos in their ceremonies; but as men had not the power of handling the clouds they should draw it on sand. This picture, a very elaborate one, not illustrated in this article, represents the *Yeïs* of the cultivated plants. It shows the central waters and the sunbeam rafts as in the first picture. It has four anthropomorphic figures extending from the center to different points of the compass, and highly conventionalized representations of the four principal domestic plants of the Indians—corn, bean, pumpkin and tobacco. The whole is surrounded on three sides by the anthropomorphic rainbow. The body of the eastern god is white; that of the southern, blue; that of the western, yellow; that of the northern, black.

Here is an appropriate occasion to speak of Navajo symbolism in color. In all cases, as far as I could learn, the south is represented by blue, the west by yellow, the upper world by blue, the lower world by black and white in spots. Usually the east is represented by white and the north by black; but sometimes these colors are interchanged and the north becomes white while the east is black. The reasons for this change are too lengthy to be discussed here.

It is related in the myth which accounts for these mysteries, that this Navajo prophet, *Dzil'-yi-neyáni,* or Reared among the Mountains, was once led by the gods to a dwelling called the Lodge of Dew; it was built of dew-drops, and the door was made of many plants of different kinds. They entered and found four goddesses called *Bitses-ninez* or long bodies. The holy ones rose as the strangers entered, and they were very tall. The plumes on their heads almost touched the sky. They said to the prophet: "In the rites that you will teach your people when you return to them, you will invoke us by drawing our pictures. We stand here, one in the east, one in the south, one in the west and one in the north; but when you draw the picture you must place us all in the east."

The third picture in the series (Ill. 2.2) is supposed to be made in accordance with these instructions. To indicate their great height the figures are twice the length of any in the other pictures, except the rainbow figures, and each is clothed in four garments, one above another; for no one garment, they say, can be made long enough to cover such giant forms. The form immediately north of the center is done first, in white, and represents the east; that next to it, on the south, comes second in order, is painted in blue and represents the south. The form next below the latter is in yellow and depicts the goddess who stood in the west of the house of dew-drops. The figure in the extreme north is drawn last of all, in black, and belongs to the north. As before stated, these bodies are first made naked and afterwards clothed. The exposed chests, arms and thighs display the colors of which the entire bodies were originally composed. Some small animal called the *gloï* is sacred to these goddesses. Two of these creatures are shown in the east, guarding the entrance to the lodge. The appendages at the sides of the heads of the goddesses represent the *glòï-bichá*, or head-dresses of *gloï* skins of different colors, which these mythic personages are said to wear. Each one bears, attached to the right hand, a rattle, a charm and a branch of choke-cherry in blossom (highly conventionalized). Some other adjuncts of the picture—the red robes embroidered with sunbeams, the forearms and legs clothed with clouds and lightning, the pendants from wrists and elbows, the blue and red armlets, bracelets and garters—are properties of nearly all the anthropomorphic gods shown in these pictures. The rainbow which encloses the group on three sides is not the anthropomorphic rainbow, it has no head, neck, arms or lower extremities. Five white eagle-plumes adorn its south-eastern end; five tail-plumes of some blue bird decorate the bend in the south-west; the tail of the red-shafted flicker is near the bend in the north-west, and the tail of the magpie terminates the north-eastern extremity. Throughout the myth not only is the house of dew spoken of as adorned with hangings and festoons of rainbows, but nearly all the holy dwellings are thus embellished.

The fourth picture represents the *Kátso-yisthan*, or great plumed arrows. These arrows are the especial great mystery, the potent healing charm of the dance. On the last night, many public *alilis* (shows, dances) may be given—shows of all sorts of societies and bands, shows adopted from alien tribes. From dark to dawn these continue around the great central fire and within the dark fence of evergreen branches. All of these may be changed, omitted, or have others substituted for them, except the dance of the great plumed arrow, this cannot be left out.

The three paintings remaining to be described are those of the *kledji-hathal* (chant of the night), or dance of the *Yeibichai* (grand-uncle of the gods). They represent some of the visions of another Navajo prophet named *Sho*. The myth recounting his adventures is interesting, but too long to be related here. In childhood and youth he showed signs of unusual wisdom. He often told his immediate relations that he held converse with the gods; but they doubted him until, as he grew older, he exhibited such unquestionable evidence of second-sight that the most skeptical were convinced. On one of his rambles he saw what he supposed to be a small herd of big-horn or Rocky-mountain sheep, and went in pursuit. Four times he waylaid them and tried to shoot them, but each time when he drew his arrow to the head it would not leave the string. Then he knew the sheep to be divinities in disguise. He approached them; they threw off their sheep-skin coverings and revealed themselves as the *gáaskidi* or gods of plenty. They bore *Sho* to their home, admitted him to their sacred rites, taught him all their mysteries, and sent him back to his people that he might teach the mysteries to man. All his adventures and visions are embodied in the myths and rites of the *kledji-hathal*. When his mission was done he was taken back by the gods to dwell among them forever.

The form of the *gáaskidi* appears several times in the pictures. It is represented as having sheep's horns on the head, wearing a crown of black clouds garnished with lightning and fringed with sunbeams, bearing on the back a great sack made of the black thunder-cloud (said to be filled with all sorts of edible seeds and fruits), and leaning on a staff to indicate that the sack of plenty is a heavy burthen. Various other important characters of the Navajo mythology appear in these pictures.

One of the *Yeibichai* paintings delineates a very singular vision or revelation of the prophet *Sho*. It is called the *tsiznaöle*, or whirling sticks. On one occasion *Sho* was led by the gods to the shores of a dark lake, on the borders of which grew four stalks of sacred corn, each of a different color. In the center of the lake lay two logs, crossing one another at right angles; near the two extremities of each sat a pair of *Yeis*, male and female, making eight in all. On the shore of the lake stood four more *Yeis*, three of whom had staves, by means of which they kept the logs whirling around with a constant motion, while the *Yeis* sitting on the logs sang songs which are still preserved in the multitudinous chants of this rite under the name of *tsiznaòle-bigin*, or songs of the whirling sticks. All the circumstances of this strange scene are duly symbolized in the painting.

The two other pictures represent scenes in the dance of the *Yeibichai*, as *Sho* witnessed it among the gods, and with some modifications they would make fair representations of the dance as it is enacted by the Navajos to-day. The pictures are beautiful, and appear of high interest when their symbolism is explained; but I have not space to describe them, and, as before stated, they are too intricate to be suitably illustrated here.

3. *Some Illustrations of the Connection between Myth and Ceremony*

Memoirs of the International Congress of Anthropology 22 (1894): 246–251

A central theme in Matthews' work was the intimate relationship between myth and ceremony in Navajo thought, with mythological story giving instructions for conduct of the ceremony and standing as a warrant of its effectiveness. While this idea is embodied in his major publications on the Mountain Chant and Night Chant, this article elaborates with specific examples from these ceremonies.

Among the Navajo Indians, as perhaps among all other peoples, rites are connected with myths or with tales which may not be all mythical. This much we can safely aver; but we cannot with equal confidence declare that all rites have originated in myths, or at least in the myths with which we now find them connected. Neither can we affirm that the myth has always preceded the associated ceremony. In some cases a Navajo rite has only one myth pertaining to it. In other cases it has many myths. The relation of the myth to the ceremony is variable. Sometimes it explains nearly everything in the ceremony and gives an account of all the important acts from beginning to end, in the order in which they now occur; at other times it describes the work in a less systematic manner and leaves you to infer that the orderly arrangement may be the result of an afterthought.

Some of the myths seem to tell only of the way in which rites, already established with other tribes were introduced among the Navajos.

The rite-myth never explains all the symbolism of the rite, although it may account for all the important acts. A primitive and underlying symbolism, which probably existed previous to the establishment of the rite, remains unexplained by the myth, as though its existence were taken as a matter of course, and required no explanation. Some explanation of this foundation symbolism may be found in the creation and migration myth or in other early legends of the tribe; but something remains unexplained even by these.

The myths which account for the origin or introduction of rites have each a central figure or hero who may be called the prophet of the rites. In one case there are twin prophets. He leaves his people; wanders among foreign tribes and among the gods, or among divine beings only; learns the rites; returns to his people; communicates his knowledge to one or more disciples, and, having performed his mission, disappears mysteriously. But he does not disappear through the portals of death or to the eternal home of ordinary men in the lower world. He is apotheosized. His everlasting home is at least above the surface of the ground if not in the heavens. After his departure he may still manifest himself to the faithful in the form of some natural phenomenon.

In connection with the adventures of this hero, an account of the rites should properly be given; but this is a part of the story which is often omitted. I have obtained rite-myths from Indians both with and without the ceremonial part. I shall briefly state the reasons for this omission. The portion of the myth relating the adventures may be told to any one and may be easily understood and remembered by any one; hence many people who are not priests of the rite may be found who know the narrative portion of the myth only, and are ready to tell it. The ritual or esoteric portion of the myth is usually known only to a priest of the rite, who is rarely inclined to part with this knowledge. Such lore interests only the priest. If a layman, unacquainted with all the work of the rite, should hear the ritual portion of the myth, he would be apt to forget it, having little knowledge of the rite to assist his memory. I have seen in print rite-myths of other tribes in which descriptions of ceremony were obviously omitted.

Probably the most important as well as the most ancient Navajo ceremony now in existence is that of the *kledji qacal*, or night chant. This rite is explained by two principal myths, each of which describes different elements in the long and intricate ceremonial, whose performance occupies nine nights and portions of ten days.

The prophet of the first myth—that of the songs and public dances—was a singular youth who early evinced the gift of second-sight and the possession of magical powers. He seemed to be one favored of the gods and in their confidence. Once, while out hunting, he was seized by certain gods, the Gaaskii—who are represented in Navajo mythology as assuming the form of the mountain sheep—and borne off to a home of the gods in certain cliff-houses in a canon north of the San Juan River, in what is now the State of Colorado. Here he made the acquaintance of the various gods who are now personated in the dances and other acts of the night chant, and he beheld scenes which are to this day depicted in the great dry paintings of this ceremony. He heard, too, numerous sacred songs of the rites and learned them by heart to repeat them to his disciples on his return to his home. While the myth describes the acts of these gods, it does not describe the gods themselves. They seem to have been well-known characters before the prophet went on his journey, and we must depend on separate accounts from the lips of learned shamans in order to discover the appearance and attributes of these mysterious beings. But this prophet was not a sick man. He was not treated by the gods for disease. If we would learn how the ceremonies of the night chant may be applied to the cure of disease we must seek the explanation in the second myth.

The prophets of this second myth were characters not unknown to the myth-makers of the Old World. One was crippled, the other was blind. The blind child bore the seeing cripple on his back, and thus they wandered through the land. This unfortunate pair were the fruit of a clandestine alliance between a Navajo woman and one of the gods of the Cañon de Chelly. Their starving relations, on their mother's side, abandoned them in the wilderness to die. They found their way after many vicissitudes to the Cañon de Chelly, where, through the intercession of their father, who long failed to acknowledge them, they were cured of their ailments by means of ceremonies which are described minutely in the myth, and which are practiced to this day. But there are now, at times, variations which the myth does not describe, made in the ceremony.

Connection between Myth and Ceremony

Out of hundreds of instances in which the specific rules of the ceremony are accounted for by incidents in the myth, I select one for illustration: The cripple and the blind boy were to be treated for their infirmities by means of a hot-air bath in a small lodge, such as the Navajos employ now, prepared for the purpose with many ritual observances. The invalids were charged to say not a word while in the sudatory. When they had been seated there awhile and were perspiring freely, the blind child became conscious that he saw a streak of light stealing in under the corner of the blanket which hung over the opening of the lodge. Forgetting, in his delight, the injunction of the gods, he cried out: "Oh, brother! I can see." At the same moment his crippled brother, beginning to experience the benefit of the bath, shouted aloud: "Oh, brother! I can move my limbs." In an instant the sweat-house, the hot stones, the carpet of leaves, all vanished, and the children, still uncured, were left sitting on the bare ground under the open sky. It was with much difficulty that the gods could be persuaded to build another sudatory and repeat the ceremonies. In consequence of the sad experience of these twins, the strictest silence is, to-day, enjoined on the occupant of the sacred sudatory.

Both of these myths refer the origin of the ceremonies to people dwelling in cliff-houses. The White House and other buildings still standing in a ruined condition in the Cañon de Chelly are specifically mentioned in the second myth. I think it not improbable that these rites may have been derived from cliff-dwellers, who still occupied the land when the first small vagrant bands of Tinne penetrated to the mountains of New Mexico and Arizona. True, the myth speaks of these cliff-dwellers as gods; but it is not difficult to believe that the rude Athabaskan wanderers, in the days when they subsisted on small mammals, such as prairie dogs, and on the seeds of wild plants (as their legends relate), may have regarded the prosperous agricultural cliff-dwellers as gods. Or it may be that the myth originally referred only to the masked characters in the cliff-dwellers' rites as gods. The Navajos say now that when one of their own number wears the mask of a god and personates a god, he is, for the time being, actually that god. A prayer to a masquerading representative of divinity is a prayer to a god.

But besides these two main myths, there are many more myths belonging to the night chant. The rite contains several groups of songs, and each of these groups has its myth accounting for its origin. Twenty-one divine characters are represented in the rite either by song, by masquerade, or by picture, and each of these characters has its own appropriate myth or myths.

In the myth of the mountain chant,* which I have already published, it is related that a ceremony of somewhat similar character existed prior to the establishment of the mountain chant, and that the rite was only enriched and improved by the prophet. This prophet, according to the story, was taken captive by the Ute Indians. In his escape from captivity he suffered much. His limbs became sore and swollen. Certain mountain gods, who were friendly to the Navajos, and whose dwellings he visited while wandering in his flight through the Carrizo and Tuincha Mountains, took pity on the fugitive, taught him the secrets of their sacrifices and showed him how their aid might be sought. The sacrifices and prayers of this rite are directed, with a poetic consistency and completeness, to the natural phenomena which occur in, and the animals which inhabit, the high mountains. The myth does not describe the acts of the rite in their consecutive order; but there is scarcely any act which is not alluded to in the course of the story. A suspicion may be aroused in the mind of the hearer, who accepts this by no means ancient tale as containing something of the truth, that the prophet may have obtained some suggestions of these rites from the Ute Indians while he was captive among them.

The most ingenious and poetic rite-myth which I have obtained is that of the *yoi-qacal*, or chant of beads. This rite is also known as the eagle medicine. It at least claims for itself a totally superhuman origin. The prophet was a veritable Navajo Lazarus. He was very poor, as the Navajos in their legends represent themselves to have been in the ancient days. Unlike other people, the Navajos have no golden age in the past—the present is the happiest period in their history. This pauper lived near one of the ancient pueblos, now in ruins, in the Chaco Cañon, and subsisted on the refuse of pueblo feasts. One day the pueblo people found on the face of a high cliff, in a small cave, an eagle's nest, which could only be reached by lowering a man with a rope over the edge of the precipice. All feared to undertake the task of descending the cliff; so they concluded to bribe the starving Navajo, with promises of abundant food for the rest of his life, to make the dangerous descent. He accepted the offer; but when he was lowered to the mouth of the cave the wind god whispered in his ear and told him that if he spared the eaglets he would meet with a great reward, while, if he stole them and delivered them to the people of the Chaco, the latter would soon forget their promises and leave him to starve as before. Hearing this, he disengaged himself from the rope and crept into the cave. In vain did the people of the pueblo plead with him and call him endearing names and renew all their promises; he heeded them not, and after a while they abandoned their efforts and went home. Later the grateful eagles (who are represented as men dressed in the feathered robes of eagles) took him out of the cave and flew with him upwards. They bore him through the sky-hole and up to the pueblo

***The Mountain Chant*: A Navajo Ceremony. Fifth Annual Report of the Bureau of Ethnology. Washington, 1888.

of the eagle-people above the sky. Here the prophet performed other valuable services for the eagle-people, and in return for his good deeds he was initiated into the ceremonies of the eagles.

A careful examination of the rites and rite-myths of the Navajos seems to reveal that some of them are not of very ancient origin, or at least have not been long known to the tribe, and we possess traditional evidence that, while new rites are being introduced, old rites are being abandoned. There are reasons for believing that suggestions for rites or parts of rites have been obtained from other tribes; but, if this is the case, such rites have been modified to conform to the fundamental rules of Navajo symbolism before being adopted. Some rites, as in one example given, appear to be but modifications of older ceremonies. The prophet of the new did not "come to destroy, but to fulfill." In the histories of other Indian tribes we find many instances of the introduction of new ceremonies in recent times.

4. *Some Sacred Objects of the Navajo Rites*

Archives of the International Folklore Association *1 (1898): 227–247*

While this article recapitulates much of the information contained in "Butts and Tips" (1892b) and "The Basket Drum" (1894a), it also provides analyses of process and function pertaining to other ritual objects. Matthews' insights concerning symbolic context underscore the pervasive nature of Navajo metaphysics in all aspects of ceremonial preparation.

Some one has said that a first-class museum would consist of a series of satisfactory labels with specimens attached. This saying might be rendered: "The label is more important than the specimen." When I have finished reading this paper, you may admit that this is true in the case of the little museum which I have here to show: a basket, a fascicle of plant fibres, a few rudely painted sticks, some beads and feathers put together as if by children in their meaningless play, form the total of the collection. You would scarcely pick these trifles up if you saw them lying in the gutter, yet when I have told all I have to tell about them, I trust they may seem of greater importance, and that some among you would be as glad to possess them as I am. I might have added largely to this collection had I time to discourse about them, for I possess many more of their kind. It is not a question of things, but of time. I shall do scant justice to this little pile within an hour. An hour it will be to you, and a tiresome hour, no doubt; but you may pass it with greater patience when you learn that this hour's monologue represents to me twelve years of hard and oft-baffled investigation. Such dry facts as I have to relate are not to be obtained by rushing up to the first Indian you meet, notebook in hand. But I have no time for further preliminary remarks, and must proceed at once to my descriptions.

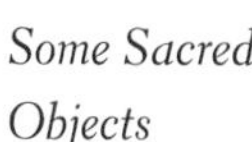

4.1 Washington Matthews

The Basket Drum

The first thing that I present to you is a basket. Wordsworth tells us of Peter Bell that:

> "*A primrose by a river's brim,*
> *A yellow primrose was to him,*
> *And it was nothing more.*"

To most observers this may seem a yellow basket, but it is much more to many an untutored savage. The art of basket-making is to-day little cultivated among the Navajos. In developing their blanket-making to the highest point of Indian art, the women of this tribe have neglected other labors. The much ruder, but cognate Apaches, who know how to weave woollen fabrics, make more baskets than the Navajos and make them in greater variety of form, color, and quality. The basket I show you is, however, of Navajo make, and it is skillfully fabricated; yet it is with one exception almost the only form and pattern of basket now made in the tribe. They buy most of their baskets from other tribes. But, having generally let the art of basketry fall into disuse, they still continue to make this form, for the reason that it is essential to their sacred rites, and must be supplied by women of the tribe who know what is required. It is made of twigs of aromatic sumac—a shrub which has many sacred uses—wound in the form of a helix. The fabricator must always put the butt-end of the twig toward the centre of the basket and the tip toward the periphery. A band of red and black, with zigzag edges, is the sole decoration. This band, it will be observed, is not continuous, but is intersected at one point by a narrow line of yellow, or, more properly speaking, of uncolored wood.

When I first observed this, years ago, I fancied that it had some relation to the "line

4.2 Basket Drum

of life" observed in the ancient and modern Pueblo pottery, and that its existence might be explained by reasons as metaphysical as those which the Pueblos give for their "line of life." But the Navajo has at least one reason of a more practical character. The line is put there to assist in the orientation of the basket, at night, in the medicine-lodge when the fire has burned low and the light is dim. In an article published in the *American Anthropologist* (October, 1892), I explained the law of butts and tips in Navajo ceremonies and shall not now repeat the explanation. It must suffice to say that throughout their ceremonies careful discrimination is made between the butt and the tip, the central and the peripheral ends, and that the butt has precedence over the tip. This law applies to the basket before you as well as to other sacred things. The butt of the first twig, placed in the centre, and the tip of the last twig, in the edge, must lie in the same radial line, and this line is marked by the hiatus in the ornamental band. The rim of the basket is often so neatly finished that the medicine-man could not easily tell where the helix ended were not the pale line there to guide him. This line must lie east and west when the basket is employed in the ceremonies.

The most important use of the basket is as a drum. In none of the ancient Navajo rites is a regular drum or tom-tom employed. The inverted basket serves the purpose of one, and the way in which it is used for this simple object is rendered devious and difficult by ceremonious observances. To illustrate, let me describe a *few* of these observances belonging to the ceremony of the Night-Chant. This ceremony lasts nine nights and nine days. During the first four nights song is accompanied only by the rattle. During the last five nights, noises are elicited from the basket-drum by means of the yucca drumstick. The drum is beaten only in the western side of the lodge. For four of these five nights, the following methods are pursued: A small Navajo blanket is laid on the ground, its longer dimension extending east and west. An incomplete circle of meal, open in the west, of the diameter of the basket, is traced on the blanket near its eastern end. A cross in meal, its ends touching the circle near the cardinal points, is then described within the circle. In making this cross a line is first drawn from east to west, and then a line is drawn from south to north. Meal is then applied sunwise to the rim of the upturned basket so as to form an incomplete circle with its opening in the east. A cross, similar to that on the blanket, is drawn in meal on the concavity of the basket, the east and west line of which cross must pass directly through the hiatus in the ornamental band. The basket is then inverted on the blanket in such a manner that the figures in meal on the one shall correspond in position to those on the other. The western half of the blanket is then folded over the convexity of the basket and the musicians are ready to begin. But before they begin to beat time to a song, they tap the basket with the drumstick at the four cardinal points in the order of east, south, west and north. The Navajos say, "We turn down the basket," when they refer to the commencement of songs in which the basket-drum is used, and, "We turn up the basket," when they refer to the ending of the songs for the night. On the last night the basket is turned down with much the same observances as on the previous nights; but the openings in the ornamental band and in the circles of meal are turned to the east instead of to the west, and the eastern half of the blanket is folded over the convexity of the basket. There are songs for turning up and for turning down the basket, and there are certain words in these songs at which the shaman prepares to turn up the basket by putting his hand under its eastern rim, and other words at which he does the turning. For four nights when the basket is turned down, the eastern part is laid on the outstretched blanket first, and it is inverted towards the west: on the fifth night, it is inverted in the opposite direction. When it is turned up, it is always lifted first at the eastern edge. As it is raised, an imaginary something is blown toward the east, in the direction of the smoke-hole of the lodge, and when it is completely turned up, hands are waved in the same direction, to drive out the evil influences which the sacred songs have collected and imprisoned under the basket.

The border of this, as of other Navajo baskets, is finished in a diagonally-woven or plaited pattern. These Indians say that the Apaches and other neighboring tribes, finish the margins of their baskets with simple circular turns of the investing fibre, like that in the rest of the basket. The Navajo basket, they believe may always be known by the peculiar finish described, and they say that if among other tribes a woman is found who makes Navajo finish she is of Navajo descent or has learned her art of a Navajo. They account for this by a legend which is perhaps not all mythical. In the ancient days a Navajo woman was seated under a juniper tree finishing a basket in the style of the other tribes as was then the Navajo custom, and while so engaged she was intently thinking if some stronger and more beautiful margin could not be devised. As she thus sat in thought, the god Qastceyelci tore from the overhanging juniper-tree a small spray and cast it into her basket. It immediately occurred to her to imitate in her work the peculiar folds of the juniper leaves and she soon devised a way of doing so. If this margin is worn through, or torn in any way the basket is unfit for sacred use. The basket is given to the shaman when the rites are done, he must not give it away, and he must be careful never to eat out of it, for, notwithstanding its sacred use it is no desecration to serve food in it.

The Drum-Stick

The next thing to be examined is the drum-stick with which this drum is beaten. I show you now only the stick used in one rite—that of the night chant. The task of making this stick does not necessarily belong to the shaman, any assistant may make it; but so intricate are the rules pertaining to its construction, that one shaman has told me he never found any one who could form it merely from verbal instructions. Practical instructions are necessary. The drum-stick is made anew for each ceremony and destroyed in a manner to be described when the ceremony is over. It is formed from the stout leaves of *Yucca baccata,* a species of Spanish bayonet. But not every plant of this kind is worthy to furnish the material. I have seen an hour spent in search for the proper plant on a hillside bristling with *Yucca baccata.* Four leaves only can be used, and they must all come from the same plant—one from each of the cardinal points of the stem. All must be of the proper length and absolutely free from wound, stain, withered point, or blemish of any kind. These conditions are not fulfilled on every yucca. The leaves may not be cut off but must be torn off downwards, at their articulations. The collector first pulls the selected leaf from the east side of the plant, making a mark with the thumb nail on the east or dorsal side of the leaf near its root, in order that he may know this leaf thereafter. He walks sunwise around the plant to the west side, marks the selected leaf near the tip on its palmar surface and culls it. He then retreats to the south side of the plant and collects his leaf there but does not mark it. Lastly he proceeds sunwise to the north and culls his last leaf,—also without marking it. When the leaves are all obtained the sharp flinty points and the curling marginal cilia are torn off and struck [*sic*], point upward, in among the remaining leaves of the plant from which they were culled. The four leaves are then taken to the medicine lodge to be made up. The leaves from the east and west are used for the centre or core of the stick and are left whole. The leaves from the north and south are torn into long shreds and used for the wrapper. But since the shaman cannot adequately explain in words, to the devotees who assist him, how the stick is made I shall not attempt the task for you tonight. I have learned how to make it; but I have, now, no fresh yucca leaves on hand to illustrate the process of making. So I shall say nothing more of the process. Any one who is not satisfied with this decision may come with me to the yucca-covered deserts of Arizona and there I may show him how to make a drum-stick. In illustration 4.3, which represents the drum-stick, you will observe that the core of the stick is divided, by a suture of yucca shred into five compartments, one for each night during which the stick is used. Into each of these sections are usually put one or more grains of corn, which, dur-

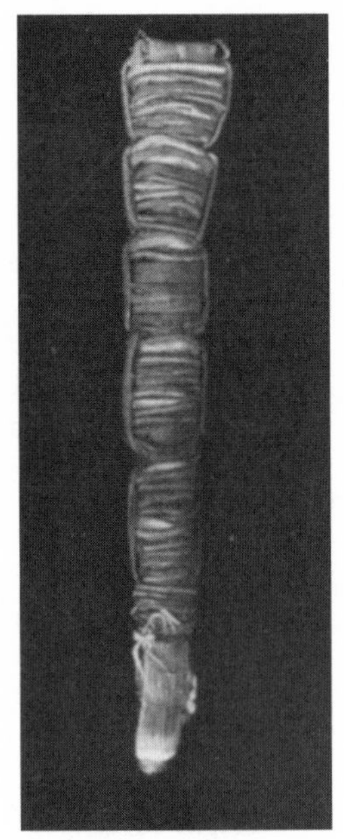

Drumstick of Yucca Leaves

ing the five nights that the implement is in use, are supposed to imbibe some sacred properties. When the ceremony is all over these grains are divided among the visiting medicine men, to be ground up and put in their medicine bags. On the last morning of the ceremony, at dawn, when the last song of sequence has been sung and the basket turned up, this drum-stick is pulled to pieces in an order the reverse of that in which it was put together. This work may only be done by the shaman who conducted the rites, and, as he proceeds with his work, he sings the song of the unravelling. As each piece is unwrapped it is straightened out and laid down with its point to the east. The debris which accumulated in the manufacture of the drum-stick and which has been carefully laid away for five days is now brought forth, and one fascicle is made of all. This is taken out of the lodge by an assistant, carried in an easterly direction and laid in the forks of a cedar tree (or in the branches of some other large plant, if a cedar tree is not at hand) where it will be safe from the trampling feet of cattle. There it is left until destroyed or scattered by the forces of nature. The man who sacrifices these fragments takes out with him in the hollow of his left hand some corn meal which he sprinkles with the same hand on the shreds from butt to tip. He takes out also in a bag some pollen, which he sprinkles on them in the same direction with his right hand. As he does this he repeats in a low voice the following prayer or benediction:

"Qojolel koçe
Qojogo nācaȼo koçe citsoi"
"Thus will it be beautiful
Thus walk in beauty my grandchild."

The drum-stick which I hold in my hand is withered, shrivelled and loose. It has long ago lost its freshness: a few taps of this on the basket would knock it all to pieces. Even during the short time that the stick is in use for its sacred purpose it would shrivel and become worthless were it not buried in moist earth all day and only taken forth from its hiding-place when needed for the ceremonies of the night.

The Plumed Wands

The next objects to be described are the Incia of the night chant. These are eight plumed wands which are set up as guardians around the sacred pictures and the sudatories of the rite. They represent ancestral Navajos of the mythic days when the people dwelt in the fourth world, before they came up to the surface of this world. They are made of willow, which should be cut only on the banks of the San Juan River—the sacred stream of the Navajos. In cutting them, the shaman begins on the south bank of the stream. He faces west and cuts the first stick; his next stick he cuts at a point west of the first and so he proceeds westward, cutting, until he has procured four sticks. These he wraps up in a bundle by themselves and observes something in their appearance by which he shall know afterwards that they are the sticks of the south. When four suitable sticks have been obtained on the south bank, the shaman scatters pollen before him in the way that he must go, and crosses the river to the north bank. Here he cuts four more sticks proceeding from west to east or in an opposite direction to that which he took on the south side, observing in his whole course the sunwise ceremonial circuit. These four sticks are wrapped in another fasces. As each willow is cut it is trimmed off to the proper length and the discarded top is placed, upright, among the growing willows, as close as possible to the stump from which it was cut. The stump is then rubbed with pollen and pollen is scattered in the air by the ascending hand, upwards from the stump in the place where the shrub grew, as if in sacrifice to the spirit of the shrub. The proper length for the wand is the natural cubit, measured from the inner condyle of the humerus to the tip of the middle finger and throughout this distance, the stick must be free from branch, knot, cicatrix or blemish. One stick measured on the arm is taken as a standard for the other sticks. The sticks are then denuded of their bark and each whittled to a point at the butt end, in order that it may be stuck in the ground. Each of the four sticks cut south of the river has then a facet cut at its tip end to represent the square domino or mask worn by the female dancer in the rites. The sticks cut on the north side of the river have no such facet, their round ends sufficiently represent the round or cap-like masks worn by the male dancers. In numerous other articles made of sticks for the Navajo rites, this distinction is made between male and female. I have observed among the Moquis a similar feature in their sacrificial sticks or bahos; but I am not aware if a similar explanation is given by the latter people. The sticks are now painted—those of the south, blue, those of the north, black. Blue in all Navajo symbolism is the color of the south and of the female; black is the color of the north and of the male. The sticks that come from the south of the San Juan represent females; those from the north, males. I might read you a separate lecture on this particular symbolism; but I can now only take time to mention a few instructive points. From various analogies in Navajo myth and language. I am led to believe that the male is assigned to the north for the reason that the north is a land of rigor and fierceness to these people. Not only do inclement and violent winds, typical of the male character, proceed from the north; but the country north of the Navajo land is very rugged and mountainous—within it lie the great peaks of Colorado. And the female is assigned to the south because thence come gentle and warm breezes and the landscape of the south is tame compared with that of the north. However this may be, all through Navajo myth and ceremony the south and all its symbolism is associated with the female; the north and all its symbolism with the male. There is a special portion of the Creation and Migration Myth of the tribe which has relation to these sticks. It is told that when the Navajos lived in the nether world, a great river, the exact counterpart of the San Juan, flowed from east to west through their land. The two sexes of the tribe quarrelled and separated; the women took the south side of the river, the men the north. It is a long story, how they fared during their separation and how they were at last reconciled and came together again, and it need not now be told. But the shamans connect the custom of cutting these sticks on the San Juan—the female sticks on the south and the male sticks on the north bank with this ancient myth.

The black sticks are painted white at their upper extremities in accordance with a fixed law of Navajo hieratic art to which I shall again refer. The facet on each blue stick is daubed with small black spots to represent the eyes and mouth of the female mask, and at its bottom is the yellow horizontal streak seen on the female mask which symbolizes the Naqotsoi or land of yellow horizontal light, *i. e.* the last streak of departing daylight. The upper extremity of each blue stick is painted black to represent the hair of the female characters in the dance, which flows out freely, not being confined by the domino; while the hair of the male dancer is hidden by the cap-like mask. When the painting is done the sticks are decked with two whorls of turkey and eagle-feathers—each whorl secured by one continuous cotton string which terminates in a downy eagle-feather. The string must be twilled from raw cotton on an old fashioned spindle, the material manufactured by the whites would never do. It must be remembered that this use of cotton shows no degeneracy of the rite, since cotton was grown and spun in New Mexico and Arizona from a remote prehistoric period and cotton fabrics are today found among the ruins of the cliffhouses. When the sticks are finished the debris of manufacture is carried to the north and thrown away among a cluster of willows on the north bank of a stream. As I have said, these sticks are, afterwards, stuck up around the sacred dry paintings and the sudatories, and when in this position the black are always erected in the north and the blue in the south. These sticks are permanent property of the shaman.

The feathers used in these plumed wands and in other more important implements of the rites must be taken from live birds. The smaller birds, whose feathers are used are captured on their nests at night. The eagles are caught in earth traps such as I have seen and described among tribes of the north a quarter of a century ago, and the Navajo eagle-hunt is accompanied by rites, prayers, and songs much like those of the same northern races. Each eagle plume must be provided with a well-developed hyporachis; otherwise, it must not be used.

Kethawns

But I must reserve a large share of my time for a description of the kethawns—the sacrifices and messages to the gods. These are perhaps the most interesting of all the sacred objects of the Navajo rites, for they are almost endless in variety and each one embodies concepts usually easy of explanation. Sacrifices of a character analogous to these are widely diffused. All the tribes of the southwest, to and beyond the Mexican line, use them or have used them, and I have found them employed by Indians residing within sixty miles of the British-American boundary. The inahos of the Ainos of Japan seem closely allied to the kethawns.

Navajo kethawns are of two principal kinds, viz.: Cigarettes made of hollow cane, and sticks made of various exogenous woods. Many of them are sacrificed with feathers, either attached or enclosed in the same bundle with them, and such are, no doubt, to be classed with the plume stick of the Zuñis. Much as these sacrifices differ from one another in size, material, painting, and modes of sacrifice, there are certain rules which apply to all, and these I shall describe at length when speaking of special kethawns.

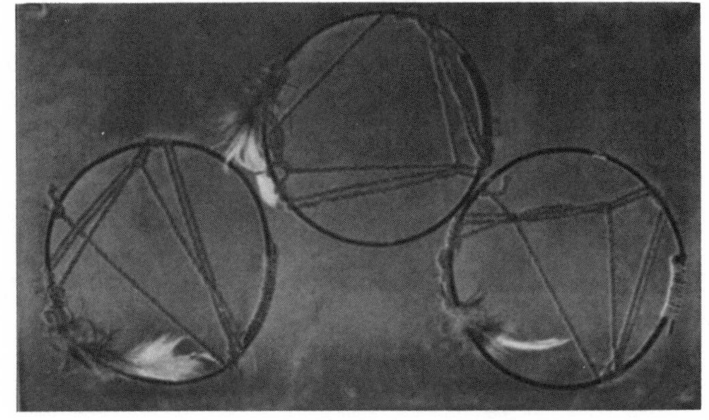

4.4 Circle Kethawns

Circle Kethawns

I shall first show you a set of kethawns made of exogenous wood and of unusual shape—circular. I present these now for an illustration only, but I shall not attempt to describe them, because I have already spoken of them at some length, in an article entitled, "A Study in Butts and Tips," already alluded to, and to this paper I refer you, although it tells by no means all that is to be told about the sacrifices.

Sacrificial Cigarettes

I shall speak next of the sacrificial cigarettes. These are usually made of the common reed or *phragmites communis,* which grows all over the United States, by the shores of Lake Michigan as well as on the banks of the San Juan. The reed designed for sacrifices is first rubbed well with a piece of sandstone—this is done, no doubt, for the very practical purpose of removing the glossy silicious surface of the reed, in order to make the paint stick. It is next rubbed with a composite plant which grows abundantly in the Navajo country, *Gutierrezia euthamiæ,* the teililgizi or scare-weed of the Navajos—this is done chiefly for metaphysical reasons. The reed must be cut up with a stone knife or arrow-point, and it must be a perfect knife. If the point has been broken off, or if it has been otherwise mutilated, it is dead, "Just the same as a dead man," the shamans have told me—and must not be used in ceremonies which are intended to cure disease and prolong life. In cutting a reed to form a series of cigarettes the operator holds the butt-end toward his body, the tip-end toward the east, and cuts off first that section which comes next to the root; for the butt, as I have told you, has precedence over the tip. This section he marks near its base, and on what he calls its front, with a single transverse notch made also with the stone knife. The severed section he lays on a clean stone, buckskin or cloth (for it must never touch the earth, at least until it is sacrificed) and proceeds to cut off another section from the remaining part of the cane which is next the root. If it is the same length as the preceding piece he marks it with two horizontal notches, in the manner described. A third section he would mark with three, and a fourth with four notches. These notches are put on in order that, throughout all subsequent manipulations—particularly if they are sacrificed in the dark—the butt may be distinguished from the tip, the front from the back, and the order in which they were cut may not be disregarded. But in making the notches, the sacred number four must never be exceeded. If there are to be more than four cigarettes of the same size in one set, the fifth must form the beginning of a new series to be marked with one notch, and the operator must depend on his memory and his care in handling to keep the sets separate. The nodal part of the stem or culm must not be used; it is carefully excluded and split into fragments with the point of the stone knife before being thrown away, lest the gods, coming for their sacrifices, might mistake empty segments for cigarettes and, meeting with disappointment, leave in anger. The god, it is said, examines and smells the cigarette to see if it is made for him; if he is pleased with it he takes it away and rewards the giver.

The second section cut off is laid south of the first and parallel to it. The last section is placed furthest to the south; the order of precedence being from north to south when sacrifices are laid out in a straight line. If there is an order of precedence among the gods to whom they are given, the higher god owns the more northern sacrifice.

The cut ends of the section are next ground smooth on a stone and a splinter of yucca leaf is inserted into each, to serve as a handle while the cigarette is being painted. A thin slice of yucca leaf is also used as a brush, and curved sections of the leaf are used as saucers to hold the paints. The decorations in paint are in great variety, a very few only will be, at present, described and exhibited.

When the painting is completed, a small pledget of feathers is inserted into the hollow of each section at the tip end and shoved down toward the opposite extremity; this is to keep the tobacco from falling out. The feathers used here are commonly those of blue-bird and yellow bird, and an owl-quill is in most cases the implement with which the wad is shoved home. The sections are then filled with tobacco, not the tobacco of commerce, *nicotiana tabacum*;—this does well enough for men, the gods despise it—but some of the species of native tobacco of the southwest. *Nicotiana attenuata*, the dsil-naco, or mountain tobacco of the Navajos, is the kind used in all the rites I have witnessed; but the Navajos tell me that *nicotiana palmeri* is used in some ceremonies, and it is not improbable that other species are used. Pollen (usually of corn) is sprinkled on the open end of the cigarette, after the tobacco is inserted, the pollen is moistened with a drop of water and thus the cigarette is sealed. There are very particular rules as to how this water is to be collected, used and disposed of, to which I must now only allude. After the cigarette is sealed, it is symbolically lighted. To do this a piece of rock crystal is held up in the direction of the smoke-hole, or in the beams of the sun, should they enter the lodge; it is then swept down from on high and touched to the tip of the cigarette. On one occasion when I saw cigarettes prepared early in the morning, the sun rose just as they were to be lighted, and shot its ruddy beams in through the doorway of the lodge over the ragged blanket which hung there as a portière. The shaman caught these first beams on his crystal and then touched the crystal to the cigarette.

I have spoken of the front or face of the cigarette, this corresponds with the side of the internode on which the alternate leaf grows, and is marked at the base of the internode in winter by the axillary pit or scar which the Navajos call the eye, this is the side which is notched and which lies next to the ground when the cigarette is sacrificed and planted.

Throughout the work on the kethawns, songs appropriate to different occasions are sung. There are songs for the painting; songs for the filling, when the tobacco is put in; songs for the lighting; songs for the application of the sacrifices to the body of the patient; songs for the application of the pollen, and songs for the sacrifice when the kethawns are taken out to their hiding-places. Some of these I have secured on the cylinder of the Edison phonograph, and I hope, ere we part, to give you a sample.

I present to you now a set of sacrifices which are all cigarettes. They belong to the morning of the third day of the ceremony of kledji-qaçal. This ceremony, or a portion of it at least, the myth tells us, originated in the Cañon de Chelly in Arizona; hence, the reeds of which these cigarettes are made should be culled only in the Cañon de Chelly. The cigarettes may be either six, eight, ten or twelve in number. The shaman who is master of the ceremonies never prepares the same number at two successive ceremonies. He changes the number constantly, and so, too, he makes changes in the songs that accompany the manufacture. In the set which I show you, and which is illustrated in illustration 4.5, there are but six cigarettes.

In the Cañon de Chelly, Arizona, there still stands, in an excellent state of preservation, a remarkable ruined cliff-house, built of yellow sandstone. Its upper portion is painted white, horizontally. As it lies in a deep rock shelter, well overshadowed by the towering cliff above, the coating of white paint has been protected from rain and snow, and looks almost as fresh and white now as when first applied, many centuries ago. The Navajos call the edifice "Keninaekai," which signifies a stone house with a white horizontal streak. Freely translating this name the Americans call it the White House. Here, according to the myth, certain divine beings once dwelt, who practised these rites and taught them to the Navajos. It is to this house, or more properly speaking, to the old divinities of this house, as the accompanying prayers indicate, that these sacrifices are offered:

"Kininaekaigi.
"Qayolkal bilnàhacináhi.
"Qayolkal bilnaciçàha.
"Qastceyalçi.
"Nigel icla'.
"Naci hila'."

In the House of Horizontal White.
He who rises with the morning light.
He who moves with the morning light.
Oh Talking God!
I have made your sacrifice.
I have prepared a smoke for you.

Thus does the first part of the prayer begin and then the devotee, following the dictation of the priest, mentions what blessings he expects to obtain in return for the present of a cigarette—restoration of all parts of his body, of his mind and voice, prosperity for all his people, increase of his flocks, long life and happiness. All these things and many more: but never one word of vengeance on his enemies or of evil to any one. Qastceyalçi, or the Talking God, is the chief in many groups of Navajo local divinities.

In the set here presented, there are two long and four short cigarettes. Like all other things made in the course of Navajo rites, they have a definite, if not a very accurate or scientific measure. The length of the small kethawns equals the width of three finger-tips: first, second, and third, pressed closely together. This measurement is much used and I shall call it three finger-widths; on my own right hand it measures about 1¾ inches. The longer kethawns, which are twice this length, are painted half yellow and half white, to symbolize this White House, as I have described it. The first kethawn is made white at its eastern extremity; the second is made white at its western extremity, for reasons that cannot be briefly explained. A cotton string is attached to each, at its centre, by means of a very peculiar knot in whose circles are included three feathers of the blue-bird *(sialia)*, and three feathers of the Yellow Warbler, or of *Pipilo chlorurus*—caçoinogáli, "he who shakes the dew," the Navajos call it. One of each kind of feather is taken from a different wing of the bird and one from the tail. Five beads are strung along each string: one of white shell for the east, one of turquoise for the south, one of haliotis shell for the west, one of cannel coal for the north, and one more of white for the east. Beyond these a bunch of three feathers is secured, by means of the peculiar knot already referred to. One of these is a downy eagle feather, the second is the breast feather of a turkey, the third is a "hair" from the "beard" of a turkey-cock. The position of the five attachments on the string are determined by stretching out, on the latter, the digits of one hand—an attachment is made where the centre of each digit falls. The string is originally two spans long, but when it is tied to the kethawn and all objects are attached, the end is cut off, three finger-widths beyond the last attachment.

The four smaller kethawns are called Naakqaigi kethawn or cigarettes sacred to the original dancers of the last night of the ceremony. But as the original dancers all lived once in the Cañon de Chelly and danced at the White House, these cigarettes go with those just described. Two of the four are painted black to symbolize males, and each is marked, near its eastern extremity, or tip end, on the right side, with a design representing the two eagle-plumes and the bunch of owl-feathers worn to this day in the dance of Naakqai by the male dancers. In figure 5*a*, I show this design; but when the kethawns are laid down on their faces to be sacrificed, the design comes only partly into view as shown in illustration 4.5. The two other small kethawns are merely painted blue to symbolize the yebaad or female characters in the dance. The black and the blue kethawns alternate just as the male and female characters alternate in the dance.

When the kethawns are completed, each is put in a separate corn-husk with twelve different articles which I will not now name and the husks are folded around their contents in a particular manner. The kethawns seen on this card, (Ill. 4.5) are arranged in the order of their proper precedence from north to south (from above downwards). This is the order in which they are made, painted, placed in the husks, folded in the husks, lifted, sacrificed and otherwise manipulated.

It takes about an hour to prepare these sacrifices. When they are done the patient sits in the west of the lodge facing the east, with lower extremities extended and with hands open resting on the knees. The shaman first puts the bundles containing the two long cigarettes into the patient's hands and says a long prayer (part of which I have repeated) which the patient recites after him, sentence by sentence. The shaman takes then the bundles and applies them to different parts of the patient's body, proceeding upwards from sole to crown. Pollen is then applied to the patient and the bundles are given to an assistant who carries them out of the lodge. The shaman lastly collects the bundles containing the smaller kethawns and repeats with them all the observances mentioned as belonging to the greater cigarettes.

The long kethawns are thus finally disposed of. The bearer carries them, running in an easterly direction from the lodge to the foot of a perpendicular rock that fronts the west, and such rocks are not hard to find in the Navajo land. This rock, some say, typifies the high-walled White House itself others say, the towering cliff on whose face the White House is built. He makes a faint mark on the ground with the outer edge of his foot from east to west, near the base of the rock. He lays down in this mark a bunch of composite plant, *Gutierrezia euthamiæ*, usually collected *en route*. Taking the first kethawn from its husk, he places it on the *Gutierrezia*, at such a distance from the rock, that when the string is stretched eastward to its fullest extent its extremity will nearly touch the rock. He puts on the kethawn, in a certain established order, the twelve other articles contained the husk and while crouching to do this he repeats in a low voice a short prayer. This finished he rises, measures off a foot's length to the southward of the first kethawn, makes at this distance, with his foot another mark, parallel with the first and places here the second kethawn with exactly the same forms which he observed in placing the first kethawn.

The smaller kethawns are also carried in an easterly direction from the lodge, until a piece of clean, level ground is found, representing the level surface on which is held the dance, wherein figure the characters symbolized by these kethawns. They are laid parallel, with their tips to the east a foot's length apart, in a row extending from north to south. In disposing of them, the observances connected with the longer kethawns are repeated. When the kethawns are all laid away the bearer returns to the lodge, observing the definite rules for return, and bearing back with him the empty corn-husks which are delivered up to the shaman to be later disposed of, according to established rules, the recital of which I shall now spare you.

I have referred to the outer or more obvious symbolism of these objects, but there is an inner and more recondite symbolism. The larger kethawns represent the White House where the devotee is supposed to stand in the centre of the world. The white cotton string is the *bike qajoni* or trail of happiness, mentioned so often in the prayers, which he hopes with the help of the gods to travel. With all around me beautiful may I travel, says the prayer, and for this reason the string passes through beads which sym-

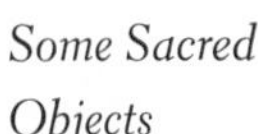

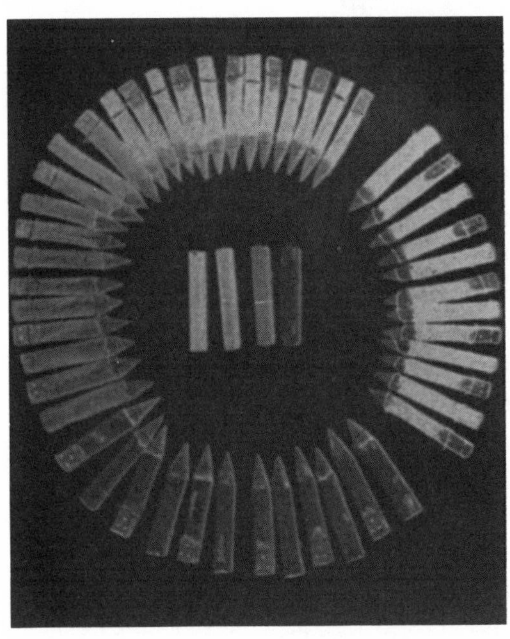

4.5 Kethawns, Sacrificial Sticks and Cigarettes

bolize by their colors the four points of the compass. "With all above me beautiful may I travel. With all below me beautiful may I travel" are again the words of the prayer, so the string includes feathers of the turkey, the bird of the earth and lower world, and a feather of the eagle, the bird of the sky; "My voice restore thou for me," and "Make beautiful my voice" are expressions of the prayers, and to typify these sentiments the string includes feathers of warbling birds, whose voices "flow in gladness" as the Navajo songs say.

I shall next describe a set of sacrifices in which both cigarettes and hard-wood sticks are employed. They are shown on this card and partly represented in illustration 4.5. The sacrifices are 52 in number; four are cigarettes cut from cane and 48 are pieces of exogenous wood. Of the 48 sticks, 12 belonging to the east, are of mountain mahogany *(Cercocarpus parrifolius)*; 12 belonging to the south, are made of a small shrub not found much beyond the borders of New Mexico and Arizona, the *Forestiera Neo-mexicana*, the maize or coyote—corn of the Navajos; 12 belonging to the west are made of juniper *(Juniperus occidentalis)*; and 12, belonging to the north are made of cherry. Mountain mahogany is probably selected for the east because its plumose fruit is white—the color of the east. Forestiera may be chosen for the south because its small olive-shaped fruit (it belongs to the Oleaceae or olive family) is blue, the color of the south. Juniper is perhaps taken for the west because the leaves of its outer branches, have a tone of yellow, the color of the west. Cherry seems to be adopted for the north, because the fruit of *Prunus demissa*, the common wild cherry of New Mexico ripens black, and black is the color of the north.

The cigarettes are each three finger-widths, the sticks, four finger-widths in length. All the pieces are not measured with the fingers; but one piece having been thus measured it is used as a gauge for others.

The four cigarettes are cut from a single cane and prepared with the usual observances. The first is painted white for the east; the second, blue for the south; the third, yellow for the west; and the fourth, black for the north; no devices are painted on them.

The wooden kethawns are painted on the bark, thus: those of mountain mahogany, white; those of Forestiera, blue; those of juniper, yellow; those of cherry, black. The outer or tip end of each male kethawn (every alternate one) is painted a contrasting color, i.e. the ends of the white sticks are painted black; the ends of the blue sticks, yellow; the ends of the yellow sticks, blue; and the ends of the black sticks, white. The tip ends of the female kethawns are painted black for reasons which I explained when speaking of the incia or plumed wands. The wooden kethawns as I have before intimated are made to represent, alternately, males and females, by means which I have described in speaking of the plumed wands, with this difference that the males are not painted black nor the females blue to symbolize sex. Only the facets, which symbolize the female masks worn in the dance, are painted blue. The bark is removed from each stick only at the but end, where it is whittled to a point. This point should be one finger width in length, so should the facet which represents the mask.

The sacred basket, previously described is used to contain these sacrifices. A little pile of corn meal is put in the centre of the basket and on this the four cigarettes are laid, one after another, in order of their precedence, from north to south. The painted sticks are laid in the same basket in four groups: the twelve white sticks are laid in the eastern quarter; the 12 blue sticks, in the southern quarter; the 12 yellow sticks, in the western quarter and the 12 black sticks, in the northern quarter of the basket. They are laid in one by one. The most northern white stick, representing a male divinity, is laid down first; the next white stick south of that, representing a female divinity, is laid down next. Thus male and female sacrifices are laid down alternately. When all the white sticks, sacred to the east, are put in place, the most easterly blue stick, sacred to the south, is placed in position and thus they proceed around the basket, in the direction of the course of the sun, until all the sticks are in the basket; the most easterly black kethawn, a female, being laid down last.

These sacrifices are made to propitiate certain local divinities called Qastcêayuhi. The four central cigarettes are for the chiefs, the sticks are for their humbler followers. They are prepared in the afternoon and laid away in a safe part of the lodge until night.

Soon after dark, four men begin to dress themselves as divinities. When their toilet is finished they leave the lodge. The kethawns are then brought forth and the shaman and his assistants begin to sing that set of sequential songs known in the rites as aga'hoàgisin or summit songs. These songs, some of which I have obtained on the phonograph, are sung unceasingly in their proper order until all the kethawns are taken out.

The four divinities are Qastcèyalsi Qastcegogan, the Home or Farm God, and two Qastcebaad or goddesses. There seem to be no bachelor gods among the Navajos and, although they are a people who practise polygamy, their gods seem to be monogamists. Each has his one accompanying goddess and no more. Each god, too, has his own peculiar cry, meaningless and often inarticulate; but the females, contrary to the custom among mankind, are silent.

Soon after the first song begins, the Talking God enters, runs towards the patient and applies his quadrangular talisman (method of application exhibited). This done he runs out of the lodge and returns instantly without his talisman. Again he approaches the patient at a run, and, being handed one of the kethawns, he applies it to certain parts of the body (soles, knees, palms, chest, back, shoulders, head) giving his characteristic whoop with each application. This done he runs with the kethawn out of the lodge. The moment he disappears his goddess (a man dressed as a goddess) rushes in, takes another kethawn from the hand of the shaman and repeats with it all the acts of the Talking God with his kethawn, uttering, however, no sound. As the goddess rushes out, the Home God enters and repeats with a kethawn all the performances already described. He is followed in turn by his goddess, who does exactly as the first goddess did. In this order they follow one another and repeat over and over again these acts, until all the kethawns are taken out. Then the Talking God returns once more and applies his folding quadrangular talisman as he did in the beginning. As there are 52 kethawns to be disposed of, each one of the gods makes 13 entries and besides these there are two visits of the Talking God to apply his quadrangle.

The kethawns are taken out in the exact order in which they were placed in the basket, and the work is so arranged that the male divinities carry out male kethawns and the female divinities, female kethawns.

Each god, as he carries out his kethawn runs a short distance from the lodge (to the east when he bears a white kethawn, to the south when he bears a blue kethawn and so on) holds the kethawn in a peculiar manner, but end foremost and face up, supported on the back of his index finger, and throws it away from him into the darkness.

This ends my descriptions. I am aware that I have made them minute to a tedious degree; but not otherwise could I have impressed on my auditors the character of these primitive observances, the thoughts and sentiments associated with these simple trifles which I have shown you. It may be some satisfaction for you, at the end of my discourse, to know that I have not told one half the particulars that I might appropriately have told you; but I trust I have said enough to show you how logical and elaborate is the symbolism of this crude people, and how, having once established for themselves a law of symbolism, they never lose sight of it, but follow it persistently and undeviatingly to the end.

5. *A Navajo Initiation*

Land of Sunshine
15 (1901): 353–356

Another example of Matthews' writing for a popular audience, this article presents a lively description of the initiation ceremonies occurring during the Night Chant. Matthews begins with comments, from his own observations, contrasting the "cruelty" of Plains Indian initiation with the more benign ceremony of the Navajos. In passing, he notes that some writers would interpret this as a social evolutionary advance; however, he himself doubts that this is "a uniform rule."

The remainder of the essay is straightforwardly descriptive. The article also reflects Matthews' penchant for synthesizing activities he witnessed during several ceremonies into one summarized account. However, this is one of the few commentaries that exclusively focuses on the initiations occurring during the fifth through ninth days of the ceremony. In other instances, this information is buried among the details of other ceremonial activities (see the discussion and chart of Nightway ceremonies in Faris 1990:40–48 and chart 4).

Many works, not without value, have been compiled on limited subjects from the constantly growing literature of ethnology, and there are many writers seeking subjects in this field. To such, I would recommend the comparative study of rites of initiation. To my knowledge, no general work on this subject has ever been written. This is an age of secret societies. Never, perhaps, in the history of our race, have these organizations been more numerous or stronger in membership. The advance of civilization seems rather to increase than diminish them. What was their origin and development? What is their tendency? With regard to such initiation rites, and to other initiations which are not secret, it is generally thought that the severities were greater in the early days than they are now, that they have gradually become milder and more symbolic; but I doubt if this is a uniform rule. I have among my scraps a number of recent cases in which members of secret societies, regarding lightly the sanctity of their oaths, have sued in open court for damages received in some rude initiation. From this we may conclude that even in this day among civilized people, some rites have elements of severity.

A Navajo Initiation

No more painful ideal of initiation has ever existed than that of the Mandan ókeepâ, seen by Catlin in 1832 and described by him in his works. So terrible was his description that many doubted its truth, yet since his day others have witnessed the ókeepâ and testified to the correctness of his account. I number myself among the corroborating witnesses; I saw the work of the last day at the ceremony in 1870. We have accounts of other Indian initiations almost if not quite as cruel as that of the ókeepâ.

But among the Navajos of New Mexico, a tribe not further advanced in civilization than the Mandans, and not less inclined to war, I have witnessed an initiatory rite in which only a semblance of punishment was enacted and no real pain inflicted. Furthermore, I have never witnessed, or heard of, a more severe ordeal except in elements of fast and vigil practiced by the Navajos.

The rite I am about to describe occurs during a great nine-days' ceremony called Klèdze Hatàl, or the Night Chant. This is really a healing ceremony. It is celebrated primarily for the cure of a rich invalid, who pays the heavy expenses; but the occasion is devoted to other purposes also, to prayers for the benefit of the people at large, and among other things, to the initiation of youths and maidens, and sometimes people of maturer years, into the secret of the Yèbitsai.

I have several times witnessed this initiation and have myself submitted to it, in order to obtain certain privileges which pertain to it. So I shall speak of it, not as I saw it on one occasion, but as I saw it on many occasions, and I shall add some information derived from the medicine men who direct it.

On the fifth night of the Night Chant, an hour or two after sunset, "the basket is turned down," as the Navajos express it; in other words, a basket is inverted to serve as a drum; this is done with many mystic observances. A crier at the door of the big medicine lodge cries, "Biké hatáli hakú!" "Come on the trail of song;" a moment later the singers begin to sing, and the drummer to pound on his basket-drum. At the same time the two men who are to enact the part of yéi or divine ones at the ceremony, begin to dress, adorn and paint themselves. At last they put on their masks. While they are dressing an assistant prepares the two yédadestsani, or implements used in the initiation of the females. A buffalo-robe is spread on a blanket west of the fire, and, after a special series of ten songs have been sung, the divine masqueraders leave the lodge.

These two implements for initiating the females consist each of an ear of yellow corn, which must be tipped with four grains arranged compactly together. To the ear, four branchlets of yucca are tied.

After the masqueraders (yéi let us call them) are gone, the singing stops and there is an expectant silence in the lodge. The yéi have gone to conduct or drive before them, rather, the candidates to the lodge. Soon the procession enters—the patient first, a number of candidates for initiation following, and the yéi bringing up the rear.

The divinities represented on this occasion are Hastséyalti, or the Talking God, and Hastsébaad or Yébaad, a goddess. Hastséyalti is also called Yébitsai, or maternal grandfather of the gods or genii. The person who enacts the goddess is a man, but feminine pronouns will be used in speaking of him. When these gods now enter the lodge, Hastséyalti carries in his hands two large leaves of yucca baccata, while Hastsébaad carries a spotted fawnskin containing pollen.

On entering, the patient sits in the south of the lodge; the candidates sit west of the central fire and buffalo robe, facing the east in a curved row. The males sit in a squatting position in the north; the females sit to the south with lower limbs extended toward the east; the mothers sit south of the girls. The candidates enter the lodge with their heads bowed and faces hidden in the folds of their blankets, and they remain thus after sitting until they are otherwise bidden. The males disrobe under their screening blankets, taking off everything but their breech-cloths. Meanwhile the yéi keep up an occasional hooting and stand facing the group of candidates. When the males are all ready the yéi stand facing that one who sits farthest north. The goddess whoops as a signal. The candidate throws off his blanket, rises and takes one step forward. The goddess applies meal transversely to the shins of the candidate from south to north. The Talking God advances and strikes the candidate in the same place with a yucca leaf. He carries a leaf in each hand; he strikes with one leaf, holding its point to the north; changes the leaves in his hand and strikes with the other leaf, holding the point to the south. The goddess then applies meal from below upward to the right side of the chest and to the left side, from nipple to collar bone, in the order mentioned. The god follows, striking in the same places and in the same order, once on each side, with his yucca leaf held upright, and changing, as before, the leaves from hand to hand between strokes. The candidate turns sunwise around with his back to the yéi, is sprinkled with meal and struck on the shoulder blades in a manner similar to that in which he was struck on the breast. He turns round again, facing the yéi, and extends his forearms, hands clinched, palm side up. Meal is applied transversely across the forearms from south to north and from north to south, and they are struck with the yucca leaves, pointing alternately in these directious in a manner similar to that in which the shins were treated. The Yébaad or goddess always applies the meal and Hastséyalti, the Talking God, always applies the yucca wands and always changes them in his hands between the strokes.

The candidate returns to his place in the line, sits down, bows his head and covers it with his blanket. The youth sitting next him in the south then rises, and submits himself to similar operations at the hands of the yéi, and so on, down the line until all the males have been powdered and flagellated.

As the leaf of this yucca, which is often called Spanish bayonet, is two feet or more in length, very stout and very much like a large bayonet in size and shape, it might be supposed that the stroke is painful; but I did not find it so in my own case, and I have questioned Indians who were initiated at a tender age and have been told that they did not suffer from the stroke. The punishment is symbolic only.

The females are not compelled to rise while the yéi are operating on them, nor to remove any of their clothing except that portion of the blanket which covers the head and shoulders. Neither are they flagellated, but they must still keep their heads bowed. Instead of yucca wands, the implements of corn and spruce, called yédadestsani, are used and merely pressed against their persons. The parts of the females, alternately sprinkled with meal and pressed with the implements are the following, in the order mentioned: The soles of the feet, the palms and forearms (which lie extended on the thighs), the upper parts of the chest, to the collar bones, the scapular regions, the top of the head on both sides of the parting of the hair. The Yébaad sprinkles the meal from below upward—for example, on the feet she sprinkles from heel to toe—and always first on the south or right side of the body and then on the north side. Hastséyalti presses his implements simultaneously on both sides, and between applications, while his companion applies the meal, he changes the implements in his hands. Throughout the work, on all the candidates, each yéi gives his own peculiar cry with the performance of each act. Each candidate covers his (or her) head with his blanket when the yéi are done with him.

The difference between the treatment of the male and the female candidates in this rite is worthy of consideration in view of the wide spread opinion that the savage has no consideration or respect for his females.

Now, while the candidates are all seated again in a row, with heads bowed and faces covered, the yéi take off their masks and lay them side by side on the buffalo robe, faces up, and tops to the east. The female mask, that of Hastsébaad, lies south of the male mask, that of Hastséyalti. The men who personated the gods then stand with uncovered faces turned toward the row of candidates. The latter are bidden to throw back their blankets and look up. They do so, and the secret of the Yébitsai is revealed.

And the secret of the Yébitsai is this: The yéi are the bugaboos of the Navajo children. These Indians rarely inflict corporal punishment on the young, but instead threaten them with the vengeance of these masked characters, if they are unruly. Up to the time of their initiation they are taught to believe, and, in most cases, probably do believe, that the yéi are genuine abnormal creatures whose function it is to chastise bad children. When the children are old enough to understand the value of obedience without resort to threats they are allowed to undergo this initiation and learn that the dreaded yéi is only some intimate friend or relation in disguise. After this initiation they are privileged to enter the medicine lodge during the performance of a rite.

Some Navajos neglect this initiation until they have reached mature years, and though it is, of course, well known that they no longer believe in the bugbear, they are not admitted into the lodges while esoteric work is in progress. On the other hand they are not anxious to intrude themselves, for the oldest among the tribe profess to believe that if they were to witness the secret ceremonies without having been duly initiated they would sooner or later be stricken blind, or would catch the disease which is being driven out of the patient.

To attain the highest priviliges in these rites one must go through this ceremony four times—twice at night and twice in the day. I have seen many adult men and women, and some even past middle life, going through their second, third or fourth ordeals. It is uot until one has submitted himself for the fourth time to the flagellation that he is permitted to wear the masks and personate the gods.

The next part of the ceremony is the application of the mask. He who masquerades as a goddess, takes the female mask and applies it in turn to the face of each of the candidates—proceeding along the row from north to south—and adjusts the mask carefully to the face so that the candidate can look out through the eye-holes and understand fully the mechanism of the mask. The mask is then laid in its former position, south of the other mask on the buffalo-robe. The actor takes good care that the eyes of the candidate are seen clearly through the eye-holes in the mask. If they are not, it is thought, blindness would result.

The next part of the performance is the act of sprinkling, or sacrificing to, the masks. Each candidate, in turn, beginning as usual in the north, rises and walks to the east of the recumbent masks, passing by way of the west and north. Standing facing the west he (or she) takes a pinch of pollen from the fawn-skin bag, which now lies west of the masks in charge of an assistant. He sprinkles it in a line downwards on each mask from the tip of the forehead to the mouth, then upwards on the right cheek or margin, and lastly upwards on the left (south) cheek or margin. He powders first the mask of Hastséyalti in the north and then that of Hastsébaad in the south. Any pollen that may adhere to his fingers is brushed off so that it may fall on the mask (but not on the eye-holes, for this would endanger the sight of the devotee.) This done, he returns to his seat and resumes his clothing. When the candidates have finished sprinkling, others in the lodge may follow their example. Each person should pray in silence for what he most desires while sprinkling. Great care is observed in sprinkling the masks, for this part of the ceremony is of the gravest import. Before they begin, the children are told carefully how to proceed, and the younger ones have their hand guided by the actors. If one sprinkles upwards on the nose of the mask it is supposed that the act may hinder the fall of rain and occasion drought; if he sprinkles downwards on the divine cheeks, the act may injure the growth of crops and even the growth of the sprinkler himself.

The last act is the fumigation. Hot coals, taken directly from the fire, are placed at intervals in front of the line of candidates; around these coals they gather in groups of three or four. The powder called yádedinil is sprinkled on the coals, and the dense odorous fumes arising therefrom are inhaled by the candidates for a few seconds. This completes the initiation. They now sit around the lodge wherever it suits their convenience and listen to the songs of sequence, which, beginning while the candidates were sacrificing to the masks, continue for abont fifteen minutes after the services are completed. The last two of the atsá'lei songs and the song for turning up the basket are sung. Then "the basket is turned up" and put in the west edge of the lodge, and the work of the night is done.

Usually the night initiation is conducted only on the fifth night of the Clédjohatál, but on one occasion I have seen candidates admitted also on the sixth night. The next repetition of the rite occurs out of doors and in the day time.

Washington, D. C.

PART THREE

Washington Matthews' Bibliography

The Guide to the Microfilm Edition of the Washington Matthews Papers *(Halpern 1985) contained a complete bibliography of Matthews' publications, which is here reproduced with a number of additions and corrections. (This bibliography had originally been assembled on the basis of Robert M. Poor's biography [Poor 1975].) Reviews and brief comments have been separated from books and articles to show more clearly the development of Matthews' own work. There is also a separate section listing publications by others who used Matthews' data and another section listing biographical publications about him. All items were examined except for a few that could not be located and those are so designated. Two journal names are abbreviated:* AA *for the* American Anthropologist, *and* JAFL *for the* Journal of American Folklore.

Books and Articles

1868–69 The Diary of Surgeon Washington Matthews, Ft. Rice, D. T., August 1, 1868 to October 4, 1869, ed. by Ray H. Mattison. North Dakota History 21 (1954): 5–74.

1870 Ft. Rice and Ft. Stevenson, Dakota Territory, Reports of Asst. Surg. Washington Matthews, U.S. Army. *In* A Report on Barracks and Hospitals with Descriptions of Military Posts, pp. 390–99. Circular No. 4, U.S. War Dept., SGO. Washington, D.C.: G.P.O. (Reprinted by Sol Lewis, New York, 1974.)

1873 Grammar and Dictionary of the Language of the Hidatsa (Minnetarees, Grosventres of the Missouri) with an Introductory Sketch of the Tribe. Shea's Library of American Linguistics, ser. ii, n. 1. New York: Cramoisy Press.

1874 Hidatsa (Minnetarees) English Dictionary. Shea's Library of American Linguistics, ser. ii, n. 2: 149–69. New York: Cramoisy Press.

1875 Ft. Stevenson, Dakota Territory, Report of Asst. Surg. Washington Matthews, U.S. Army. *In* A Report on the Hygiene of the U.S. Army with Descriptions of Military Posts, pp. 438–41. Circular No. 8, U.S. War Dept., SGO. Washington, D.C.: G.P.O. (Reprinted by Sol Lewis, New York, 1974.)

1877 Ethnography and Philology of the Hidatsa Indians. U.S. Geological and Geographical Survey, Miscellaneous Publication no. 7. Washington: G.P.O. Reprinted 1969 in Plains Anthropologist 14 (45) and 1971 by Johnson Reprint editions, New York and London.

1882 "The Pagan Martyrs," anonymous poem accompanying article: The Tenacity of the Indian Customs, by Sylvester Baxter. American Architect and Building News (Boston, October 21) n. 356: 196. (Not seen.) Three stanzas are reprinted in W. W. Newell's obituary of Matthews, JAFL 18, 1905: 245–47.

1883a Navajo Silversmiths. Bureau of [American] Ethnology, 2nd Annual Report for 1880–81: 167–78 (pl. 16–20). Reprinted 1968 by Filter Press, Palmer Lake, Colo.

1883b A Part of the Navajo's Mythology. American Antiquarian 5: 207–24. A German translation of this was published in Der Westen 10-14-83.

1884a Navajo Weavers. Bureau of [American] Ethnology, 3rd Annual Report for 1881–1882: 371–91 (pl. 24–38). Reprinted 1968 by Filter Press, Palmer Lake, Colo.

1884b A Night with the Navajos, by Zay Elini (pseudonym). Forest and Stream 23 (15) (N.Y. November 6): 282–83.

1885a Natural Naturalists. Philosophical Society of Washington, Bulletin 7 for 1884: 73–74. Abstract of paper read by J. S. Billings for Matthews 10-25-84. Also published in Smithsonian Miscellaneous Collection, vol. 33, 1888.

1885b The Cubature of the Skull. Anthropological Society of Washington, Transactions vol. 3: 171–72. Abstract of paper read 5-19-85.

1885c The Origin of the Utes, A Navajo Myth. American Antiquarian 7: 271–74.

1885d Mythic Dry-Paintings of the Navajos. American Naturalist 19: 931–39. Also abstract of this paper published in Philosophical Society of Washington, Bulletin 8 for 1885: 14–16 and reproduced in Smithsonian Miscellaneous Collection, v. 33, 1888. Another abstract published in Anthropological Society of Washington, Transactions 3: 139–40.

1885e Anthropometric and Reaction-time Apparatus. Philosophical Society of Washington, Bulletin 8 for 1885: 25. Also published Smithsonian Miscellaneous Collection, v. 33, 1888. Report of a meeting 10-10-85 at which Matthews and J. S. Billings exhibited Francis Galton's anthropometric apparatus.

1886a On Measuring the Cubic Capacity of Skulls. Memoirs of the National Academy of Sciences 3, pt. 2, 13th Memoir: 107–16.

1886b (with John S. Billings) On a New Craniophore for Use in Making Composite Photographs of Skulls. Memoirs of the National Academy of Sciences 3, pt. 2, 14th Memoir: 117–19.

1886c Apparatus for Tracing Orthogonal Projections of the Skull in the U.S. Army Medical Museum. Journal of Anatomy and Physiology 21: 43–45.

1886d An Apparatus for Determining the Angle of Torsion of the Humerus. Journal of Anatomy and Physiology 21: 536–38.

1886e Navajo Names for Plants. American Naturalist 20: 767–77.

1886f Some Deities and Demons of the Navajos. American Naturalist 20: 841–50.

1886g Consumption among the Indians. American Climatological Association, Transactions: 234–41.

1887a The Mountain Chant: A Navajo Ceremony. Bureau of [American] Ethnology, 5th Annual Report for 1883–84: 379–467 (pl. 10–18). Reprinted 1952 under title Dance with Fire, by Grabhorn Press (Leslie and William Denman) and 1970 by Rio Grande Press, Glorieta, N. M. For the "Suppressed Part of the Mountain Chant," see 1892c.

1887b How the Navajo Indians Make Blankets. Scientific American (February 12): 99–100.

1887c Consumption among the Indians. New York Medical Journal 45 (January 1): 1–3.

1887d The Study of Consumption among the Indians, A Reply to Dr. Thomas J. Mays. New York Medical Journal 46 (July 30): 127–28.

1888a The Prayer of a Navajo Shaman. AA o.s. 1: 149–71.

1888b Two Mandan Chiefs. American Antiquarian 10: 269–72.

1888c A Further Contribution to the Study of Consumption among the Indians. American Climatological Association, Transactions of 5th Annual Meeting: 136–55.

1888d Medical and Surgical History of the War of the Rebellion, Medical History:

pt. 3, v. 1. Washington, D.C.: G.P.O. Matthews' cases are described on pp. 348, 666, 667, 670, 694, 714, 773, 774, 796, 814, 826, 969.

1889a The Inca Bone and Kindred Formations among the Ancient Arizonians. AA o.s. 2: 337–45.

1889b Navajo Gambling Songs. AA o.s. 2: 1–19.

1889c Nquoilpi, the Gambler: A Navajo Myth. JAFL 2 (5): 89–94.

1890a The Gentile System of the Navajo Indians. JAFL 3 (9): 89–110.

1891a Marriage Prohibitions on the Father's Side among Navajos. JAFL 4 (12): 78–79.

1891b The Catlin Collection of Indian Paintings. Report of U.S. National Museum for 1890: 593–610.

1892a Meaning of the Word "Arikara." AA o.s. 5: 35–36.

1892b A Study in Butts and Tips. AA o.s. 5: 345–50.

1892c The Suppressed Part of the Mountain Chant. This is a printed pamphlet of two inserts, one at par. 130, p. 433, and the other at par. 145, p. 441, of the Mountain Chant 1887a, published privately Fort Wingate, N. M. (Margaret Schevill Link made a typescript of this pamphlet in 1950, which is in the National Anthropological Archives, Smithsonian Institution, NAVAJO 4834.)

1892d The Ceremonial Circuit, JAFL 5 (19): 334–35.

1893a The Human Bones of the Hemenway Collection in the U.S. Army Medical Museum, with Observations on the Hyoid Bones of the Collection by J. L. Wortman. Memoirs of the National Academy of Science v. 6, 7th Memoir: 141–286 (pl. 1–59).

1893b Navajo Dye Stuffs. Smithsonian Annual Report for 1891:613–16.

1894a The Basket Drum. AA o.s. 7: 202–8.

1894b Songs of Sequence of the Navajos. JAFL 7 (26): 185–94.

1894c Some Illustrations of the Connection between Myth and Ceremony. *In* Memoirs of the International Congress of Anthropology, ed. by C. Staniland Wake, v. 22: 246–51. Chicago: The Schulte Publishing Co.

1894d Explorations in the Salado Valley. The Archaeologist (Waterloo, Indiana) 2 (12) (December): 351–66. This repeats introduction to 1893a, with some omissions.

1894e The Terrace or Stepped Figure. American Antiquarian 16:114. (A paragraph in "Correspondence" section.)

1895a Mt. Taylor. American Antiquarian 17:294. (In "Correspondence.")

1896a A Vigil of the Gods—A Navaho Ceremony. AA o.s. 9: 50–57.

1896b Songs of the Navajos. Land of Sunshine 5: 197–201.

1896c In Memoriam: John Gregory Bourke. Science 4: 820–22.

1897a Navaho Legends. Memoirs of the American Folklore Society, Memoir 5. Boston: Houghton Mifflin.

1897b The Study of Ceremony. JAFL 10 (39): 257–63.

1898a Use of Rubber Bags in Gauging Cranial Capacity. AA o.s. 11: 171–76.

1898b Icthyophobia. JAFL 11 (41): 105–12. Reprinted in Folklore of the Great West, ed. by John Greenway, pp. 95–100 (Palo Alto: American West, 1970).

1898c Serpent Worship among the Navajos. Land of Sunshine 9: 228–35.

1898d Some Sacred Objects of the Navajo Rites. Archives of the International Folklore Association 1: 227–47. Chicago: Charles H. Sergel Co. (Paper given at International Folklore Congress of the World's Columbian Exposition, Chicago, 1893. Helen Wheeler Bassett and Frederick Starr, eds. Reprinted New York: Arno Press, 1980.)

1899a Seeking the Lost Adam. Land of Sunshine 10: 113–25.

1899b The Study of Ethics among the Lower Races. JAFL 12 (44): 1–9. (A note in AA 3 (1901): 369 says this was translated into French by Henriette Rynenbroeck, "L'étude de l'éthique chez les races inférieures," Humanité Nouvelle, Paris, 1901, V, 140–48.)

1900a In Memoriam: Frank Hamilton Cushing, 1857–1900. AA 2: 370–76.

1900b A Two-Faced Navaho Blanket. AA 2: 638–42.

1900c The Cities of the Dead. Land of Sunshine 12: 213–21.

1901a Navaho Night Chant. JAFL 14 (52): 12–19.

1901b The Treatment of Ailing Gods. JAFL 14 (52): 20–23.

1901c A Navajo Initiation. Land of Sunshine 15: 353–56.

1901d A Goose Hunt with Two Hearts (by Roderick Heron, pseudonym). Forest and Stream (June 15).

1901e Sustained by the Supreme Court. Land of Sunshine 14: 238.

1902a The Night Chant: A Navaho Ceremony. Memoirs of the American Museum of Natural History, Anthropology, v. 6.

1902b Myths of Gestation and Parturition. AA 4: 737–42.

1902c The Earth Lodge in Art. AA 4: 1–12.

1903a Was Willow Bark Smoked by Indians? AA 5: 170–71.

1903b Sturnella's Song. Out West 18: 613–15. Poem.

1904a The Navaho Yellow Dye. AA 6: 194.

1904b The Navaho Clan. AA 6: 758–59. Abstract of paper read at Anthropological Society of Washington 11-29-04.

1904c The First Model for a Statue of Sacajewea. Lewis and Clark Journal 1 (March): 17–18.

1905a The Eyes of Judah. Out West 22: 68. Poem.

1905b The Contrast. Out West 22: 304–5. Poem with picture of Matthews.

1906 Three Short Words. Out West 24: 216. Poem.

1907 (with Pliny Earle Goddard) Navaho Myths, Prayers, and Songs. University of California Publications in American Archaeology and Ethnology 5: 21–63.

1907 and 1910 The following articles. *In* Handbook of American Indians, edited by F. W. Hodge, Bureau of American Ethnology, Bulletin 30.
Vol. I Color Symbolism, pp. 325–26; Dry-Painting, pp. 403–4; Ethics and Morals (with Alice C. Fletcher), pp. 441–42; Measurements, pp. 828–29; Magic, pp. 783–85.
Vol. II Navaho, pp. 41–45.

Reviews and Comments

1885f A New Cranial Race Character. American Naturalist 19: 1244. Comment on and quote from Dr. Lissauer, Untersuchungen über die sagittale Krümmung des Schädels bei den Anthropoiden und den verschiedenen Menschrassen . . . Separat-Abdruck aus dem Archive für Anthropologie, XV Band, Supplement.

1888e Review of: Archives de biologie, Tome VII Fascicule III, 1887—La race humaine de Néanderthal ou de Canstadt en Belgique, par Julien Fraipont. AA o.s. 1: 286–87.

1888f Review of: Revue d'anthropologie, March 15, 1888—Le tibia dans le race de Néanderthal, par Julien Fraiport. AA o.s. 1: 287.

1889d Plume-Sticks (Kethawns bahos) among the Northern Tribes. AA o.s. 2: 46. Comment on and quote from a "Fort Berthold Item" in Word Carrier, Santee Agency, Nebraska, 1888.

1889e One More Skull of the Neanderthal Race. AA o.s. 2: 53–54. Comment on and quote from an article by Hamy in Revue d'anthropologie, 5-15-88.

1889f The Descent of Man. AA o.s. 2: 20. Quote from an article by Paul Topinard in Revue d'anthropologie, 1888.

1889g Are There Totem-Clans in the Old Testament? AA o.s. 2: 345. Comment on an article by Joseph Jacobs in Archaeological Review, May 1889.

1889h Counting-Out Rhymes among Indian Children. AA o.s. 2: 320. Comment on and quote from a paper on Wabanaki Indians by Mrs. W. W. Brown read before the Royal Society of Canada 5-23-88.

1889i Review of: L'archéologie Préhistorique par Le Baron J. de Baye, 1888. AA o.s. 2: 183.

1889j Review of: Tatooing, Cicatricial Marking, and Body-Painting, by Wilhelm Joest, 1887. AA o.s. 2: 85.

1889k Review of: De l'oreille au point de vue anthropologique et médico-legal, par le Dr. J. Julia, 1889. AA o.s. 2: 366–67.

1889l Review of: Boletin de le Sociedad Anthropologica de la Isla de Cuba. AA o.s. 2: 367–68.

1889m Review of: Ueber vier Koreaner Schädel, by Dr. Koganei, 1888, in Mittheilungen aus der Medicinischen Facultät der Kaeserlich-japaneschen Universatät, Tokio. AA o.s. 2: 368.

1889n Review of: Heredite et Alcoholisme, par le Dr. M. Legrain, 1889. AA o.s. 2: 368–69.

1890b Olecranon Perforation. AA o.s. 3: 173–74. Comment on paper by D. L. Lamb.

1890c Review of: Die Forschungsreise S. M. S. Gazelle in den Jahren 1874 bis 1876 unter Kommando des Kapitän zur See Freihern von Schleinitz, herausgegeben von den Hydrographischen Amt des Reichs-Marine-Amts. AA o.s. 3: 285–86.

1890d Review of: Among the Cannibals, by Carl Lumholtz, 1889. AA o.s. 3: 89–92.

1891c Review of: The Klamath Indians of Southwestern Oregon, by Albert S. Gatschet. AA o.s. 4: 294–97.

1893c Review of: Dakota-English Dictionary, by Stephen R. Riggs. AA o.s. 6: 96–98.

1893d Review of: Bibliography of the Athapascan Languages, by James C. Pilling. AA o.s. 6: 105–6.

1893e Review of: The Song of the Ancient People, by Edna Dean Proctor. AA o.s. 6: 340–41.

1894f Review of: The Snake Ceremonials at Walpi, by J. Walter Fewkes, with A. M. Stephen and J. G. Owens. AA o.s. 7: 420–22.

1895b Review of: Proceedings of the Fourth Annual Meeting of the Association of Military Surgeons. Journal of the Military Service Institution of the U.S. 16: 165–69.

1896d Review of: Outline of Zuni Creation Myths, by Frank H. Cushing. JAFL 9 (34): 233–35.

1897c Review of: The Ghost Dance Religion, by James Mooney, JAFL 10 (38): 248–49.

1899c Review of: Creation Myths of Primitive America, by Jeremiah Curtin, 1898. AA 1: 377–78.

1899d Review of: Anthropologie des Anciens Habitants de la Région Calchaquie, by Herman F. C. ten Kate. AA 1: 563–64.

1899e Review of: The Magic of the Horseshoe, with Other Folklore Notes, by Robert Means Lawrence. AA 1: 378–79.

1900d Review of: Indian Story and Song from North America, by Alice C. Fletcher. AA 2: 748–49.

1901f Review of: Calendar History of the Kiowa Indians, by James C. Mooney. AA 3: 542–44.

1902d Review of: Zuni Folk Tales, by Frank H. Cushing. AA 4: 144–45.

Publications Using Matthews' Observations and Data

Matthews was often called on to contribute his own observations to the work of colleagues, especially during the years of his association with the Smithsonian Institution. A number of publications containing such comments came to our attention and have been listed below. This list is not intended to be exhaustive.

Darwin, Charles

1896 The Expression of Emotions in Man and Animals. New York: D. Appleton. (In this edition pp. 22, 230, 257, 268, 276, 289 acknowledge correspondence with Matthews and his help and examples from Indian tribes of the Upper Missouri. Earlier edition was not available.)

Fillmore, John Comfort

1896 Songs of the Navajos. Land of Sunshine 5: 238–41. (A companion piece to Matthews 1896b, analyzing songs from Matthews' Cylinders 38, 41, 49, and 62.)

1899 The Harmonic Structure of Indian Music. AA 1: 297–318 (posthumous). (Acknowledges debt to Matthews.)

Hrdlicka, Ales

1900 Physical and Physiological Observations on the Navajo. AA 2: 339–45. (Matthews made measurements on adult Navajos at 1893 Chicago World's Fair and gave permission to incorporate them in this article.)

Larpenteur, Charles

1898 Forty Years a Fur Trader on the Upper Missouri. Edited by Elliott Coues. New York: F. P. Harper, 2 vols. (Reprinted, two vols. in one, Minneapolis: Ross and Haines, Inc. 1962). (Matthews' comments and quotes in footnotes.)

Mallery, Garrick

1881 Sign Language among the North American Indians. First Annual Report of the Bureau of [American] Ethnology for 1879–80, pp. 263–552. Washington, D.C.

1886 Pictographs of North American Indians. Fourth Annual Report of the Bureau of [American] Ethnology for 1882–83, pp. 13–256. Washington, D.C. (Matthews furnished comments for both of these publications.)

Mooney, James

1896 The Ghost Dance Religion. Fourteenth Annual Report of the Bureau of [American] Ethnology for 1892–93, pt. 2: 641–1136. (Matthews provided comments re absence of Ghost Dance among the Navajos.)

Pilling, James C.

1892 Bibliography of the Athapascan Languages. Bureau of [American] Ethnology, Bulletin 14, pp. 63–65. Washington, D.C. (Comments by Matthews regarding the state of his linguistic work and a bibliography of his publications.)

Stephen, Alexander M.

1888 Legend of the Snake Order of the Moquis as Told by Outsiders. JAFL 1 (2): 109–14. (Letter introducing this article is by Matthews.)

Yarrow, H. C.

1881 A Further Contribution to the Study of the Mortuary Customs of the North American Indians. First Annual Report of the Bureau of [American] Ethnology for 1879–80, pp. 87–203. Washington, D.C. (Comments by Matthews.)

Biographical References

Lamb, D. S.

n.d. A History of the U.S. Army Medical Museum, 1862–1917, compiled from official records. Typescript. (Matthews' activities at the Museum are mentioned, pp. 50–51, 86–93, 103–4, 116, 123.)

Hough, Walter

1933 Washington Matthews. Dictionary of American Biography, v. 12, p. 420. New York: Scribners.

Journal of the American Medical Association

1905 Washington Matthews. v. 44: 1630.

(Lummis, Charles F.)

1897 Authorities on the Southwest: Dr. Washington Matthews. Land of Sunshine 6: 109–11. (Contains brief appreciation of Matthews.)

1905a The Passing of the Dean. Land of Sunshine 22: 426–27. (Tribute to Matthews.)

1905b The Nation 81, no. 2090, July 20. (A single paragraph on Matthews presumably written by Lummis.)

Mooney, James

1905 In Memoriam: Washington Matthews. American Anthropologist 7: 514–23.

Newell, W. W.

1905 In Memoriam: Washington Matthews. Journal of American Folklore 18: 245–47.

Poor, Robert M.

1975 Washington Matthews: An Intellectual Biography. Master's Thesis, University of Nevada, Reno. 148, p., mimeo. (University Microfilms, No. M-8323)

Schevill Link, Margaret E.

1947 Beautiful on the Earth. Santa Fe: Hazel Deris Editions.

1948–49 Dr. Washington Matthews (1843–1905). Kiva 14: 2–6.

1960 From the Desk of Washington Matthews. Journal of American Folklore 73: 317–25. (Contains reference to Matthews' son Berthold, also an unpublished and abridged mythological excerpt from Matthews' Notebook 674, pp. 36–50.)

Spencer, Robert F.

1970 Introduction to: Ethnography and Philology of the Hidatsa Indians, pp. xxii–xxv. New York: Johnson Reprint Edition.

Watson, I. A.

1896 (Biographical notice) In Physicians and Surgeons of America. Concord, N.Y.: Republican Press Asssociation. (Not seen).

Wedel, Waldo R.

1969 Washington Matthews: His Constribution to Plains Anthropology. Plains Anthropology 14: 175–76.

Who Was Who in America 1897–1942

1943 Washington Matthews. Chicago: Marquis.

References Cited

The following journal names are abbreviated: AA for the *American Anthropologist* and JAFL for the *Journal of American Folklore.* The essays in Part One reference Matthews' unpublished papers by citing page and item number in the *Guide to the Microfilm Edition of the Washington Matthews Papers* (see Halpern 1985). In a few cases, the microfilm roll number is also given. Other archival references are explained in the individual essays, as are references to personal communications.

Aberle, David F.

1960 The Peyote Religion among the Navaho. Viking Fund Publications in Anthropology 42. New York: Wenner-Gren Foundation for Anthropological Research.

1967 The Navaho Singer's Fee: Payment or Prestation. *In* Studies in Southwestern Ethnolinguistics. Dell H. Hymes and W. E. Bittle, eds. pp. 15–32. The Hague: Mouton.

1982 The Future of Navajo Religion. *In* Navajo Religion and Culture: Selected Views. Papers in Honor of Leland C. Wyman. David M. Brugge and Charlotte J. Frisbie, eds. Museum of New Mexico Papers in Anthropology 17:219–31.

Abrams, M. H.

1986 The Norton Anthology of English Literature. Fifth Edition, vol. 2. New York: W. W. Norton and Co.

Adair, John

1944 The Navajo and Pueblo Silversmiths. Norman: University of Oklahoma Press.

Amsden, Charles Avery

1934 Navajo Weaving, Its Technic and History. Santa Ana, California: Fine Arts Press. (2nd edition, University of New Mexico Press, 1946; reprinted Rio Grande Press, 1972)

Astrov, Margot

1946 The Winged Serpent: An Anthology of American Indian Prose and Poetry. New York: John Day Co.

Bailey, Garrick, and Roberta Glenn Bailey
1986 A History of the Navajos: The Reservation Years. Santa Fe: School of American Research Press.

Baird, Spencer
1889 Annual Report of the Smithsonian Institution for 1886. Washington, D.C.: G.P.O.

Baker, Frank
1895 Review of: The Human Bones of the Hemenway Collection in the U.S. Army Medical Museum. AA o.s. 8: 86–89.

Bandelier, Adolph F.
1970 The Southwestern Journals of Adolph F. Bandelier, 1883–84. Charles H. Lange, Carroll L. Riley, and Elizabeth M. Lange, eds. Albuquerque: University of New Mexico Press.
1890 The Historical Archives of the Hemenway Southwestern Archaeological Expedition. International Congress of Americanists, Berlin, 1888: 450–59.

Barnes, Nellie
1921 American Indian Verse: Characteristics of Style. University of Kansas Bulletin XXII, no. 18.

Baxter, Sylvester
1882 The Tenacity of Indian Customs. The American Architect and Building News, October 21: 195–97. (Contains Matthews' poem "The Pagan Martyrs")

Benedict, Ruth
1935 Zuni Mythology. Columbia University Contributions to Anthropology, v. 21.

Bierhorst, John
1974 Four Masterworks of American Literature. New York: Farrar, Straus and Giroux.

Boas, Franz
1935 Kwakiutl Culture as Reflected in Mythology. American Folklore Society, Memoir 28.

Bourke, John G.
1936 Bourke on the Southwest, VIII–X. Lansing E. Bloom, ed. New Mexico Historical Review 11:77–122, 188–207, 217–82.

Brody, J. J.
1991 Anasazi and Pueblo Pottery in the 20th Century and Beyond. American Indian Art 16:2.

Buckland, A. W.
1893 Points of Contact between Old World Customs and Navajo Myth Entitled the Mountain Chant. Journal of the Royal Anthropological Institute 22:346–55.

Brinton, Daniel
1881–1933 Library of Aboriginal Literature. 5 vols. Washington, D.C.: Bureau of American Ethnology.

Brotherston, Gordon
1979 Image of the New World: The American Continent Portrayed in Native Texts. London: Thames and Hudson.

Child, F. J.
1822–1898 The English and Scottish Popular Ballad. 5 vols. Boston: Houghton Mifflin.

Clements, William M.
1990 Schoolcraft as Textmaker. JAFL 103 (408): 177–92.

Clifford, James
1984 On Ethnographic Allegory. *In* Writing Culture: The Poetics and Politics of Ethnography. James Clifford and George E. Marcus, eds. pp. 98–121. Berkeley: University of California Press.

Coleridge, Samuel Taylor
1936 Miscellaneous Criticism. T. M. Raysor, ed. London: Constable.

Coolidge, Dane C., and Mary Roberts Coolidge
1930 The Navajo Indians. Boston: Houghton Mifflin.

Cronyn, George W.
1918 The Path of the Rainbow: An Anthology of Songs and Chants from the Indians of North America. New York: Boni and Liveright.

Culin, Stewart
1903 The Brooklyn Museum Archives, Culin Archival Collection. Report on a Collecting Expedition among the Indians of New Mexico and Arizona. September, 1903.

Curtis, Edward S.
1907 The North American Indian. Vol. 1: Apache, Jicarillas, Navaho. New York: Johnson Reprint Corporation. (Reprint edition, 1970)

Cushing, Frank H. (see also Green, Jesse)
1890 Preliminary Notes on the Origin, Working Hypothesis, and Primary Researches of the Hemenway Southwestern Archaeological Expedition. International Congress of Americanists, Berlin, 1888: 151–94.

Dante Aleghieri
1892 Letter XI: "To the Magnificent and Victorious Lord, the Lord Can Grande della Scala." *In* A Translation of Dante's Eleven Letters. Charles Sterrett Latham, ed. pp. 187–216. Boston: Houghton Mifflin.

Darnell, Regna
1974 Daniel G. Brinton and the Professionalizaion of American Anthropology. *In* American Anthropology: The Early Years. J. V. Murra, ed. Pp. 69–98. Proceedings of the American Ethnological Society. St. Paul: West Publishing Co.

Day, A. George
1951 The Sky Clears: Poetry of the American Indians. New York: Macmillan. (Reprinted by University of Nebraska Press, 1964)

de Laguna, Frederica, ed.
1960 Selected Papers from the American Anthropologist, 1888–1920. New York: Row, Peterson.

Derrida, Jacques
1976 Of Grammatology. Translated by Gayatri Chakravorty Spivak. Baltimore: Johns Hopkins University Press.

Durkheim, Emile, and Marcel Mauss
1963 Primitive Classification. Chicago: University of Chicago Press. (Original publication date 1903)

Earle, Alice Morse
1904 Child Life in Colonial Days. New York: MacMillan.

Edwards, B. B.
1832 The Eclectic Reader. Boston: Perkins and Marvin. (Quoted in Elson, p. 78)

Ehrlich, Clara
1937 Tribal Culture in Crow Mythology. JAFL 50: 307–408.

Elson, Ruth Miller
1964 Guardians of Tradition: American Schoolbooks of the Nineteenth Century. Lincoln: University of Nebraska Press.

Faris, James C.
1986 The Nightway: Yesterday and Today. Paper presented at the Navajo Studies Conference, University of New Mexico, Albuquerque, February 20–22. (Later published as Faris 1988)
1988 Navajo Nightway Chant History: A Report. Diné Be'iiná I (2): 107–17.
1990 The Nightway: A History and a History of Documentation of a Navajo Ceremonial. Albuquerque: University of New Mexico Press.

Faris, James C., and Harry Walters
1990 Navajo History: Some Implications of Contrasts of Navajo Ceremonial Discourse. History of Anthropology 5 (1): 1–18.

Fillmore, John Comfort
1896 Songs of the Navajos. Land of Sunshine 5:238–41.

Franciscan Fathers
1910 An Ethnologic Dictionary of the Navaho Language. St. Michaels, Arizona: Saint Michaels Press.

Frisbie, Charlotte J.
1967 Kinaaldá, A Study of the Navaho Girl's Puberty Ceremony. Middletown, Connecticut: Wesleyan University Press.
1975 Review of Diné' ba'alííl of Navajoland, U.S.A. Canyon Record 6117. Ethnomusicology 19 (3): 503–506.
1977 Music and Dance Research of Southwestern United States Indians: Past Trends, Present Activities and Suggestions for Future Research. Detroit Studies in Music Bibliography 36. Detroit: Information Coordinators, Inc.
1980 Vocables in Navajo Ceremonial Music. Ethnomusicology 24 (3):347–92.
1981 Review of: Interview with American Indian Musicians, videotapes by Charlotte Heth. Navajo Videos, III A and B. Ethnomusicology 25 (2): 365–81. (Review essay)
1985 Temporal Change in Navajo Religion, 1868–1896. Paper presented in Advanced Seminar in Temporal Change and Regional Variability in Navajo Culture, School of American Research, Santa Fe, October 7–11.
1986 Navajo Ceremonialists in the Pre-1970 Political World. *In* Explorations in Ethnomusicology: Essays in Honor of David P. McAllester. Charlotte J. Frisbie, ed. Detroit Monographs in Musicology 9: 79–96. Detroit: Information Coordinators, Inc.
1987 Navajo Medicine Bundles or Jish: Acquistion, Transmission, and Disposition in the Past and Present. Albuquerque: University of New Mexico Press.
1989 Gender and Navajo Music: Unanswered Questions. *In* Women in North American Indian Music: Six Essays. Richard Keeling, ed. Society for Ethnomusicology Special Series 6: 22–38.
1992 Temporal Change in Navajo Religion, 1868–1990. Journal of the Southwest 34 (4): 457–514.

Frisbie, Charlotte J., and Eddie Tso
1993 The Navajo Ceremonial Practitioner Registry. Journal of the Southwest 35 (1): 53–92.

Gill, Sam D.
1979 Songs of Life: An Introduction to Navajo Religious Culture. Leiden: E. J. Brill.
1981 Sacred Words: A Study of Navajo Religion and Prayer. Westport, Connecticut: Greenwood Press.

Green, Jesse, ed.
1990 Cushing at Zuni: Correspondence and Journals of Frank Hamilton Cushing, 1879–1884. Albuquerque: University of New Mexico Press.

Gruber, J. W.
1970 Ethnographic Salvage and the Shaping of Anthropology. AA 72: 1289–99.

Guide (references are to the Guide to the Microfilm Edition of the Washington Matthews Papers, see Halpern 1985)

Haile, Father Berard
1946 The Navaho Fire Dance. St Michaels, Arizone: St Michaels Press.
1947 Head and Face Masks in Navaho Ceremonialism. St Michaels, Arizona: St Michaels Press.
1981 The Upward-Moving and Emergence Way. American Tribal Religions, v. 7. Karl W. Luckert, ed. Lincoln: University of Nebraska Press.

Halpern, Katherine Spencer (see also Spencer)
1985 Guide to the Microfilm Edition of the Washington Matthews Papers. (See also: Wheelwright Museum of the American Indian.) Note: Throughout the present volume this Guide is cited simply as "Guide," followed by page reference.

Halpern, Katherine Spencer, and Susan Brown McGreevy
1986 Navajo Field Work in the Papers of Washington Matthews: A Report on the Microfilm Edition. Paper presented at the Navajo Studies Conference, University of New Mexico, Albuquerque, February 20–22.

Haury, Emil W.
1945 The excavation of Los Muertos and Neighboring Ruins in the Salt River Valley, Southern Arizona. Papers of the Peabody Museum of American Archaeology and Ethnology, Harvard University, v. 24, no. 1. Cambridge.

Heininger, Mary Lynn Stevens
1984 Children, Childhood and Change in America. *In* A Century of Change in America. Rochester, N.Y.: The Margaret Wordsby Strong Museum.

Hinsley, Curtis
1981 Savages and Scientists, the Smithsonian Institution and the Development of American Anthropology, 1846–1910. Washington, D.C.: Smithsonian Institution Press.
1983 Ethnographic Charisma and Scientific Routine: Cushing and Fewkes in the American Southwest, 1879–1893. *In* Observers Observed: Essays on Ethnographic Field Work. G. W. Stocking, Jr., ed. History of Anthropology, v. 1. Madison: University of Wisconsin Press.

Hobbes, Thomas
1983 Leviathan. C. B. Macpherson, ed. New York: Penguin.

Hodge, Frederick Webb

1903 Review of: The Night Chant by Washington Matthews. AA 5: 130–32.

1907 and 1910 Handbook of the American Indians. Bureau of American Ethnology, Bulletin 30. Vols. 1 and 2. Washington: G.P.O. (Also later edition 1911)

Hollister, U. S.

1903 The Navajo and His Blanket. Denver: U. S. Hollister. (Reprinted 1972 and 1974 by Rio Grande Press, Glorieta, New Mexico)

Hrdlicka, Ales

1909 Tuberculosis among Certain Indian Tribes of the United States. Bureau of American Ethnology, Bulletin 42. Washington, D.C.: G.P.O.

1914 Physical Anthropology in America. AA 16: 508–54.

Hymes, Dell

1965 Some North Pacific Coast Poems: A Problem in Anthropological Philology. AA 67 (2): 316–41.

1981 In Vain I Tried to Tell You: Essays in Native American Poetics. Philadelphia: University of Pennsylvania Press.

Journal of American Folklore

1895 Notes, v. 8: 339.

1896 Notes, v. 9: 69.

Judd, Neil M.

1967 The Bureau of American Ethnology: A Partial History. Norman: University of Oklahoma Press.

Kent, Kate Peck

1985 Navajo Weaving: Three Centuries of Change. Santa Fe, N. M.: School of American Research Press.

Ker, W. P.

1908 Epic and Romance. Oxford: Oxford University Press. (Reprinted 1957 by Dover Publications, New York)

Kernan, Alvin

1987 Printing Technology, Letters and Samuel Johnson. Princeton: Princeton University Press.

1990 The Death of Literature. New Haven: Yale University Press.

Kluckhohn, Clyde

1923 The Dance of Hasjelti. El Palacio 15: 187–92.

Kluckhohn, Clyde, W. W. Hill, and Lucy Wales Kluckhohn

1971 Navajo Material Culture. Cambridge: Belknap Press of Harvard University.

Kluckhohn, Clyde, and Leland C. Wyman

1940 An Introduction to Navaho Chant Practice. American Anthropological Association, Memoir 53.

Koenig, Seymour H.

1982 Drawings of Nightway Sandpaintings in the Bush Collection. *In* Navajo Religion and Culture: Selected Views. Papers in Honor of Leland C. Wyman. David M. Brugge and Charlotte J. Frisbie, eds. pp. 28–44. Museum of New Mexico Papers in Anthropology, v. 17.

Kunitz, Stephen J.
1986 The Medical Writings of Washington Matthews. Symposium Paper, American Anthropological Association, 85th Annual Meeting, Philadelphia.

Lamb, D. S.
n.d. A History of the U.S. Army Medical Museum, 1862–1917, Compiled from Official Records. Typescript.

Leach, MacEdward
1955 The Ballad Book. New York: A. S. Barnes Company.

Leach, MacEdward, and Tristam P. Coffin
1961 The Critics and the Ballad. Carbondale: Southern Illinois University Press.

Letherman, Jonathan
1856 Sketch of the Navahoe Tribe of Indians, Territory of New Mexico. Smithsonian Institution, 10th Annual Report for 1854–1855. pp. 283–97. Washington, D.C.: A.O.P. Nicholson.

Levitas, Glorio, Frank Robert Vivelo, and Jacqueline Vivelo
1974 American Indian Prose and Poetry: We Wait in Darkness. New York: G.P. Putnam and Sons.

Lewis, C. S.
1936 Allegory of Love. Oxford: Oxford University Press.

Littell, Norman
1967 Proposed Findings of Fact in Behalf of the Navajo Tribe of Indians in Area of the Overall Navajo Claim (Docket 229). Washington, D.C.: Privately printed.

Locke, John
1975 An Essay Concerning Human Understanding. Alexander C. Fraser, ed. 2 vols. Oxford: Clarendon Press.

Loh, Jules
1971 Lords of the Earth: A History of the Navajo Indians. New York: Crowell-Collier.

Lord, Albert B.
1971 The Singer of Tales. New York: Atheneum. (Originally published by Harvard University Press as Harvard Studies in Comparative Literature 24)

Lummis, Charles F.
1905 The Passing of the Dean (memorial comment). Out West (formerly Land of Sunshine) 22 (6):426–27.

Lyon, Luke
1986 History of the Prohibition of Photography of Southwestern Indian Ceremonies. Paper presented at the Conference on Researching Dance Through Film and Video, Washington, D.C., April 12.

McAllester, David P.
1971 Review of: Night and Daylight Yeibichei. Indian House 1502. Ethnomusicology 15 (1):167–70.
1979 A Paradigm of Navajo Dance. Parabola 4 (2):28–35.
1880a The First Snake Song. *In* Theory and Practice: Essays Presented to Gene Weltfish. Stanley Diamond, ed. pp. 1–27. The Hague: Mouton.
1880b Coyote's Song. Parabola 5 (2):47–54.
1986 Review of: Navajo: Songs of the Diné; Apache; Songs by Philip and Patsy Cassadore of the San Carlos Tribe (2 records). Ethnomusicology 12 (3):470–73.

McAllester, David P., and Susan W. McAllester
1987 Hogans, Navajo Houses and House Songs. Middletown, Connecticut: Wesleyan University Press. (First printing 1981)

McAllester, David P., and Douglas F. Mitchell
1983 Navajo Music. *In* Handbook of North American Indians, vol. 10 (2), The Southwest. Alfonso Ortiz, ed. pp. 605–23. Washington, D.C.: Smithsonian Institution.

McGreevy, Susan Brown (see also Wheelwright Museum)
1985 The Other Weavers: Navajo Basket Makers. Phoebus 4, Arizona State University College of Fine Arts:54–61.
1986 Translating Tradition: Contemporary Basketry Arts. *In* Translating Tradition: Basketry Arts of the San Juan Paiutes. pp. 25–31. Santa Fe: Wheelwright Museum of the American Indian.
1989 What Makes Sally Weave? Survival and Innovation in Navajo Basketry Trays. American Indian Art 14 (3):38–45.

McGuire, R.
1987 Economics and Modes of Production in the Prehistoric Southwestern Periphery. *In* Ripples in the Chichimec Sea: New Consideration of Southwestern-Meso-American Interactions. F. Joan Mathien and Randall H. McGuire, eds. pp. 243–69. Carbondale: Southern Illinois University Press.

McNeil, William J.
1985 The Chicago Folklore Society and the International Folklore Congress of 1893. Midwestern Journal of Language and Folklore 11 (1):5–19.

McNeley, Grace Anna
1994 Foreword to the reprint of Navaho Legends by Washington Matthews. pp. ix–xv. Salt Lake City: University of Utah Press.

Matthews, Washington (see separate bibliography)

Merbs, Charles F.
1986 Washington Matthews and the Paleopathology of the Hohokam. Symposium Paper, American Anthropological Association, 85th Annual Meeting. Philadelphia.

Mooney, James
1905 In Memoriam: Washington Matthews. AA 7:514–23.

Morgan, Lewis H.
1851 League of the Ho-de-no-sau-nee or Iroquois. Rochester and Sage: M.H. Newman. (Reprinted as League of the Iroquois, New York: Corinth Books, 1962)

Morse, Jedidiah
1784 Geography Made Easy. New Haven, Connecticut: Meigs, Bowen and Dana. (Quoted in Elson, p. 78)

Moses, L. G.
1984 The Indian Man: A Biography of James Mooney. Chicago: University of Chicago Press.

Newell, W. W.
1903 Review of: Washington Matthews' The Night Chant. JAFL 16:61–64.
1905 In Memoriam: Washington Matthews. JAFL 18:245–47.

O'Bryan, Aileen
1956 The Dîné: Origin Myths of the Navaho Indians. Bureau of American Ethnology Bulletin 163.

Olin, Caroline B.
1982 Four Mountainway Sandpaintings of Sam Tilden, 'Ayóó 'Aníłnézí. *In* Navajo Religion and Culture: Selected Views. Papers in Honor of Leland C. Wyman. David M. Brugge and Charlotte J. Frisbie, eds. pp. 45–57. Museum of New Mexico Papers in Anthropology, v. 17.

Parezo, Nancy J.
1983a Navajo Sandpainting: From Religious Act to Commercial Art. Tucson: University of Arizona Press.
1983b Navajo Singers: Keepers of Tradition, Agents of Change. *In* Woven Holy People: Navaho Sandpainting Textiles. Susan B. McGreevy, ed. pp. 19–26. Santa Fe: Wheelwright Museum of the American Indian.
1984 Cushing as Part of the Team: The Collecting Activities of the Smithsonian Institution at Zuni. American Ethnologist 12 (4):763–74.
1987 The Formation of Ethnographic Collections: The Smithsonian Institution in the American Southwest. *In* Advances in Archaeological Theory and Method, v. 10. Michael Schiffer, ed. pp. 1–47. Orlando, Florida: Academic.

Pearce, Roy Harvey
1965 Savagism and Civilization. Baltimore: Johns Hopkins University Press.

Pilling, James C.
1892 Bibliography of Athapascan Languages. Bureau of American Ethnology, Bulletin 14. Washington, D.C.: G.P.O.

Poor, Robert M.
1975 Washington Matthews: An Intellectual Biography. Master's Thesis, University of Nevada, Reno. 148 pp., mimeographed. (University Microfilms, No. M-8323)

Porter, Joseph C.
1986 Paper Medicine Man: John Gregory Bourke and His American West. Norman: University of Oklahoma Press.

Powell, John W.
1885 Introduction to Fourth Annual Report of the Bureau of [American] Ethnology for 1882–83. Washington, D.C.: G.P.O.
1887 Introduction to Mountain Chant, pp. xliv–xlviii, Fifth Annual Report of the Bureau of [American] Ethnology for 1883–84. Washington, D.C.: G.P.O.
1888 Introduction to Sixth Annual Report of the Bureau of [American] Ethnology for 1884–85. Washington, D.C.: G.P.O.

Preminger, Alex
1974 Princeton Encyclopedia of Poetry and Poetics. Princeton: Princeton University Press.

Proctor, Edna Dean
1893 The Song of the Ancient People. With Preface and Notes by John Fiske and Commentary by F. H. Cushing. Boston and New York: Houghton, Mifflin.

Reagan, Albert B.
1934 A Navaho Fire Dance. AA 36:434–37.

Reichard, Gladys A.
1936 Navajo Shepherd and Weaver. New York: J. J. Augustin.
1939 Navajo Medicine Man. New York: J. J. Augustin.
1944 Prayer: The Compulsive Word. New York: J. J. Augustin.

1950 Navaho Religion, A Study of Symbolism. New York: Pantheon Books. Bollingen Series 18. Princeton: Princeton University Press. (Later printing 1963)

n.d. Another Look at the Navajo. Unpublished manuscript. Wheelwright Museum of the American Indian, Santa Fe, N. M.

Rodee, Marian

1987 Weaving of the Southwest, from the Maxwell Museum of Anthropology, University of New Mexico. West Chester, Pa.: Schiffer Publishing Co.

Sapir, Edward, and Harry Hoijer

1942 Navaho Texts. Iowa City: Linguistic Society of America.

Schaafsma, Polly

1980 Indian Rock Art of the Southwest. Santa Fe and Albuquerque: School of American Research and University of New Mexico Press.

Schoolcraft, Henry Rowe

1839 Algic Researches. New York: Harper and Brothers.

Schevill Link, Margaret E.

1948–1949 Dr. Washington Matthews (1843–1905). Kiva 14:2–5.

1960 From the Desk of Washington Matthews. JAFL 73:317–25. (Contains unpublished and abridged origin myth from Matthews' Notebook #674, pp. 36–50)

Sherzer, Joel, and Anthony C. Woodbury, eds.

1987 Native American Discourse: Poetics and Rhetoric. Cambridge and New York: Cambridge University Press.

Silver, Bruce

1982 Reason and Primitivism in the American Wilderness. Journal of American Culture 5 (3):72–83.

Singleton, Charles

1986 Two Kinds of Allegory. *In* Dante. Harold Bloom, ed. pp. 11–19. New York: Chelsea House.

Sledzik, Paul

1989 The Army Medical Museum, the Anthropological Society of Washington, and the American Anthropologist: A Brief History. Symposium Paper, American Anthropological Association, 88th Annual Meeting, Washington.

Spencer, Katherine (see also Halpern)

1947 Reflection of Social Life in the Navaho Origin Myth. University of New Mexico Publications in Anthropology, no. 3.

1957 Mythology and Values: An Analysis of Navaho Chantway Myths. American Folklore Society, Memoir 48.

Spencer, Robert F.

1971 Introduction to: Ethnography and Philology of the Hidatsa Indians, 1887, pp. xxii–xxv. New York and London: Johnson Reprint Editions.

Steichen, Edward

1955 The Family of Man. New York: The Museum of Modern Art.

Stephen, Alexander M.

1893 The Navajo. AA, o.s. 6:345–62.

1930 Navajo Origin Legend. JAFL 43:88–104. Recorded by Stephen in 1885, Olive Bushnell, ed.

1936 Hopi Journal of Alexander M. Stephen. E. C. Parsons, ed. Columbia University Contributions to Anthropology, v. 23. New York: Columbia University Press.

Stevenson, James

1891 Ceremonial of Hasjelti Dailjis and Mythical Sand Painting of the Navajo Indians. Bureau of American Ethnology, Eighth Annual Report for 1886–1887:229–85. Washington, D.C.: G.P.O.

Tedlock, Dennis

1972 Pueblo Literature: Style and Verisimilitude. *In* New Perspectives on the Pueblos. Alfonso Ortiz, ed. Albuquerque: University of New Mexico Press.

1983 The Spoken Word and the Work of Interpretation. Philadelphia: University of Pennsylvania Press.

ten Kate, Herman, F. C.

1892 Somatological Observations on Indians of the Southwest. (Hemenway Southwestern Archaeological Expedition.) Journal of American Ethnology and Archaeology (ed. by J. W. Fewkes) 3 (11):117–44.

Toelken, Barre

1986 Figurative Language and Cultural Contexts in the Traditional Ballads. Western Folklore 45:128–37.

Tozzer, Alfred M.

1905 A Navajo Sand Picture of the Rain Gods and Its Attendant Ceremony. Proceedings of the Thirteenth International Congress of Americanists, New York, 1902:147–56.

1908 A Note on Star-Lore Among the Navajos. JAFL 21:28–32.

1909 Notes on Religious Ceremonials of the Navaho. *In* Putnam Anniversary Volume. pp. 299–343. New York: G. E. Stechert and Co.

Tschopik, Harry, Jr.

1938 Taboo as a Possible Factor in the Obsolescence of Navajo Pottery and Basketry. AA 40:257–62.

Walton, Eda Kay, and T. T. Waterman

1925 American Indian Poetry. AA 27:25–52.

Waters, Frank J.

1970 Book of the Hopi. New York: Ballantine.

Wedel, Waldo R.

1969 Washington Matthews: His Contribution to Plains Anthropology. Plains Anthropologist 14:175–76.

Welsh, Andrew

1978 Roots of Lyric: Primitive Poetry and Modern Poetics. Princeton: Princeton University Press.

Wheat, Joe Ben

1981 Early Navajo Weaving. *In* Tension and Harmony: The Navajo Rug. Plateau 52 (4):3–9.

Wheelwright, Mary Cabot

1938 Tleji or Yehbechai Myth by Hasteen Klah. Retold in shorter form from the myth by Wheelwright. Museum of Navajo Ceremonial Art, Bulletin 1. Santa Fe: Museum of Navajo Ceremonial Art.

1942 Navajo Creation Myth. The Story of the Emergence. Santa Fe: Museum of Navajo Ceremonial Art.

1951 Myth of the Mountain Chant told by Hasteen Klah and Beauty Chant by Hasteen Gahni. Museum of Navajo Ceremonial Art, Bulletin 5. Santa Fe: Museum of Navajo Ceremonial Art.

1955 Journey Towards Understanding. Typescript. Archives of the Wheelwright Museum of the American Indian.

Wheelwright Museum of the American Indian

1985 A Microfilm Edition of the Washington Matthews Papers. Katherine Spencer Halpern, Research Anthropologist; Mary E. Holt, Archivist; Susan Brown McGreevy, Project Director. 10 Rolls. Distributed by the University of New Mexico Press, Albuquerque. (For Guide to the Microfilm, see Halpern 1985)

Whitaker, Kathleen

1992 The Trials and New Trails of Charles F. Lummis. Paper, American Anthropological Association, 91st Annual Meeting, San Francisco.

Williams, Aubrey

1970 Navajo Political Process. Smithsonian Contributions to Anthropology, v. 9. Washington, D.C.: Smithsonian Institution Press.

Witherspoon, Gary

1987 Navajo Weaving, Art in its Cultural Context. Flagstaff: Museum of Northern Arizona.

Wittfogel, Karl A., and Esther L. Goldfrank

1943 Some Aspects of Pueblo Mythology and Society. JAFL 56:17–30.

Wortman, J. L., and Herman F. C. ten Kate

1890 On an Anatomical Characteristic of the Hyoid Bone of Pre-Columbian Pueblo Indians of Arizona, USA. International Congress of Americanists, Berlin, 1888:263–70.

Wyman, Leland C.

1962 The Windways of the Navaho. The Taylor Museum of the Colorado Fine Arts Center.

1970 Blessingway. Tucson: University of Arizona Press.

1973 The Red Antway of the Navajo. Navajo Religion Series, v. 5. Santa Fe: Museum of Navajo Ceremonial Art.

1975 The Mountainway of the Navajo. Tucson: University of Arizona Press.

1983a Southwest Indian Drypanting. Santa Fe and Albuquerque: School of American Research and University of New Mexico Press.

1983b Navajo Ceremonial System. *In* Handbook of North American Indians, v. 10 (2), The Southwest. Alfonso Ortiz, ed. pp. 536–57. Washington, D.C.: Smithsonian Institution Press.

Wyman, Leland C., and Stuart K. Harris

1941 Navajo Indian Ethnobotany. University of New Mexico Bulletin, Anthropological Series, v. 3, no.5 (whole no. 366).

Young, Robert W.

1994 A Note on Orthogrophy. *In* Reprint of Navaho Legends by Washington Matthews. pp. 301–303. Salt Lake City: University of Utah Press.

Young, Robert W., and William Morgan, Sr.

1987 The Navajo Language, A Grammar and Colloquial Dictionary. Albuquerque: University of New Mexico Press. (Earlier edition 1980)

Zolbrod, Paul

1984 Diné Bahane': The Navajo Creation Story. Albuquerque: University of New Mexico Press.

Index